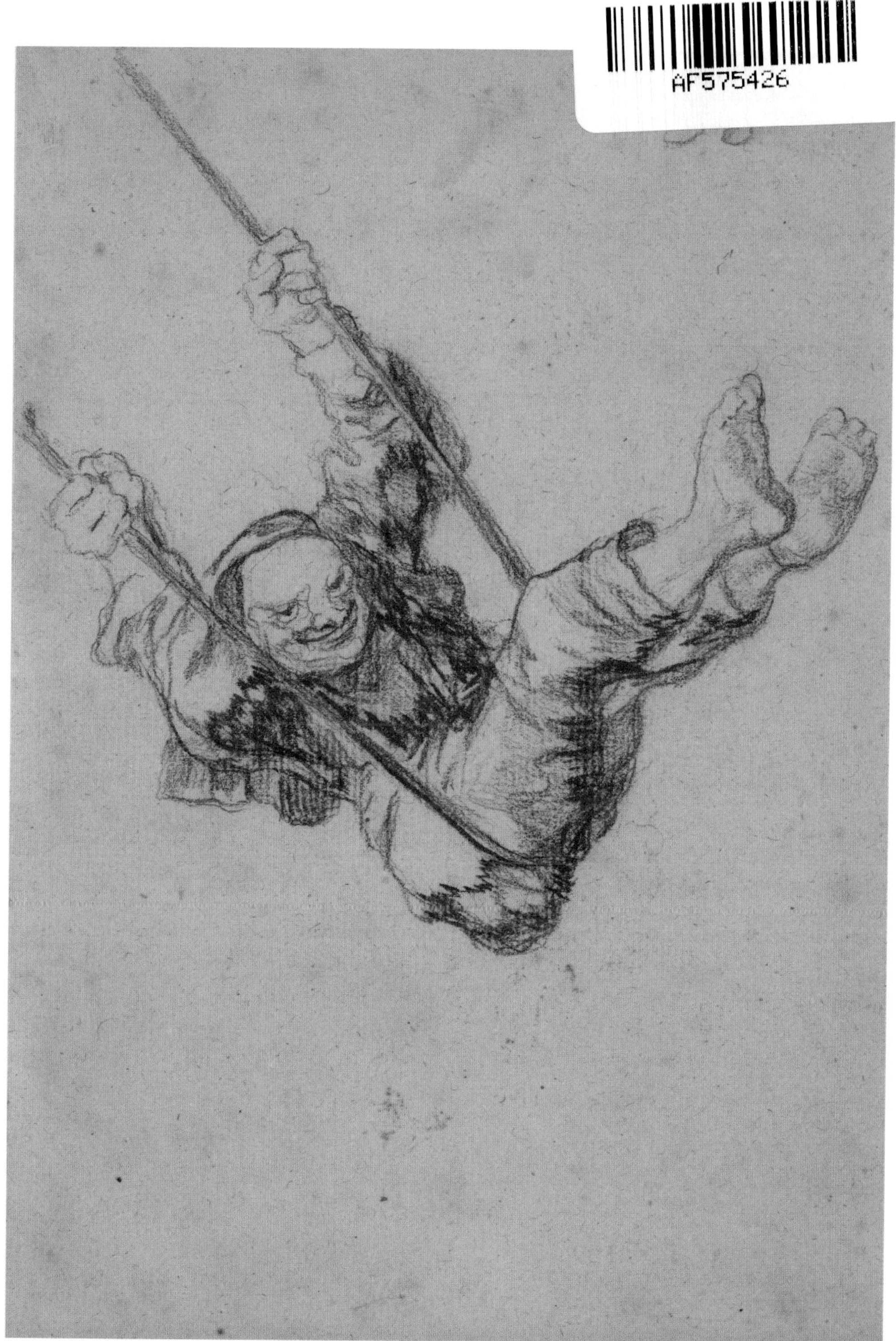

Goya, *Old Man on a Swing*, 1824–1828, Hispanic Society of America, New York

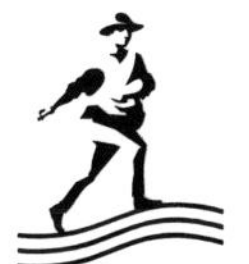

LAST LIGHT

How Six Great Artists Made Old Age a Time of Triumph

Richard Lacayo

SIMON & SCHUSTER

New York London Toronto Sydney New Delhi

Simon & Schuster
1230 Avenue of the Americas
New York, NY 10020

First Simon & Schuster hardcover edition October 2022

Interior design by Ruth Lee-Mui

Manufactured in China

1 3 5 7 9 10 8 6 4 2

Library of Congress Cataloging-in-Publication Data has been applied for.

ISBN 978-1-5011-4658-9
ISBN 978-1-5011-4660-2 (ebook)

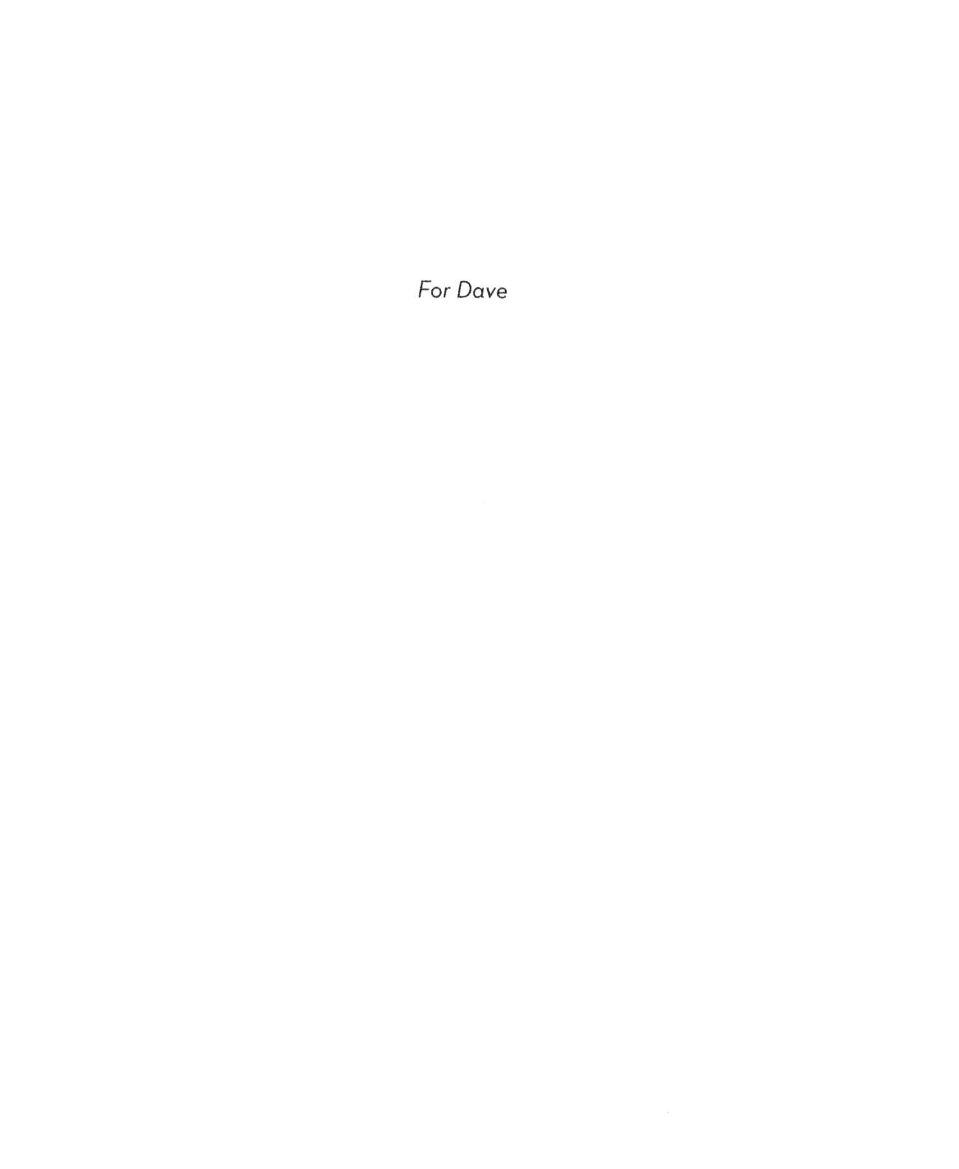

For Dave

CONTENTS:

For then I saw
That fires, not I,
Burn down and die;
That flare of gold
Turns old, turns cold.
Not I. I grow.

May Sarton
from "On a Winter Night"

INTRODUCTION

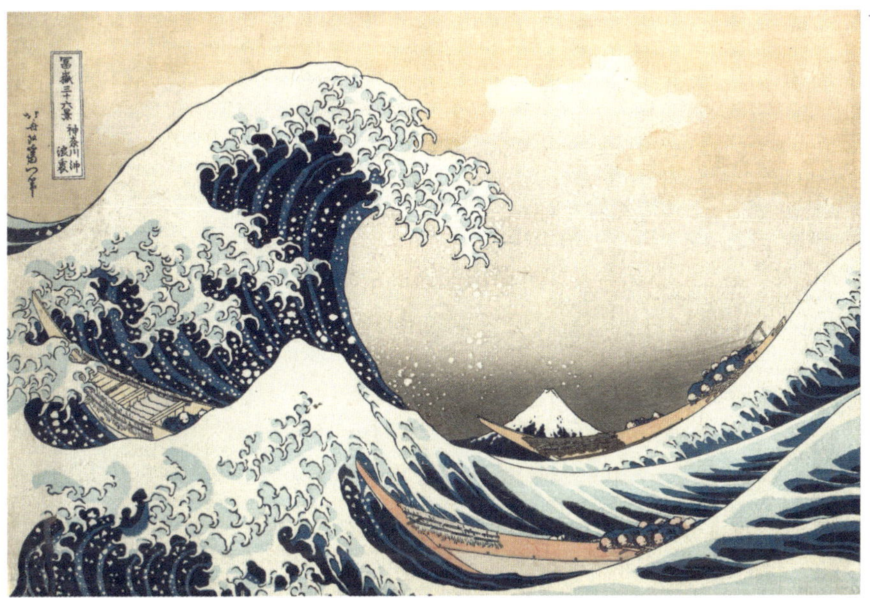 1

Under the Wave Off Kanagawa, ca. 1830–32, polychrome woodblock print; ink and color on paper, 25.7 × 37.9 cm, The Metropolitan Museum of Art, New York

Probably the most famous reflection on old age from any artist is the whimsical testimony offered in the 1830s by Katsushika Hokusai, the great Japanese painter and printmaker.

> All I have produced before the age of seventy is not worth taking into account. At seventy-three I have learned a little about the real structure of nature. . . . When I am eighty, I shall have made still more progress. At ninety I shall penetrate the mystery of things; at a hundred I shall have

reached a marvelous stage; and when I am one hundred and ten, everything I do, be it a dot or a line, will be alive.

As it happens, Hokusai lived only to eighty-nine. That's more than two decades short of 110. Even so, not bad. And he was right. It was in his last years that he produced some of his most enduring works. They include his most famous, *Under the Wave Off Kanagawa,* a woodblock print he first published between 1831 and 1833. He was then in his early seventies, around the very time he issued his declaration on the benefits of old age. In that roller-coastering picture Hokusai presents a titanic claw of surf lifting above and bearing down on three slim boats and their huddled crews. The image is a freeze-frame of deadly energies, pitting a carnivorous sea against a few flimsy trays of helpless humans. Off in the distance rises the serene cone of Mt. Fuji, majestically indifferent to their fate. In its combination of graphic force and cold-eyed philosophical perspective, it's not just a powerful image but a wise one. And everything in it is alive.

"And when I am one hundred and ten . . ." That wasn't such a crazy boast either. It's surprising how many artists have lived well past seventy. Even in centuries when life expectancy, held in check by bad hygiene, poor nutrition, and guessing-game medicine, was a fraction of what it is now, they often made it to a remarkable age. For every Raphael or Van Gogh who left this world in his or her thirties, there's a very long A-list of artists who reached their eighties and nineties. And older. It's not just that Grandma Moses lived to be 101. At her death in 2022, the hard-edge abstractionist Carmen Herrera was 106. It was just six years earlier that the Whitney Museum of American Art had mounted her first major museum show.

Better still, many of those men and women remained productive to the end. Almost by definition artists are people who spend a lifetime doing what they love. As Simone de Beauvoir wrote in *The Coming of Age,* her book-length examination of later life: "There is only one solution if old age is not to be an absurd parody of our former life, and that is to go on pursuing ends that give our existence a meaning . . . social, political, intellectual or creative work." If it's true, as some researchers tell us, that contentment correlates with longevity, is it any surprise that the people who do this kind of thing for a living rarely retire? "Happiness is work." Words the aging Paul Cézanne fixed to the wall of his studio in Provence.

Throughout history, countless artists have lived in accord with Cézanne's motto. Crippled by arthritis, the elderly Auguste Renoir went on painting with his hands strapped tightly in bandages. On the day before he died he completed a still life. Until nearly the end of her very long life, in 2010, Louise Bourgeois drew almost every day. (Or night—she was an insomniac and drawing helped her sleep.) Around 1515, the year before he died, Giovanni Bellini produced his first full-length nude, an elegant young woman coolly appraising her own charms in a handheld mirror. He was eighty-five when he had the pleasure of revisiting her image regularly in his studio, gently touching her up with his brush. Happiness is work.

This is not to say that the work itself is always so lighthearted. The old can make art that's a final cry of anguish—think of Goya. Even then it can be a triumph of articulate despair, a dark victory but a victory all the same. Again, think of Goya. Or it can be a determined repudiation of pain, as it was for Matisse. A semi-invalid by age seventy, to the end he was exuberant in his art, especially in the joyous cut-outs that consumed his last years. And when Renoir's crippled hands were so tightly bandaged, he was using them to produce his long final series of peachy, sun dappled nudes.

But while artists can end up in very different places in their last years, there's almost always a sense that age has changed them, and changed their work. The purpose of this book is to examine those changes in the life and work of six artists who lived into their eighties—Titian, Goya, Monet, Matisse, Edward Hopper, and Louise Nevelson. I want to consider what might have made the old artist depart from his or her younger self, to grasp the differences between an earlier practice and a later one, and to think about how old age can inform art and the process of making it. This is not a self-help book. I make no promises that there are life lessons to be gained from lives as unique as these. Yet we might still learn something from the paths they went down through the final stretch that awaits us all—if we live long enough.

I'm hardly the first writer to ask how artists are changed as they advance into old age, but until the last century the literature was skimpy. There are brief reflections on the topic in Plato and Cicero, but for the first notable discussion we have to wait for Giorgio Vasari, the busy Florentine painter, architect, and writer. His enduring anthology of mini-biographies, *The Lives of the Artists*, published in 1549 and expanded in 1568, is generally considered the first work of art history. (And fan fiction. Not all his stories can be taken at face value.) At one point Vasari tells us that elderly artists produce work that displays "a certain impatience with the rules of craft, a rugged freedom of execution . . . an insistence on very basic structure"—effectively, a crusty renunciation of the very skills and finesse it took a lifetime to achieve.

In the years after Vasari's book appeared, a number of thinkers turned their attention to the subject of older artists, mostly to lament the shortcomings of late work by particular figures like Michelangelo. A century later, in 1699, the French critic, diplomat, and sometime painter Roger de Piles made a first attempt to lay out a universal theory of old-age style. In a recent book, *The Artist Grows Old*, the art historian Philip Sohm describes the three stages of an artist's career as mapped out by de Piles. "The first style of youth, where artists follow their masters; the second style of maturity, where they become truly themselves, and the third style of old age, when they become mannered or caricatures of themselves."

Not until the twentieth century did a succession of German-speaking art historians begin the kind of serious examination of the question you would expect from German-speaking art historians. One of them, A. E. Brinckmann, was among the first to consider the elements of what came to be called *altersstil*—the "old-age style"—a name that remains in use today. He counted as some of these a reduction of forms to their essences and a preference for unfinished surfaces. But it's not just Germanic scholars who have wondered what to make of last works. When it doesn't seem merely repetitive—the product of a once mighty talent on autopilot—the late output of some artists has bewildered their own contemporaries. The slashing brushwork of Titian's final years, which looks to us like a climactic expression of genius and originality, made his last pictures seem patchy and incomplete to some who first saw them. Vasari, one of Titian's qualified admirers, said he should never have let his later works out of the studio, because they simply cast a shadow across the reputation he had earned by his earlier masterpieces. Better if he had just puttered around on canvas for his own enjoyment and kept the results to himself.

In his final years, J. M. W. Turner, a peculiar, growling man at the best of times, produced nearly phosphorescent pictures, force fields of misty light in which solid figures, such as they were, all but dissolved. In Victorian England, where Turner was often regarded as Lear on the heath with a paint box, these looked to many people like the work of a grunting madman. They appear now as early signposts of twentieth-century abstraction. Likewise Claude Monet's final series of water lilies, the panoramic canvases that curve all around two large oval galleries of the Orangerie in Paris. When those opened in 1927, five months after Monet's death, impressionism had long been accepted by the once uncomprehending French public. Even so, these complex last examples of Monet's art again left many people puzzled or indifferent, or worse still, wondering if they weren't best explained by the cataracts he famously suffered in old age. But in the 1950s, after decades of neglect, they enjoyed an immense posthumous validation. Now they were recognized as precursors of postwar abstract expressionism, of Jackson Pollock's vaporous drip paintings, Philip Guston's shimmering fields of color, and Mark Rothko's rectangular fogs. Those artists may not have looked to late Monet for inspiration, if they knew his last paintings at all, but two decades after his death they arrived at a pictorial space he had developed first. And with that, the image of old man Monet went in no time from "squinting geezer" to "visionary."

Probably the best-known attempt by an English-speaking expert to characterize late style came from the regal British art historian Sir Kenneth Clark in a lecture he delivered at Cambridge University in 1970. Then sixty-seven and at the height of his fame as host of the BBC documentary series *Civilisation*, Clark began with a cheerful proposition. While poets almost always decline in old age, artists often flourish. And he agreed there was indeed "a special character" common to the work of nearly all old artists, one that he defined in psychological more than stylistic terms.

And what was it? Now the bad news started. "A sense of isolation, a feeling of holy rage, developing into . . . a transcendental pessimism; a mistrust of reason, a belief in instinct." All in all, "a very poor view of human life." There was more. Old artists, he assured us, "are solitary; like all old people they are bored and irritated by the company of their fellow bipeds and yet find their isolation depressing." More than that, they find the creative act itself an exhausting ordeal and take no pleasure from their work, however brilliant.

But is bleakness of that kind the "special character" of all late work? Pessimism is certainly the preexisting condition behind some of the unflinching last paintings of Titian and the most abject among the late works of Goya. It no doubt also explains the sense of tragedy in late Donatello, the Renaissance sculptor whose risen Christ, a bronze relief that's one of his last works, looks burdened and weary even as he arrives at the triumph of his own resurrection. But the notion of "transcendental pessimism" doesn't help us much to understand the torrents of light in those late canvases of Turner or any of Renoir's dozens of rosy nudes. It may say something true of the black clouds hovering in some of Mark Rothko's later pictures—or not; he was a complicated man—but what good does it do before the explosive last coils of Cy Twombly? As for the sculptor Louise Nevelson, she was never so happy and fulfilled as she was in the old age that finally brought her the recognition she always knew she deserved.

And looking for "a feeling of holy rage" will get you nowhere when considering the paper cut-outs of Henri Matisse. It's true that, for those who can decode them, a few of the earliest disguise dark memories of wartime Europe. But for the most part they remain some of the most joyful art ever produced, and all the more so when you recall that Matisse was a semi-invalid in frequent pain when he made them. It was the buoyancy of youth the old man summoned in that work. Charles Baudelaire said that "genius is nothing other than the ability to retrieve childhood at will." Almost a century later there was Matisse, showing how true that could be.

So maybe we should put aside any attempt to find a single rule uniting the last achievements of every artist who, as the old Irish expression has it, lived to comb gray hairs. A better approach might be a case-by-case examination of how some very different artists made use of their final decades. That is what I'm doing here, in reflections on the life and work of a half dozen who lived from the sixteenth to the twentieth centuries. Yet however different their later lives may have been, in one way they were the same. They kept working, long enough to express their final insights into life and art through the great last unfolding of their gifts. Or as Matisse put it: "It took me sixty years to organize my brain."

Something else they had in common—their late work was daring. Ordinarily we think of young artists as the bomb throwers. Monet and Renoir were still in their twenties when they embarked on what would eventually be called impressionism. So were Picasso and Braque, when they ventured into cubism. But old age can be no less liberating, if it brings with it the confidence to try new things. Young artists may experiment because they have nothing to lose. More established ones can do the same because they have nothing to fear. Because their legacies are a settled matter, they're free to play the provocateur. Consider Titian—by his seventies, when he began to work regularly with the loose brushwork of his late style, he had long been regarded as one of the greatest painters of his time. Though he never said so, at least not in any record that has come down to us, his reputation was so assured that he could afford to depart from the firm modeling and fine finish of his early triumphs.

Likewise for Monet. Though the panoramic water lily canvases that consumed his last years did not so much break from his earlier practices as bring them to a powerful culmination, they are still such complex pictures that he risked once again confusing the public that had taken decades to embrace impressionism. And as we've seen, many people dismissed them. But by the time he produced them, in the years after World War I, Monet was not just a French cultural celebrity but a kind of national monument. A man of his stature, who had always gone his own way, could go right on doing that. At the urging of his good friend Georges Clemenceau, the prime minister of France, the cash-strapped French government had even promised these canvases the costly permanent home in the Orangerie that they occupy today. Though with the challenging late *Water Lilies* he was by no means resting on his laurels, it can't have hurt to know they were there.

Even Hopper, whose late work mostly extends the traditions of realism he had mastered as a young man, in old age sometimes detoured into the deadpan surreal. Just look at *Rooms by the Sea*, where an improbable wall of ocean mounts up just outside an open doorway, with no intervening strip of land to locate the house on terra firma. The effect is very deliberately unreal. If you didn't know this was a Hopper, you might think it was a Magritte.

And in his last years, when Matisse turned to paper cut-outs, they were something almost no one thought of as a fine art. For centuries skilled craft workers and ordinary hobbyists had cut paper into silhouettes and even whole intricate scenes. But no matter how skillfully made, these were largely regarded as handicraft or folk art, something akin to glued seashell arrangements. Matisse was confident enough to step outside the realms of painting and sculpture that were the foundations of the high art tradition, while bringing to cut paper a modernist sensibility that made of it something new. All the same, most French critics found his cut-outs childish and negligible.

Even Christian Zervos, who had commissioned Matisse in 1936 to design a cover for his magazine, *Cahiers d'Art,* one that Matisse assembled from colored paper, dismissed his later scissors work as "an agreeable distraction." Matisse didn't care. The inspired child's play of the cut-outs would remain one of the chief pursuits of his old age. As he wrote to another friend, "I hope however old we might become, we will die *young*."

In the course of researching and writing this book, one unexpected similarity emerged among four of the six artists I was looking at. In old age all four devoted years to producing a grand work of art that was some kind of enclosure. Goya made a toxic womb of his entire house outside Madrid, laying down his Black Paintings on nearly every interior wall. Monet designed his last water lily panels as wraparound installations, completely surrounding visitors in his two oval galleries in the Orangerie. And having already covered the walls of his Paris apartment with dozens of paper cut-outs, Matisse went on to conceive every part of a chapel in Vence. Even the sunlight that enters through his stained glass windows comes wearing colors assigned by him.

As for Louise Nevelson, not only were the works that first bought her fame at age sixty sculptural environments that filled entire rooms, but in her seventies she produced an enormous castle keep. A massive rectangular box, measuring twenty by eleven feet, *Mrs. N's Palace* is a sculpture that's also a mysterious dwelling. Designed to be entered, it's covered inside and out with sculptural assemblages.

Was there something in the psychology of these four that inclined them in their last years to produce a primal space of their own invention? Or might these enveloping projects have been ultimate acts of sovereignty, 360-degree projections of the self? Having spent a lifetime taking in the world as they found it, did they feel inclined in their last years to produce one entirely their own?

One thing all six of these artists shared was the experience of physical decline. Some visitors to Titian's studio said that in old age he had trouble holding the brush. Monet suffered from cataracts. Matisse was mostly bedridden. But their need to go on making art drove them back to their easels and sketch pads, just like the elderly Bellini with his belated first nude. For them art was literally therapeutic.

Just not so therapeutic it could fend off the inevitable. By their last years they all knew death was on the near horizon, but only some of them said so in their work, and all of them broached mortality in different ways. In his somber late devotional art, Titian painted himself a few times in close proximity to Christ. He knew he was approaching the moment when they would meet at last. So here he is in *The Entombment* of 1559, when he was around seventy, appearing in the role of Nicodemus, helping to lower his Lord and Savior into a carved sarcophagus. And there he is as St. Jerome, prostrate and appearing to crawl toward the dead Christ in a *Pietà* Titian intended for his own tomb.

Goya didn't turn toward God. True to his sympathy with the values of the Enlightenment in deeply unenlightened Spain, in late life he instead made a powerful tribute to science and reason. At the age of seventy-four he produced a portrait of himself near death from an illness he had suffered the year before, being tenderly propped up from behind by the doctor who eventually nursed him back to health, and who is reaching around to bring a cup of lifesaving medicine to his patient's lips.

As for Monet, though not one to dwell on mortality in his work, with the immense final views of his water garden he created a world that dissolves into a liquid infinitude, a fathomless viewshed where hints of eternity come easily to mind. At the same age Matisse would opt for the defiant joy of his cut-outs and the light and color of the chapel in Vence that the God-skeptical artist was only too happy to create from the ground up. Hopper went out with a wink. In his final painting, from 1965, he appears on a proscenium stage with his wife, Josephine, both dressed as clowns taking a final bow. But in a picture he completed two years earlier, the most affecting and most nearly abstract of his late paintings, he had already offered a more subtle farewell. He shows us sunlight flooding through the windows of an empty room and striking the walls in such a way as to produce two upright rectangles of light, one much taller than the other, just like him and his diminutive wife. Those fleeting zones of brightness, soon to fade, can only be stand-ins for himself and Jo, all the frictions of their difficult marriage reconciled in the pure light that was the lifelong essence of his art.

Nevelson was even more indirect. Among her last works is a numbered series of black wooden wall assemblages, each called *Mirror Shadow*. Many of them contain circles, arcs, or crescents that suggest mirror frames or fragments of curving mirrors. None of them makes any plain reference to the grave; they don't need to. That title tells us all we need to know about the gathering darkness in her own mirror, the surface where we all spend a lifetime watching time perform, as Charles Dickens dryly put it, "his deeper operations."

The American abstractionist Joan Mitchell once called painting "the opposite of death." It would take nothing less than death to keep these six from doing more of what they had done all their lives, to probe last questions of life and art, with their last work as both the instrument and the product of those final inquiries. And now the resonant art of their final years remains as proof of their vitality and relevance in old age. So this will be a book about six artists who played forceful, inventive endgames that produced lasting outcomes. One was Italian and one Spanish. Two were French and two were Americans. Their lives spanned the centuries from the Renaissance to the Reagan administration. And though they differed in many respects, they shared one thing—a determination to continue, to go on creating, driven not by the bouncing energies of youth but that all-powerful last imperative, the ticking clock.

In his eighties Hopper was asked by an interviewer what advice he would give to a young painter.

"Work," he said.

It's the word they all lived by to the end.

2

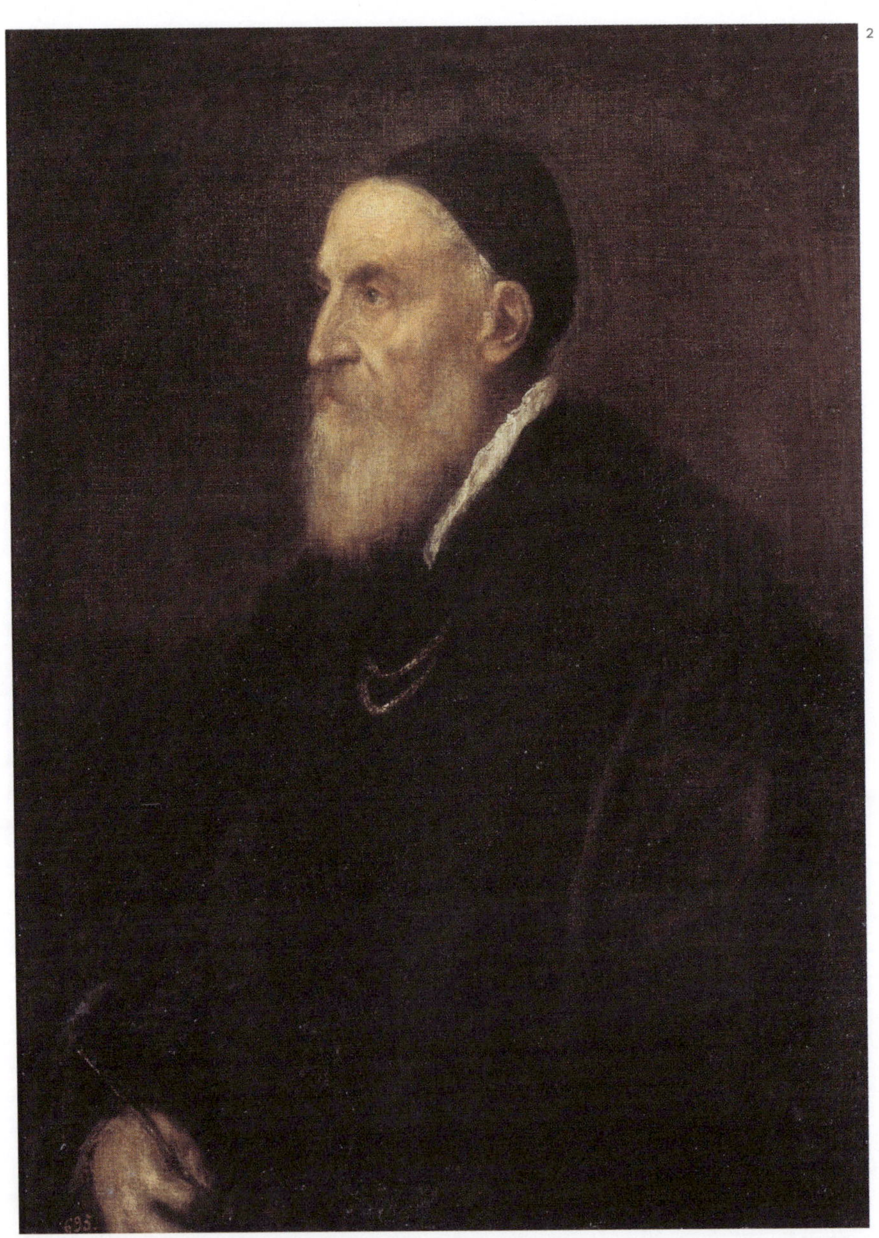

Self-Portrait, ca. 1562, oil on canvas, 86 × 65 cm, Museo Nacional del Prado, Madrid

1

TITIAN

The Modern Artist

In the summer of 1576, Venice was in chaos. For centuries, plague had been a grim leitmotif in the history of the city, one of the busiest ports on the Mediterranean, arriving again and again on merchant ships and the flea-infested rats they carried. But this time was different. It was worse than the epidemic almost fifty years earlier that had swept away a fifth of the city and left bodies floating in the canals. Worse than anything since the Black Death that killed off much of Europe in the mid-1300s. On some days religious processions filed through the narrow streets, beseeching God's mercy. God wasn't listening. When it started the population may have been about 171,000. Before it was over more than a fourth of them would be dead—46,721 men, women, and children.

Those who could flee, did. But in the terrible silence of this stricken city, one of its most famous residents stayed behind. As the dying and dead mounted up all around him, the ancient Tiziano Vecellio—the man we know as Titian—stayed where he was, at his home in the neighborhood called Biri Grande, overlooking a lagoon on the north side of Venice. Though not a palace, his house was still the headquarters of a rich man, with a garden that caused one visitor to sigh when he wrote to a friend about a dinner he once enjoyed there. In the hills outside the city, in the region of his birthplace and boyhood, Titian also owned a stone house built for him by the villagers of Castel Roganzuolo, payment for an altarpiece he had done for their church. He might easily have escaped there. Why didn't he?

He left us no explanation. Perhaps at his age the trip seemed too taxing. And besides, he never liked to leave Venice. Though he well understood Rome's importance to any artist, he was in his late fifties before he could rouse himself to make the obligatory visit. More than once Philip II of Spain, the great patron of his later years, tried and failed to tempt him to Madrid. Titian was Venetian in the way that Samuel Johnson would be a Londoner and Walter Winchell would be a New Yorker. He had spent a lifetime at the center of the universe. Why budge? But perhaps this time he lingered simply because his house was also his studio. Filled with the many canvases he worked on continually, sometimes for years at a time, it was a centrifugal force he was constantly borne back into, the place where, day after day, he forged himself.

Whatever his reasons in that awful summer, he would certainly be aware that he had already enjoyed a very long life. In sixteenth-century Venice, when the average male life span was fortysomething, to live into your seventies was unusual. To carry on for another decade, as he had done, was extraordinary. At his death, Titian was somewhere in his mid-to-late eighties, though no one was sure just how old he was, not even him. For years he had been claiming to be much older than his real age. In a gerontocracy like Venice, where the Doge was almost always elderly and his council was chosen from the ranks of old men, great age was no disadvantage. No matter that Venetian law designated the elderly as *persone inutile*—"useless people"—advanced age could still be a sign of distinction. It was the crowning distinction for Titian, who for decades had been renowned as the greatest artist in Venice, and since the death of Michelangelo in 1564 the greatest in Italy. For many people, and not just Italians, that meant the supreme artist of Europe. And for most Europeans, though the concept was just emerging and no one would yet call themselves that, Europe was the world.

Yet for all the wealth and prestige he acquired over his long life, climbing ever upward, adding more important patrons and commissions, Titian never lost touch with the little mountain town in the Italian Alps where he was born. He would always maintain an umbilical relationship with Pieve di Cadore, making frequent trips home, choosing the daughter of a local barber as his first wife, operating a timber business there with his brother Francesco, and hoping, in vain as it turned out, to be buried in the local church. Given his fondness for Pieve, can it have been coincidental that his Venetian house and studio looked north onto the mountains he never entirely left behind? The house was sufficiently grand to host a luncheon in 1574 for King Henry III of France. But day after day in his studio, the great man worked with a more humble past looking over his shoulder.

At his death, there were many pictures still in that studio, some that he had been promising forever to his patron Philip II. Even as a younger man, he was not an artist who liked to be rushed. One of the triumphs of his early career, the Pesaro family altarpiece in the great Gothic church of the Frari, took him seven years to complete. He spent decades sweating out a commission from the city fathers for paintings in the Chamber of the Great Council in the Doge's Palace. But in his last years he simply couldn't bring himself to part with many of the canvases he was working on, never satisfied that they were done. Palma Giovane, who would one day be the principal painter in Venice, was Titian's pupil and studio assistant in the old man's last years. He left us this report of his elderly master's working methods: "He would leave a painting for months without looking at, until he returned to it, and stared critically at it, as if it were a mortal enemy." Then he would set to work on it again, Palma wrote, "like a surgeon."

The art of Titian's old age has fascinated and perplexed generations because it was so unlike his earlier manner, the one that had conquered the world. Along with the plenipotentiary genius Michelangelo, Titian was actually among the first European artists to adopt a "late style." Michelangelo's was expressed chiefly in the way he depicted the human body. Where his earlier achievements, like *David*, were the quintessence of classical harmony, balance, and restraint, his late work, especially in the contorted bodies of *The Last Judgment*, is full of the straining, twisting figures of the Renaissance endgame we call mannerism. For Titian the late style was a different matter, not a new approach to form but a startling new kind of paint handling. By the time he reached his sixties he was fascinated by the effects he could achieve with loose brushwork, a flurry of rapid marks that could gently outline figures and landscape or dissolve them into a hectic storm of strokes. If late Michelangelo was all twisted muscle, late Titian was flickering fog, in images that sometimes require you to step back to make them out clearly. Yet these soft-edged pictures still come at you with such force, stepping back is what you do by reflex.

Titian's gamble in his late work was to liberate pigment— the viscous goo that was the literal substance of his art— from the obligation to produce the smoothly expressed illusions he had spent many years perfecting. He cut it loose from its purely descriptive purposes to give it a life of its own, so that its visible movements on the canvas transmit moods and energies that no tightly controlled execution could convey. All by itself, his brushwork can have an electrical charge as powerful as any of the people or scenes he uses it to describe. When applied in a gently pulsing way, it can produce a sensation of sexual intermingling, an effect that intensifies the drowsy eroticism of his languid *Nymph and Shepherd*. When executed con brio, it can signal energy and excitement. Or anxiety, dissolution, and morbid agitation—Titian uses it to that end in some of the greatest pictures of his last years, scenes of divine cruelty and injustice that include *The Death of Actaeon* and *The Flaying of Marsyas*. Both were executed with a very free hand, in the whiplashing soft focus that Italians call *non-finito*—meaning "unfinished," even when the picture is, in the artist's judgment, *finito*.

This was a significant departure from the firmly modeled forms and smooth surfaces that characterized most painting of the High Renaissance, and for that matter much of Titian's work from earlier in his career. With the dynamic brushwork of his late work Titian broke the confines of European painting almost as soon as they had been put in place—in good part by him. And when we talk about Titian's hand, we sometimes mean that literally. Palma Giovane recalled that in the last stages of reworking a picture, the old man "used his fingers more than his brush." To this day you can see on some of his canvases the evidence of his literal "touch," marks left by his fingertips where he dabbed and pushed the pigment.

Counting among the first generations of Italian artists to spend a lifetime with oil paint, working with it from their earliest years, Titian was also among the first to discover its range of possibilities. He delighted in how it could suggest the watery sheen of silk, the luster of metal, or the flushed pliancy of flesh. And toward the end of his life, he demonstrated one more possibility, when he showed that paint itself, the oily paste, not just the things it depicted, could transmit feeling to the canvas. With this, he immensely widened the expressive possibilities of the magical substance he worked with every day. Centuries before Marshall McLuhan, he discovered that the medium is the message.

• • •

Precisely because it provided artists with a third means, along with form and color, to express emotion on the canvas, a third front in their campaign to maximize the capabilities of their art, the influence of Titian's late style spread quickly after his death. It also gained fame because he was already so widely known. He was the first international artist, the first whose renown and clientele extended, in his own lifetime, far beyond his home turf. Even Michelangelo, one of the few Renaissance artists whose stature rivaled his, saw only a handful of his works move beyond Italy, notably into the collection of Francis I of France. Even Leonardo, who would spend his last days in France, as guest of the same Francis, devoted nearly his entire life to the service of Italian patrons. Yet by his forties Titian was supplying pictures all around the continent. In a sense his work was an early example of Italian luxury export.

It's customary to say that after the fifteenth century, when Filippo Brunelleschi and Leon Battista Alberti rediscovered and codified single-point perspective, nearly any painting by a Western artist was designed to be a kind of window onto the scene it depicted, a device to draw the viewer into an illusion of three-dimensional space. Only with the first stirrings of modernism in the nineteenth century did artists begin to draw the viewer's attention back to the surface of the canvas, to the "picture plane." It was a process that's often said to have begun as early as Manet in the 1840s before exploding in the twentieth century with the shallow space of cubism, the broad expanses of single color in the work of Matisse, and the two-dimensional abstractions of Malevich and Mondrian. It reached a kind of apotheosis in the United States after World War II, in the all-over compositions of Jackson Pollock and Mark Rothko, and then in the resolute flatness of work by painters like Morris Louis, Ad Reinhardt, Ellsworth Kelly, and Frank Stella.

That at least is the usual telling of the story. But it's important to remember that this emphasis on the canvas as a surface had its first stirrings in the Venetian Renaissance, in the art of Giorgione, and then with late Titian. His visible brushwork never lets you forget that his paintings aren't just windows onto a view but things created on a stretch of woven cloth, holding droplets and smudges of pigment very near to your vision. No matter how much your eye dives into the scene, you never entirely shake the simultaneous sensation of looking at marks deposited on a flat surface. Having spent a lifetime mastering illusion, in late life Titian saw fit to break his own spell.

Why did he turn to this kind of rough brushwork? In his sixties, when he was beginning to work more often in the new way, he offered one visitor to his studio the not quite convincing rationale that it was due to the simple desire to forge a uniquely personal manner. The visitor was Francisco de Vargas, the Holy Roman Empire's ambassador to Venice, who recorded Titian's words this way:

> Sir, I am not confident of achieving the delicacy and beauty of the brushwork of Michelangelo, Raphael, Correggio, and Parmigianino. And even if I succeeded in emulating them, I would be judged with them or considered an imitator. But ambition, which is as natural in my art as in any other, urges me to choose a new path to make myself famous, much as the others acquired their own fame from the way which they followed.

It's true that Titan offered that rationale some years after having made his only visit to Rome, a monthslong working trip during which he at last saw for himself the works of the great artists of central Italy. He may well have felt afterward that it would be to his advantage to adopt a very different signature style. But could that have been the only reason? The younger Titian had already won over the world with a refined surface not unlike theirs. Very possibly a deeper, more intimate motive was in play, one rooted in the circumstances of Titian's old age. When the late style emerges, events all around him were taking an unsettling turn and his mood appears to have been darkening in reply. Old friends were dying. Venice was enduring a succession of crises. There was also a mysterious and nearly successful attempt on the life of his beloved younger son, Orazio, and a final break with his long-estranged older son, Pomponio. On multiple fronts, life must have seemed as though it was drifting out of control.

Even without taking into account his new paint handling, we can sense the pressure of these events on other aspects of his work. He turns away from portraiture—glorifying earthly vanity seems to have lost its appeal. In his mythological canvases he's attracted to stories about the cruelty of the gods, the way they turn mere mortals into their helpless playthings. In his religious work, scenes of Christ's suffering and death start to dominate. Even his famously bright palette subsides. In that context, the agitated brushwork of his later years looks in part like a vehicle to express an uneasy state of mind. At the end of a career during which he had revolutionized one genre after another, he may well have arrived at this final innovation because he needed to. The evidence is not conclusive, but the circumstances of his later life, the glum reflections in some of his letters, his turn toward darker subjects on canvas, all suggest a man ready for a means to convey a more distressed outlook, which his broken brushwork can certainly do. Yet at the same time, and paradoxically, that brushwork can suggest the continuing vitality and spontaneity of the man who applied it. And by substituting the vivid evidence of his hand for the conventions of clear representation, it was also the literal sign of Titian's creative autonomy, his freedom as an artist.

To understand the elderly Titian it's important first to have an idea of how he began and what he became over time. His international prestige was a sizable achievement in itself, but even more so because he came from nowhere. He was born in Pieve di Cadore, a little village in the Veneto, about sixty miles north of Venice. It stands at the foot of the Italian Alps, mountains that all his life would appear as a distant landscape in his paintings. For most of the Middle Ages the region had been part of the Holy Roman Empire. But in 1420, after a series of negotiations that secured its citizens a variety of privileges, Cadore agreed to be absorbed into the mainland territories of Venice. Heavily forested, it was a logging area, and for many years Titian and his brother Francesco—also a painter, though of modest gifts—would run a significant family sideline in timber.

Because the records were lost long ago, Titian's birth date is uncertain. Most scholars now believe it was somewhere between 1488 and 1490. Though not of the nobility, the Vecellio family was old, reasonably prosperous, and occasionally distinguished. Titian's father, Gregorio, would serve as a militia captain in the Battle of Cadore, where, in 1508, in the fields and woods below the town, the Venetians beat back a siege organized by the Holy Roman Emperor Maximilian I. In civilian life, however, he mostly held a succession of minor municipal jobs. It's Titian's grandfather, called Conte, who appears to have been the real capo of the clan. It was he who presided over family affairs until Titian was in his twenties, a shrewd businessman, a lawyer, and a local dignitary who sometimes represented Cadore in the councils of Venice.

Perhaps it was to Conte, a man who moved in higher circles than Titian's father, that Titian owed the refined manners that people often remarked on in later years, a quiet poise that allowed him to mix comfortably with aristocratic patrons. "Mild, tractable, and easy to deal with," as one contemporary described him in his fifties in a letter to Cardinal Alessandro Farnese, who would become another of Titian's high-born clients.

We don't know much about his education, except that he learned to read and write. Though we have letters in his own hand, his correspondence was often composed by hired professionals, a common practice of his day. Some were the work of highly literate friends, like the poet Lodovico Dolce. But after it became obvious he could draw, his family resolved to have him properly trained. At around the age of ten or twelve he made the long journey down the twisting mountain roads from Cadore to Venice, probably with his brother Francesco, to live with an uncle and take up an apprenticeship in the workshop of Sebastiano Zuccato, a minor painter and mosaic artist. He, too, quickly recognized Titian's exceptional gifts and arranged for him to move on to the much more prestigious studio of Gentile Bellini, head of the city's preeminent family of artists. In time, Titian transferred to the studio of Gentile's younger brother Giovanni, by then the city's most esteemed painter, and a man whose sensuous art would have more to offer Titian than Gentile's drier manner. With that, the teenage prodigy was on his way.

Crucially for Titian, Giovanni Bellini was an early adopter of oil paint, the compound of powdered pigment and oil that had originated in northern Europe, and arrived in Venice in the 1460s. Venetians were also among the first Italian artists to paint on canvas. These two innovations changed everything. Artists elsewhere in Italy were slower to make the transition, preferring fresco—the wet plaster technique used for wall paintings like Michelangelo's Sistine ceiling—or else egg-based tempera applied on wood panels. But in the damp climate of Venice, plaster crumbled and wood warped. Canvas was an obvious alternative. As a seafaring power and shipbuilding center, the city had plenty of sailcloth to experiment with, in weaves ranging from fine linen to a coarseness near to burlap. Each permitted a different range of surface effects, from smooth to nappy.

As a young man Titian favored tightly woven canvas with an even surface, which he primed with heavy layers of white gesso that smoothed it further to permit finely detailed brushwork. But as he grew older he preferred thicker, more nubbly weaves coated with just a thin layer of gesso. That let the coarse fabric emerge more visibly through the paint to amplify the rougher appearance of his late style. Unlike paintings on walls or wood panel, pictures on canvas could also be crated and even rolled for easy transport, which fostered the emergence of an international market, the faraway patrons and buyers who would make Titian rich.

Even more than the variety of canvas, an artist's choice of paint medium—tempera or oil—determined the appearance of any picture. Tempera produced a precise and meticulous surface, partly because it set so quickly, so it couldn't be reworked for long or blended easily with adjoining colors. Oil paint dried slowly, which meant that individual passages could be revisited and adjusted over hours, days, or even weeks, offering new possibilities of depth and atmosphere. Depending on how much oil you blended into the powdered pigment, you could concoct a muck that spread thickly like soft butter, or a thin wash that could be settled onto the canvas in layer after layer. Titian liked to lay down many, often over a layer of opaque underpainting, to produce a complex translucence. Better still, you could do both those things in the same picture, as he often did, with no end of complicated results. It would be oil paint that would make possible Titian's sensuous art. And he in turn would be one of its greatest innovators, spending a lifetime drawing out the subtle capabilities of this mesmerizing new substance, until in old age he discovered its most unexpected potential.

It was around 1508, in Bellini's workshop, that young Titian came to know one of the pivotal artists of his generation. The brilliant and doomed Giorgio Barbarella, known as Giorgione, was one of those charismatic geniuses, like the poet Percy Shelley or the actor James Dean, who revolutionized their art before dying young. He was at most thirty-five, maybe younger, when he was swept away in 1510 in yet another outbreak of the plague. In his book *The Lives of the Most Excellent Painters, Sculptors, and Architects*, the sixteenth-century painter and writer Giorgio Vasari credits Giorgione, as we still do, with being the first Venetian to master Leonardo da Vinci's "modern manner," an art of soft forms, delicately rendered moods, and smoky atmospheres the Italians called "sfumato."

These lessons of "modern art" Giorgione would transmit to Titian. All of them are on view in *Le Concert Champêtre*, or *The Pastoral Concert*, an enigmatic scene in which two well-dressed young gentlemen, one fingering a lute, idle on a hillside in the company of two languorous nude women. One of the defining achievements of Western art, that painting establishes an enduring new type of image, the pastoral—pictures of cultivated people at leisure in an idealized nature. It was a tradition Manet was still drawing upon more than four centuries later for his *Déjeuner sur l'herbe*. For centuries *The Pastoral Concert* was attributed to Giorgione, but now most scholars credit it to Titian, as does the Louvre, which owns it. If so, it would merely be the first in a line of painterly genres that Titian either created entirely or utterly transformed.

For a long time, there was something like a consensus that both men collaborated on another groundbreaking work. *The Sleeping Venus* is the first painting on canvas of a reclining female nude, a genre that Titian would electrify in later years. The woman was presumed to be by Giorgione, with the landscape and sky added by Titian after his friend's death. Though the Gemaldegalerie in Dresden, which owns the painting, still credits it to both men, a number of scholars now attribute it mostly or entirely to Titian. No matter whether that picture is a solo or a duet, it's a virtuoso performance. The woman lies outdoors on silk sheets in wine red and ocher, her eyes closed, in rolling landscape that "rhymes" with the curves of her body. Her right arm raised behind her head, her left hand rests suggestively between her legs, the fingers bent gently into the crevice.

As with Giorgione, Titian's genius announced itself early. His master Giovanni Bellini was by far the most important Venetian artist of his generation, and Titian would show signs of Bellini's valuable influence in many of his earliest works. Certainly his many informal Madonnas in outdoor settings owe a lot to Bellini's example. In those, Titian would entirely reimagine the genre called the "sacra conversazione." These are images of the Holy Mother seated with the Christ child and surrounded by saints in such a way that the figures appear to be in some silent, purely spiritual communion—the sacred conversation. We credit Bellini not with inventing that formula but brilliantly relaxing it, again and again playing with the enthroned Madonna to place her in less conventional settings. In some he even removed the figures from the customary arched interior and took them outdoors, under an open sky. Titian built spectacularly on Bellini's innovations. In many of his pictures he, too, freed the Holy Mother from her throne entirely. In one, *Virgin and Child with Saint Catherine, Saint Dominic and a Donor*, she sits outdoors before a cloth backdrop, amid a landscape of hills and trees. Her bare foot peeks from beneath her skirt to rest on the dirt—a stunningly realistic device.

Two years after Bellini's death in 1516, Titian, then somewhere in his mid-to-late twenties, unveiled his most important commission to date, a picture that made his name in Venice. *The Assumption of the Virgin* hangs above the high altar in the city's largest Gothic church, Santa Maria Gloriosa dei Frari, known to everyone as the Frari. For his debut on this sizable stage Titian produced the largest altarpiece of its day, composed of twenty-one cedar panels and measuring nearly twenty-three feet high and eleven and a half wide. A monumental scene of airborne majesty, *The Assumption* shows us the bodily ascent into heaven of the Holy Mother after her death. At ground level you find Christ's awestruck disciples, excitedly gazing and pointing skyward, in nothing like the subdued way Venetians were accustomed to seeing their saints. In the sunbursting heavens above them is the ascending Madonna, perched on a cloud and attended by a crescent-shaped flock of infant angels. God himself looks down from up top, as though urging the Holy Mother upward.

So this is no contemplative devotional picture. It's a geyser, a vertical jet stream of light, color, and movement. In a city where Bellini's more restrained figures were still the standard, the celestial tumult of Titian's altarpiece was an astonishment. The dramatic energies of the picture, operatic before opera was invented—and baroque, well before the theatrical art of the baroque first appeared in the next century—created a sensation among the Venetians who first saw it.

One year after unveiling

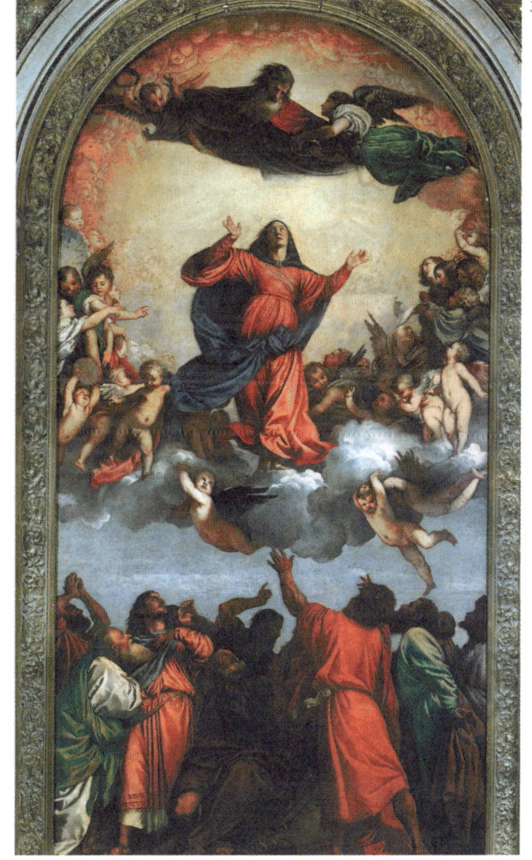

3

The Assumption of the Virgin, 1516–18, oil on panel, 685.8 × 355.6 cm, Basilica di Santa Maria Gloriosa dei Frari, Venice

the *Assumption*, Titian returned to the Frari to begin another large altarpiece that would—when it was completed, seven years later—once more excite the Most Serene Republic by exploding the conventions of the sacred conversation he had already so greatly enlarged. As he did with the *Assumption*, in the *Madonna di Ca' Pesaro*—"the Pesaro family Madonna," named after the donors—he created a drama of energetic ascent, but this time on a rightward diagonal, in a teeming stairstep composition with the Madonna at its apex. We see her seated before the base of a wide column that rises beyond the top of the picture and into the blue sky behind her. Near the bottom left a soldier who may be Saint George flourishes the large red banner of the papal arms.

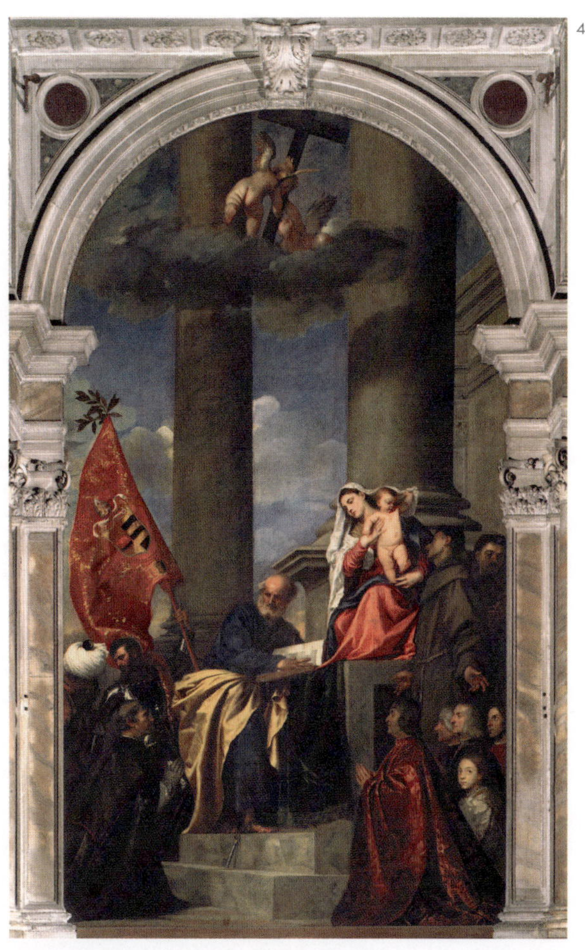 4

The Madonna di Ca' Pesaro, 1519–26, oil on canvas, 478 × 266, Basilica di Santa Maria Gloriosa dei Frari, Venice

This would be in honor of Jacopo Pesaro, the warrior bishop of Cyprus who commissioned the painting. In 1502 he had led a papal fleet into victorious battle against the Turks. We see him in a prayerful pose in the lower left corner, being presented to the Holy Mother by Saint Peter, a large figure who sits below her, midway on the descending diagonal. With both hands she supports the standing figure of the infant Christ. By her side Saint Francis points toward the lower right corner, where a kneeling cluster of Pesaro men gaze upward. Or most of them do. A spotlit boy, Jacopo's favored nephew Leonardo, turns to look directly at you, the viewer, as if asking—how about *this*? And yes, how about this? There had never been anything like it.

By the time he unveiled the Pesaro *Madonna*, Titian had also completed his magnificent cycle of mythological paintings for Alfonso I d'Este, the Duke of Ferrara, as well as *Sacred and Profane Love*, an outdoor scene of two women, one sumptuously clothed, the other no less sumptuously naked, that now ranks among the touchstone pictures of Western art. Having transformed religious and secular imagery, what was left to revolutionize but portraiture? Just as with Gainsborough, Sargent, and Warhol, it was portraits that would make Titian's fortune. When he first attempted them in his twenties, paintings of individual men and women were a relatively new genre in Venice, one dating back only to about the 1460s. For the most part artists made them to confirm the sitter's station in the world, through the clothing, jewelry, and weaponry that proclaimed it. Hints of personality and character were rare. This is true even in one of the best of the Venetian portraits, Giovanni Bellini's meticulous image of the Doge Leonardo Loredan, from around 1501. An iridescent likeness, incredible in its high-resolution realism, it's immobile all the same, a magnificent cut-out in which the man is subordinate to his embroidered robe and doge's cap. Only in the hands of a few of the greatest painters, like Leonardo da Vinci, endlessly fiddling with the *Mona Lisa*, had portraiture become a more subtle instrument.

Titian would be among them. With the profound fluency he possessed even as a young man, he brought to his subjects a new dynamism, an ample life that announces the beating pulse beneath their tightly buttoned finery. The men and women in his canvases, though they might be princes and queens, admirals and popes, weren't inert emblems of officialdom or social status. They were lustrous mammals, robust, subtle, and complex. They possessed the space of the canvas the way they occupied the world, with force and assurance, in a supple, lifelike way. Through the eloquence of Titian's brush they offer us a glimpse of their intelligence and wit, their love of life, their vanity and ambition. And even their wary cunning. Just look at the coiled energies in Titian's portrait of the very worldly Pope Paul III, a ferret in red velvet, hunched between the grandsons he had made sure to raise to high station, but also to manipulate and betray—a man bent but ever ready to spring.

So by the 1550s, when the aging Titian begins to work often with the free brushwork of his late style, he had been for decades the acknowledged master of every consequential genre of painting. As the fabled art historian Bernard Berenson would say of him, Titian's art contained "nearly all of the Renaissance that could be expressed in painting."

And what did this much sought-after man look like in his last years? We have a good idea from the second of his two surviving self-portraits, which he produced around 1562. He offers himself dressed as a prosperous but sober Venetian. Except for his white linen collar he's all in black, a color prized in his day and ours for being elegant without ostentation. His outfit includes the black skullcap that was a trademark for him, much as Andy Warhol's wig or Louise Nevelson's false eyelashes would be for them. But look closely and you can see two glinting trickles of ornament on his costume, a double-strand gold chain. To those who knew, it was a discreet signifier of prestige, the chain of the Knight of the Golden Spur, an honor presented to him by the Holy Roman Emperor, Charles V, when he knighted Titian in 1533.

In the self-portrait Titian shows himself to us in profile—unusual, since it was a pose he almost always avoided in his work as stiff and outdated. But for many centuries it was in profile that kings and emperors were represented on coins. So maybe this is Titian proposing himself as the king of European painting. In the lower left corner of the canvas he discreetly grips what appears to be a slender paintbrush. Some scholars think it's actually a drawing stylus, included perhaps to dismiss Florentine criticism that Venetian painters, in their devotion to soft color, neglected firm draftsmanship. Whichever it is, it's an instrument of his art, making this one of the first self-portraits by a painter to include any reference to his occupation. Before Titian (and Leonardo and Michelangelo and Raphael) even the greatest painters were likely to be considered mere tradesmen, but by the mid-sixteenth century genius had earned the ones who had it a higher status, none higher than him. So why not show himself holding one of the little tools that got him there?

For good measure, Titian had achieved this high status in one of the greatest and richest cities in Europe. Glittery, hedonistic, and prideful, Venice in the sixteenth century was also still a consequential power, though a declining one. A republic ruled by a sizable oligarchy of around twenty-five hundred noblemen, it had never been subject to foreign control. This was a novelty on the Italian peninsula, where city-states like Milan and Naples were regularly devoured by France, Spain, or one another. The two and a half miles of water that separated Venice from the Italian mainland discouraged would-be invaders. But though it held itself apart from the rest of Italy, as a trading center it was also thoroughly cosmopolitan, a place where Turks, Greeks, Levantines, Germans, and Jews all did business. And unlike the feudal monarchies that dominated the rest of Europe, places where most artistic commissions that did not come from the church came from a single royal court, the merchant republic of Venice had countless civic and business associations to support artists to suit every taste.

Naturally, this congregation of wealthy families was also a city of luxury. While the worldly people of the Most Serene Republic might sometimes ask for images of Christ or the Madonna, it was themselves they most loved to see projected onto canvas, usually as epitomes of lusty materialism, happily at large among their precious goods. Even as he probed their character more adroitly than earlier painters, Titian would be their consummate enabler. Like teenagers in their look-at-me selfies, the women in his portraits are fashionistas, encased in embroidered silk, some with pearls strung in their hair in the Venetian style, fine gold chains on their wrists, and more pearls dangling from their ears. They gaze at their reflections in mirrors, a new kind of deluxe merchandise from Murano, the Venetian glass-producing island. As for the men, they offer themselves in the regalia of a power elite, in plush fur capes or embossed armor. Titian's famous early portrait of Gerolamo Barbarigo, one richly clothed arm ballooning toward us from its elbow perch, might as well be called "portrait of a big blue sleeve." As it nearly is. The title we know it by is *A Man with a Quilted Sleeve*.

But already by Titian's early adulthood, cracks were beginning to show in the city's rich façade. In 1508 Pope Julius II assembled a collection of European powers, the League of Cambrai, to successfully retake territories that

Venice had conquered on the Italian mainland, which it had done to acquire buffers against the host of warring principalities there. Though Venice eventually regained the lost possessions, its status as a military power on land was henceforth put permanently into question. As for its command of the sea, which was crucial to its wealth and position, it was under constant challenge from the ascendant Turks. Since the mid-fifteenth century a series of Ottoman sultans had been pressing hard against Venetian power in the eastern Mediterranean. So by the 1540s, when Titian was understood everywhere as one of the greatest artists in Europe, the city he represented was in a decline that would prove to be irreversible, unable to resist Turkish advances and constantly courting bankruptcy.

All the same, its slide would be gradual enough that throughout Titian's life the Most Serene Republic would continue to sparkle like the mosaics the city was famous for. It was a crossroads of commerce. (And not incidentally, the center of the European trade in first-quality artist pigments from the East, like costly ultramarine, the rich blue made from ground lapis lazuli that found its way from mines in Afghanistan into Titian's magnificent skies.) If anything, in his day the city's piazzas and waterways would become even more lustrous, with new churches, palaces, and public buildings. Its carnivals and masked balls would remain the scandalous envy of Europe, its courtesans so famous that inns in other cities would eventually use the name "Venice" in their signboards as a winking signal they were brothels. In much the same way that Britain's dwindling role in global affairs after World War II would be masked by the rise of Swinging England, with the Beatles, the Stones, and Carnaby Street offering distractions from the loss of empire, Venice disguised its growing weakness by applying heavier makeup and putting out party lights.

And among the brightest ornaments of the city was the trio composed of Titian and his two closest friends, the great architect Jacopo Tatti, known as Il Sansovino, and the boisterous writer Pietro Aretino, one of the most infamous personalities of his day. A Renaissance mini–Rat Pack, known everywhere as "the Triumvirate of Taste" or "the Three Accomplices," they were tireless drinking and feasting buddies, inseparable confidants, constantly furthering one another's careers.

Aretino and Sansovino were transplants from Rome who came separately to Venice in 1527 and stayed. Both arrived on the run. Aretino was a poet, playwright, dinner table wit, and sometime pornographer, author not only of the notorious *Lewd Sonnets*, which more than lived up to their name, but of *The School of Whoredom*, a sex manual. Having made serious enemies in Rome through his scurrilous satires, and then scandalized the city with the publication of those sonnets, he had found it prudent to leave town and to wander about Italy until he ended up in Venice.

As for Sansovino, he came as a refugee from the Sack of Rome, an outrage carried out by unpaid troops of the Holy Roman Emperor Charles V, who decided to compensate themselves by plundering the city. In the week-long orgy of rape, slaughter, and arson, tens of thousands of Romans died and untold numbers fled the smoldering ruins, Sansovino among them. But his genius was portable. Very soon he would be the most prominent architect in Venice, the man behind many of its new and rebuilt churches and public buildings. Named the city's chief architect the very year he got there, he would become the principal figure in a turn away from the ornate Gothic that had long characterized much of Venice to a more subdued classical style like the one he used for his great library of St. Mark.

For decades the three men were constantly in one another's company. You were sure to find them at the parties Aretino threw once he somehow scored a rent-free apartment on the Grand Canal, with its servants, reception hall, and rotating troupes of beautiful young women. (And young men; he went both ways.) If Aretino is to be believed, Titian the good family man usually peeled off when the dissolute poet was ready for yet another visit to this or

5 *Portrait of Pietro Aretino*, 1545, oil on canvas, 108 × 76 cm, Galleria Palatina, Florence

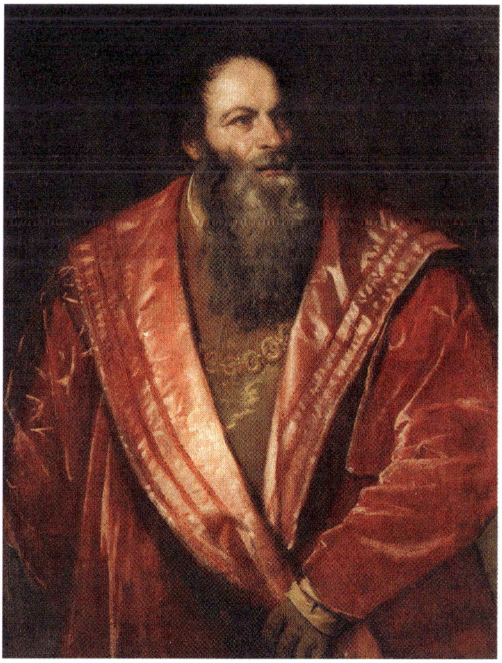

that brothel. All the same the painter adored his reprobate friend. And the high-living Aretino repaid him with poems, pamphlets, and letters, all published, even the "private" correspondence, to broadcast the news of Titian's genius and drum up business for his studio.

For his part Titian produced at least three portraits of Aretino, including one, from 1545, that appears to be a forecast of his late style. Though he would have been only in his middle or late fifties when he painted it, areas of the picture plainly feature the free brushwork he would adopt often in later years—so much of it that Aretino once suggested, perhaps in jest, that if he had paid his friend more for the portrait Titian might have taken the trouble to finish it.

So for much of Titian's life, life was good. This was due especially to his long connection to Charles V. The same emperor whose troops had sacked Rome was also the man who, not long after that atrocity, would launch Titian into European stardom. Charles was one of the pivotal figures of the sixteenth century, with an empire that covered half the continent. His paternal grandfather had been the Emperor Maximilian I, who had greatly enlarged the Habsburg territories that Charles ruled. On his mother's side his grandparents were Ferdinand and Isabella of Spain, the monarchs who had bankrolled Christopher Columbus, a bet that paid handsomely. After their deaths, Charles would assume their thrones, along with what were by then Spain's vast and profitable New World possessions. For decades he was a hinge on which European affairs constantly turned. His lengthy struggle against the rising power of France consumed the continent for decades. He was at the forefront of the fight to suppress the Protestant Reformation. His complex dealings with a succession of popes continually shifted the European balance of power back and forth.

By the time of his death, in 1558, Charles and Titian had enjoyed a close and mutually rewarding relationship for more than twenty-five years. The emperor had brought Titian to the attention of patrons all across Europe, many of them members of his extensive Habsburg clan. Over time Titian and his studio would produce for the Habsburgs alone more than 150 paintings. In turn Titian had given Charles, a man well aware of the propaganda power of art, incomparable images of himself in all his glory, as well as devotional paintings that were cherished by the pious Catholic emperor.

Titian's first encounter with Charles, in 1529, did not go well. The emperor declined to sit for a portrait, then dismissed the artist with a single ducat, the Renaissance equivalent of chump change. But in 1532, when Charles returned to Italy, he agreed at last to pose for Titian, for a portrait in armor that's now lost. But we still have Titian's next picture of Charles, in a fur-lined silver cloak beside an immense adoring hound. Though that picture was based on a very similar portrait of Charles by his Austrian painter Jacob Seisenegger, by the time Titian completed it, in 1533, Charles was persuaded that this was the man to put his image before the world. He paid Titian five hundred scudi—real money at a time when a thousand was the annual income typical for a prosperous man and a skilled shipbuilder might bring in only fifty. But much more than that, Charles took the extraordinary step of raising him to the aristocracy by making him a count and conferring upon him a knighthood, the one represented by that golden chain in the self-portrait Titian produced decades later. He also named him as his court painter. That would be a considerable honor at any time. It was more remarkable for the fact that Titian, the man who hated to leave Venice, had no intention of hauling himself and his family to the emperor's principal court in the ancient Bavarian city of Augsburg, much less to follow Charles and his retinue on their constant movements around his empire, to palaces in Hungary, Italy, Spain, and the Netherlands.

While he would never relocate to Augsburg, Titian made two lengthy visits. First summoned there in 1547, fully fourteen years after being named court painter, he arrived early the following year, already nearing sixty, after a difficult winter journey across the Alps. He remained for eight months, installed in apartments adjacent to the emperor's chambers and granted so many private meetings that it puzzled some of the emperor's jealous courtiers. What could explain this intimacy between an emperor and a mere painter?

But why not? While Charles had very little grasp of the aesthetic pleasures to be gotten from art, he understood well its political uses. And he plainly saw that Titian could provide him with potent representations of himself and his rule. It was on that first visit to Augsburg that Titian produced for Charles a particularly powerful invention, the mounted equestrian portrait. It would prove to be yet another enduring new genre of Western painting that Titian inaugurated. In a canvas intended to commemorate the emperor's victory the year before at the Battle of Mühlberg, where imperial troops defeated a league of German Protestant armies, Titian gives us Charles literally dressed to kill, on a capering warhorse, in the embossed black armor with glinting gold trim that he wore on the day of battle. But this Charles is also a paragon of thoughtful action, looking somehow both implacable and meditative, bellicose and introspective, a man of war with a life of the mind. The picture made an impression of mastery so compelling to future generations that portraits on horseback would become the must-have emblem for every weaponized leader of men from Charles I of England to Napoleon and beyond.

Titian's seventeenth-century biographer Carlo Ridolfi reports a famous anecdote from that first visit, a story that has come to symbolize the emperor's extravagant regard for his court painter. Ridolfi tells us that one day when Charles and his retinue were visiting Titian at his Augsburg studio, the master accidentally dropped his brush. To the astonishment of everyone in the room, including Titian, Charles stooped to pick it up. Titian hastened to tell the emperor, "Sire, I am not worthy of such a servant." Charles is said to have replied, "Titian is worthy to be served by Caesar."

Did this charming scene really take place? Baroque-era biographers were not the first, or the last, to have an easygoing notion of fact checking. But even if it's a story too good to confirm, it says something true about the profound appreciation Charles had by that time for Titian's genius. This man wasn't just his hired hand. He was his evangelist. And to the extent possible between an emperor and a commoner, however brilliant, his intimate.

Maybe that exchange even happened. Charles was a complicated and contradictory man. Ever mindful of himself as the most powerful leader in Europe, the Christian Caesar, he was also capable of acts of surprising humility, never more so than in one he undertook toward the end of his life. Two years before he relinquished his soul, he handed away his empire. Like King Lear, though half a century before Shakespeare set down Lear's tale, he voluntarily gave up his throne and all the territories under his rule.

It was a step he had been contemplating for some time, but he was moved to take it at last by the conclusion of the Peace of Augsburg in 1555. A complex agreement negotiated by his younger brother, Ferdinand, it aimed to settle the constant turmoil in Germany between Catholics and Lutherans. One of its provisions stipulated that in each of Germany's many principalities and free cities the religion of the ruler would be adopted by all his subjects.

However coercive its terms—certainly from the point of view of the subject populations—the treaty did for a while establish a measure of peace. But because it allowed Lutheranism to be recognized for the first time as a legitimate faith in whichever states it was adopted, it was a bitter compromise for Charles. One of the chief opponents of the Reformation, for decades he had hoped to become the secular leader of an all-Catholic Europe. With that ambition dashed, better to relinquish the crown and retreat to a pious retirement in Spain, to a villa attached to a monastery in Yuste, in the hill country of the Extremadura.

When he arrived there is 1557, Charles brought with him three precious Titians. One was a posthumous portrait of his late wife, Isabella, that Titian had done for him ten years earlier, long after her death from a miscarriage in 1539. Another was an *Ecce Homo*—an image of Christ crowned with thorns—that Titian had presented to him during the artist's first stay in Augsburg. The third was the most spectacular. During Titian's second and final visit to Augsburg, in 1550–51, Charles commissioned him to produce a painting for his private religious devotion. When completed in 1554, *The Adoration of the Trinity*, also sometimes called *Glory*, was a kind of heavenly whirlwind. Titian shows a tumultuous throng of airborne figures who include Adam and Eve, Moses with his tablets, and Noah with his ark, with Charles and his family among them. They all gesture up rapturously toward God, Christ, and the Holy Spirit, perched at top amid sunlit clouds, with just below them to our left the Virgin and John the Baptist. On the right edge of this teeming canvas Titian has even included himself as a pious graybeard. Remarkably, the old man we see beside him is very possibly his roguish buddy Aretino, libertine, glutton, and sometime pornographer, the last person you would expect to find in heaven. But Titian, you might say, was working the door.

At Yuste, Charles had this enormous picture, over eleven feet high and nearly eight feet wide, placed at first above the high altar of the church. But on his deathbed in 1558 he had it transferred to his room, to join the portrait of Isabella. So it was with his eyes fastened on Titian's *Adoration*, a swirling portal through which his soul might be suctioned from this world, that the fifty-eight-year-old emperor went to meet the King of Kings.

At his abdication, Charles had divided his domains between his son Philip and his brother Ferdinand. To Ferdinand he granted the Holy Roman Empire, extending across what is now Germany, parts of Austria, Poland, the Czech Republic, and Switzerland. To Philip went Milan, the Kingdom of Naples, and the Netherlands, but above all the rich prize of Spain and its New World territories with their silver mines. Those would fund Spain's ambitions to be the preeminent European power, which included the ill-fated Spanish Armada that Philip hoped would force England back into the Catholic fold.

From his father, Philip would gain one other precious inheritance—Titian. By the time of the emperor's death his son was already Titian's enthusiastic patron, able to appreciate not only the propaganda value of the portraits that Charles so admired but the wider range of Titian's gifts, especially for mythological scenes, the more coyly erotic the better. For the remaining eighteen years of Titian's life, Philip would be his most constant and discerning patron.

The two men had first met in Milan in 1548, where Philip commissioned several portraits. He would do that again when Titian made his second trip to Augsburg, two years later. Not long after his father's death, Philip also saw to it that Titian should be paid the accumulated arrears of an annual pension promised to him by Charles, but never disbursed. Philip directed his governor in Milan to issue the full remaining sum of twenty-two hundred scudi, a sizable amount.

However much Titian benefited from Philip's patronage, after decades that had taken him from one triumph to another, his last years would be a trying time. Like anyone tipping into their seventies, he was outliving his circle of familiars. In 1556, death had claimed his rollicking comrade Aretino. The enormous man was at dinner with friends when he leaned back in his chair to roar at someone's joke. The chair collapsed beneath him, leading him to suffer an attack of some kind from which he died soon after. Though the official verdict was apoplexy, friends liked to say he had laughed himself to death, a conclusion he would have loved. Four years after Aretino's death, Titian also lost his brother Francesco, whom he had always regarded fondly and kept close, working with him to oversee the family timber business, as well as some iron mines they eventually owned in the Cadore.

By that time Titian had also suffered a blow that haunted and enraged him, a near-fatal attempt on the life of his beloved younger son, Orazio. The circumstances remain murky. In the Venetian tradition of family workshops, Orazio had not only become a painter himself but also handled the business affairs of his father's studio. Early in 1559, Titian dispatched him to Milan to collect the pension money Philip had promised. While there Orazio was invited by Leone Leoni, court sculptor to the Habsburgs, to stay for a while at his palazzo, itself a gift from Charles.

Leoni was a notoriously volatile character. He had twice been accused of attempted murder, spent time as a galley slave in the papal fleet as punishment for one of those attempts, and conducted a counterfeiting scheme in collusion with none other than Titian's friend Aretino. All the same he was a longtime friend of Titian's as well, so Orazio duly arrived at Leoni's. For reasons we don't know, he decided after a time to move back to his lodgings at an inn. Even less do we know why, when Orazio returned to the palazzo to gather some belongings, he was brutally attacked by Leoni, his son Alessandro, and another henchman. After throwing a cloak or bag over Orazio's head, they stabbed and slashed him seven times with daggers and swords. He survived only because his servant, with his own blade drawn, was able to fend off the attackers long enough for his cries to bring neighbors, who helped the men, now both wounded, to make their escape.

How to explain this sudden assault? Since Leoni knew Orazio was carrying the pension money, one likely motive is robbery. Orazio may also have become involved somehow with Leoni's mistress. Whatever the reason, Titian learned of the attack several weeks later through a letter from Orazio. For months afterward, he was beside himself. Hoping to move Philip to punish his son's assailants, Titian wrote to him at once. "If Orazio had been killed I swear to you with all my faith that from the pain of it I, who have placed all my life and my hope in his wellbeing in this my impotent old age, would have been deprived of spirit and consequently of the ability to serve my most potent Catholic King." Titian may even have worried that Orazio might be tracked down and ambushed again by the incorrigible Leoni, a fear that would haunt Orazio for years. Because what the aged painter seems to have been hinting, none too subtly, is that if Orazio were to die Titian would have had to put down his brush. Philip wouldn't have been getting any more of those pictures he liked so much.

In subsequent letters Titian would urge the Spanish king repeatedly to take action against Leoni, who was after all a Habsburg court sculptor and medallion maker. But the would-be assassin was also a gifted artist who had made many images of Charles V—pendants, medals, cameos, and busts. No less than Titian's portraits, these were important devices in the imperial propaganda machine. Perhaps Leoni was simply of too much potential value to Philip, now that the machinery was devoted to him. The king simply ignored Titian's pleas, until finally the old man took the hint. Leoni stood trial but would get off with a fine. After a brief banishment from Milan, he would return to go on living splendidly in his palace, one more thing to fuel a deepening cynicism in Titian's old age.

Titian's distress over the attack was only heightened by the fact that Orazio was by far the favorite of his two sons. Meanwhile relations with his elder son, Pomponio, were a constant trial that reached a sour crescendo as Titian neared eighty. Both boys were Titian's children by his first wife, Cecilia, a barber's daughter from a village near his hometown. Originally his housekeeper, she bore Titian's sons out of wedlock before he married her in 1525 to legitimize them. Five years later she died, perhaps after giving birth to Titian's daughter Lavinia. Then again, Lavinia's mother may have been Titian's second wife, about whom we know nothing, not even her name. Later there would be another daughter, possibly born to a household servant whom Titian never married.

The old man's dealings with Pomponio were difficult largely because he had long ago pushed the unwilling boy into the priesthood, which he saw as a promising career path for a young man of common birth. No matter that Titian had been made a count by Charles and might be treated everywhere like an aristocrat; he wasn't one and he knew it. There would be no hereditary titles for his children. What he also knew was that well-connected priests could monetize their calling, settling into comfortable lives through "benefices," church positions that came with income from vineyards and farmland.

From Pomponio's earliest years, Titian struggled to secure for his son a number of these benefices, getting the first when the boy was just six, long before he became an ordained priest at around forty. Though he would always resent the way his father took control of his fate, for many years he went along with it. After all, the money was good. But by the 1550s, when he had already taken the minor orders that were preparation for the priesthood, he had thoroughly stopped aspiring to a priestly way of life, much less any pretense to celibacy. Titian's loyal friend Aretino wrote repeatedly to plead with Pomponio, for his father's sake, to give up his "riotous living" and "lewd doings." Interestingly, the young man sometimes undertook these escapades with none other than Francesco Sansovino, son of his father's other cherished friend, the great architect Jacopo Sansovino. If nothing else, the wayward boys could commiserate about the burden of having famous fathers.

Things finally came to a head in 1567, when Titian, exasperated by his son's way of life, decided to take for himself the revenue from two of Pomponio's ecclesiastical cash cows, setting off a final crisis in their relations. Only after an intervention by church authorities did the estranged father and son draw up an agreement settling the matter, but the damage was done. Titian would live for nine more years, but Pomponio would never see or even write to him again.

No wonder then that in old age Titian's correspondence with Philip was full of complaints about what he called the "calamities" of his time, both public and private. But there was one place he could always retreat from these: to the refuge of the canvas, and the new possibilities he was discovering there—the late style.

The more fluid brushwork of that style took to new lengths what a number of Renaissance commentators, notably Giorgio Vasari, had already identified as a tendency in Venetian painting generally, one that distinguished it from that of Tuscan artists based mainly in Florence. In this dichotomy, Florentine work was characterized by *disegno*—the Italian word for "drawing" or "design"—the attribute of pictures with firm contours, the crisp lines and clearly outlined forms you find in any painting by Botticelli, Raphael, or Michelangelo. Those paintings usually rested upon many preparatory drawings, which could then be copied onto the canvas as "underdrawing" before pigment was carefully applied within the lines.

By contrast, the work of Venetian artists was said to be based upon the contrary principle of *colore*, the use of color as a fundamental expressive and compositional element. It was characteristic of Venetians like Titian and Paolo Veronese to blend and layer color, softening the contours of human or landscape forms. And they often built up those forms directly on the canvas, without extensive underdrawing, sometimes with none at all.

It's often remarked that, in all this, Venetian painters seemed to express the liquid character of Venice itself, a place penetrated everywhere by the sea, a city of moist air, atmospheric fogs, and shimmering reflections in the rippling water of its canals. For most of his life, Titian's art, with its sensuous modeling, would epitomize this soft, lustrous aspect of *colore*. But in his last decades, though his actual palette became more subdued, with grays and ochers elbowing in among his more characteristic rose and blue, Titian's more energetic brushwork drove this idea of soft contour and permeable form into utterly new realms, almost sometimes to the point of disintegration. His liquid surroundings appear to have entered his imagination and to flow through his brush to such an extent that his people fluctuate and his landscapes tremble.

A reason that the aging Titian could afford to experiment along these lines was that he had in Philip II a sophisticated patron who gave him free rein. By his seventies, though his ever-busy studio was turning out "Titians" produced largely by his assistants, the canvases painted almost entirely by the master were intended, with few exceptions, for Philip. In him Titian had a learned and receptive audience, a man with "approving eyes," as Titian described the royal response to his work in a letter to the Spanish king himself. So in 1551, after his second and last trip to the emperor's court in Augsburg, Titian agreed that over the next decade he would supply Philip with around ten large paintings on a mixture of religious and mythological subjects that were left unspecified. Six of them would be mythological canvases that Titian would call *poesies*, "poetic inventions," a term in use at that time to describe paintings drawn from classical literature. His would be based mostly on episodes in the *Metamorphoses*, a retelling of stories from Greek mythology by the Latin poet Ovid. By calling these great pictures *poesies*, Titian appears to have intended not only to point to their sources in ancient texts, but to signal that they were poems of a sort themselves, that as an art form his images were—at the very least—the equal of words, with the narrative force and nuance of literature.

One can't really talk about the *poesies*, some of the greatest and most revealing products of Titian's last years, without first touching upon the reservations that complicate any understanding of his late work. So different were many of his late pictures, so hasty looking, that some people, then and now, have wondered whether his new kind of brushwork was simply a sign of infirmity, one more consequence of old age. In his lifetime, there were visitors to his studio who saw in what Vasari called Titian's *pittura a macchia*— "patchy painting"—not an intended style but an accidental one, a sign that he was losing it, that his eyesight was too weak and his hand too shaky to accomplish the more assured finish of his earlier work.

This is the suspicion raised in 1568 by a Venetian art dealer, Niccolò Stoppio, when he mentioned Titian in a letter to the German banker and art collector Max Fugger. "Everyone says he no longer sees what he is doing, and his hand trembles so much that he cannot bring anything to completion, but leaves this to his pupils." The gossip-loving Stoppio had some personal issues with Titian. He resented Titian's close professional relationship with one of Stoppio's competitors, the dealer Jacopo Strada. He had also quarreled with Titian's son Orazio. So his malicious report to Fugger may be payback from a jealous man.

All the same he raised a question that has been endlessly debated by Titian scholars and will probably never be settled. Could it be that the rough passages in some of Titian's late paintings are simply the stumblings of a dwindling master who couldn't do any better? Most scholars are persuaded that the free brushwork was intentional. For one thing, Titian had sometimes painted that way when he was still in his fifties and his physical capabilities were not in question. As early as 1545, his great friend Aretino was complaining that Titian's most recent portrait of him—the first picture we know of in which Titian worked freely—looked so dashed off that it was more like an oil sketch than a finished painting.

Meanwhile, after he reached genuine old age, even as he was regularly indulging in the rough brushwork of his late style, he was also turning out occasional canvases with a more conventional finish. This would describe the first two of his three versions of *Tarquin and Lucretia*. When Titian completed them, in the early 1570s, he would have been in his early eighties. All three show us a rape in progress, as the ancient Roman prince Sextus Tarquinius, dagger in hand, moves in on a cowering but resistant Lucretia, the chaste wife of a Roman nobleman. One version was produced for Philip, and in a letter to the Spanish monarch from 1568 Titian makes assurances that he was hard at work personally on this exciting new picture: "Because I desire to close the days of this my extreme old age in the service of the Catholic king, my Lord, I promise you that I am composing another invention of painting of much greater labor and ingenuity than perhaps any I have produced for many years until now."

If by that year Titian were only capable of a shaky, stutter-step brushstroke, then how to explain the much smoother execution of that work? Likewise his last surviving portrait, from 1568, an image of Jacopo Strada, the art dealer whom Stoppio so much resented. Though the brushwork is feathery over much of the canvas, the details are realized with an acute eye and a confident hand. Even in one of the last pictures to leave his studio, a version of *The Penitent Saint Jerome* that he sent to Philip in 1575, a few months before his death, the figure of the saint is executed at a high degree of finish. None of these is the work of a man who can't hold a steady brush or see what that brush is doing. And though we have no record of Titian's using eyeglasses, they were available in his day. He even shows us a man wearing a pair of pince-nez in *The Tribute Money,* a painting he completed in his early seventies.

One way to think about Titian's late style is as an early instance of an artist exercising a right to self-expression, to make his own rules and work in his own fashion. This was a concept still just emerging in the 1500s, one that would later become central to the very idea of the artist. Even in the sixteenth century, when Michelangelo, Leonardo, Titian, and a few others were producing highly original and personal work, most artists were still regarded as tradesmen for hire. They belonged to guilds that combined them with decorators and sign painters. But by his sixties, Titian was exercising a rare degree of autonomy. This was especially true for the *poesies*. For all of them, Philip did not dictate the subject but left the choice to Titian. This was something very unusual in an artist/patron relationship, especially when the patron was a king. But then, Titian was Titian.

What this meant was that he was free to choose stories that might hold a personal meaning for him. And what he largely chose were ever darker episodes on the theme of divine injustice, the capriciousness and cruelty of the gods and their indifference to the suffering of lesser creatures. In his final decades, this was the problem he found so compelling that in the *poesies*, some of the greatest works he would ever produce, he returned to it again and again. Often he would customize these tales, departing from Ovid's text when it suited his purpose, generally to make them even more bitter. Perhaps because Titian worked on this series in the first decades of the Counter-Reformation, with the church ever on the lookout for heresy or impiety, it may have seemed prudent to ascribe those sentiments to pagan divinities than to indict the Christian God.

The first of the *poesies* was *Danaë*, which Titian sent to Philip in 1553. No doubt it was calculated to please the still youthful king, a very frisky heterosexual, in part because it's plainly a slice of mythological cheesecake, with enough naked flesh to qualify as a Renaissance centerfold. (All the *poesies* would feature female nudity. For that reason, after Philip's death in 1599 they would be sequestered in the most private apartments of the Royal Alcázar in Madrid, away from the eyes of pious visitors.) The mythical Danaë was the daughter of Acrisius, king of Argos. Because an oracle had prophesied that his daughter would one day give birth to a son who would kill him, the king kept her locked up in a bronze tower. In vain. Zeus—or Jupiter in Ovid's Roman retelling—became smitten by the girl and had recourse to supernatural means of entry. Taking the form of a shower of golden particles, he arrived in her chamber and rained down upon her as she lay back in bed. In due time Danaë would give birth to the son Acrisius feared, the hero Perseus. As a young man he would kill the Gorgon Medusa, she of the snaky head, and free the princess Andromeda, cruelly chained to a rock by the sea god Neptune.

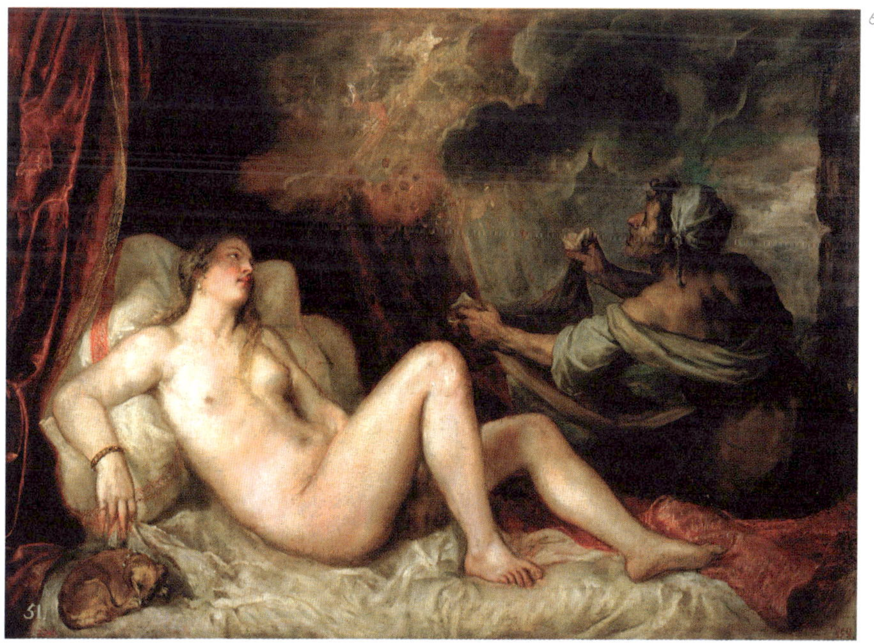
6

Danaë, 1560–65, oil on canvas, 129.8 × 181.2 cm, Museo Nacional del Prado, Madrid

En route home from these adventures he would stop in Thessaly to take part in athletic games. As fate would have it—quite literally—Acrisius would be in attendance, and Perseus would unintentionally strike him dead with a discus. Prophecy fulfilled.

But for now that's all in the future. What we see in Titian's picture is the spectacular moment in which Perseus is conceived. Before a backdrop of wine-red curtains, Danaë lies naked on white silk sheets. Her languorous pose, with her right leg bent at the knee and pulled up toward her, echoes Michelangelo's *Night*, a sculpture he made for the tomb of Lorenzo de Medici in Florence. It may also owe something to his painting *Leda and the Swan*, now lost, another scene of a mortal woman coupling with a transformed Jupiter that Titian could have known through copies. But Titian has considerably softened the muscular woman Michelangelo fashioned for *Night*. Though plainly Jupiter has not asked the young woman's permission for this surprise visitation, she doesn't appear to be experiencing it as an assault. As a cloudburst of golden droplets descends toward her, Danaë leans back on a pile of silk pillows in what looks like a carnal stupor, her legs open, a dreamy expression on her upturned face and her right hand lightly fingering a white handkerchief. At the foot of her bed sits a much older nurse. No doubt remembering her younger days, she gathers up one end of her flowing shawl in hope of catching a splash of the divine ejaculate.

The *Danaë* Titian sent to Philip was actually his second version of the scene. The first, produced about five years earlier, had been made for Cardinal Alessandro Farnese, one of the grandsons of Pope Paul III. There would be at least four others, some mostly from Titian's hand, others mostly products of his studio. Of the ones that were plainly his, the most interesting is the version he completed around 1565, now in the Prado. (Long thought to be the picture Titian sent to Philip, most scholars now believe it's one of eighteen canvases that were sold in the next century to Philip's grandson, Philip IV, by his court painter Velázquez.) Completed when Titian was in his mid-to-late seventies, this later canvas shows clear evidence of his increasingly free paint application. You see it especially in the flickering rapids of the sheets that the young woman rests on, fabric she grips hard with the excited fingers of her right hand as she accepts the god's golden penetration. No more of that lightly fingered handkerchief. Those sheets are painted in slashing strokes of white, equivalents for the crackling sexual charge of the scene.

Titian's next *poesie* for Philip would be *Venus and Adonis*, another scene he had painted before. In Ovid's poem the goddess Venus worries that her famously beautiful lover Adonis, a mortal and avid huntsman, might be killed while on the chase after some dangerous beast. Titian shows the pair on the morning that an unwitting Adonis is setting out to meet that very fate on the tusks of a wild boar. Fearing what's in store, Venus is frantically attempting to hold him back, wrapping her upraised arms around his torso while his impatient dogs are already pulling him away.

It so happens that in Ovid there is no such scene. In his poem, when Adonis heads out on the fatal morning, Venus is busy coursing through the skies in her chariot. Titian invents their fraught parting or may have borrowed it from a Renaissance poet's retelling of the story. He shows us Venus

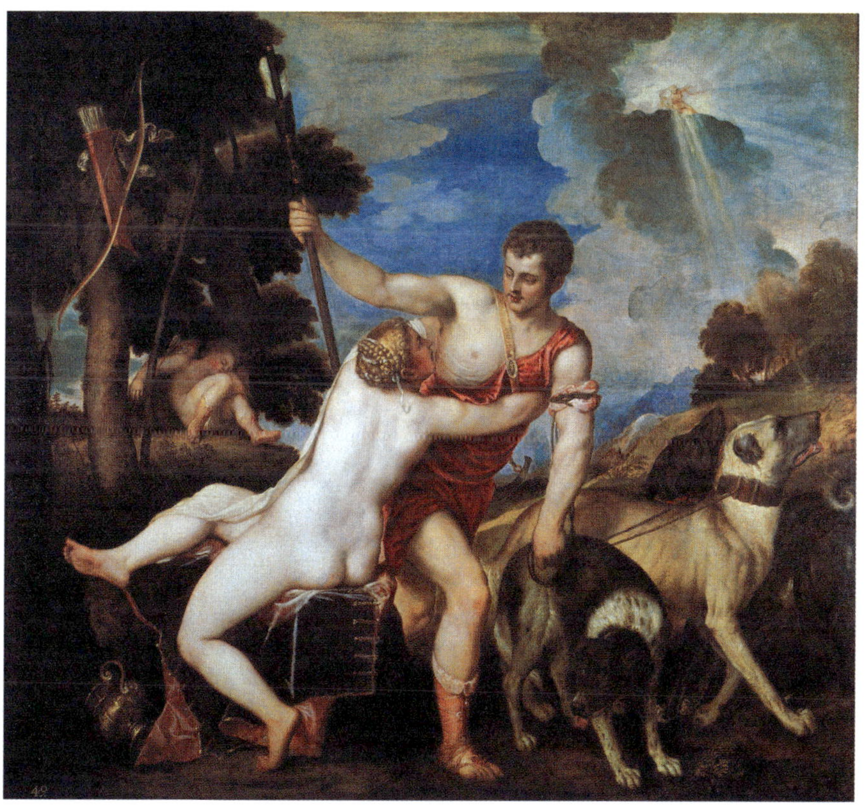 7

Venus and Adonis, ca. 1554, oil on canvas, 186 × 207 cm, Museo Nacional del Prado, Madrid

unclothed and from behind, sitting awkwardly on a rock covered by a purple cloth. Awkwardly but unforgettably, her legs askew and her rump flattened slightly against its hard seat. One of his hunting dogs, straining at the leash, attempts to drag Adonis away. Titian's profound conflation of mad love and naked flesh would make this one of his most popular images. In all he would produce at least five versions, his studio turned out more, and it was the subject of countless engravings. Philip reported back that it was "perfect."

Titian would finish Philip's version of *Venus and Adonis* in 1554 and ship it to him in London, where at his father's behest the twenty-seven-year-old Philip had recently wed the queen of England, Mary Tudor, who at thirty-eight was eleven years his senior. Daughter of the late Henry VIII, she would soon become the notorious "Bloody Mary." An ultramilitant Catholic, she would stop at nothing to suppress the Protestant faith in England, jailing and burning heretics before dying suddenly of the flu in 1558, no doubt to the relief of Philip. He approved her religious fervor but shared her bed without enthusiasm. While Mary lived, Philip was probably glad to have another slice of classical soft core from Titian, even if the story it was based on ended in tragedy.

By the time he dispatched *Venus and Adonis*, Titian was already at work on his next *poesie*. *Perseus and Andromeda* offers us the moment when an almost somersaulting Perseus—that same spectacular offspring of Danaë and Jupiter who had recently slain Medusa—swoops in headfirst from the top of the canvas to fight off a sea monster headed for the captive and nearly naked Andromeda. In yet another instance of divine injustice, she's been chained to a rock by Neptune, god of the sea, to punish her mother, Queen Cassiopeia of Ethiopia, for bragging that she and her daughter were more beautiful than the sea nymphs who served Neptune.

This damaged picture—the pigment has decayed, and one subsequent owner hung it in an open courtyard—is the first of Philip's *poesies* to be executed in Titian's looser style. And again, the flickering brushwork transmits the headlong energies of the scene. Perseus plummets into the picture upside down, racing to defeat the menacing sea creature before it can reach the fetching Andromeda, who somehow manages to struggle with her chains in a graceful balletic pose. The head-over-heels figure of Perseus may be Titian's response to a tour de force that his rival Jacopo Tintoretto completed six years earlier to much acclaim, the vividly inverted apostle who dives into

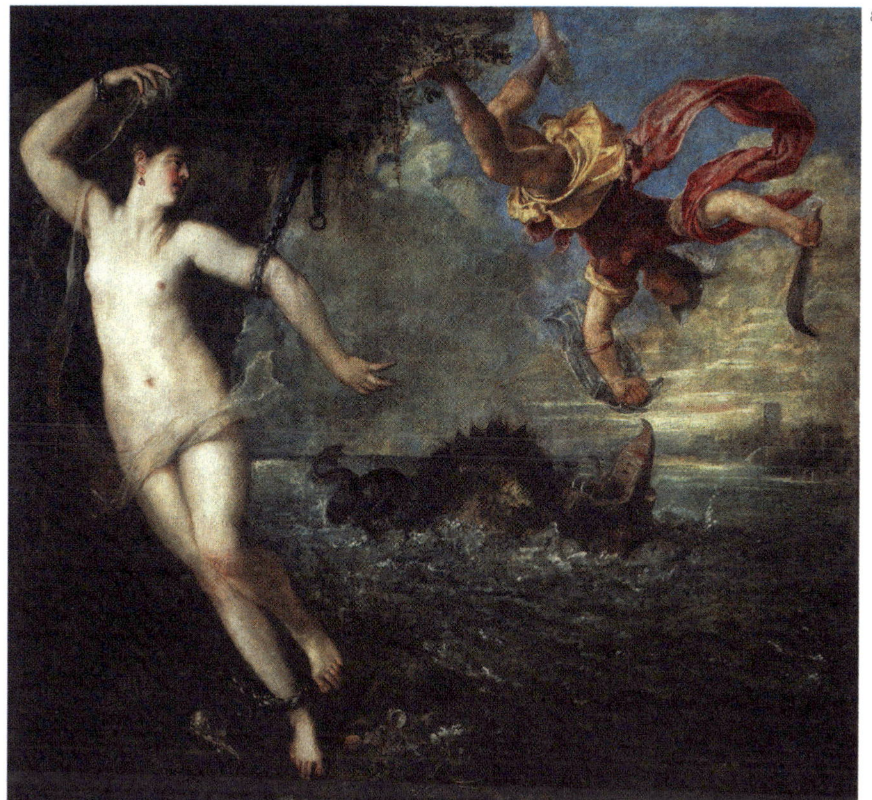

8

Perseus and Andromeda, ca. 1554–56, oil on canvas, 183.3 × 199.3 cm, The Wallace Collection, London

The Miracle of the Slave (also known as *The Miracle of Saint Mark*). Some three decades Titian's junior, Tintoretto had once been his studio assistant, then struck out on his own to become his sometime antagonist within the small universe of first-tier Venetian painters. Titian generally disdained Tintoretto, who generally returned the favor, but he may have intended here to show that the old man could play some of the younger man's tricks.

Titian completed *Perseus* in 1556, the year his friend Aretino died. Around the same time he set to work on two truly ominous paintings drawn from Ovid, both concerning the goddess Diana. He would finish them in 1559, and in both, though the palettes have their bright passages, the actions of the goddess are capricious and cruel. *Diana and Callisto* is drawn from a fraught episode in Ovid involving one of her attendants, the nymph Callisto.

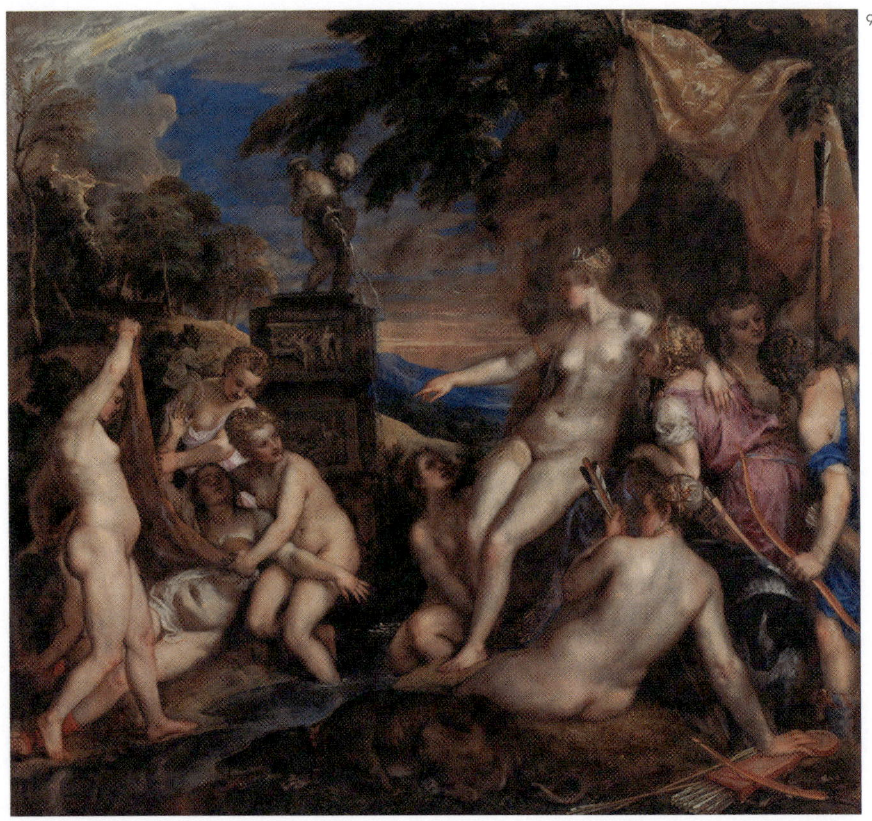
9

Diana and Callisto, 1556–59, oil on canvas, 187 × 204.5, The National Gallery, London, and National Galleries of Scotland, Edinburgh

Nymphs were young women who both inhabited and personified elements of nature like woodlands and streams. Among the many who waited upon Diana, Callisto was a favorite, at least until she suffered the ultimate rejection. In the story as related by Ovid, she's forced to strip and bathe by Diana's other nymphs, who suspect she's hiding something. They're right, she's pregnant, a condition that will lead to her expulsion from the virgin retinue of the chaste goddess.

Titian shows us the moment in which her pregnancy is revealed to Diana, who appears on the right side of the scene, upright, imperial and, all the same, naked—this is after all a painting intended for Phillip. With a pitiless gaze and a long, accusatory finger, she points across the canvas to Callisto, restrained by three of Diana's attendants so a fourth can expose her swollen belly. It doesn't matter to the impassive goddess that Callisto had been raped by none other than that tireless reprobate Jupiter. Worse still, to trick the nymph into receiving his embrace, he had first assumed the form of Diana. (It's complicated.) But mercy is not a divine attribute. In the harsh justice of the gods, no extenuating circumstances apply. This is a lesson Callisto will learn yet again when Jupiter's furious wife, Juno, after learning of her husband's transgression, turns the helpless nymph into a bear. After many further plot developments, Jupiter will fling her and her son into the sky to become the constellations Ursa Major and Ursa Minor.

Does Titian intend for us to conclude that the fate of Callisto holds a lesson for humans too? By his choice of subject is he implying that mere mortals are also the playthings of the gods? Almost certainly, and not for the last time. As he moves into his seventies this is where his disposition often appears to be heading, into a mournful disenchantment.

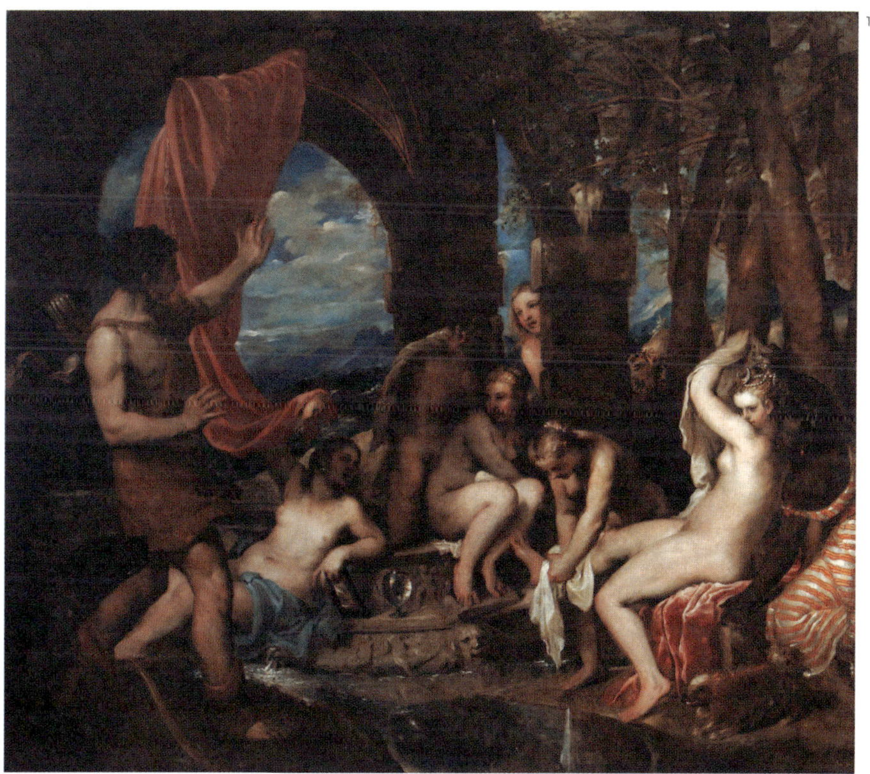
10

Diana and Actaeon, 1556–59, oil on canvas, 184.5 × 202.2 cm, The National Gallery, London, and National Galleries of Scotland, Edinburgh

The second of the Diana *poesies* from 1559 is *Diana and Actaeon,* one of two paintings Titian would devote to the story of Actaeon, a hunter who stumbled upon the naked goddess bathing with her attendants. He finds them in an odd hybrid setting, a leafy grotto semi-enclosed by some arched classical ruins, where the water of Diana's sacred spring is pooling around a carved fountain as it tilts into the soft ground. Titian shows us the moment when Actaeon, looking to quench his thirst, happens upon the scene and glimpses the lordly Diana unclothed—in Ovid's words, "as the water beads like diamonds to deck the breast of the goddess." However unintended, this is a sight forbidden to mere mortals, and she will impose a terrible punishment. She will change the accidental invader into a stag, and in that form he will be torn apart by his own hunting dogs.

But for now the scene has not yet devolved into tragedy. The fatal error has only just occurred, and Titian's palette is subdued but not yet somber, its dominant browns highlighted with areas of burgundy, rose, and blue. The flesh of Diana and her nymphs plays across the painting in shades of ocher, pale pink, and ivory, as well as the dark brown of a Black attendant who presses closely behind her. We know from Ovid that in a moment Diana will rise to splash Actaeon with water and that "a rack of impressive antlers" will sprout from the places where the droplets touch his head, the first stage of his transformation.

Not long after he completed those pictures Titian would learn of the attack on his son, a blow worsened by Philip's failure to punish the assailants despite Titian's pleas. It was in that frame of mind that he began work on *The Death of Actaeon,* the last brutal chapter of the story. A painting he would promise to Philip but never deliver, it would still be in his studio at the time of his own death. It's a literally dark picture. In a subdued palette keyed to gray-green and ocher, colors that may have darkened even further over time, Titian shows us the moment when Actaeon is attacked by his hounds. We see him as an upright figure fleeing through the woods in midtransition, still with the body of a man but already with the head of a stag.

Oddly, Titian has chosen to push that crucial action off to the right and into a murky middle distance, as if the death of the mere human is less important than the cruelty of the goddess who inflicts it. So in the left foreground we see the much larger figure of Diana, outlined in well-lit profile and holding a curved bow in her outstretched left hand, a pose that reminds us

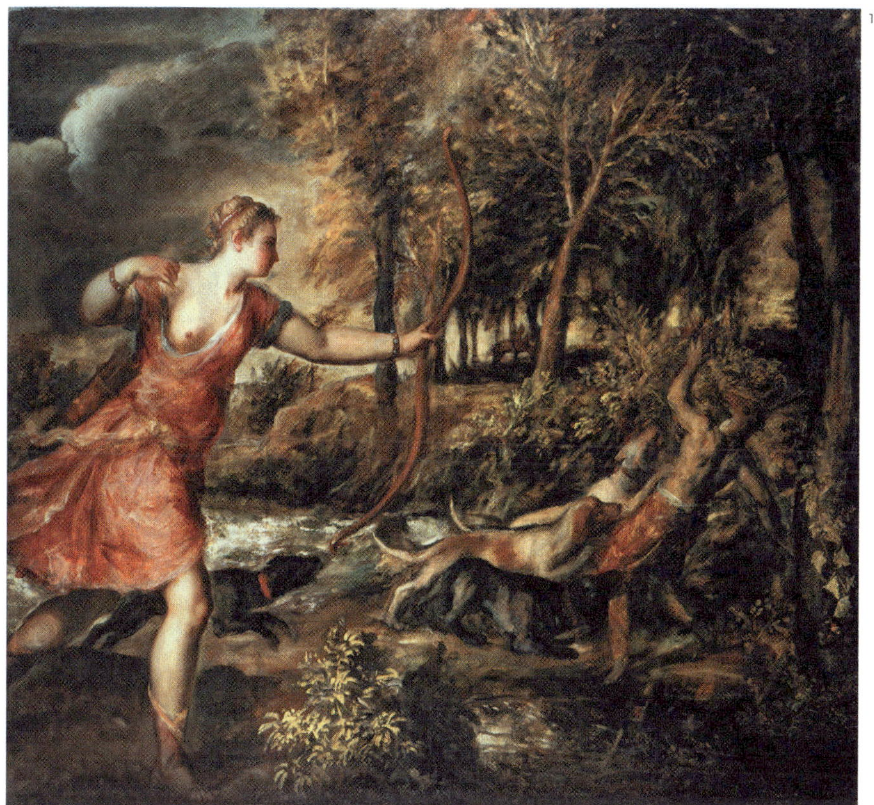
11

The Death of Actaeon, ca.1559–75, oil on canvas, 178.8 × 197.8 cm, The National Gallery, London

she is also goddess of the hunt. With the neckline of her reddish tunic lowered to reveal her right breast, she's in a running posture that makes her appear to be hunting down Actaeon. Strangely she has her right hand pulled back as though drawing a bowstring, but her bow has neither a string nor an arrow in place. Perhaps Titian was still pondering to the end how best to add those. Whatever the case, there's no scene of Diana pursuing Actaeon in Ovid's poem, where she's not even present at his death. But it's an invention that dramatizes her role as the hapless man's executioner and drives home the moral of the picture—the gods care nothing for the suffering of mortals.

Titian's virtuoso touch is visible everywhere here. In a canvas where water churns, clouds roll, dogs come bounding into the picture, and the very trees appear to tremble at Diana's vengeance, he doubles down on the ability of his free brushwork to be the instrument of feeling. The surface agitation is amplified by the thick twill of his canvas. This quintessence of late-style turbulence and flickering form is what the painter Francis Bacon was getting at four centuries later when he told an interviewer in 1972 that the images in this second *Actaeon* picture "are never absolutely definite and yet they are the suggestion of a tremendously tragic act."

Though it would not be that scene of Actaeon's death, Philip would get one last *poesie*. Delivered to him in 1562, *The Rape of Europa* is Titian's penultimate reflection on how the gods do with us as they please. Once again the story concerns that serial seducer Jupiter. Smitten this time with the princess Europa, he has transformed himself into a dazzling white bull. Though his strength, as Ovid tells us, is "eloquent in the carved musculature of his neck and shoulders," his eyes are (deceptively) gentle. After a bit of cross-species

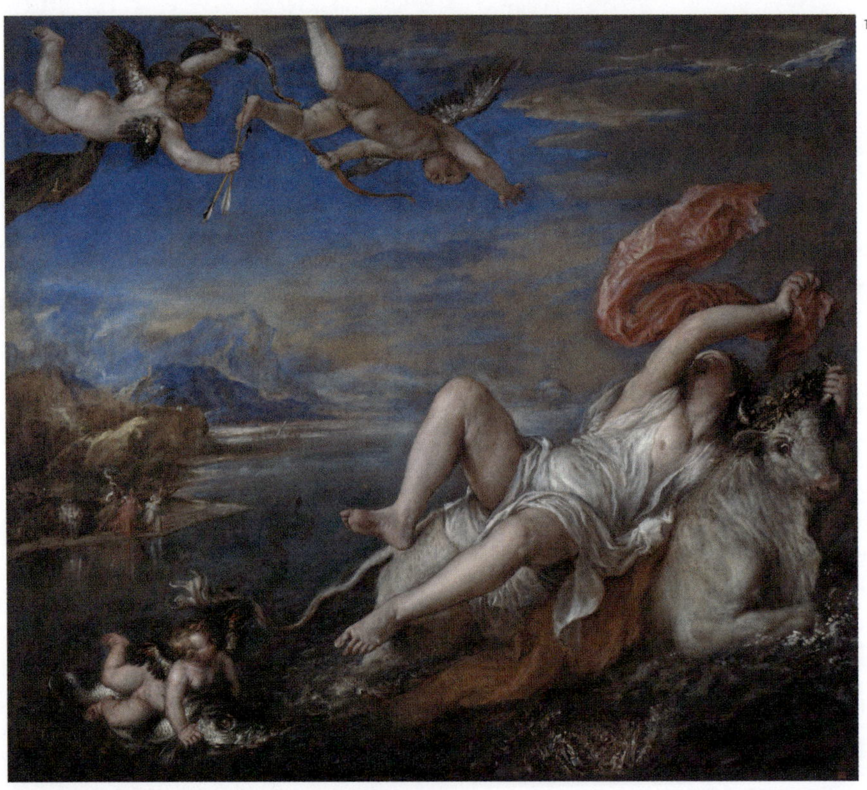 12

The Rape of Europa, 1559–62, oil on canvas, 178 × 205 cm, Isabella Stewart Gardner Museum, Boston

flirtation with the virgin princess, who is thrilled by "the enormous lips that nuzzled her open palm," he entices her to climb aboard for a ride. Bad idea.

In Titian's painting we see the cunning bull making off across the Mediterranean toward Crete, the princess flung half naked over his back. Racing after them in the picture's lower left corner is a winged putto riding a silver dolphin like a jet ski. (However outrageous the transgression here, there's a plain whiff of slapstick in this painting.) While hanging on for dear life to one of the bull's horns, waving a long pennant of red silk as a distress flag, Europa manages to keep an eye on two winged cupids tumbling through the sky, Perseus-style, in the upper left corner. On the now distant beach her attendants gesture frantically, but it's too late. Meanwhile, in the lower right, the bull has turned his head to look directly at us with a wide-eyed expression of feigned innocence. He knows it's too late, too.

As it turns out, this abduction and rape is not just one more of Jupiter's self-gratifying transgressions. It's the literally seminal event of Western civilization. After Jupiter brings Europa ashore at Crete, he will resume his godly form and consummate his lust. From that will spring a child who will grow up to be Minos, first king of Crete, in legend the island birthplace of civilization, the one that will spread across the continent that now bears Europa's name. In this pagan account of first things, the one Titian has chosen to give us, it's not Adam and Eve who are guilty of original sin. It's an indifferent and all-powerful god.

When he finished *Europa* Titian was somewhere in his early-to mid-seventies. For years he had been leaving much of the portrait work to his studio assistants, satisfied to do no more than add a few finishing touches with his own experienced brush. He did, however, go on to produce a handful of revealing self-portraits, but now in disguise, pictures of himself mingled among the faces and figures in some of his late religious and mythological paintings. He had done this sometimes as a younger man, but in old age he appears in more anguished guises. In 1559, we see him in *The Entombment*, one of several devotional pictures he did for Philip during the same years as the *poesie*. Though the gray-bearded figure at upper left, helping lay Christ to rest, is probably meant to represent the Pharisee Nicodemus, he bears the unmistakable features of Titian.

And there he is again in *The Flaying of Marsyas*, now as the hapless King

13

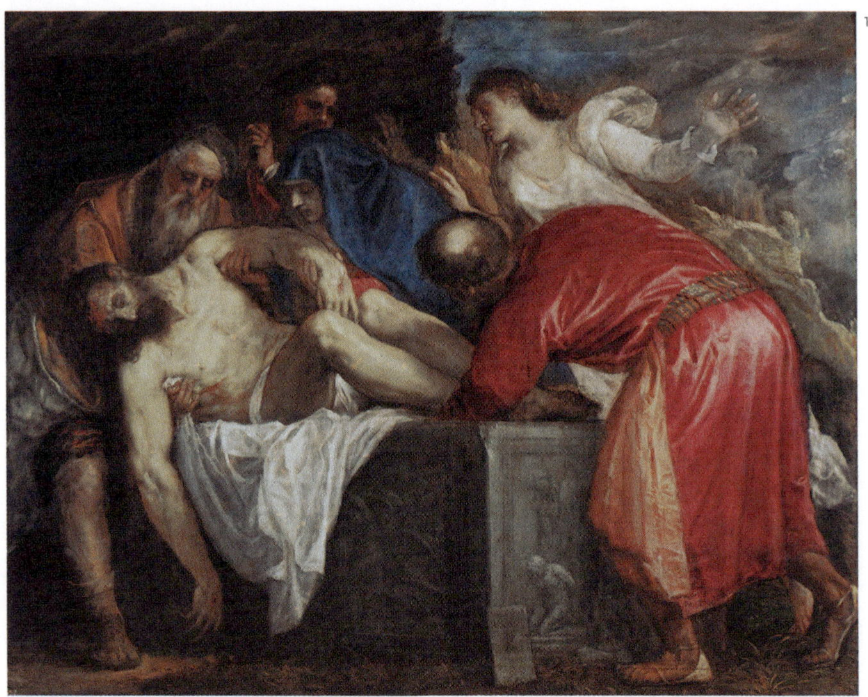

The Entombment, 1559, oil on canvas, 136 × 174.5 cm, Museo Nacional del Prado, Madrid

Midas, the man once granted his foolish wish that everything he touched should turn to gold. Though in a letter of 1562 Titian told Philip that *The Rape of Europa* was the last of the *poesie*, this picture, begun sometime around 1570, is often considered the real culmination of the series, the most brutal and despairing, and in terms of its staccato brushwork the most radical. We don't know who commissioned it, or even if anyone did, which opens the possibility that this painting was one Titian produced for his own grim delectation.

Again it's a story taken from Ovid, in combination with other sources, and again it represents the cruelty of divine justice, more spectacularly than any of the canonical *poesie*. The protagonist this time is Apollo, the elegant god of music, poetry, and the sun, among other distinctions, who is serenly wielding a slender blade. The victim is the satyr Marsyas, who is bound upside down and hung from a tree limb as Apollo skins him alive. Marsyas had presumed to challenge the god to a musical contest—his peasant flute against the god's more courtly instrument, a lyre. Marsyas lost, and this atrocious penalty is Apollo's idea of what should happen to the loser. Worse, it's a group endeavor. Above the kneeling god stands a Scythian shepherd who is assisting in the torture, cutting skin from the satyr's leg like a butcher carving a ham. Behind him an obliging youth with a stringed instrument provides musical accompaniment. At right another satyr approaches with a bucket, perhaps to catch the blood. It must be delicious, because in a grotesque detail at the bottom of the canvas, a little spaniel is lapping it up.

Like *The Death of Actaeon*, this is a painting that is assumed to have been

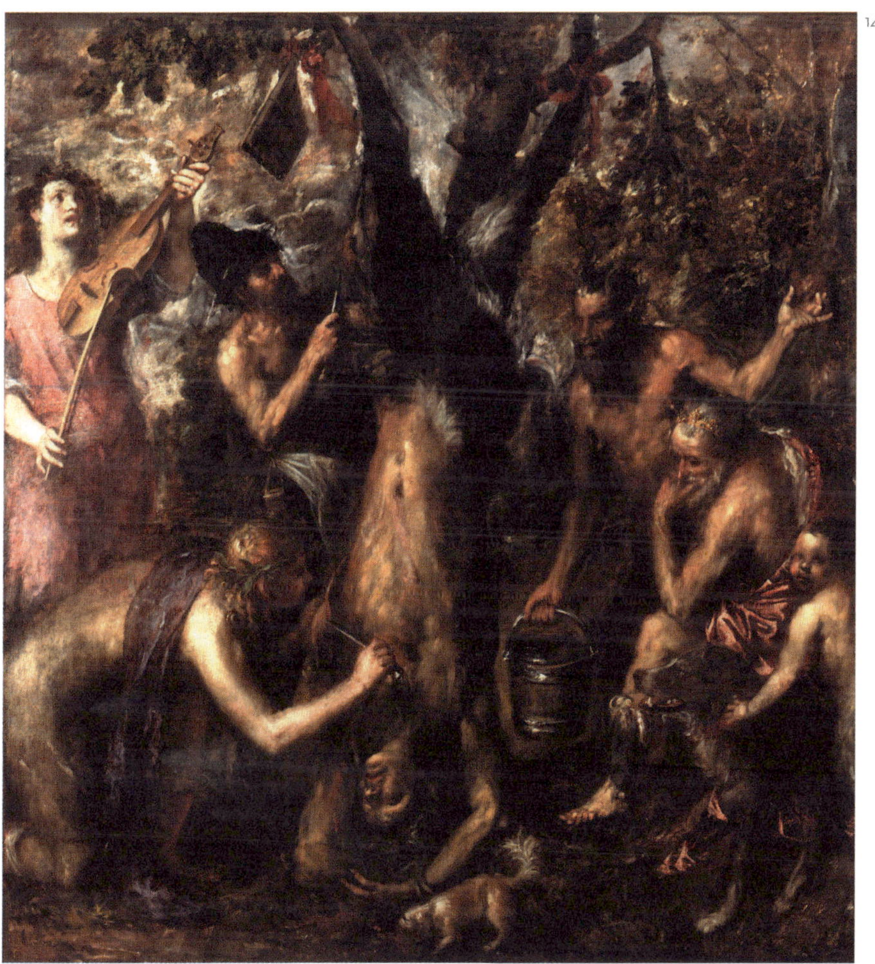 14

The Flaying of Marsyas, ca. 1570–76, oil on canvas, 220 × 204 cm, Archdiocese Olomuoc, Archiepiscopal Palace, Picture Gallery, Kromeriz, Czech Republic

in Titian's studio at his own death and, like *Actaeon*, had apparently been worked and reworked for years, as though Titian couldn't bring himself to part with it. If so, then why? Is it because the subject—a creature tormented for his art—was too close to the heart of an increasingly somber old painter? Because there he is on the right of the picture, Titian as Midas. In some versions of the story Midas had been asked to judge the musical competition and had found in favor of Marsyas, but his verdict had been overruled by the Muses. Now he sits watching the merciless god wield his blade. He's in a contemplative pose, his left elbow propped on his knee and his left hand stroking his beard, while he glumly eyes this awful scene the world allows.

Look closely and you discover that the ears of Midas are misshapen. In fact, they're donkey ears, a punishment imposed by Apollo after Midas protested the god's victory in an earlier musical competition, this one against the woodland god Pan. So here is Titian depicting himself in old age, not just as a thwarted king—which in a sense he was, the king of the Renaissance art world—but as an ass, crushed and humiliated by an implacable god.

But couldn't Titian also be identifying with Apollo, whose dainty knife, disposed just so in his sharply lit hand, looks very much like a paintbrush or drawing stylus, the instrument we see Titian holding in his self-portrait of almost two decades earlier? And finally, can't we also catch a glimpse of him in the tormented Marsyas, a creature suffering for his hubris as an artist, his presumption to compete with the gods and his failure to understand, until too late, that it's a game you can't win? In the painting's most chilling detail, the inverted Marsyas casts one cool eye directly toward the viewer, drawing us that much more deeply into the scene and implicating us, at least as bystanders, in the crime being committed against him.

So is this picture Titian's last judgment on himself and his plight, the failure of his art to protect him from his fate as a dying old man, or to exempt him from the human predicament generally? When you look at this canvas in that light, you realize something about that other picture Titian never let go of, *The Death of Actaeon*—that it too might be an allegory for the plight of the artist, of Titian himself. Because as the Titian biographer Sheila Hale has pointed out, the crime for which Actaeon was punished was any painter's most basic transaction with the world: the simple act of seeing.

With *The Flaying of Marsyas*, we come to the fullest expression of late Titian and his bravura paint handling. And this in a picture that he signed, an important evidence that he considered it to be finished, even if he never sent it out. Its almost blistered surface turns the whole canvas into a unified force field, infected in every corner by the pain and anxiety of the pleading satyr. More than that, what *Marsyas* also demonstrates is that not only could pigment amplify the mood produced by faces and figures, it could, if you wanted it to, play *against* them. As Apollo tortures the hapless creature, his face carries a serene expression of what can truly be called Apollonian detachment. So, oddly, does the face of Marsyas. All the same, everywhere around the canvas, the frantic brushstrokes, crackling signifiers of torment, tell the real story. Either way, the agitated paint becomes the vehicle of feeling and meaning, and the artist's hand, just like Apollo's, literally carries out the anguish of the scene, of the tormented satyr—and very likely of the artist who produced it.

By the time Titian reached his eighties, Venice was in another of its mounting crises. In 1570, around the year he started the Marsyas picture, the whole of Italy experienced hunger after a disastrous harvest. Venice was not spared. In March of that year the new Turkish sultan Selim II, the dissolute but capable son of Suleiman the Magnificent, demanded the island of Cyprus, for almost a century the easternmost part of the Venetian empire. To resist his demand, the next month Venice put to sea a fleet of 144 ships. It was supplemented by a small papal armada and a larger but strangely reluctant one from Titian's patron Phillip II. Reluctant because the admiral Gian Andrea Doria was under secret instructions from Philip to hold back, so as to make sure the Venetians did all the fighting.

When the joint expedition got to Cyprus in September it was too late. Two months earlier a Turkish fleet of some 350 ships had appeared off the island's coast. In short order the Turks seized Nicosia, the capital, beheading its Venetian governor before embarking on a week of massacre, rape, and looting. Without so much as having sighted the Turks, the Venetians and their listless allies simply turned around and went home. In the words of the historian John Julius Norwich: "So ended one of the most humiliating episodes in the history of Venice."

Still to come was a grotesque coda, an event that would certainly have weighed on the Titian who produced *The Flaying of Marsyas*. On September 17, the Turks moved down the coast of Cyprus to blockade the port of

Famagusta. By the following August the city's Venetian generals decided to ask for terms of surrender. Once those were agreed to, a Venetian captain, Marcantonio Bragadin, called on the Turkish commander to present him with the keys to the city. The Turks abruptly seized him, cut off his ears and nose, slaughtered the Venetian delegation that was with him—perhaps 350 men—and threw their mutilated captive into a dungeon. Two weeks later, Bragadin was taken to Famagusta's main square, tied naked to a column, and skinned alive. His tormentors had peeled him to his waist before he died. When news of his grotesque fate reached Venice, the city was shaken. Certainly Titian would have been.

By the time Famagusta fell, the prospect of further Turkish advances in the Mediterranean had finally pushed Venice, Spain, and Pope Pius V into a real alliance. In May 1571, the new league launched a more sizable fleet of more than two hundred fighting galleys and seventy-two thousand men. On October 7, in the Gulf of Lepanto, near the island of Corfu, the Christian armada met and faced off against a comparable Turkish force in one of the largest and most famous naval engagements in history. An astonishing victory for the Holy League, the Battle of Lepanto resulted in the near annihilation of the Turkish fleet—fifty ships sank, 137 captured, and their mainly Christian slave crews freed, plus some thirty thousand Turkish soldiers and sailors killed. The Christian side lost just thirteen ships and perhaps fifteen thousand men.

Lepanto was a triumph both for Venice and for Spain, which faced constant pressure from Moors in North Africa. To commemorate the victory Philip commissioned a painting from Titian. Before a backdrop of the naval battle, it shows us the Spanish king offering his infant son to heaven while a shackled Turkish prisoner sits at his feet. But the advantage to the Venetians, who went all out in celebration when news of the outcome arrived, would be short lived. The Turks would quickly rebuild their lost navy, and just two years later Venice would conclude a treaty renouncing all claim to Cyprus. No single victory at sea, however tremendous, could stem the city's decline.

By that time Titian may have been beyond caring. Like so many old people, as he entered his last decades he began to dwell on last things. This most worldly of men, for decades the supreme chronicler of the rich, famous, and beautiful, in old age took a new interest in religious subjects. Starting as early as his sixties, Titian turns ever more often to producing portraits of saints and scenes from the Bible. And the mood of his devotional art changes. As a younger man it was likely to have had an optimistic glow, as it does in his pictures of the Virgin outdoors, in settings that subtly conflated the Christian story with pagan ideas of the Golden Age, a connection newly circulating among Renaissance thinkers. His later religious work is darker in palette and more anguished in his choice of subjects. Scenes from Christ's passion and crucifixion become a frequent theme. This may in part represent the new direction in Catholic church doctrine in the later sixteenth century, the Counter-Reformation emphasis on the redemption of mankind through Christ's suffering. It could also be a corollary for his own more somber disposition. Maybe both.

With the growing religious preoccupations of his late work, it's not surprising that his last canvas, one of the most freely worked, was a *Pietà,* a picture he originally produced to go above his own tomb in the Christ chapel of the Frari, the same Franciscan church that held his early triumphs *The Assumption* and the *Madonna di Ca' Pesaro*. But before his death the Franciscans had rejected his *Pietà* as inappropriate in subject for a chapel devoted to the Crucifixion. Or maybe they just thought it would be one too many Titians in their church. In any event, the painting was returned to the old man, to become another of the many canvases still in his workshop at the time of his death.

After that it was acquired by his assistant Palma Giovane, who held on to it for decades. At some point he made a number of small changes and added an inscription at the bottom. It reads: "What Titian began, his pupil Palma brought to a state of completion." As further evidence that Titian's late style was deliberate, it's interesting that Palma, who had worked with the old man for years, did very little to the canvas other than add an angel at top and a few layers of touch up. But he did nothing to smooth out the briskly, even brutally rendered central figures. This at least suggests that he assumed that in Titian's view these parts of the picture were finished and their free brushwork was as he wanted it.

Like so much of his late work, Titian's funerary *Pietà* is a strange picture. And like so much of his work from all throughout his life, it expands its genre in powerful ways. The action—and that's just what it is in this remarkably frenzied Pietà—takes place before a stone chapel with a half-dome niche and an enormous triangular keystone, symbol of the Holy Trinity at the center

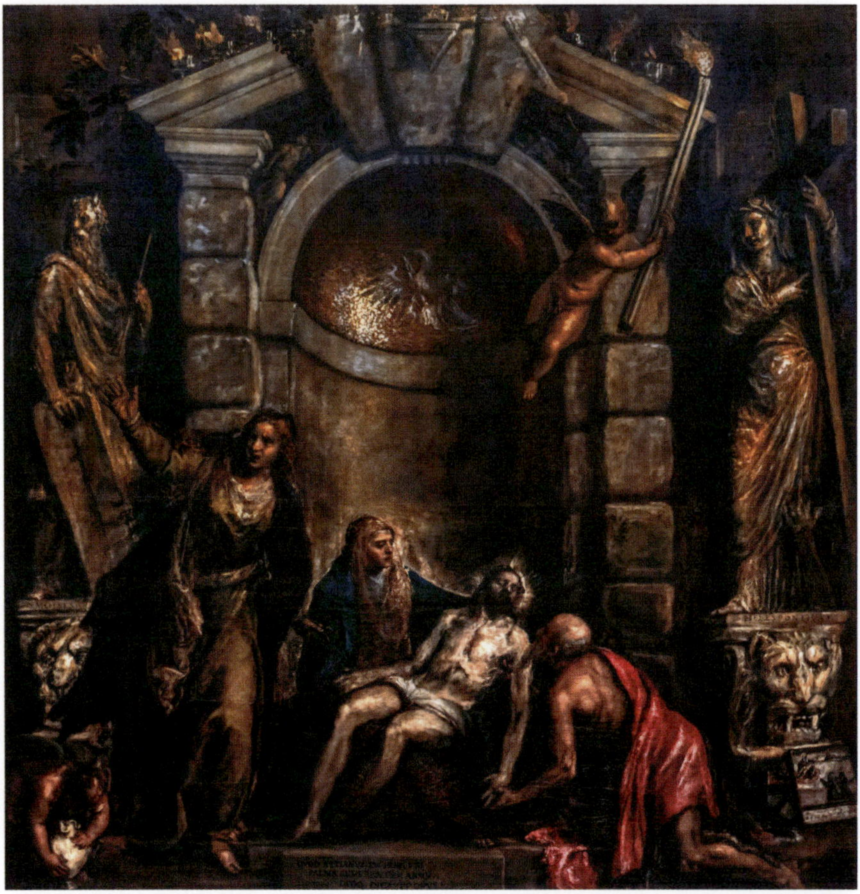

15

Pietà, 1575–76, oil on canvas, 389 x 351 cm, Gallerie dell'Accademia, Venice

of the Christian faith. Arched chapels of the kind Titian represents here had long been a convention of Renaissance religious art. But in most such pictures the chapel is a stabilizing device—it encloses the figures in a serene composition. They may sometimes step or stand just beyond the arch, but they don't, as Mary Magdalene does on the left side of Titian's picture, seem to explode from it, waving one arm in a gesture of something like alarm. For that matter, a Pietà is typically a quiet arrangement of grieving figures, nothing like this roiling ensemble that the Magdalene seems to be fleeing. Even the Virgin, though she bears her son's body on her lap, appears almost to hold him at arm's length.

The old man on the right of Titian's *Pietà*, approaching the dead Christ on his knees, is probably intended to be St. Jerome, a penitent saint who fled to the desert to flagellate himself and commune with God. Like portraits of Mary Magdalene, pictures of Jerome were something of a product line of Titian's later studio. His story suited the penitential mood of the Counter-Reformation. But in the *Pietà* Jerome now also suits Titian. Here he's yet another, and the last, of Titian's disguised self-portraits. Just as Michelangelo had supplied his own features to the figure of Nicodemus in the late marble *Pietà* he had intended for *his* tomb, Titian casts himself as Jerome, literally crawling toward the Son of God, a posture suggesting both repentance and prostrating grief. And more. The abject artist grasps Christ's hand and stares deeply into his face, the face of the Savior he fully expects to stand before very soon.

Very soon. In the lower right-hand corner of the *Pietà* there's a picture within the picture—a little canvas, leaning against a stone at the base of a pillar, showing Titian and his son Orazio in a prayerful posture before the Virgin, as though imploring her to be spared from the contagion. In vain. In that pestilential summer, the Christian heavens were as indifferent to human suffering as Apollo with his little blade or Diana with her pointing finger. Humans were the playthings of the gods.

Titian would go first, on August 27, with Orazio at his bedside. But the epidemic may not have been the cause. In Venice that year anyone showing its symptoms was usually quarantined. He never was. And his body wasn't burned or dumped in a lime pit, as was customary for contaminated corpses. Instead, as we've seen, it was interred one day later in the chapel of the great Church of the Frari. Is it because he was a very distinguished citizen that Titian was accorded special treatment? Or was he simply not a victim of the plague at all, just a very old man who died of other causes in the middle of a terrible time? A doctor who examined his body claims to have found no sign of the disease. His death certificate says he died of a fever. What we do know is that it was the plague that claimed Orazio, not long after his father. Titian's funeral at the Frari was quick and relatively modest. With the epidemic still raging, it may have seemed best to keep things simple, and to avoid assembling a large crowd that could spread contagion. Even in the sixteenth century they had figured out social distancing.

Titian died without a will. Likewise Orazio. It fell to Pomponio to sort out the old man's affairs. In a peculiar development of the following year, Titian's house on Biri Grande is reported to have been looted. A proclamation of the criminal court declared that "many goods of enormous value . . . and numerous paintings" had disappeared. But the culprit may have been Titian's son-in-law, Cornelio Sarcinelli. The husband of his late daughter Lavinia, Sarcinelli was living in the house with Pomponio's assent. He would turn out to be a scoundrel, scheming, with some success, to have Titian's entire estate diverted to his own sons by Lavinia. But amid years of suits and countersuits, Pomponio was eventually able to lease the Biri Grande place.

Though the old man was gone, the late work would gradually come to be more widely known and to exert its pull on other artists. It was a thunderbolt he threw in old age, and it traveled a long way. In the next century and beyond, his whiplashing brushwork would be hugely influential, both as a signifier of life and spontaneity, or conversely of anxiety and anguish. Early in the seventeenth century, a number of the great private collections of northern Italy, the precious property of the dukes who had been among Titian's patrons, were sold off or otherwise dispersed, releasing many Titians into wider circulation and visibility.

Diego Velázquez, himself one of the most influential artists of all time, had his own means for studying the late work. As court painter to Philip IV of Spain and curator of the king's collections, he had only to wander the halls of the Spanish royal palaces to see the many pictures that Titian had produced for Philip II. The Flemish painter Peter Paul Rubens was still in his twenties when he began seeking out and copying Titians in Rome and Venice, and then much later at the Spanish court as well. In the late 1620s he made almost two dozen copies of canvases by Titian at the Alcázar, including four of the *poesie,* in time bringing them back with him to Antwerp. Through them, and through his own work that was profoundly indebted to Titian, Rubens would transmit the vital energies of his great predecessor.

Over time, the legacy of Titian's free hand became so widespread it influenced painters who never saw an actual late Titian. Did Frans Hals, whose Dutch portraits look like they were produced under Titian's baton? Probably not. Later still it would reach to Delacroix, Turner, and Manet, and from them to the twentieth-century expressionists. By now, it's no longer unusual to find critics and scholars who value Titian's late work above the lush masterpieces that came before, reasoning that with its freely applied paint it has more to offer young artists.

With that, his posthumous triumph is complete. More than four centuries after his death, and largely through his prophetic late work, the old man who drew from his last self his last art is a modern artist again.

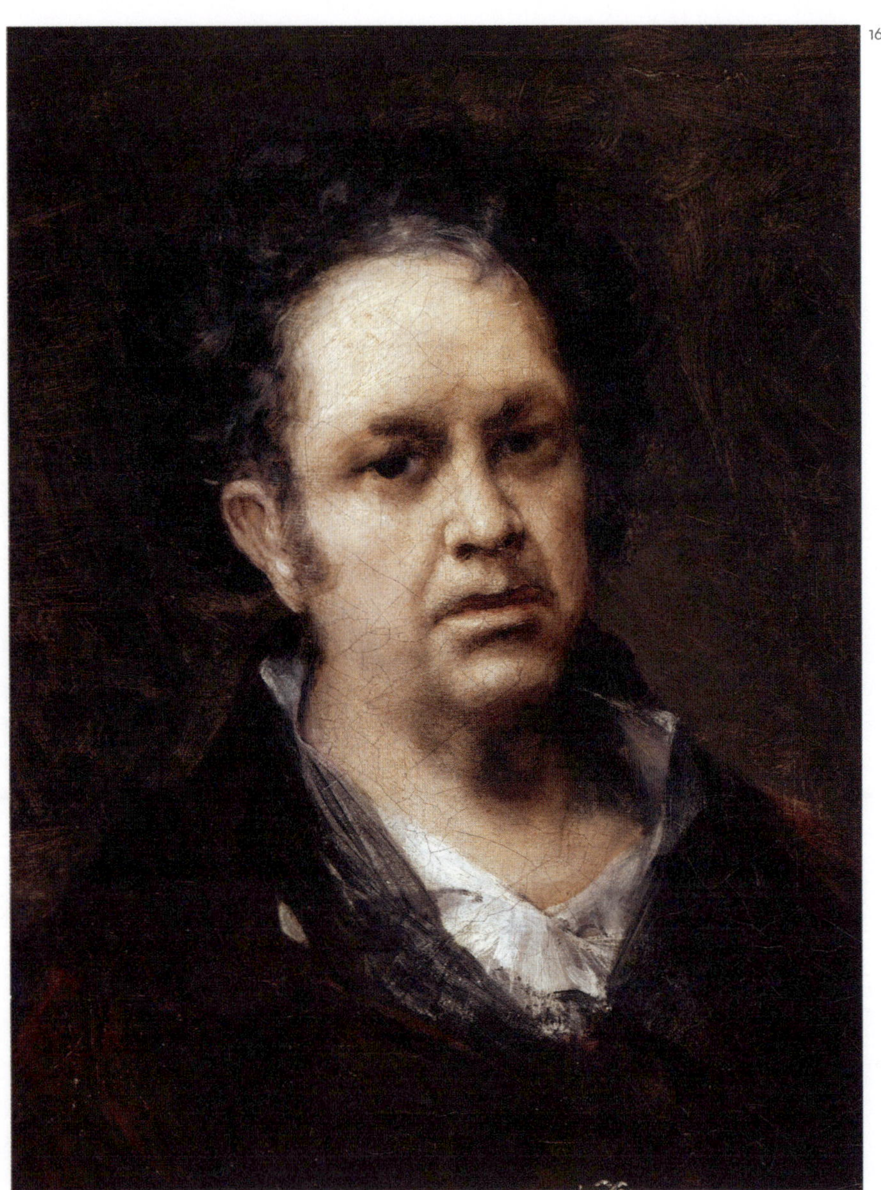

Self-Portrait, 1815, oil on canvas, 45.8 × 35.6 cm, Museo Nacional del Prado, Madrid

2

GOYA

Darkness Visible

In 1819, the year he turned seventy-three, Francisco José de Goya y Lucientes, first court painter to the king of Spain and longtime resident of Madrid, bought himself a new house in farm country just west of the city. Though he left us no record of the reason for his move, and there may have been more than one, his timing makes it hard not to suspect he was looking for a literal getaway. Not just a country retreat, but a sanctuary, an escape from the oppressive atmosphere of Madrid as it suffered under the thumb of Ferdinand VII, the vengeful and reactionary monarch whom the aging Goya served.

Ferdinand had returned to the throne five years earlier, at the close of the Peninsular War. That harrowing conflict had ended in defeat for the French, who for a time had installed Napoleon's brother on the Spanish throne. Once back in power, Ferdinand set out to reverse whatever liberal innovations had been put in place during the war, not only by the French "intruder king" but by the parliament of Spanish reformers that had convened in his absence and dared to adopt a constitution. Soon after his return, he brushed the offending document aside. As he pursued his campaign to restore royal absolutism, hitting out in all directions, his rule became an ordeal for his opponents, at times a literal reign of terror.

Though Goya's sympathies were no doubt with the reformers, for the most part he had managed to dodge the king's pinwheeling wrath. All the same, by 1819 it would have seemed prudent to put some distance between himself and the turbulent Ferdinand. Not only was reform in Spain an aborted mission, the king never called upon him anyway. He much preferred another court painter, Vicente López, a neoclassicist and skilled illusionist with a gift for the kind of high finish that royals found flattering and Goya had little use for. It was time to get out of Madrid.

Goya found his new home on the other side of the Manzanares, a river that had appeared in some of his early paintings of Madrileños partying and picnicking along its banks. The house was spacious but not grand, two floors of stucco and brick, set on about twenty-three acres.

Goya's *quinta*, Spanish for "country house," has entered history as the Quinta del Sordo, the "House of the Deaf Man," which is what the locals called it even before Goya arrived. Some of his biographers say that was because the previous owner was deaf. Others believe it was the house next door, once the property of a deaf farmer, that was first known by that name, which then passed to Goya's place after he moved in. Because Goya, too, was deaf, profoundly deaf for twenty-six years. Though he could speak intelligibly, he could hear nothing. For a long time, the world had gone gliding past him in silence. But in that silence, his mind had gone on furiously ticking.

The most powerful evidence of how acutely he had felt the events of his time, and how deeply he had reflected upon the cruelty, stupidity, and superstition he saw all around him, is the great project he undertook in his new home. During the four years he would spend there, before fleeing Spain entirely, Goya would produce some of the most anguished and unnerving art not just of his time but of ours. In the fourteen large paintings he would lay down directly across its interior walls, he would translate his worst conclusions about humanity into bleak allegories. In those pictures he would distill the lessons of a lifetime about human nature, none of them pretty.

These are the works that we now call the Black Paintings, one of the greatest achievements of Goya's old age. Along with the series of etchings called *The Disasters of War*, and another called the *Disparates*, as well as the powerful canvases known as *The Second of May, 1808 in Madrid* and *The Third of May, 1808 in Madrid*, the Black Paintings have secured his position as one of the most indispensable artists in the Western canon. If he had died in his early sixties, he would still be remembered as an artist of charming genre scenes in his youth, a superb portraitist and printmaker in his maturity, and a gifted satirist, but not as one of the most influential artists of all time. Instead, he lived to be eighty-two, time enough to plumb his own depths.

When Goya bought the house, on February 27, he paid cash—60,000 reales, ten thousand more than his considerable annual salary as first painter, but he could afford it. Though the restored king asked almost nothing of him, Goya still drew his full pay, a sizable amount, and one he had been enjoying—except during the war years—since being named first painter twenty years earlier. In a letter to his childhood friend Martín Zapater, himself a successful businessman, Goya once even boasted: "I spend a lot because my position demands it." Then he added, "Besides, I like it."

Goya would have relished his success all the more because like Titian he came from nowhere. Nowhere in his case was Fuendetodos, a dusty backwater in Aragón, the region of northeastern Spain adjoining Catalonia, where he was born on March 30, 1746, the fourth of six children. His parents actually lived about thirty miles to the north, in Aragón's capital, Zaragoza, where his father, José, was a master gilder, burnishing picture frames, candlesticks, and altar screens. In Spain, it was a steady but modest living. It may be that when Goya's mother, Gracia Lucientes, was pregnant with the future artist, José was regilding an altar in Fuendetodos, which was her hometown. Whatever the reason they found themselves there, during their stay her family gave the couple use of the bare-bones stone house set amid parched hills where Goya was born. Not long after, the Goyas moved back to Zaragoza. Goya would later recall himself there as a boy, already drawing on any free surface he could find.

However modest his parents' circumstances, Goya, like Titian, could still claim a mildly distinguished bloodline, thanks to one of the countless diluted routes of European pedigree. His mother was a hidalgo. A minor subcategory of Spanish nobility, that title signified merely that she was descended from someone who once had the right to live off income from property—who once, however long ago, didn't toil with his hands. It was a distinction that bestowed upon her a family coat of arms, the right to be addressed as "Doña"—"Lady"—and precious little else.

So despite his mother's slender claim to status, in Zaragoza Goya would attend a school for children of the poor, and when his father died in 1781 he left no property. But after a youthful period of struggle, Goya would prosper far beyond the dreams of his parents. A few years after his move to the quinta, he was able to pass control of two substantial homes in Madrid to his hapless only child, Javier, an idler ever in need of assistance from his indulgent dad.

Goya arrived at his new country house as a widower. His wife of thirty-nine years, Josefa Bayeu, had died in 1812. But he would not live there alone. Leocadia Weiss, a distant cousin of his son's wife, would be joining him. A handsome woman in her early thirties, she had already lived with Goya in Madrid, ostensibly as his housekeeper. Very possibly she was something more. Though we have no firm evidence of what their relationship was, Weiss is often presumed to have been Goya's bedmate and life partner, in effect a common-law wife. If that's true theirs would have been a relationship to be discreet about, because Leocadia already had a husband, and under Ferdinand's conservative reign sexual and marital propriety were being enforced more strictly.

What we know for sure is that, as a young woman, Leocadia had wed a jeweler, Isidoro Weiss, and had two children by him. In 1811, he formally accused her of "illicit conduct," probably meaning infidelity. All the same, they never divorced and may even have resumed sexual relations, because in 1814 she gave birth to a daughter, Rosario. Or could the little girl have been fathered by Goya? That's often been suspected as well, but again, we have no proof. What we do know is that when she moved to the quinta, Leocadia brought Rosario with her, along with her son Guillermo, and that Goya doted on the girl as if she were his own. He loved teaching her to draw. She would grow up to become an artist herself. Goya urged at least one friend to regard her as his daughter.

If Goya did indeed buy the quinta in part as a retreat from the tense atmosphere of Madrid, he was not entirely successful, because he couldn't retreat from himself. After years of war and political repression, there were dark imaginings in his head, an uneasy take on the world that he carried within himself, one that would soon find expression in the Black Paintings. Nearly all of them are angry or haunted or both, evidence of a pessimism so unconditional and free-ranging it no longer needs to account for itself by way of reference to any specific events. We can take for granted that Goya's harsh judgment of human nature grew largely out of the war he had just lived through and the reaction that followed. He had seen or heard about too much. But unlike *The Disasters of War,* which are mostly scenes of wartime suffering and cruelty, the Black Paintings don't rely on images from daily life, however awful. Instead, in them Goya lays down general emblems of darkness and folly. In *Witches Sabbath*, we see Satan as a preening he-goat, worshipped by wretched human followers. In another there are two men locked in an eternal struggle, bashing at each other with cudgels. Then there's the religious procession coming down a long road, a parade of howling imbeciles. And the strangest—a dog looking up abjectly into a wan, empty sky, from a pit into which the wretched animal appears to be sinking. Pictures like these don't critique this or that injustice. They're a howl against humanity itself, one that he'd been moving toward for decades. This is the Goya whose art Baudelaire—who never saw the Black Paintings but knew Goya's earlier prints—would describe perfectly as "a nightmare of things unguessed."

The Black Paintings were nightmares Goya can't have expected many people to see. They were a personal phantasmagoria, locked down in a villa where he lived in semi-seclusion. It was only long after his death that they began their slow progress into the world, after the quinta was sold in the 1870s to Baron Frédéric Émile d'Erlanger, a Paris banker of German descent. The baron arranged to remove Goya's paintings from the walls and have them transferred to canvas, a complicated process that involved significant repainting. The transfer and subsequent retouching almost certainly distorted the pictures, which had already suffered water damage from seepage that occurred after Goya's death. So the paintings we have are by no means exactly what he laid down. But we know from photographs taken when they were still on the walls that most of them are, in essence, still Goya's work, an expression of his intentions. The monsters he put in our heads were the ones that burst from his.

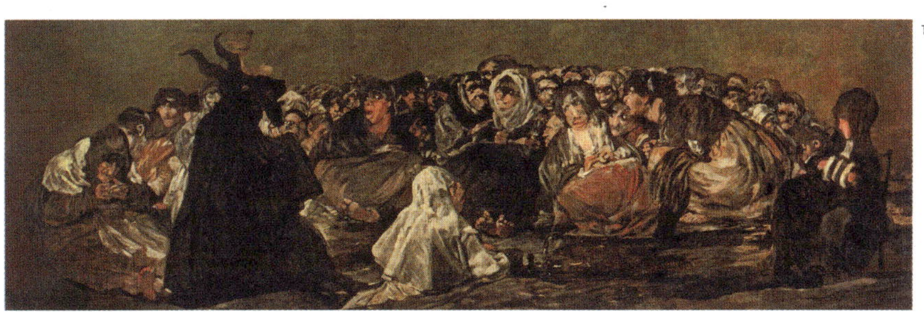 17

Witches' Sabbath, or the Great He-Goat, 1820–23, mixed media mural transferred to canvas, 140.5 × 435.7 cm, Museo Nacional del Prado, Madrid

In the hope of selling some or all of them, d'Erlanger arranged for the Black Paintings to be exhibited at the Universal Exposition in Paris in 1878, where they hung in the Trocadéro, across the Seine from the city's new symbol of progress, the Eiffel Tower. There they puzzled and appalled some people but delighted the impressionists, who saw in Goya's free paint handling a precursor to their own. When no buyer emerged, the baron gave them to the Spanish government, which passed them over to the Prado in Madrid.

Today they bear down on visitors there from all sides of one large, dimly lighted gallery. If it's the Halloween House of the museum world, it's also something much more profound. Once they were placed on permanent display, the Black Paintings would work their way into the collective consciousness of later generations until they reached our own. Goya's late work was an incendiary device that didn't explode until it landed in the lap of the twentieth century, an era terrible enough to understand it, to find in the raging visions of his old age signs and signifiers of its own calamities.

It's for reasons like those that Goya has often been called "the last of the old masters and the first of the moderns." The last of the old masters is debatable. That title might better fit Ingres, the French neoclassical painter who outlived Goya by almost forty years. But the first of the moderns? Absolutely, and not just because of his fiercely original artistry and his insistence, still unusual for his time, on the sovereignty of his imagination. But he was also modern because of his militant pessimism. Goya, of all people, living in what was then backward Spain, is one of the key points of entry into art—which means, into our shared awareness—of a clear-eyed recognition that chaos and madness are inextricable elements of the human predicament. By way of his fearless reckonings with human nature, he's one of the first visual artists to tell us how precarious the arrangements of civilization are, what thin ice we skate across and how quickly the beast within us bares it fangs. This can make for some difficult pictures, images of an almost voluptuous despair. But even as some of his work foreshadows nineteenth-century Symbolism and twentieth-century surrealism—and it does that, too—it's this inconsolable judgment that makes Goya modern.

Certainly there were artists before him who knew how to cast a cold eye on the times they lived in. The eighteenth-century English painter and printmaker William Hogarth was expert at waspish takedowns of the manners and hypocrisies of his day. Goya would have known the work of Hogarth and others like him. Very possibly he would have seen some at the home of the wealthy Cádiz merchant and art collector Sebastián Martínez, where Goya spent several months recuperating after he went deaf in his midforties. But the elderly Goya operated in a deeper key than mere satirist, with a focus on truly lethal vices, the consequence of ignorance and superstition. He converted these into images more profound and unnerving than any of Hogarth's drawing room fops. The leering madmen of Goya's late work, the levitating witches and flying animals, the witless giants—these aren't mere figures of fun to him, or to us. Monsters inhabit his world, not just drunks and party girls. And what Goya came to tell us is that they lurk within us all.

Goya knew this in part because he had observed the life of his tumultuous time like few artists before him, and not just because his decades as a court painter to a succession of very different kings had equipped him with the survival skills of an expert courtier. By his late thirties his gifts as a portraitist had also brought him into contact with the circles of educated and reform-minded Spanish men and women known as *ilustrados*. Never numerous but for a time influential, sometimes in high ministerial positions, their shared mission was to introduce into Spain some trickle of the new streams of thought unleashed by the European Enlightenment.

This was a development that powerful elements of Spanish society had long resisted. For more than a century, notions like the universal rights of man, equality before the law, and free philosophical inquiry had been developing in Europe and then North America. All the while, a reactionary Spanish aristocracy, allied to a deeply conservative Church and its all-seeing Inquisition, had worked hard to keep Spain uncontaminated by liberal humanism, advances in the physical sciences, or any other byproduct of the Age of Reason. But by the 1780s, though Spain was still largely a paradise for reactionaries, the ideas of Rousseau, Montesquieu, John Locke, and their Spanish disciples were in somewhat freer circulation, often by way of books and periodicals introduced from France. Because of their interest in French thinking, Spanish liberals were often labeled as *afrescandos*—"the Frenchified"—an identity that did them no good once French troops, and not just French ideas, came pouring over the border.

No doubt the *ilustrados* Goya came to know played some role in exposing him to these new ideas, which he may already have been predisposed to approve. But what exactly were Goya's politics? He left us no written account of his thinking, not even in letters—probably a smart idea for a court painter in a lifetime of shifting court politics. All the same, do we need that? We only have to look at his art to know where his sympathies lay, and it wasn't with ignorance, authoritarianism, and dogma. Goya was not a systematic thinker, much less someone given to producing treatises or manifestos. He was an artist, a man who expressed himself in images. As a window onto his beliefs, they could be as eloquent as any essay. He didn't need to speak out or write in praise of the Spanish Enlightenment. In his many pictures of injustice, stupidity, and cruelty he served brilliantly as its silent partner.

In Goya's last decades he witnessed an era in Spanish history not so different from the early twenty-first century. It was a time of populist revolt against sophisticated elites, when many ordinary people looked to an authoritarian leader to deliver them from a modernity they feared, resented, and wanted no part of. If in the 1780s and '90s reformist thinking was circulating more freely, by 1815, with Ferdinand back on the throne, all that had changed. By then mobs of the king's supporters were coursing through the streets of Madrid, trashing the parliament building, destroying symbols of constitutional rule, and shouting poisonous idiocies. "Long live our chains" and "Long live oppression!" "We the people" were not words those people were ready for.

Goya would reflect on those riots in a drawing, an image in brush and wash of a workman on a ladder that leans against a pedestal. Still brandishing his pickax, the man has just smashed a classical bust of a woman that lies in pieces on the ground. Goya's caption echoes Christ's words on the cross to his heavenly Father: "He doesn't know what he's doing."

But Ferdinand did. If the king had his way, Spain would become the graveyard of reason. And as Goya entered his seventies, the king was having his way. Yet even he couldn't prevent his first painter from making his own reply, if only in work that very few would see until long after both were dead.

The powerful indictment of human nature that we find in Goya's late work could only have been produced by him in his old age, and not just because it was then that he was at the peak of his gifts as a painter and printmaker. That wouldn't have mattered if he hadn't carried those gifts through the furnace of the war and the reaction that followed, and then judged those events in light of the fully developed moral sense of his maturity. Very little that we see in the work of young Goya suggests a man who could have comprehended and expressed the wretchedness of that later time, much less made it into something larger, a pathway into an all-encompassing tragic vision. But old man Goya was fully equipped. As an artist, a moralist, and an experienced soul, only the elderly Goya had the means to become what he is for us now—a teacher, an exemplary sufferer, and much more than that, a spiritual contemporary, just one who happened to live two centuries ago.

And now he enters the grounds of his new house. A place he would soon start turning into a wall-to-wall canvas for his worst imaginings—and ours.

When he took possession of that house, Goya knew something few others did—that he had been working for years on a ferocious series of etchings, most of them bearing witness to the Peninsular War. Like the Black Paintings, the suite of eighty-two aquatint etchings called *The Disasters of War* would not be made public during Goya's lifetime. Not until 1863 would they finally be published, thirty-five years after his death. But like the Black Paintings, once they were unveiled they would seep ever more widely into the world's awareness and give shape to our darkest intuitions about ourselves. They may have arrived late but they were printed in indelible ink.

The Peninsular War—or the War of Independence, as the Spanish call it—was a prolonged and brutal struggle. An outgrowth of Napoleon's march across Europe in the first years of the nineteenth century, it was a contest in which Spain's barely sufficient army—undermanned, undersupplied, and badly led—would enter an uneasy but essential alliance with England and Portugal to beat back French occupiers. The year 1807 had been a high-water mark for Bonaparte. In June, he crushed a large Russian force at the Battle of Friedland, in what was then East Prussia. That decisive defeat persuaded Russia's Tsar Alexander I to conclude a reluctant peace that allied his nation to France and to the French embargo on all trade with England. Since by that time Napoleon had also subdued Prussia and Austria, the Russian capitulation meant that France was left with no real adversaries on the continent other than Sweden. Though Britain remained a formidable opponent, the little colonel was now the undisputed master of Europe.

In a textbook example of hubris, he then badly overstepped, and in a campaign he originally thought of as a mere sideshow. Looking to deprive

Britain of an unofficial but de facto ally, Napoleon decided to seize Portugal, which continued to trade with Britain in defiance of the French embargo. Very soon he began contemplating a bigger prize. As he saw it, Spain was grotesquely mismanaged. It had a feckless and distracted king, a semifeudal aristocracy, and a parasitic clergy. Why shouldn't that nation, too, along with its immense New World empire, be gathered into the improving embrace of enlightened France?

Bonaparte's intention was never to annex Spain but simply to make of it an obedient French satellite. To do that required him first to enlist the unwitting cooperation of Spain's King Charles IV and his widely unpopular prime minister, Manuel de Godoy. As a first step, in October 1807 the emperor concluded a secret treaty with Charles at Fontainebleau. They agreed that once the conquest of Portugal was complete, they would divide it into three parts. The northern portion would be ceded to the king of Etruria, who was the grandson of Charles. The fate of the middle territories would be determined later, but meanwhile they would be placed under French military occupation. The sizable southern section would be given entirely to the control of one man—Godoy. By this arrangement France would gain ports on Portugal's Atlantic coast from which to launch attacks against British shipping. Spain would retrieve at least a part of the Portuguese kingdom that had united with it in 1580, only to break away in 1640. And Godoy would get an immense personal domain. That might seem a disproportionate prize for one man, but then, what better way to ensure that the powerful royal adviser, whom Napoleon distrusted, would raise no objections to a scheme allowing tens of thousands of French soldiers to freely cross into Spanish territory? Or, to put it another way, to invade. Even before the treaty was ratified, Napoleon began sending troops across the Pyrenees.

To understand the events that shaped Goya's outlook in his later years, it's worth pausing for a moment on Godoy, a pivotal figure in the chain of misfortunes that would lead to the Peninsular War. Because few artists in any century have produced work so profoundly affected by the upheavals of their time, that war, and the man who helped unwittingly to bring it on, are essential to any understanding of Goya. A would-be reformer, world-class narcissist, peerless opportunist, and—by reputation at least—tireless stud, Godoy was born into a family of impoverished minor aristocrats in Spain's remote Extremadura. By 1784 the good-looking seventeen-year-old had arrived in

Madrid and joined the royal bodyguard. Before long he caught the attention of the future King Charles and—no less important—of his wife, Maria Luisa of Parma. After Charles assumed the throne in 1789, the handsome and personable Godoy enjoyed a rapid and improbable rise to power, quickly entering the royals' inner circle and—possibly—the queen's bedroom.

That the two were intimately involved is a rumor some historians find plausible, though unproven. Much of Spain however was entirely sure that Godoy was Maria Luisa's lover. Everyone but the king. When one of Godoy's predecessors as first minister tried to convince Charles of what everybody "knew," his royal highness wouldn't hear of it. Anyway, he never cared much for governing, not the way he cared about hunting, so why not leave affairs of state to his capable young friend? The queen agreed.

In 1792, the twenty-six-year-old Godoy arrived at his apotheosis when he was named by the king as first minister. But very soon all the knives were out for the young upstart, his presumed liaison with Maria Luisa being just one reason. He offended conservatives by pursuing "enlightened" reforms in manufacturing, agriculture, and education. He earned enemies throughout Spain's powerful clergy when he lent himself to a campaign to expropriate the sizable properties of the Catholic Church, or at least to force it to sell lands that weren't in useful cultivation. And when he proclaimed a ban on bullfighting in 1805 he alienated almost everybody. Though a segment of educated opinion regarded the ritual bloodletting of the bullring as a sadistic holdover from the past, most Spaniards revered it as fundamental to their identity as a people.

Godoy was also reportedly always ready to capitalize on the sexual opportunities his rising position offered him. Rumor had it that in the sizable palace Charles awarded him as prime minister he hosted orgies with prostitutes, and that favor-seekers hoping for his blessing knew to bribe him with their wives and daughters. However much of that was true, it's thanks to Godoy's formidable libido that we have two of Goya's most famous paintings, *The Naked Maja* and *The Clothed Maja*, two nearly identical images of a reclining woman, except that only one of them is dressed. Both are almost certainly portraits of Godoy's favorite mistress, Pepita Tudó.

One last provocation to his enemies was Godoy's foreign policy. It tilted back and forth, toward and away from France, but to the multitude of Spanish reactionaries, too often toward. To them, France, with its dangerous ideas about liberty, equality, and free inquiry, was a threat to Spain's ancient traditions of royal absolutism and rockbound Catholic dogma. It didn't help that just weeks after Godoy came to the pinnacle of power the revolutionaries in Paris guillotined Louis XVI, a Bourbon monarch and first cousin to Charles. That outrage further marginalized Spain's small cohort of liberal reformers, many of them Goya's patrons and friends, who tended to be Francophiles. In 1798 Godoy fell from the position of first minister, until three years later when Charles restored him to power.

So by early 1808, Godoy was the wrong man in the wrong place at the wrong time, just as Napoleon was turning his hungry gaze toward Spain. French troops had already entered Lisbon, with more headed toward Madrid. Meanwhile King Charles was getting old. His fretful son Ferdinand was eager to assume the throne and afraid that when his father died, Godoy, whom Ferdinand detested, might somehow claim the crown or impose a regency. In the previous year the prince had even taken part in a vain plot to oust Godoy, depose his own father, and maybe even poison his mother—the evidence is murky on that last point—only to be discovered by Godoy and forced to beg the king's forgiveness.

By that time, the twenty-three-year-old Ferdinand had long been a flag of convenience around which Godoy's enemies of all kinds gathered, knowing that the pliant young prince was wildly popular among the common people. They called him *El Deseado*—the "Desired One"—the man they looked to to save them from Godoy's chronic misrule. Meanwhile Godoy's enemies in the old aristocracy and the church looked to Ferdinand to inspire the commoners to stage a revolt that their betters could then take in hand and turn to their own purposes.

The moment arrived on March 18, when Charles and his queen, having finally grasped Napoleon's real intentions, were fleeing Madrid, hoping to reach Seville and from there perhaps escape to Spanish colonies in South America. On that night they were lodged at the royal palace at Aranjuez, with Godoy housed luxuriously nearby. Ferdinand was in Aranjuez as well. Determined to thwart Godoy, head off war with France, and present himself to Napoleon as a king who would do his bidding, Ferdinand had set another plot in motion. He gave the signal to his followers by placing a candle in his bedroom window. At that a mob duly assembled, rioted, and sacked Godoy's residence. At first they couldn't find the man himself. He was hiding in an attic, rolled in a rug, where he spent the next thirty-six hours. But once discovered he was brought before Ferdinand, who agreed to spare his life so long as the king and queen allowed him to be hustled off to prison. Then Charles, who had been persuaded that Spain's all-important army was throwing its allegiance to his impertinent son, brought the situation into further turmoil by abdicating in Ferdinand's favor, a step he and his queen hoped would ensure Godoy's safety.

By the time of the "Mutiny of Aranjuez," as the episode came to be known, there were some fifty thousand French troops in Spain. On March 23, a sizable contingent arrived in Madrid, still posing as allies. At the emperor's direction, their captain, Marshal Joachim Murat, refused to recognize Ferdinand's claim to the throne. And besides, Charles had now disowned his abdication and wanted his crown back. Who was the rightful king? Eventually it was agreed that Bonaparte would arbitrate the question.

Now the emperor had his chance. He summoned Charles, Maria Luisa, Ferdinand, and Godoy to meet with him in France, in the southern city of Bayonne. Soon after they arrived, at the end of April, Bonaparte sprang his trap. He informed them they would not be going home. What's more, Ferdinand would be required to return the Spanish crown to his father, who would then be obliged to surrender it again, this time to Napoleon. A few weeks later, on June 6, the emperor, who for years had been placing members of his family at the head of kingdoms and principalities all around Europe, would reach for his older brother Joseph, whom he had already made the king of Naples. Now Napoleon would transfer him to the much more consequential throne of Spain, the one that had a valuable New World empire attached. Mission—*civilisatrice*—accomplished.

Neither Charles, Maria Luisa, nor Godoy would ever see Spain again. With Godoy's mistress Pepita in tow, they would live for some years in lavish exile, with a sizable allowance provided by the emperor, fetching up eventually in Rome. Ferdinand would languish for the next six years in a chateau—owned by Talleyrand, no less—in Valençay, France. Once the French were finally expelled from Spain, he alone would return home. In a rage.

Very soon after the Spanish royals fell victim to the emperor's subterfuge, Madrid exploded. On May 2, 1808, its citizens, stirred up by reports that members of the royal family still in the capital were being hurried out of town by the French, set upon French troops in bloody skirmishes all around the city. The French replied in force and the next day rounded up and executed any Madrileños suspected of having taken part in the uprisings. This was the development that years later Goya would make the subject of his most famous painting, *The Third of May, 1808 in Madrid*. In the two days of fighting and firing squads, hundreds died. As news of those events spread, spontaneous insurrections sprang up all around Spain. And with that, the war was underway.

That grinding struggle, along with the political repression that followed it, were the decisive misfortunes in the last decades of Goya's life, upheavals that crystallized his bleak disposition at the very moment his gifts as an artist were at their mature peak. It was a prolonged and brutal conflict, one that gave us the word "guerrilla"—"little war"—to describe resistance mounted by bands of peasant irregulars, many of them bandits and army deserters. Early on they began ambushing the startled French, who were no more prepared to respond than the marching formations of British troops who had been caught off guard at Lexington and Concord by hit-and-run American snipers. Because the guerrillas cared nothing for the rules of war, such as they were, atrocities were routine. Ordinary Spanish villagers would set upon French stragglers and couriers with stunning savagery. Letters and journals of French and even British soldiers—who often looked down on their Spanish allies—are filled with accounts of French soldiers mutilated, burned alive, gutted, castrated, sawn in half, thrown from cliffs, and even crucified on barn doors, in one case upside down above a slow fire.

That Bonaparte's troops were in uniform did only so much to make them more civilized. Hostage taking and the summary execution of Spanish prisoners and civilians were common. Women and even children were hanged. As reprisal for guerrilla attacks, French punitive missions would set fire to whole villages and mow down the fleeing inhabitants. They were no less brutal with captured cities. During the two prolonged sieges and bombardments of Zaragoza, the city where Goya grew up, more than half its citizens—fifty-four thousand people—died. For good measure even the British, though allied with Spain, sometimes plundered Spanish villages. So for that matter did the lawless guerrillas, who terrorized everyone, both foreigners and fellow Spaniards, wherever they operated.

Thanks to the British, the Peninsular War was also one of the first to see the use of a particularly nasty innovation in weaponry, shrapnel artillery, exploding shells packed with pellets that fired scattershot into enemy flesh. Wellington employed it against the French and wrote warmly of its bloody effectiveness. As for rape, everybody knew it was a fringe benefit of war and part of the wipe-up operations for all sides.

That Goya observed all this within the isolation booth of his deafness, and through the saturnine disposition of his increasing years, can only have concentrated his attention as he was producing the first masterwork of his old age, his lithograph series *The Disasters of War*. We think he made the first plates in 1810, the year he turned sixty-four, but may not have etched the last of them until about a decade later. Altogether they amount to the bitter testimony of an old man, meditating in silence for years, impervious all the while to the drums and bugles of military glory meant to distract him from bearing witness to the truth.

Every one of the eighty-two *Disasters* is captioned, mostly with brief,

18

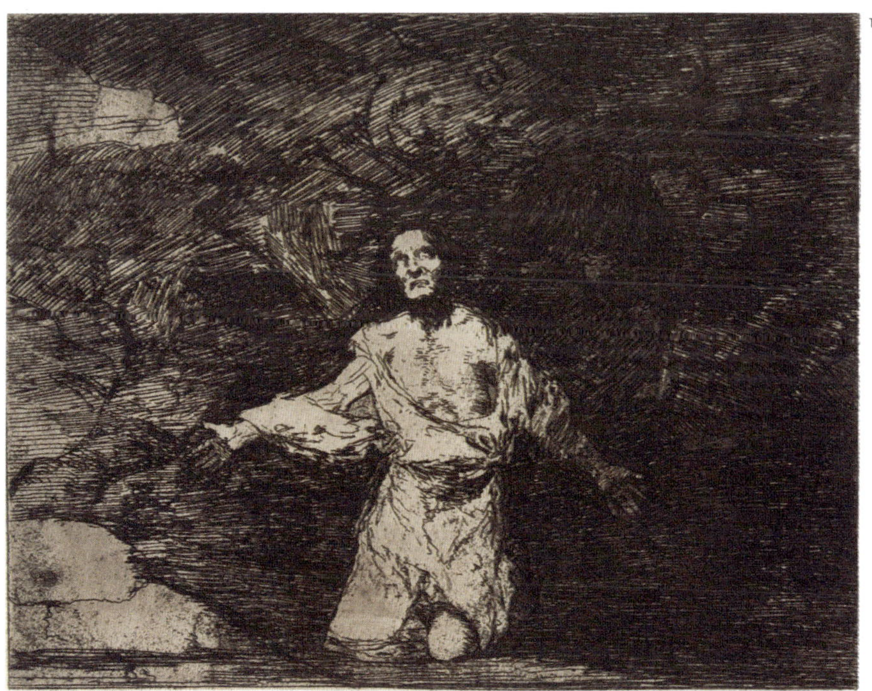

Sad foreboding of what is to come, ca. 1815, etching, drypoint, burin, burnisher, 17.8 × 22 cm, The Metropolitan Museum of Art, New York

anguished phrases that serve as titles: “One can’t look.” “I saw it.” “And this too.” The series opens with one titled *Sad foreboding of what is to come,* in which a wretched man on his knees looms out at us from a dark rocky recess of some kind, his eyes raised beseechingly toward heaven. He’s here to prepare us for the grotesque images that will follow.

Almost half are scenes from the war—atrocity vignettes, masterfully compressed, sheet after sheet of assaults of all kinds, heaped corpses, mass graves, and refugees in flight. Goya probably hadn’t witnessed most of these scenes personally, though late in 1808, during the brief interval between the first and second siege of Zaragoza, he was invited by the Spanish general José de Palafox to see for himself the devastation. But more commonly he would simply have gathered reports from newspapers, eyewitnesses, or even secondhand accounts, whatever was available from the stockpile of reported outrages, then translated those into the imaginings he passed on to us.

In the war scenes, rape is a recurring theme. That’s the crime about to be

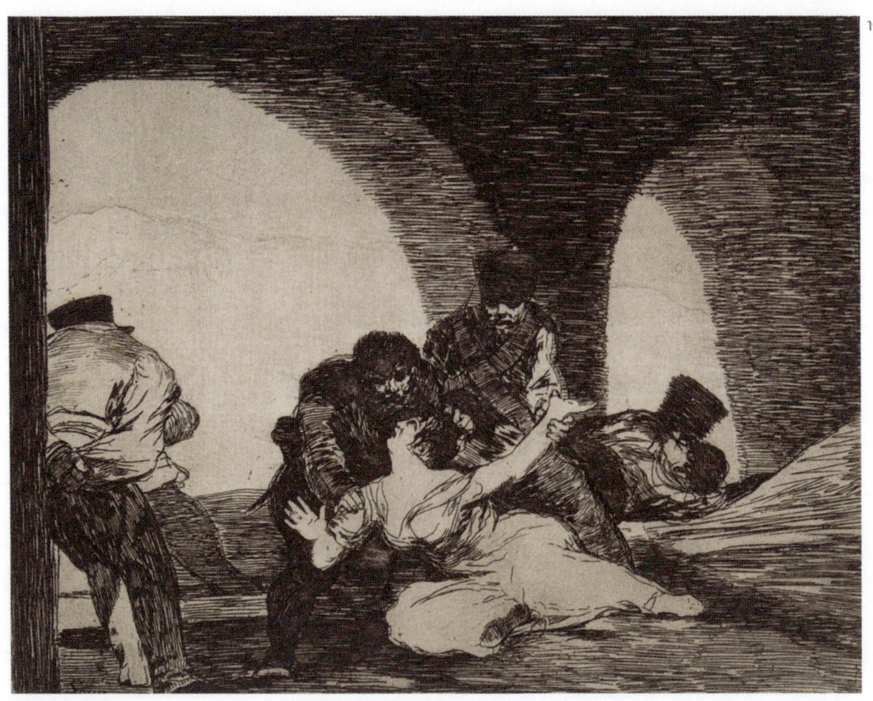 19

Bitter to be present, 1810, etching, burin, 14 × 17 cm, The Metropolitan Museum of Art, New York

carried out in the plate titled *Bitter to be present*, in which a group of French soldiers manhandle a Spanish woman who has fallen to the ground. To their left is one of the "bitter" witnesses to this assault, a man seen from behind with his hands tied behind his back. He's no doubt a member of the woman's family, perhaps her husband. In the background we see the indistinct figure of another woman slumped in despair, perhaps another relative.

Execution is another motif of the *Disasters*. One of those images, and one of the most brutally effective, is titled *And there is no help*. It shows us Spanish prisoners being dispatched by French firing squads. In the foreground one body already lies in the dirt. At rear three soldiers point their rifles at another man tied to a post. In the center is a third man, also bound to a post. Three guns are pointed at him as well, but we don't see who holds them. Instead Goya shows us just the front ends of their long barrels, jutting weirdly—almost cartoonishly—into the picture from the right edge. It's a

20

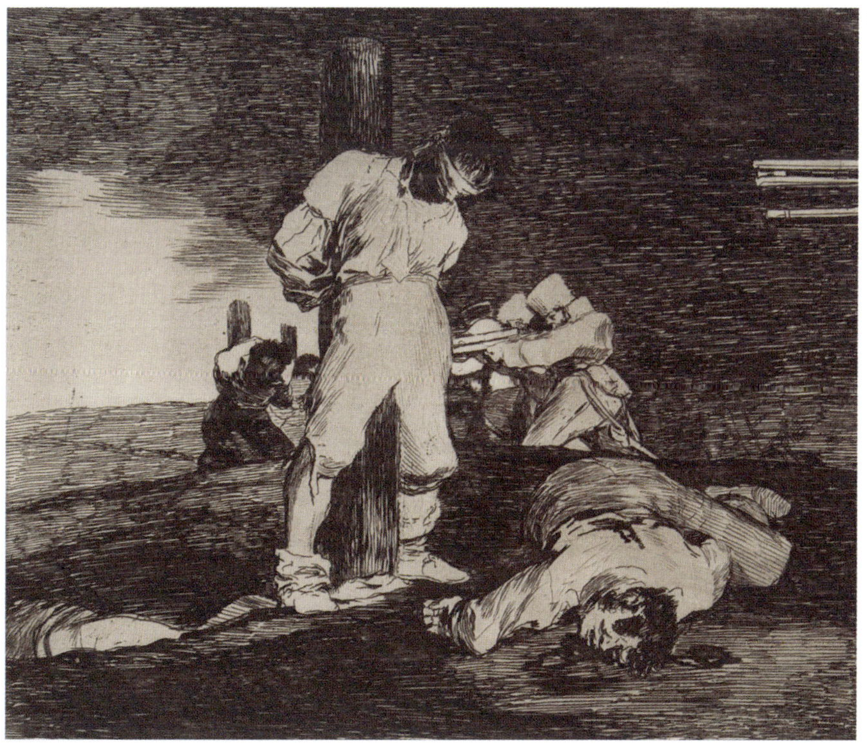

And there is no help, 1810, etching and dry point, 14 × 16.7 cm, the Metropolitan Museum of Art, New York

brilliant imaginative device that makes the guns instruments of an anonymous killing machine. Decades before the invention of photography, Goya is using the kind of incongruous, fragmented imagery that the next century would call the "snapshot aesthetic."

Even dismemberment is one of Goya's themes. Among the most famous of the *Disasters* is the one captioned *An heroic Feat! With dead men!* It shows a tree hung with naked bodies and disassembled body parts, a head here, two arms dangling there, both probably hacked from the headless torso that hangs upside down beside them. It's not just a nightmare image but a brutal parody of neoclassicism and its ideal anatomies, now mocked, butchered and, weirdly, reduced to something like the broken fragments of ancient statuary that neoclassicists revered.

Finally there's castration, explicit or implied. In one of those images, a naked man is held upside down by three soldiers who spread his legs, while a fourth applies a sword to his groin. (The caption says it all: *What more can one do?*) Given the indiscriminate savagery of the fighting, maybe it was

21

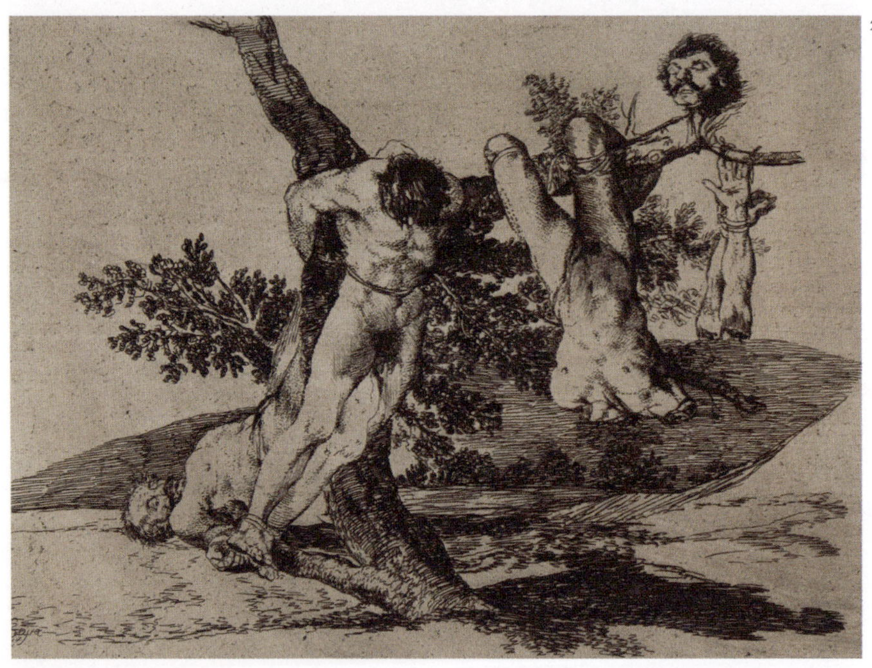

An heroic Feat! With dead men!, 1810, etching and dry point, 15.5 × 20.5 cm, the Metropolitan Museum of Art, New York

inevitable that castration would be one of Goya's themes. All the same you wonder if the deaf painter wasn't specially attuned to the pain of losing a vital sense organ, a literal means of intercourse with the world.

Some years after the American Civil War, Walt Whitman made a bitter prediction. "The real war will never get into the books." Because of Goya, the Peninsular War did. But more than that. While the *Disasters* are a chronicle of that particular conflict and the poisons it unleashed, they are also a toxicology report on humankind generally. That sense of universality is enhanced by the fact that Goya almost never illustrates specific incidents of the war, engagements that we can identify by place and date. But his purpose wasn't to produce a chronology of the fighting; it was to imagine the array of cruelties the war gave rise to and to challenge us to contemplate the beast within ourselves that could carry them out. What we learn from him is that war, any war, unleashes our worst impulses, whatever murderous drives civilization is supposed to have subdued. As Edmund says in *King Lear*: "Men are as the time is." Goya may not have known Shakespeare's play, but he would have understood those words.

So what he shows us is a war without battlefield heroics, though there are a few scenes of individual bravery. Most of these are images in which Spanish civilians, especially women, put up a desperate fight. In one, an old woman lunges with a knife at a soldier forcing himself upon a young beauty. In another, a group of women armed with just blades and a pike—and one heaving a large rock—lay into some French riflemen. In another, one of the few images that show us a more or less identifiable historical figure, a steadfast woman prepares to fire a cannon. She stands atop a pile of male corpses, defenders she has risen to replace. (The caption: "What courage!") Though we only see her from behind, she would certainly be Agustina of Aragón, a heroine of the siege of Zaragoza who took over a cannon from a dying gunner who was said to have been her lover.

But mostly it's anonymous mayhem that Goya offers us. There are no panoramic scenes of clashing military formations in these etchings, no generals on rearing horseback, no dying officers expiring gallantly in the arms of their brothers. There's even very little of anything that could be described as combat, if combat means armed men facing off against other armed men. The cruelties Goya shows are mostly ad hoc, war crimes committed along the side of the road, in the shadows and odd corners of what the next century would call the "theater of operations," a theater of the absurd where the official performances don't interest him. He's old enough to know better.

In as much as the villains in those etchings are usually identifiable as French soldiers, the *Disasters* are a "patriotic" project. But Goya has a broader agenda. He doesn't flinch from also showing us Spaniards torturing French soldiers or even their Spanish sympathizers. In one of them—titled, simply, *Mob*—a man is stretched out facedown on the ground while a Spanish villager shoves a blade-tipped pole into his rectum. The convulsive madness of war is Goya's subject, not just the nobility of the Spanish cause. He almost certainly supported that cause, though his sympathies were complicated by the fact that throughout the war he continued to serve as a court painter to the French "intruder king" Joseph. Though he wisely didn't draw his salary in those years, he produced at least one portrait of the imported monarch.

What's more, under more ordinary circumstances Goya may well have been pleased by the reforms undertaken by Joseph, who was eager to be accepted as an enlightened ruler, Spain's first constitutional monarch. In July 1808, a few months after relieving Charles and Ferdinand of the Spanish crown, Napoleon himself had bestowed upon Spain its first constitution, which guaranteed individual liberties and an independent judiciary, things long dreamt of by reformist circles in Spain. But in the chaotic circumstances of the war it was never enforced. And anyway, it did nothing for the prestige of Enlightenment ideas that they arrived in Spain at bayonet point.

So even while he served the enlightened French king, Goya worked away privately at home on his images of a world where madness ruled. It's often observed that, with the *Disasters*, Goya became in effect the pioneer of wartime visual reporting, producing images so graphic that even now most news outlets wouldn't show them. (The internet, of course, is another matter.) As a sustained witness to war he had few predecessors among artists. He also offered to the next century the example of wartime art with an unprecedented cynicism about war. After World War I, when much of Europe was a blast crater, Goya was the example the unflinching German artist Otto Dix would turn to. His 1924 series of etchings called *The War* is an explicit homage to Goya but brought to an even more grotesque pitch. And that same year, in the same spirit, a militant German pacifist, Ernst Friedrich, published *War Against War*, a volume of photos he had collected from various sources of blasted churches, dying soldiers, and bloated corpses. It climaxes in a long, unbearable sequence that it's hard to imagine being published today—twenty-four separate close-ups of soldiers whose faces had been partly shot away. Those men are mangled citizens of the world Goya gave us a glimpse of in his own time and predicted for ours, in the pictures he left behind so we could show them to ourselves as a warning.

In a later section of the *Disasters* there's a sequence of sixteen images from the yearlong famine that hit Madrid in 1811, midway through the war. This was an ordeal that Goya, who remained in the capital throughout the war, would certainly have known firsthand. As a man of some means, he might not have gone hungry himself, but he would have seen the suffering all around him. So through his eyes we see skeletal beggars, people dying in the streets, the body of a woman being carried away as her child follows behind in tears.

The *Disasters* series ends with a group of etchings done after the war, some made in the period before Ferdinand returned to the throne in 1814, others probably dating from the turbulent times that followed. Goya called them "emphatic caprices," and they're very different from anything that precedes them. Not scenes from wartime, more like surreal political cartoons, many appear to glumly forecast or lament Ferdinand's postwar repression in symbolic terms. They're full of allegorical images, an angry funhouse of fantastical cats, wolves, bats, and birds, gathered to warn against, satirize, or deplore Spain's descent into the madness of Ferdinand's reactionary regime. They alone might explain why Goya chose not to publish the *Disasters* during his lifetime. Once Ferdinand returned to power, satire and lamentation were the sort of thing that got you arrested and worse.

Among these last etchings is one of the most desolate images of the entire series. In the foreground is a half-rotted corpse partly dislodged from its grave. Behind it is a mass of onlookers. The dead body clutches a sheet of paper that carries a one-word message: *Nada*. Nothing. The suffering, the death, the war itself—it was all for nothing. And beyond that, in Goya's bleak image there's more than a hint of what the word would convey more than a century later in Ernest Hemingway's story "A Clean Well-Lighted Place," where an aging waiter drops it into a profane prayer. "Our nada who art in nada, nada be thy name thy kingdom nada . . ." It's a word that repudiates God himself. *Nada*.

In 1815, one year after the war ended, Goya painted a self-portrait, one of the most profound and candid made by any artist in old age, a self-examination to compare with any by Rembrandt, Picasso, or Lucian Freud. Goya's face emerges into the light from shadows. He's in three-quarter pose, so that his head is cocked and slightly turned away and he offers to us just one of his long ears. Did the deaf artist paint that ear wistfully, thinking how by that time it had been for many years a closed portal? Or is he thrusting it toward us as a taunt—a way to insist on how much still goes on within him? Because while this particular door to the world may be shut, the mind furiously operating behind it is still very much alive.

As for his expression, it's situated just so, not so much pained as wary and tentative. His mouth turns down at the corners. He questions the viewer with eyes that are dark pools. He looks like a man who may be encased in silence, but whose head is still teeming with what he has lived through and wishes he hadn't. Above all he still bears the weight of that hideous war. It's the face of a man who wants you to know that he knows what suffering is, what cruelties we are capable of inflicting, and capable of enduring, and that he wonders what's coming next.

But first, what came before? Was Goya always this grim? Not at all. Given the saturnine artist he became, the work of the young Goya, produced in a much more buoyant key, is a surprise. In 1763, after studying for four years in Zaragoza with José Luzán, a painter who had trained in Naples, the seventeen-year-old Goya relocated to Madrid to join the studio of Francisco Bayeu, himself once Luzán's apprentice. This would turn out to be a crucial step in Goya's gradual career ascent. Bayeu was by that time an assistant to the German artist Anton Raphael Mengs, first court painter to Spain's King Charles III and *capo di tutti* over all artistic endeavors at court.

It would take some time for the connection to Mengs to pay off, in part because in Madrid Goya would fail twice in competitions for a scholarship at the Royal Academy of Fine Arts. With his career off to that less than promising start, Goya left Spain in 1769 to further his education in Italy. His aim was to acquaint himself firsthand with the Italian art the Spanish court favored, while also mastering the neoclassical style that Mengs epitomized. After two years abroad Goya went back to Spain, but not to Madrid. He returned instead to Zaragoza, where there was less competition for a young artist and where Goya found steady employment, chiefly through a series of church commissions. He also soon married Josefa Bayeu, sister of the same Francisco Bayeu he had apprenticed with during his first stay in Madrid. Though they would remain together for thirty-nine years, until her death in 1812, not much is known about her or their marriage. Baptismal records tell us that she gave birth to at least seven children. In an age of high infant and childhood mortality, only one would survive into adulthood, the last of them, a son born in 1784 whom the parents named Francisco Javier.

Certainly Goya's marriage to Josefa solidified his relationship with her brother, a very useful in-law, at least until the two men fell out years later over a disastrous commission in Zaragoza's most prestigious church. But in 1773, when Goya and Josefa wed, Bayeu was a court painter to King Charles III, a priceless connection. A mildly enlightened despot, Charles had an interest in fostering the arts. He would soon decide to reopen the royal tapestry works of Santa Bárbara, which would assure a supply of woven wall hangings for the royal palaces. The king put Mengs in charge, with Bayeu as his assistant. It may have been at Bayeu's urging that in January 1775 Mengs summoned the twenty-eight-year-old Goya back to Madrid.

Mengs set the young man to producing tapestry "cartoons," full-scale paintings that weavers would copy in dyed wool. The position was a mixed blessing. The work of tapestry painters was rarely seen by the public, so it did little to secure an artist's reputation. (That most of Goya's cartoons now hang in the Prado is due only to the fact that they were rediscovered forty years after his death, in a basement of the Royal Palace.) But the job still represented an invitation to the threshold of the royal court. And with that, the boy from a modest background at last achieved escape velocity.

Over the next seventeen years, Goya would produce sixty-three tapestry paintings. In 1779 he even had the pleasure of seeing some of them praised in public by Charles and by his son the crown prince and the prince's wife. "I kissed their hands," he wrote excitedly to his boyhood friend Martín Zapater, "for I have never been so happy." In these sizable canvases he was an artist almost nothing like the ferocious pessimist he would later become. Of course these were work-for-hire pictures, not personal projects, made to order for patrons looking only for buoyant scenes. But Goya plainly had a gift for those. In his cartoons peasants fling themselves around in festival-day games or brawl outside a country inn. Here's a girl on a swing and here, in *The Picnic*, are some tipsy young majos taking in the charms of an orange seller who may be selling more than oranges. And here's a man launching a kite into a cornflower-blue sky while his friends idle around him. Everything in these pictures says that life is good.

Yet even in these lighthearted canvases, Goya is already taking the measure of the world he finds himself in. The future satirist was already fascinated by the full, foolish array of the society in his time, a society he will later judge through much harsher eyes. For now, those eyes roam up and down the class ladder with considerable amusement. Though his tapestry paintings include people of high station, they are even fuller of the middling and lower orders, to say nothing of shady figures who probably have arrest records. Among the tumbling men and women at his roadside inns and street festivals there are servants, peasants, coachmen, and vendors of all kinds, including young women who may be marketing themselves. A lot of his men are strutting versions of what eighteenth-century Spain called "majos"—paragons of

22

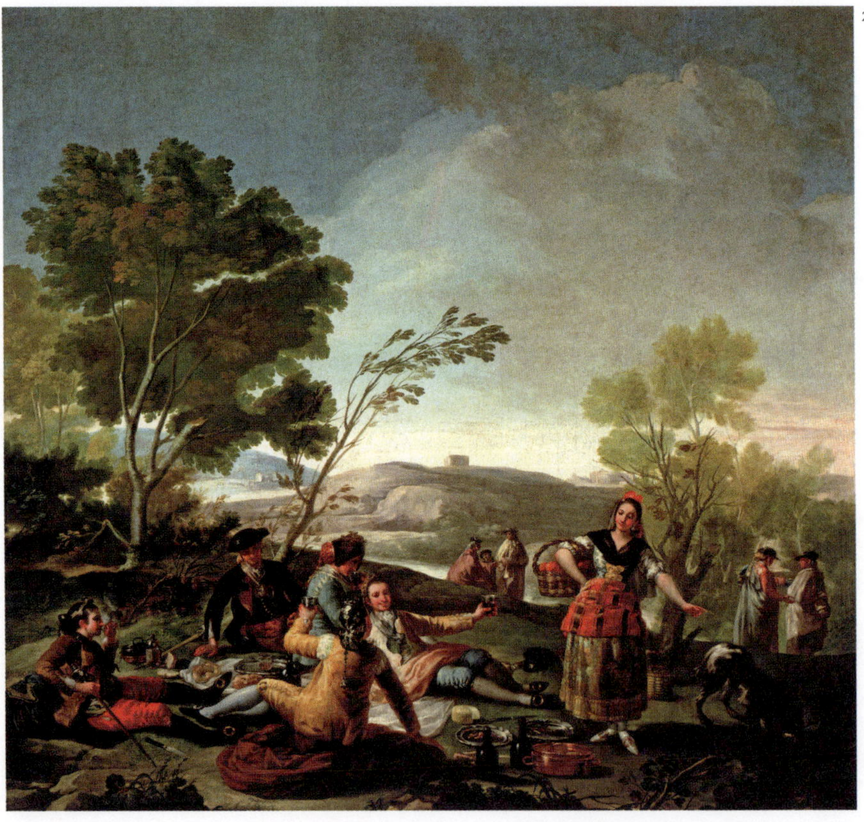

The Picnic, 1776, oil on canvas, 272 × 295 cm, Museo Nacional del Prado, Madrid

machismo in everything from their embroidered jackets to their louche swagger. Quite a few of his women are voluptuous "majas," the pretty young things of his day. Style conscious but not high born, a self-regarding breed of fashionable riffraff, the majos and majas were the street people of eighteenth-century Spain, the supreme specimens and most boisterous players in the carnival of city life. And under Goya's shrewdly appraising eye they fight, flirt, and caper with great charm.

Pictures of that world would have appealed in particular to the tastes of the king's adult son, Crown Prince Charles, and his Italian wife, Maria Luisa, who found the ceremonious court life around Charles III stuffy and boring. At the Pardo Palace where they lived, they would have welcomed some cheeky decor, with flighty girls, posturing boys, and comic lowbrows, the very characters Goya would provide. As for the king, he went in more for hunting scenes. Goya also loved to hunt, and scenes from the chase filled his first series of tapestry paintings, on subjects provided by Bayeu and Mengs. But by the time he completed his next series, composed of vignettes from contemporary life for the crown prince and Maria Luisa, Goya was making sure to point out that now he was the principal author of his pictures. In the invoices he had to submit for payment on each series, he was careful to point out that these were scenes "of my invention." It was a standard contract term used by tapestry painters who came up with their own ideas for a picture, but it showed that Goya, still in his twenties, was wasting no time in asserting his sovereignty as an artist and the value of his imagination.

It was in the 1780s that Goya also began to enjoy the patronage of the wealthy ilustrados, who may have introduced him to the new currents in Spanish thinking. Charles III, who had come to the throne in 1759, gave hope to these small circles of Spanish liberals. He was no Voltaire, but he was cautiously receptive to reform ideas. He appointed some of them as royal ministers, to pursue goals like improving Spain's infamous rural roads and establishing its first central bank. They would introduce tax incentives for industry, promote agrarian reform, and modernize the kingdom's medieval universities. And though a very devout Catholic, Charles was even open to curbing the power of the church, especially when it challenged his.

Goya got to know these ilustrados as he drew closer to court circles and found portrait commissions there. The first would be from the Count of Floridablanca, then Spain's first minister, whom Goya painted in 1783. The portrait is ultimately unsatisfying, a bit stiff, with the spotlit mask of Floridablanca's face more inert than dignified. But a figure on the sidelines may be of more interest—it's Goya. The artist painted himself into the picture, the way Velázquez included himself in *Las Meninas*, his famous group portrait of the royal household of Philip IV. We see Goya on the left of the canvas, as he humbly approaches the king's minister to show him a framed picture.

It's a device Goya would return to more than once. Like Alfred Hitchcock, though not as regularly, he liked to make cameo appearances in his own pictures, perhaps as a reminder to the viewer that this skillful illusion had emerged from his hand. And perhaps too, they were intended as discretely boastful evidence of his remarkable proximity to wealth and power. Soon after completing the Floridablanca portrait, Goya was invited to paint the king's younger brother, Don Luis de Borbón, and his family. The tour de force that emerged from that commission was a large and complex multi-figure canvas daringly modeled on English "conversation pieces," scenes of gentlefolk relaxing and talking, a rarity in Spanish art of the time. Goya shows us a darkened room lit by a single candle, where Don Luis pauses from a card game while surrounded by family, servants, and visitors. Once again Goya puts himself into the picture, off to the left, crouching before a large blank canvas and ready to begin work. This near-panoramic canvas, almost eleven feet wide, was more than a picture. It was an announcement. Unlike his tapestry paintings, all destined to be stashed out of sight for decades, this suavely conceived and executed glimpse of the don's household was sure to be seen and talked about by the many visitors to his estate, a brash self-advertisement by an artist on the rise.

In the two years following his completion of that picture in 1784, Goya was named Assistant Director of Painting at the Royal Academy, where he had finally been admitted in 1780, and then attained the salaried position of painter to the king, one of several artists simultaneously holding that title. In time he was making enough money to equip himself with fashionable clothing and well-made hunting rifles. In a letter to Zapater he boasted about his fancy new carriage, "so light that it leaves everyone else behind, with its iron work excellently gilded and shiny; what a beauty." After researching his family history he started styling himself Francisco de Goya, appropriating the aristocratic *de* that his wealthy patrons so often had in their names.

But it's now, when his success is assured as never before, that an unaccustomed note of darkness enters his work, in early instances of the forbidding subjects he would later give himself over to, the pictures of banditry, madness, injustice, and witchcraft that would be spiritual and psychological tributaries to the great floodtide of the *Disasters* and the Black Paintings. There had been just one precursor to these images that we know of. Around 1779 Goya had made an etching of a corpse. It showed the seated body of a condemned man who had been garroted—bound to a chair and then executed by means of an iron collar tightened around his throat. But that image remained an outlier in his art until 1786, when he began a series of large paintings for the walls of the country estate of the Duke and Duchess of Osuna.

Immensely wealthy ilustrados and supporters of the arts—their library contained some sixty-five hundred volumes, including works forbidden by the Inquisition that they somehow got permission to own—the Osunas would become two of Goya's most faithful patrons. Most of the first paintings he made for them were in the cheerful manner of his tapestry cartoons, a girl on a swing, children at play, and so forth. But then there was the one we now call *Highwaymen Attacking a Coach*. There Goya presents us with a pastoral setting that could have come straight out of Fragonard, all blue sky and bright greenery, except that it's a crime scene, and the crime is still in progress. On one of Spain's notoriously dangerous country roads, four armed bandits have set upon a group of travelers. Two of them, the coachman and a military officer, appear already to be dead, bleeding out amid the foliage and under that fine blue sky. A third is on his back, fending off the knife of an attacker leaning in for the kill. Two others are pleading for mercy, including a young woman whose fate we can pretty well guess. One bandit stands before them holding an ominous length of rope.

Certainly the Osunas must have preapproved this brutal bit of home decor. Goya wouldn't just spring it on them. Perhaps they even suggested it. Yet even if the idea wasn't entirely his own, the picture represents a crucial eruption into Goya's art of the real-world terror and pain that would become preoccupations. And one year later, in a devotional picture commissioned by the Osunas for a chapel, he would bring onstage for the first time the ogres and goblins that would populate the haunted work of his old age. In *St. Francis Borja at the Deathbed of an Impenitent*, the saint is attempting to rescue the soul of a dying man who has refused absolution. All around the head of the man's bed, crouched in an infernal glow, his impending damnation is eagerly awaited by a host of ghoulish figures. We haven't seen faces quite like these in any of Goya's earlier work, but we'll see them again and again.

In December of 1788, Charles III died. Little more than a month later his son was crowned Charles IV, with his wife, Maria Luisa, as queen. They came to the throne well disposed toward the artist who had created their playful tapestry scenes at the Pardo Palace. Goya was quickly promoted from painter to the king to the loftier position of court painter. But one year later the whole of Europe would be shaken by the cataclysm of the French Revolution and the ripple effects of that event. These would include the Peninsular War and the postwar crackdown engineered by Charles's son Ferdinand.

As we have seen, these upheavals would profoundly shape the remainder of Goya's life. So would another, more personal misfortune. Late in 1792, and into the first months of the following year, when he was forty-six years old, he was felled by the mysterious illness that left him deaf for the rest of his life. We don't know what the disease was. Botulism? Meningitis? An inflammation of the nerves of the inner ear? Or maybe it was a long-brewing reaction to the toxic white lead pigment he had been using for years to prime canvases. All we know for certain is that his symptoms included dizziness, fainting spells, noises in his head, and deafness. All but one of them receded in time. The deafness was complete and permanent.

Goya spent his initial months of convalescence in Cádiz, at the home of his friend Sebastián Martínez, a wealthy merchant and art collector whose sizable store of English art may have given Goya a chance to study Hogarth's satirical prints. Not until the summer of 1793 would Goya recover sufficiently to return to Madrid, where in time he would resume his work as a court painter and sought-after portraitist. But he was a changed man, changed in ways that show up in the pictures he soon started making on his own initiative.

The very fact that he set to work without waiting for commissions is itself one of the signs that he was different, more than ever compelled to set down his own ideas. By the first weeks of 1794, he had completed a dozen cabinet paintings on tin plate. These were small pictures, portable merchandise, created on spec, that anyone could buy. As he described them in a letter to the vice president of the Royal Academy, they allowed him to make "observations which are usually not permitted by commissioned work."

And what were those observations? Six were bullfight scenes, a favorite subject for Goya that he might reasonably expect would find buyers among

Spain's many aficionados. Another, an image of an itinerant theater troupe on an outdoor stage, even seems to hark back to his lighthearted tapestry cartoons. But the rest? More tableaux of misfortune and degradation. One was even a reworking of the Osunas' coach robbery picture, this time in a much bleaker and dustier landscape and with all the passengers but one already dead. In the aftermath of his illness, the brooding imagination of the mature Goya was coming forward.

At least two of the pictures bring to mind a fashion outside Spain for scenes of catastrophe, both natural and manmade, a fascination that our own time has mostly ceded to disaster movies, YouTube videos, and television news. But in the eighteenth century an artist like the French marine painter Claude-Joseph Vernet could have an entire sideline in pictures of storm-tossed sailing vessels and exhausted castaways struggling to reach shore. In that line Goya now produced *The Shipwreck*, in which fifteen or so battered survivors struggle in the surf to gain a rocky perch. Only one has managed to get back on her feet, a woman in a flimsy and waterlogged gown. Not one to forgo the chance for a bit of calamity porn, Goya shows her holding both arms up to heaven imploringly, the better to display the bare breasts that have escaped from her blouse.

As for *Fire at Night*, it's a scene that could have come out of Dante, in which a confused scrum of people is fleeing a conflagration we can't see ourselves. In a cruel reversal of the ancient trope of divine light descending from the heavens, the fire appears to us only as an ominous explosion in the night sky, an irregular burst of white, ocher, and red utterly surrounded by dense black clouds of smoke.

The most chilling of the cabinet pictures is *Yard with Lunatics*, where two naked men wrestle in the shadowy outdoor enclosure of an asylum. For good measure a warden rears back to beat them with a stick or whip. All around the struggling men are leering or vacant-eyed inmates, looking something like the evil spirits in that painting of St. Francis Borja—with the difference that this time the monsters are entirely human. A cold light lingers in the wedge of sky you can see above the walls of the yard, as though even the sunlight were incarcerated. It's around this time that Goya begins to produce in certain of his pictures daytime skies unlike any other artist's. Gone is the cornflower blue of his tapestry cartoons. What he offers in its place is not storm clouds but something even more sinister, a void, an oppressive and mostly featureless atmosphere of pale gray, something no one would think to call the heavens.

Yard with Lunatics is also a first evidence of Goya's growing interest in madness. He wrote to a friend that he had personally witnessed a scene like this at the mental hospital in Zaragoza, where he grew up, and where both an aunt and uncle of his may have been confined when he was young. The treatment and mistreatment of the mentally ill was also a topic of interest among his ilustrado friends. But for Goya insanity appears as well to have been a metaphor, a base element of human nature and a kind of spiritual default mode that confounds the optimism of the Spanish Enlightenment he elsewhere appears to identify with. And there's a final, more personal reason for his attention. For a time after his deafness first set in, his head was full of inexplicable noises. He feared he was going mad himself.

Finally, there's *Interior of a Prison*, another of his exercises in confinement and gray gloom, a vision of seven desolate men chained inside a courtyard. Just like madness, incarceration may have taken on a personal meaning for Goya. The critic and Goya biographer Robert Hughes surely had it right when he wrote of that prison that "this place whose walls are too thick for outside sounds to penetrate . . . served Goya as a metaphor for his deafness."

It's true. Though he learned sign language, Goya's deafness cast him into a kind of solitary confinement and periodic melancholy. In a letter to Zapater from the first full year of his deafness, he confesses to his friend that sleep has become a refuge "when my sadness afflicts me." Hoping for a cure, he even allowed himself to be subjected to electrical shock treatment, in a session that was aborted when the electrical device broke.

In 1796, three years after he lost his hearing, the emotionally vulnerable Goya appears to have come under the spell of the famously beautiful and fabulously wealthy Duchess of Alba, who invited him to stay for a time at Sanlúcar de Barrameda, her estate near Cádiz. It was an attraction that led to some extraordinary portraits of the duchess but probably did not gain Goya access to her bed, however badly he may have wished it. Yet the isolation deafness imposed upon him also appears to have set him free. Goya began to produce yet more of his own art on his own terms, terms that now included the freedom to explore cruelty, calamity, and the irrational.

Around 1798, working again for the Osunas, Goya made his first paintings concerned with witchcraft and the diabolical, themes that would thread through his work for the rest of his life. This was a realm that fascinated Spain's lower classes, who sincerely believed in and feared the supernatural. But it also had its appeal to unbelieving sophisticates like the Osunas. Just as their literate English contemporaries were turning to Gothic horror novels like *Vathek* and *The Castle of Otranto*, many ilustrados liked to indulge a condescending taste for tales and imagery of witchcraft. For them it was an amusement, something bordering on what a later century would call camp.

And there *is* something almost campy in at least two of the half dozen witch paintings Goya provided the Osunas. Both resort to touches of Grand Guignol to mock the superstitious belief that witches snatched infants from their cradles to offer as sacrifices to Satan. So in *Witches' Sabbath*, Goya shows us the Evil One sitting upright in a meadow eerily lit by a predawn crescent moon. He has taken the form of a giant he-goat, his tall lyre-shaped horns garlanded with oak leaves. All around him mostly hideous female acolytes—witches—present him a selection of emaciated infants, which he eyes like a customer in a butcher shop. To double down on the hint of a blood feast, on a branch behind him a line of dead fetuses is strung up like so many game birds.

Satan is missing from another of these pictures, *The Spell*, but now there's a whole basket of dead babies. It's being held by one of five shriveled hags who menace a man crouching in terror on an isolated road at night. Another of the women holds a candle, while one of her weird sisters sticks a pin into a doll. One more bears down from a sky teeming with lamp-eyed owls, drumming the air with a pair of human thighbones. The man wears what appears to be a white nightshirt. Is this just a bad dream? Or have the witches transported him to this place in his sleep?

So over the top are the devices Goya resorts to in these two paintings, you can easily believe they were meant as satires of peasant superstition. But another of the Osuna canvases is too unnerving to dismiss so easily as a joke. In *Witches Flight* we see two terrified men on another road at night. One is lying facedown in the dirt with his hands covering his ears. The other is stumbling forward with a white cloak pulled over his head, both his fists balled into the *figa*, a hand sign meant to ward off evil.

We also see what it is that has frightened these men. Hovering vertically in the sky above them are a trio of shirtless and barefoot men in loose-fitting short

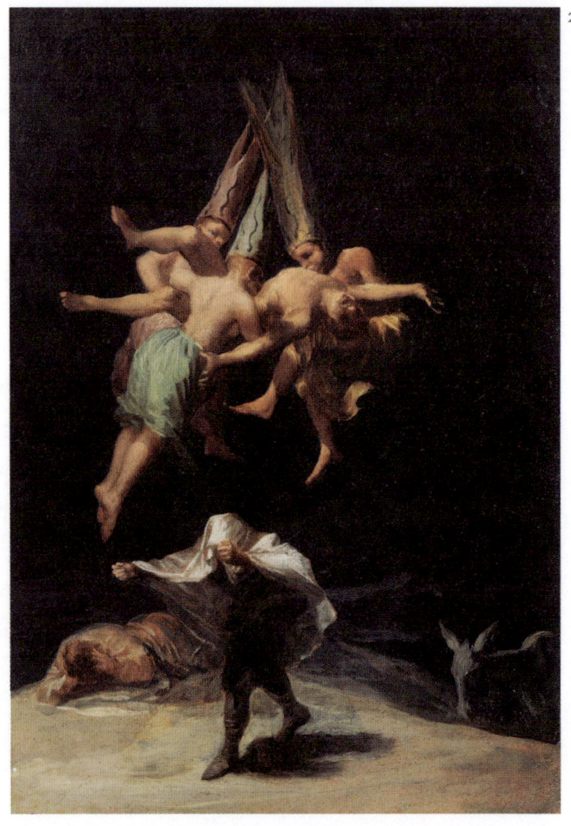

23

Witches Flight, 1797–98, oil on canvas, 43.5 × 30.5 cm, Museo Nacional del Prado, Madrid

pants. All three wear the tall conical caps, called *carozas*, that the Inquisition assigned to the accused and condemned, though theirs are also split lengthwise, like bishops' miters. Horribly, they appear to be feeding like sucker fish on a living man they've encircled. With his head flung back in terror and pain, they support him horizontally as though in some awful midair ballet. Though Goya may still just be mocking peasant delusions, there's nothing funny about this scene, even if it's imaginary. Men in the sky feasting on another man—it's a shock image of a disordered universe, like Linda Blair's full-circle head spin in *The Exorcist*.

When it came to witchcraft, Goya was almost certainly not a believer. As he once described himself in a letter to Zapater, "Ya ya ya. I'm not afraid of witches, apparitions, hobgoblins, boastful giants, knaves, or varlets, etc., nor indeed of any kind of beings except human beings." All the same he returned to the subject again and again. Witches, goblins, and other infernal creatures figure in roughly a fourth of the *Caprichos*, the eighty etchings satirizing Spanish society that Goya would publish when he was fifty-two. They also appear among his drawings, in the pages where he downloaded his most personal observations and imaginings. In their manifold reappearances,

Goya's nocturnal creatures no longer seem like lampoons of peasant superstition but metaphors for the all-too-real wickedness and irrationality forever at large in the world.

The emergence in late middle age of Goya the mordant fantasist closely tracks the appearance of the other essential strain in the art of his last years, Goya the moralist. In 1799, the year after he completed the witchcraft images, Goya published the series of etchings we know as the *Caprichos*. His first lengthy public exercise in satire, they were in some ways a prelude to the *Disasters*. In Spanish *capricho* is a word meaning "caprice," a light fancy or fantasy, with a further implication of "invention," a product of the artist's mind. But while they never descend into the bleakness of his Peninsular War images, "lighthearted" would not be quite the word to describe most of the Caprichos. "Bilious" would be better, also "sour," "indignant," and even "outraged." As he entered late middle age, the bemused response to the human comedy you find in some of his tapestry paintings was no longer Goya's emotional default mode.

So in the *Caprichos* what you get instead is a cavalcade of old women pimping out younger ones, plus venal priests and medical quacks. Gluttony, lust, vanity, and hypocrisy are mocked, along with faithless women, goatish geezers, and marriages contracted for money alone. Aristocratic donkeys ride atop lowborn laborers and the Wheel of Fortune flings men this way and that—just the image for a time when it seemed the king's ministers rose and fell in the blink of an eye. But there are also much darker spirits among these pictures. Victims of the Inquisition are grimly abused; monsters of all kinds roam free. Once again witches are everywhere, flying naked on brooms—or in one, mounted on a crippled woman—roasting children on spits, inducting newcomers into their diabolical sisterhood.

Midway through the series we come to one of Goya's most famous images, the one he captioned with words that have resonated for centuries: *The Sleep of Reason Produces Monsters*. He shows a man, probably himself, slumbering facedown on a table, his head cradled in his arms. All around him flutters a sinister flock of birds, mostly owls, which in Goya's day represented ignorance, not wisdom. So this world isn't just foolish, it's haunted, menaced by whatever might explode from the darkest reaches of the human psyche. It's notable that Goya developed this print from an earlier drawing in which above the sleeping man we see a crowd of faces, animal and human. Two of them are Goya's. Is he telling us that no one is immune; even he might be capable of becoming one of the monsters?

And yet, compared with what Goya will begin producing a decade later in the *Disasters*, the overall mood of the *Caprichos* is less despairing. Goya is still enough of a disciple of the Enlightenment in these images to believe, or to want to believe, that the foibles he ridicules are mostly just that, behavioral misdemeanors, things that might be corrected if exposed to the light and subjected to the remedial powers of reason. But some years later, the man who produces the *Disasters* will have none of that. There's nothing funny about the acts of willful sadism he will show us in the war zone, where the human heart is what Yeats would call it in the next century, a "foul rag and bone shop" that the sunlight of mere reason is powerless to disinfect.

On February 6, 1799, Goya announced the publication of the *Caprichos* with an advertisement in a Madrid newspaper. The ad served as an opportunity for him to set out at length another chapter of his perennial argument in favor of the importance and relevance of his personal vision as an artist. "The author is convinced," he begins, "that it is as proper for painting to criticize human error and vice as it is for poetry and prose to do so, although criticism is usually taken to be exclusively the business of literature."

Goya may have hoped that the *Caprichos* would be a big seller. He printed about three hundred sets for the steep price of 320 reales. But just two days after publishing his advertisement, Goya withdrew them all from circulation, or so he would later claim. If true, he may have done that because he feared his lampoons of corrupt clergy had offended the Inquisition, though we don't truly know the reason. He later claimed only twenty-seven sets were sold, four to his friends the Osunas.

In any event, he didn't really need the money, however much it pleased him to accumulate it. Later that same year, after completing two portraits of the queen, one astride the horse recently given to her by her favorite, Godoy, Goya advanced to the highest possible career rung for an artist in Spain. As first painter to the king he was now granted the sumptuous annual salary of 50,000 reales—more than three times his former pay. He bragged in a letter to Zapater: "The king and queen are crazy about your friend."

His ascent to that pinnacle is a reminder that even as his mood darkened and his critique of society sharpened, Goya remained a nimble courtier, a well-compensated servant of the king and a consummate insider. It was in that role that in 1800 he began one of his most famous canvases, a standing group portrait of Charles IV and his family, with the matronly queen at center, the king at right, looking a bit out of it, with various royal siblings and offspring here and there, and Goya in the background before his easel. At one time it was common to interpret this somewhat bovine ensemble as Goya's sneaky satire of the royals—in Renoir's famous description, "like a butcher's family in their Sunday best." But it would not be like the ever-ambitious Goya to insult the patrons to whom he owed so much, and who in any case had approved their likenesses in advance. A more common reading now sees the picture as an assertion of Spanish Bourbon stability and continuity—all those dynastic sashes and medals! all those children!—an important statement just a decade after the execution of Louis XVI had ended the Bourbon line in France.

Yet in that same year, in more personal work, Goya was dwelling once more on troubling things, in a series of eleven paintings that relate to bloody crimes and other outrages, both real and imagined. Two amount to a kind of fine-art tabloid reporting, episodes from a sensational murder that once had all Madrid talking. Three others are of an imagined crime, an armed holdup in a bleak, rocky landscape. In the first of the sequence, a group of bandits, having ambushed some travelers, are gunning down the surviving men, while a woman from their party flings her hands to the indifferent heavens in despair. In the next, one of the women, having been taken to a cave, is being stripped naked. She knows what's coming, because in the background another woman is being raped. In the last and most terrible a fully dressed man has a woman pinned to the ground. She may be the one we've seen in the earlier painting being stripped. Undoubtedly, she too has been raped. Now she's being murdered. The man is about to plunge a dagger into her throat while she issues a final open-mouthed scream of grief and terror.

More than a decade before he will begin the *Disasters*, Goya also produced as part of this group an imagined scene of wartime atrocity, a chaotic nighttime shooting attack at an army camp. The invaders emerge from the inky darkness on the right side of the canvas, their rifles blazing. Some soldiers at the camp already lie dying or dead. Others are fleeing. In the foreground a terrified woman in the line of fire runs with a baby cradled in her arms. Remarkably, there was sufficient taste for such things in Spain that the eleven pictures found a single buyer. A Majorcan collector, Juan de Salas, purchased the full group and later left them to his son-in-law, the Marquess of La Romana, whose descendants still own them.

In images like these, of madness and sadistic criminality, Goya appears to cast doubt on the optimistic faith in reason that underlay the European Enlightenment and its Spanish branches. Rationality and progress might be the hope of mankind, but barbarism and cruelty were the facts on the ground, the incurable realities of human nature. In a way it's remarkable that Goya did not end up an arch-reactionary like the political philosopher Joseph de Maistre, the Sardinian opponent of the French Revolution so convinced of the innate depravity of humankind that he saw despotism as the only sure bulwark against it.

That does not appear to be the position Goya arrived at, but that pessimistic line of thought surely helped make Goya the sunny tapestry artist into the man capable of the *Disasters* and the Black Paintings. So with his disposition by now suitably darkened, and his image bank of horrors well supplied, Goya is ready for the events that will tip him into the bitterness of his final years, the Peninsular War and its aftermath.

Awful as it was, the war could have been worse. After six years of bloodshed and privation, Spain could well have lost. There were many times when it looked like it would. But after years of shifting fortunes for both sides and long stretches of stalemate, the allied armies of Spain, Portugal, and England prevailed. This happened in part because by the end of 1812 Napoleon's disastrous invasion of Russia compelled the emperor to withdraw thousands of troops from Spain, weakening the already precarious French position there. On June 21, 1813, a decisive defeat at the Battle of Vitoria, a town in Spain's northern Basque country, signaled the beginning of the end of French power on the Iberian Peninsula. A few months earlier Joseph Bonaparte had already fled Madrid.

Such was the resurgence of the Spanish cause that in the autumn the armies of Britain and Spain invaded France, to play out the war's endgame on French soil. Meanwhile the combined armies of Prussia, Austria, and Russia, emboldened by Napoleon's setbacks in Spain, would converge on Paris. Soon after they arrived there at the end of March 1814, Napoleon was forced to abdicate. Within days the Peninsular War was over. Though not all modern historians would agree, Napoleon would remain convinced for the rest of his life that his invasion of Spain had been his undoing. In his final exile on Saint Helena, he would bitterly remark, "All my disasters can be traced back to this fatal knot."

The end of the war would not bring to a close the misfortunes of Spain. In March, Ferdinand had been released from his forced exile in France. Soon he would begin a monthslong victory lap through a succession of Spanish cities, culminating in a triumphal reentry into Madrid. Once there he lost no time in moving brutally against the Spanish liberals who might challenge his reassertion of unchecked royal and clerical power. Before his return, the reformers had gotten him to promise to swear an oath to uphold the constitution that had been adopted in 1812 by Spain's first-ever parliament, the Cortes, part of a government in exile that had convened during the war in the city of Cádiz. That pioneering document guaranteed a constitutional monarchy, with universal male suffrage, land reform, and a free press. Once back on Spanish soil Ferdinand broke his promise without hesitation. He abolished the Cortes, abrogated the constitution, and annulled any laws that flowed from it. Then he went after the liberals themselves. On the night of May 10, 1814, three days before he arrived in the capital, police began dragging prominent reformers out of their homes and into jail cells. It was the beginning of what would be a yearslong campaign of lawless imprisonment, torture, executions, and property confiscation.

Just six months later, the sixty-eight year old Goya found himself called before a body of inquiry established to determine the wartime loyalty of those who worked in government positions during the French occupation. He had to summon witnesses to testify in his favor. Some of them would claim in his defense that at one point during the war Goya had fled Madrid, hoping to find sanctuary in another country, only to be forced home by a police order threatening to confiscate his family's property. Did it happen? We have no other evidence, but there are many stretches of Goya's life for which we have scant record. If true, that foiled attempt at escape would tell us how difficult it had been for Goya to live with the daily contradiction of serving the French-imposed king while sympathizing, in his conflicted way, with the Spanish cause. In any event, by the following April Goya would be formally exonerated by the loyalty board.

Another of Ferdinand's early actions was to restore the Spanish Inquisition, which had been abolished by Joseph Bonaparte. The revived "Holy

Office," as it was known, was something of a paper tiger. Though it could ban books and conduct inquiries, its torture chambers had long been a thing of the past. All the same, it could still intimidate and harass its targets. Soon Goya was one of them. In March 1815 he was called to appear before the Inquisition on a charge of obscenity. The offense, of course, was a painting. The painting, of course, was *The Naked Maja*, completed fifteen years earlier and almost certainly commissioned by Godoy as a portrait of his mistress, Pepita Tudó. After Godoy's fall from power, it was discovered in his palace and eventually identified as a Goya. Now the Inquisition wanted to know why he had produced such a "lascivious" picture.

And naked she certainly was and is, a briskly matter-of-fact young woman on a cushioned chaise, her arms raised languidly above her head, her whole body torquing slightly in your direction, as if to make sure you don't miss a thing. Looking right at you with a half-amused and entirely immodest stare, she's a plain precursor of *Olympia,* the imperturbable nude that Édouard Manet, who revered Goya, would produce in 1863. There's no attempt by Goya to idealize or mythologize this woman, to connect her to classical predecessors, to pretend she's Venus. Utterly contented and self-possessed, she's entirely of the here and now. That was a point made explicit some years later when Goya produced the picture's companion piece. *The Clothed Maja* is a portrait of the same woman, in the same pose, but dressed in the fashions of her time, a lower-class gauzy maja outfit that, like a thong today, was intended to be hotter than mere nudity.

It would be wonderful to have a transcript of Goya's appearance before the Inquisition, to see what he would have said to defend not just that painting but his right to paint as he pleased. But there is none, because he may not have put in an appearance. His connections at court may have been sufficient to make the whole matter go away without his having to suffer the humiliation of being interrogated. Or maybe the Inquisitors simply decided it wasn't worth their time to pursue a deaf painter pushing seventy. They had bigger prey in their sights.

Even before his run-ins with the loyalty board and the Inquisition, Goya understood he needed to do something to allay any concerns about his fealty to Ferdinand. Bad enough that with the excitable king back in power the whole of Spain was strapped to a bomb. So much the worse should Goya be personally under suspicion, putting at risk his court salary and possibly much more.

Not only had he continued occasionally to work for Joseph Bonaparte—while prudently declining to take any salary—but he had made several portraits of Joseph's courtiers and very possibly one of Joseph. The French "intruder king" had even given him an award for loyal service that he had designed himself. The Royal Order of Spain was a deep red star on a ribbon that Spaniards mocked as "the eggplant." Goya claimed never to have worn his, but still . . .

With all of that in mind, in February 1814, a few months before Ferdinand's return, Goya had asked Spain's temporary governing authority, called the Council of Regency, to commission him to make work commemorating episodes in his nation's struggle against France. That request is generally believed to have led to the creation of Goya's famous paintings related to two momentous dates. The first of these was May 2, 1808, when citizens of Madrid had risen up at various points around the city against the French troops they now realized were not allies but an army of occupation. The second was May 3, when the French summarily executed anyone they suspected of having taken part in the previous day's bloody disturbances.

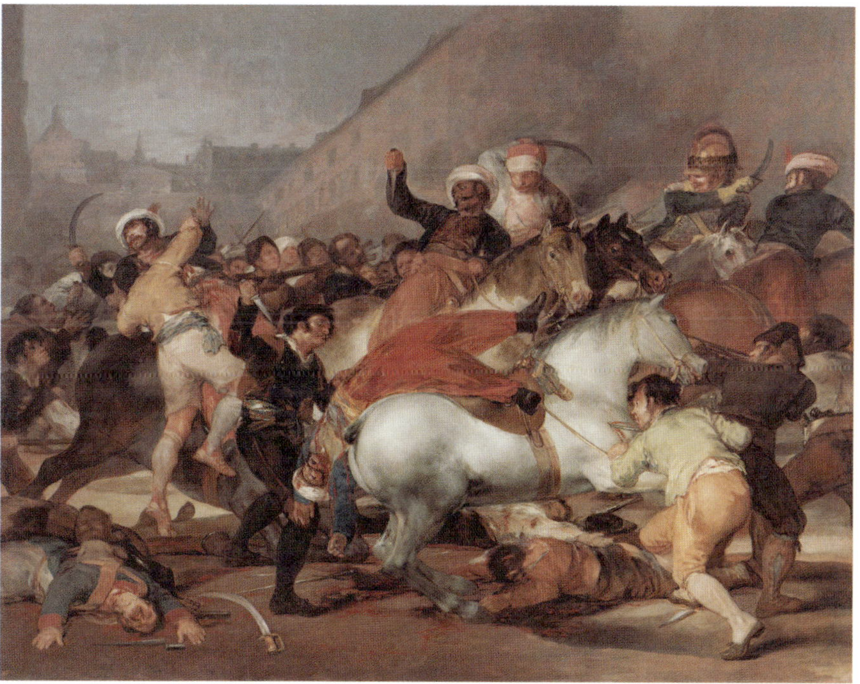 24

The Second of May, 1808 in Madrid, 1814, oil on canvas, 268.5 × 347.5 cm, Museo Nacional del Prado, Madrid

Before the year was out Goya had completed both pictures, very much a related pair. *The Second of May, 1808 in Madrid,* to use the first painting's full title, could be said to be another of his images of madness, albeit madness unleashed by the Spanish people in their own defense. It shows us an actual incident from that day's multiple uprisings, a lethal skirmish at one of the city gates, the Puerta del Sol. That fight had pitted armed Madrileños on foot against mounted French dragoons in their brass helmets, along with turbaned Mamelukes, the much-feared Egyptian fighters in Napoleon's Guard. Goya shows us a wild scrum of men and horses in which one of the Mamelukes has fallen backward from his saddle. Now he hangs upside down across the rump of his white horse, blood streaming down his face and chest from stab wounds in his midsection. Lunging toward him is a man in the distinctive dress of a lower-class majo, who prepares to plunge a dagger into the helpless man.

There's more chaos in the lower right corner of the canvas, where a crouching young man thrusts a long, thin blade directly into the flesh of the same Mameluke's horse. At stage left another Madrileño throws himself at a mounted Mameluke who rears back in alarm, flourishing a scimitar. And on the right-hand side again, a trio of horse's heads rise from within the turbulent scene to lock eyes with the viewer, like the satyr Marsyas as he's being skinned in Titian's painting, creating a weird locus of calm within the surrounding chaos. Much as he did in the *Disasters,* Goya has departed from the convention of representing war as any kind of noble combat to describe it instead as a bloody free-for-all.

In the next canvas comes the payback. *The Third of May, 1808 in Madrid* is a scene of pitiless retribution by the French that has also become one of the most famous paintings in the Western canon, an image so familiar that for once it justifies being described by that weary cliché "iconic." It's a nighttime tableau. A group of frightened men, their backs almost literally against the wall—actually a hill that rears up steeply behind them—confront a faceless French firing squad. At the lower left of the canvas there's already a bloody pile of corpses. One of the men still standing, a tonsured monk, pleads on bended knees to avoid the same fate. Or perhaps he's praying, no doubt in vain. Others bury their faces in their hands.

In the forefront is the pivotal figure, a kneeling man who might possibly be the one we see in the earlier picture about to stab the inverted Mameluke.

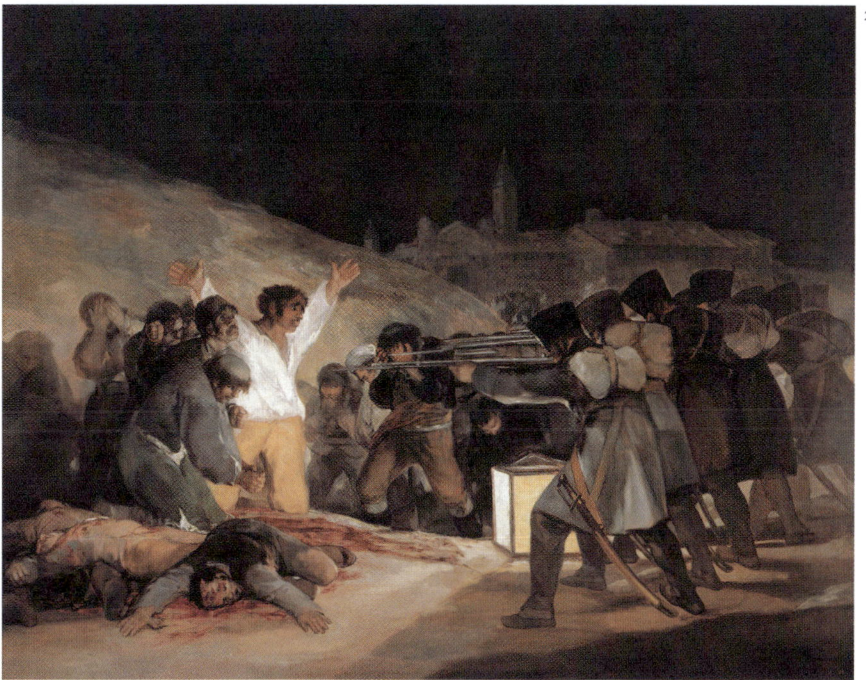

25

The Third of May, 1808 in Madrid, 1814, oil on canvas, 268 × 347 cm, Museo Nacional del Prado, Madrid

Here he throws his hands in the air in entreaty. No matter that he appears in the left side of the canvas, he's the emotional center of this picture. His white shirt and yellow pants are brilliantly lit by the large boxlike lantern that sits on the ground between the soldiers and their victims. That harsh illumination throws him into sharp relief against the other men, who are clothed mostly in subdued browns and grays. And his shirt seems almost to be alive on its own, rendered in electric sweeps of free brushwork.

He's also plainly a Christ figure, and not just because of his outstretched arms. On the upraised palm of his right hand we can see a scar lightly indicated, something surely meant to suggest a stigmata. But he's not Christ as Salvator Mundi, the savior of the world. He's Christ as sacrificial lamb, and his face, with an expression both pained and puzzled, is the face of every anguished and anonymous victim of history, from Goya's murderous time to our own.

While the left side of this great painting is a scene of high emotion, the affectless right side complicates and deepens its impact. Goya shows us the members of the firing squad from behind, so that the French soldiers are almost literally faceless. What little we can see of their features is as cold and imperturbable as their rifle barrels, which reach into the crucial dead center of the canvas with their dull metal luster and fixed bayonets. Though ranks of impassive killers are a warrior convention going back to Assyrian wall carvings, and though early nineteenth-century Spain had nothing in the way of mass production, Goya's way of representing the soldiers as impassive killing machines feels new for the way it prefigures twentieth-century industrial imagery. The French executioners are like pistons, the machinery of oppression, uniform and interchangeable, and all the more deadly for that.

And what to make of that box lantern on the ground? It sheds an icy glow on this official massacre, illumination that offers no hope in the moment, but all the same literally brings this outrage to light for future generations. Picasso would pay homage to that lantern in the image of a blazing electric bulb he placed at the top of *Guernica*, a light to represent the eyes of the world being turned toward another infamous event, this time a Nazi bombing raid, almost 130 years later, on a Basque village during the Spanish Civil War.

We're not sure how these paintings were first displayed or for how long, though they may have been placed on a triumphal arch that greeted Ferdinand on his return to Madrid. But after they were completed there's no mention of them until 1834, when they turn up in an inventory of pictures in storage at the Prado.

In the years after Ferdinand's return, to burnish his "patriotic" credentials, Goya was sure to make portraits of the heroes of the war against Napoleon. As early as 1812, he produced one drawing and two paintings of the Duke of Wellington, who had commanded the British armies in Spain and would later defeat Napoleon at Waterloo. One of these was a large equestrian portrait of Wellington that appears to have been painted over another equestrian portrait—also by Goya—that may have depicted Joseph Bonaparte. If it is indeed Joseph under there, then Goya's ingratiating new image of Wellington would conveniently sweep away his incriminating prior tribute to the French intruder. For an artist trying to smooth his transition between opposing sovereigns, concealment of past services might well have been a useful stratagem.

Meanwhile Goya worked very little for Ferdinand himself. Though after the war he made three portraits of the king, none were commissioned by

Ferdinand or made from life. All three were tributes of varying quality to a monarch who, at least on the evidence of Goya's brush, looked something like Quentin Tarantino. In 1817, the year he turned seventy-one, he completed his last royal commission, for a painting of Saint Isabel of Portugal, intended for the palace dressing room of Ferdinand's queen, Isabel of Braganza. Thereafter he would have all the time in the world for work of his own invention.

And even before the outpouring of the Black Paintings, some of that work would continue his meditations on madness and injustice. These include the last of his *Disasters of War* etchings, those oblique commentaries on the postwar situation he called "emphatic caprices." In some Goya comes close to the role of editorial cartoonist, as he does in the one titled *They do not know the way*, in which a long line of men, roped together, stumbles through the countryside led by a blind man. Even if the allusion to Spain under the wretched misguidance of Ferdinand is never made explicit, it's hard not to suspect that may have been Goya's message. Three that feature an allegorical female figure in distress—*Truth has died, Will she live again?* and *This is truth*—may lament Ferdinand's rejection of the Constitution of 1812.

Others are much harder to pin down, though some may have meanings that were clearer in his time than they are to us now, two centuries later. In these Goya introduces a bestiary of fantastical animals. Here's a giant carnivorous vulture that capers before a crowd on its hind legs while a man prepares to poke it with a pitchfork. And here's a dog—"Proud monster"—that devours (or is it vomits up?) an entire pile of humans.

In addition to producing a series of thirty-three bullfight prints in the postwar years—the *Tauromaquia*, which failed to sell even in *corrida*-crazed Spain—Goya also continued painting more of his imagined scenes of injustice and cruelty. In a series of oils on wood panel, he envisioned an Inquisition trial of heretics taking place in some unspecified past, as well as a procession of religious penitents whipping themselves bloody. This spectacle too would have taken place in the past, since even in ultra-pious Spain self-flagellation parades had been banned since 1777. There was as well a raucous village festival with what appears to be a distinctly manic edge, plus yet another madhouse, one where inmates in outlandish costumes parody the princes and judges of the "sane" world outside.

Around 1816, Goya also began the third of the four great undertakings of his last years, the quizzical series of twenty-two etchings called the

Disparates. A *disparate* is, roughly translated, a folly, an act of foolishness. Like the *Disasters*, these prints were never published in Goya's lifetime, not appearing until 1864. With many of them Goya ventures into realms of very private meaning, images of a kind that would rarely appear in European painting until the Symbolists of the later nineteenth century, via the riddles and fantasies of artists like Odilon Redon and Gustave Moreau. In their strangeness and hermeticism, they even offer a preview of twentieth-century surrealism. Maybe Goya didn't publish them because he suspected only he could fully decipher them.

The most approachable of the *Disparates* are bits of social satire, especially of relations between men and women, which are not so different from much of what's in the *Caprichos*. The one called *Marital Folly* reads easily enough. It's a cynical emblem of domestic misery, a man and a woman conjoined freakishly at their backs in a maddening and permanent union—to adapt a phrase from Shakespeare, the beast with two fronts. Yet even in these there can be some powerful perplexities. *Big Fool* is a wonderful image, but of what? An ungainly carnival giant of the kind the Spanish called a *bobalicón*—a "big booby"—is dancing goofily while flourishing a pair of castanets. Two enigmatic heads with wild expressions loom out of the darkness behind him. They may be singing—unless they're not. The giant meanwhile is looming over a very intimidated man holding a life-size wooden statue of a woman. Is the hooded man a friar? Is the statue a saint? So could this be a parody of foolish idolatry, the worship of statues? Or is the giant simply a grinning personification of male lust?

Yet, for the purposes of a modern viewer it doesn't matter. These images are all the more fascinating now for their enigmas. They represent the work of Goya's imagination in its freest register, unbound by mere reality. If the *Disasters* were the work of Goya in extremis, the *Disparates* are Goya in excelsis. They are Goya inventing fantastical images more extravagantly perhaps than any artist since Hieronymus Bosch, whose *Garden of Earthly Delights*, with its scores of improbable creatures, Goya might have known from the Spanish royal collection. For that reason, maybe the most representative etchings in the series are the several that show men and animals airborne, set free entirely from earthly constraints. No witches this time, but a herd of bulls tumbling through an empty sky, a man on the back on an immense

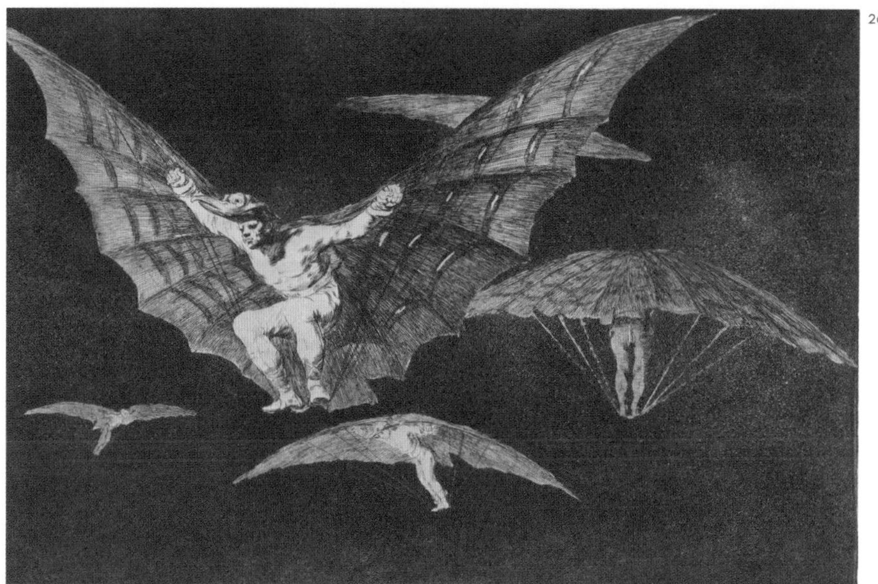
26

A Way of Flying, ca. 1815–16, etching, aquatint, drypoint, 24.5 × 35.3 cm, the Metropolitan Museum of Art, New York

winged beast, and, in the image called *A Way of Flying*, a whole flock of men sailing through the sky on mechanical wings.

Goya probably finished the *Disparates* around 1819, a time when flight may well have been something on his mind—away from the turbulence of Madrid, out to his newly acquired house in the country, a place where his fully achieved imaginative freedom would reach its final crescendo. But in the years before he made that leap, Goya also produced one other powerful and enigmatic image, a freestanding aquatint, not part of any series, that he appears to have executed by 1818 and that we call *Seated Giant*.

In a nighttime or predawn setting, the naked giant is seated with his back toward us. Perched hugely on the horizon of a desolate landscape, he looks back at us across one shoulder, his expression tentative and a bit questioning. Is he somehow representative of postwar Spain itself, all too well acquainted with the horrors of the recent past and contemplating what may be yet to come? Considered that way, you realize he somewhat resembles the Goya of that guarded self-portrait from 1815. His features are not the same,

27 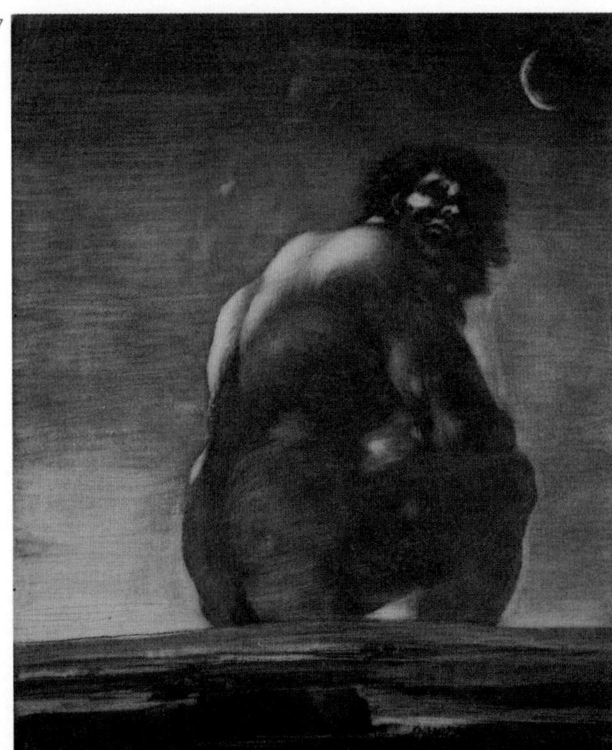

Seated Giant, by 1818, aquatint, with burnishing and scraping, 28.5 × 21 cm, Museum of Fine Arts, Boston

but his expression is similar, the face of a creature whose wary take on the world is conditioned by what he now knows of its awful ways.

Late in 1819, the same the year he moved out to the countryside, Goya was hit again by a severe illness. It was probably not a recurrence of whatever disease had left him deaf twenty-six years earlier, but life-threatening all the same. We know how serious it was, and how grateful he was to be delivered from it, because of his *Self-Portrait with Doctor Arrieta*, one of the most harrowing depictions ever made of human frailty, and more than that, of an artist's personal proximity to death.

Goya shows himself alive, but just barely, propped up from behind in his bed by the doctor, who is bringing to his lips a cup of medicine. In the background, weird faces flicker in the darkness, barely visible and perhaps

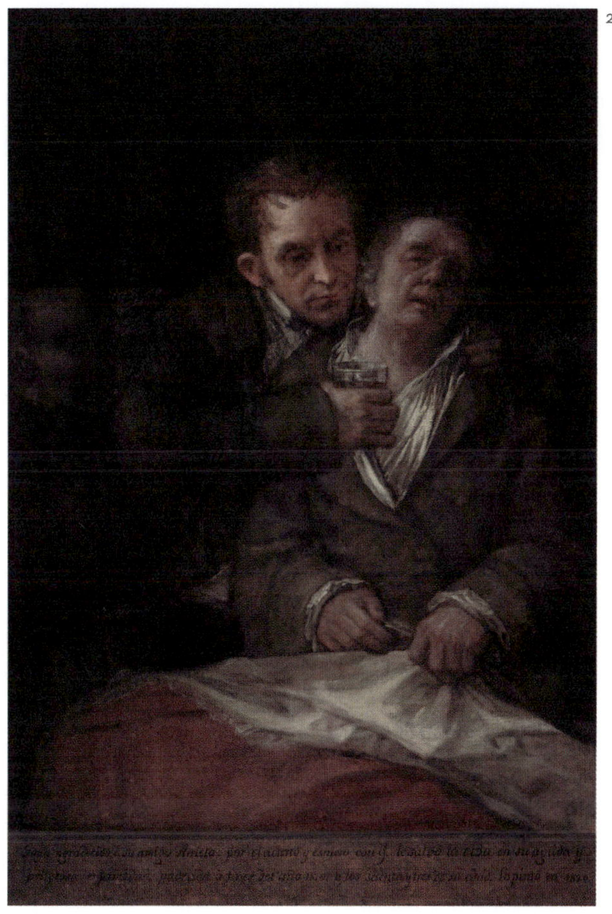

Self-Portrait with Dr. Arrieta, 1820, oil on canvas, 114.62 × 76.52, Minneapolis Institute of Art, Minneapolis

supernatural, but we don't know who or even what they are. At the bottom of the canvas, which he made as a gift for the doctor, he inscribed a dedication. "Goya gives thanks to his friend Arrieta for the expert care with which he saved his life from an acute and dangerous illness which he suffered at the close of the year 1819 when he was seventy-three years old."

A tribute to the healing power of a physician's care—this is something new for Goya. In the *Caprichos* he had featured doctors a few times as quacks, more dangerous than the illnesses they treated. Now he casts the power of at least one of them in sacred terms, a man bearing a curative cup that's very much like a chalice. What it offers is not just therapeutic but sacramental.

The two men are posed as a secular Pietà. The doctor's arms encircle the exhausted artist the way the Virgin cradles the dead Christ. And the entire image is plainly modeled after the ex-votos that were then—as now—common throughout Spain, pictures made to give thanks for heaven's intercession in some personal misfortune that befell the owner. Each consists of a scene of the crisis itself, with the Virgin or saint hovering above, and a text at the bottom proclaiming the success of the supernatural intervention.

And just as, in Christ's death, his resurrection is implied, so with Goya. When he made this picture, he had already recovered from whatever his illness was, so it's an image of deliverance, not despair. Even in this haunted sickroom, the hint of spring-renewal green in the men's coats and the rosy palette of the bedclothes tells us as much. The way Goya grips the sheet, however faintly, as though clawing his way back to life, is also a sign of just that—life. He would go on to live another nine years. But he would never again produce anything as tenderly autobiographical as this, his last self-portrait.

At some point after he rose from that bed, Goya was ready to begin work on the Black Paintings, which he would produce between 1820 and 1823. Each floor of his house was largely taken up by a single rectangular room measuring about thirty-three by fifteen feet. With few windows, the rooms on both floors offered plenty of usable wall space. Remarkably, though nearly all the Black Paintings ended as nightmare images, many didn't begin that way. We know from X-ray study that when Goya first started "decorating" the walls of his new home, what he laid down were happier scenes. (Assuming the underpaintings were his. They may well have been there when he bought the house.) One of the most famous of the works that we know are from his own hand is *Saturn Devouring His Son*. What we see is a wild-eyed graybeard gripping in both fists a much smaller figure of indeterminate gender, while taking a big, blood-squirting bite of his victim's upper body. But X-rays show it began as a picture of an ordinary man doing a dance step. If both pictures were indeed by Goya, was he trying at first to recapture a youthful love of life and then decided to hell with it?

In any case, what was Goya trying to say in that grotesque image? Saturn was one of the Titans, the parents of the Olympian gods. Because it had been prophesied to him that one of his children would someday overthrow him—shades of Titian's Danaë and her doomed father, King Acrisius—he took to devouring them at birth, to the great distress of his wife. She chose to save

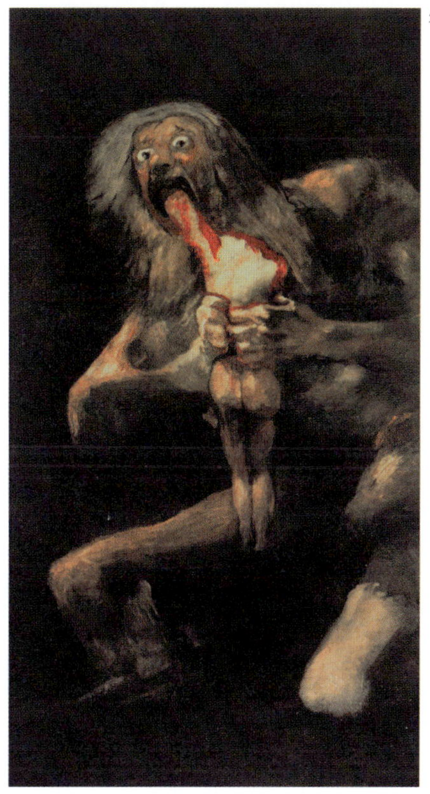

29

Saturn Devouring His Son, 1820–23, mixed media mural transferred to canvas, 143.5 cm × 81.4 cm, Museo Nacional del Prado, Madrid

one by fooling her husband into swallowing a rock wrapped in swaddling clothes. The rescued boy escaped, grew up to be Jupiter, and fulfilled the prophecy.

The Greeks had a different name for Saturn. They called him Cronus, and by the time of the Renaissance he had become identified with Chronos, whom European artists developed into the figure of Father Time. Goya would certainly have known of that association. He had made images of Father Time himself. So in this picture the aging Goya may be showing us Time devouring one of his children as he devours us all. Now well into his seventies and weakened by successive illnesses, Goya would certainly have had reason to be thinking of time as a monster that chews us up before it delivers us to the grave.

Actually, he had been thinking about it for decades. As early as 1787 he wrote to his friend Zapater and asked, "Has time passed as quickly [with you] as with me? I've aged, with many wrinkles, and you wouldn't recognize me except for my snub nose and sunken eyes." In that year, he was all of forty-one. And whatever else it was, this image of high-stepping cosmic cannibalism was also a very dark joke. It looked out from one wall of the first-floor room where Goya and his household took their meals. Bon appétit.

In the same room Goya laid down *Two Old Men Eating,* in which the fellow on the right has a skull for a head. Memento mori—even at mealtime. Nearby was *Two Old Men,* a vertical panel in which a tall standing figure with a goblin's face whispers into the ear of a fully human codger who has long white hair and a flowing white beard. Or is the goblin shouting, in which case the old man may be the deaf Goya himself?

Goya executed that painting down one side of the quinta's first-floor doorway, on the narrow end of the house. Bordering the other side of that entry was the only light image among the Black Paintings, a full-length portrait of a woman assumed to be Goya's companion Leocadia, leaning against what began as a mantelpiece but was repainted to resemble a large stone. (Some commentators have seen in it the outlines of a tomb, perhaps Goya's—so maybe the image isn't that light after all.) That placement would support the idea that the ancient man is Goya, sharing the threshold of his home across from his lady. And, possibly, across from his tomb.

There's another woman in that first-floor room, this one wielding a knife. The only one of the Black Paintings that draws on the Bible, *Judith and Holofernes* illustrates the Old Testament story of the Hebrew widow who seduced and beheaded Holofernes, a Babylonian general dispatched by King Nebuchadnezzar II to menace the Jewish people. Her tale had already provided Artemisia Gentileschi and Caravaggio with the opportunity to paint scenes combining female flesh with blood-spurting gore, the same formula that would much later launch a thousand slasher movies. Goya spares us the blood—we see Judith in the moment before the decapitation. As with late Titian, the violence in this image is all in the paint application, the shocking broad strokes of thick brown and black. And as with his image of Saturn, this would be another painting that referred to the idea of a powerful man losing his power.

Those pictures shared the first floor with two of the largest and most unnerving of the Black Paintings, one of them a vision of humanity as a crowd of braying imbeciles. It's known as *The Pilgrimage of San Isidro,* but as with all the wall paintings removed from the quinta, that title was assigned after Goya's death. We can't be sure if that was his intended subject, though the

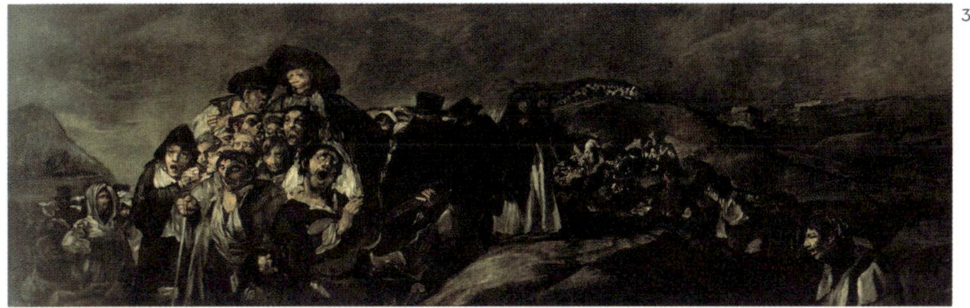 30

The Pilgrimage of San Isidro, 1820–23, mixed media mural transferred to canvas, 138.5 × 436 cm, Museo Nacional del Prado, Madrid

Madrid procession of that name traveled down a slope he could see from his house, and its outdoor festival was an annual event he knew well. He had even made it the subject of one of his tapestry paintings more than thirty years earlier, though in a much more cheerful vein. What we can be sure of is that the later painting, a forbidding tableau more than fourteen feet wide, is one of the most purely misanthropic images he would ever produce. For the man who left us the *Caprichos* and *Disasters*, that's saying something.

Goya shows a long rank of people parading toward us on a dark road. The hills behind them are a sooty gray-black. The sky is so dark it might as well be the roof of a cave. Leading the crowd is a group of men and a few women whose expressions are repulsive, coarse, and stupid, each in its own way. At their forefront is a blind guitar player singing in open-mouthed, bug-eyed excitement. This is old man Goya's portrait of "the people" as "the mob," a herd of idiots in which the moronic verges into the demonic.

Just across the room from that picture, the literally demonic heaves up from its companion piece, *The Witches' Sabbath, or the Great He-Goat*. Another panorama in the same lugubrious palette, it features yet another assembly of near bestial humans, this time seated worshipfully around Satan himself. Just as Goya had done years earlier in one of his witch paintings for the Osunas, he represents the Prince of Darkness as a giant he-goat. This time he's a black silhouette who preaches before dozens of his apish acolytes in a perverse parody of the Sermon on the Mount.

So much for the first floor. There were no laughs on the upper story either. Certainly there are none in the scene of two men in a field battering each other with long poles—a hopeless tableau of eternal violence. That we

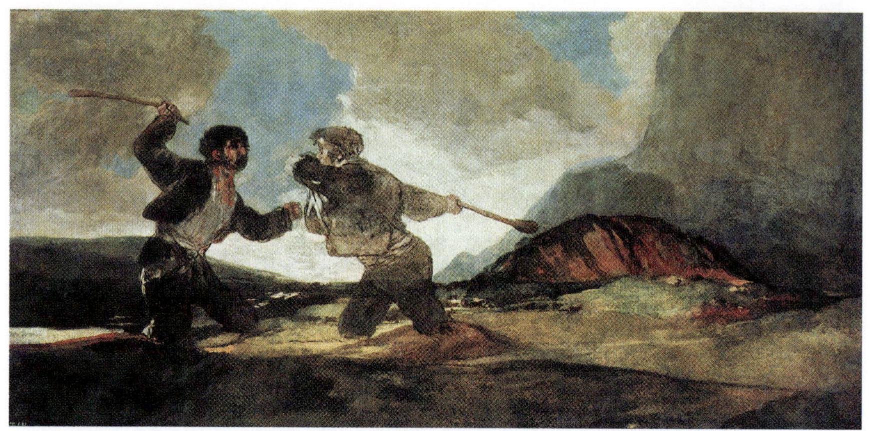

31

Duel with Cudgels, 1820–23, mixed media mural transferred to canvas, 125 × 261 cm, Museo Nacional del Prado, Madrid

also see them sunken into the ground up to their knees amplifies the image wonderfully, but it may not be Goya's doing. It may be a distortion of his original image, one that took place during the posthumous transfer of the mural to canvas and subsequent retouching.

Nearby was Goya's eerie version of the three fates, the mythical trio who spin the thread of life, measure it out, and cut it off at life's end. Goya shows them flying, or maybe just floating, a haunted hovercraft above another dank landscape. The three appear to be joined in a bedsheet that holds them in flight. It also carries an unidentified fourth passenger, a man whose arms are bound and whose fate they may be deciding.

Goya's picture of two women laughing at a man in deep shadow may be an eruption of both his blunt approach to sex and his own sexual anxiety—the man appears to be masturbating. It's hard to be sure. The shadows are just deep enough to make the action uncertain, and in photographs taken of the Black Paintings before they were removed from the walls the man appears to be holding a piece of paper. So maybe it's his writing and not his wrist action that's being mocked. As for the wide image of two women floating or flying across a mountainous landscape while one points to a distant mesa and the town that sits across it—no one has any real idea what it means.

On that floor is also the emotional terminus of the Black Paintings, the most indelible image of the entire suite and a premonition of the twentieth-century absurd. It's that dog. We only see his head, popping out from near

32

The Drowning Dog, 1820–23, mixed media mural transferred to canvas, 131 × 79 cm, Museo Nacional del Prado, Madrid

the bottom of the picture. The rest of him appears to have sunk into a pit of quicksand, or behind some earthen barrier. With his tapering snout and beseeching eyes pointed upward, he looks into the empty sky, as though for the return of a master who is not coming back. It's the final appearance of Goya's sicklied-over white heavens, the bleak yonder that no God occupies. This is where he leaves us, staring expectantly into what the poet Wallace Stevens would describe more than a century later as "nothing that is not there and the nothing that is."

Or as Goya had already put it: *Nada*.

And then, incredibly, the clouds parted—though not all at once. In his last years, Goya uncoiled, easing into a period of what was by all reports genuine contentment, effectively a new lease on life. Certainly his art suggests as much. You can almost hear the laughter that courses through so many of the drawings he made in that final stretch, when he also mastered complex new practices like lithography and a novel way of producing ivory miniatures. In all, an extraordinary burst of late-life creativity. But to get to that place he had to leave Spain entirely, by way of a self-imposed exile in France.

Events in Spain had developed rapidly after he first moved to the quinta. By 1820 Ferdinand's captious misrule had alienated even his allies in the Spanish military, the very men who had helped him regain absolute power six years earlier. His government was in a state of perpetual chaos. His ministers rarely lasted more than six months. The economy sank into depression.

Worse, Ferdinand would not give up a hopeless ambition to regain Spain's New World territories and their all-important silver. All around South America, colonials, notably including Simón Bolívar, had used the chaos of the Peninsular War years as an opportunity to launch independence movements. Now Ferdinand insisted on assembling a military contingent in Aragón to reinforce a dwindling Spanish army of reconquest already in South America. The prospect of being sent into the frightful jungles there was deeply unpopular within the military. It didn't help that Ferdinand also lacked the funds to pay his soldiers. So in 1820 two Spanish officers staged a coup. But this would be a military takeover with a progressive agenda, pledged to restore the liberal Constitution of 1812. Ferdinand would be permitted to remain on the throne, but his powers would be curtailed by the very document he had nullified on his return to Spain.

The era of constitutional rule would last only three years—the *Trienio Liberal* (the "Liberal Triennium"), as they are now known. In 1822, Ferdinand appealed to Europe's conservative powers to launch a military expedition to defeat his opponents. Though wary of the tempestuous Ferdinand, they were warier still of rebellions anywhere in Europe against the royal absolutism they believed in as fervently as he did. In the spring of the following year, a coalition of France, Russia, Prussia, and Austria sent a French-led army into Spain, where, by that time, the Spanish parliament had gone so far as to depose Ferdinand and establish a regency. The invaders made quick work of the liberals, scoring a final victory over them at the fortress of Trocadero on August 31. Almost immediately, the dashing young officer who had led the revolt against Ferdinand, General Rafael del Riego y Núñez, was arrested. In November he was executed.

In no time Ferdinand, now restored yet again to the throne, was back on the warpath against liberals, constitutionalists, and Freemasons, this time more viciously than ever. Arrests and executions became routine. Ultraroyalist death squads went on a killing spree throughout Spain, targeting anyone who had played a part in trying to abridge the king's power.

We can tell from Goya's actions that he feared being caught up in this whirlwind. Less than three weeks after the liberal defeat at Trocadero, he signed over the quinta to his seventeen-year-old grandson Mariano, Javier's son, a move that he might have hoped would shield the property from seizure should Goya become a target of Ferdinand's reprisals. Then in January 1824, when Ferdinand was organizing tribunals to hear charges against his opponents, Goya apparently sought refuge for a few months with a scholarly and moderately liberal priest, José Duaso y Latre. Like Goya a member of the Royal Academy of Fine Arts, Duaso would harbor a number of refugees from Ferdinand's wrath. Assuming Goya was one of them, then the portrait he made of Duaso early in that year might be a token of his gratitude.

Eventually Ferdinand's crackdown became too much even for his European allies. After they warned him to pull back or risk losing their support, he prudently responded on May 1 with a general amnesty, which many liberals took as an opportunity to pack up and leave. Certainly Goya lost no time. On May 2, he petitioned the king for permission to spend six months in France, ostensibly to take the medicinal waters at a spa near Vosges. The implied prospect of his return after six months meant he could continue to collect his salary as a court painter, but the spa vacation was a pretext, a cover story that would not make him look like one more political exile. Goya would depart for France in June, but he would never get to Vosges. Instead, he would settle in Bordeaux, where Leocadia and two of her children would join him in the fall. Though he would make two brief return trips to Spain, he would never live there again.

Yet while Goya was profoundly and eternally Spanish, life in France would not be an unhappy circumstance for him. He was free at last from the daily turmoil of events back at home. Bordeaux also had a large community of Spanish expatriates, many having left as early as 1814, the year of Ferdinand's first return to power. Some were Goya's longtime friends, like the playwright Leandro Fernandez de Moratín. Soon after Goya arrived in Bordeaux, it was Moratín who hosted him for a time. In a letter to a mutual friend in Madrid, Juan Antonio Melón, he described his seventy-eight-year-old houseguest:

"Goya arrived, deaf, old, clumsy and weak, and without knowing a word of French and without bringing a servant (which no one needs more than he) and so content and so desirous of seeing the world. He was here three days; on two of them he ate with us as if he were a young student."

Goya didn't linger at Moratín's. He was eager to reach Paris, where he had never been before. In his letter to Melon, Moratín explains that "I urged him to return by September and not get tied up in Paris and let himself be caught by the winter, which would be his end."

In Paris, we catch another glimpse of Goya, this time through the odd lens of a police report. As they often did with refugees from Ferdinand's Spain, Paris police were keeping tabs on their new visitor. Their purpose was to see whether Goya was entering into "suspicious relations," meaning plots against Ferdinand. He turned out to be a disappointing target of surveillance. On July 15, the prefect of police wrote to inform the Spanish minister that the officers tailing him had not found that he had "habitual relations with any of his compatriots. He receives no one at his place and the difficulties he has with speaking and understanding French often keeps him at home, from where he does not leave except to visit monuments and take a walk in public places."

Too bad the police didn't include in their report whether Goya visited the Louvre, and if he did which works he paused in front of. And did he look in on the Salon of the French Academy, the annual group show of the latest art acceptable to its largely conservative juries? It was showing new pictures that year by Delacroix, Constable, and Ingres. Very little of Goya's work was known yet in Paris, but the *Caprichos* had circulated a bit. Delacroix in particular admired them and had even copied a few. He would no doubt have been delighted to meet the man who created them, but apparently they never crossed paths.

Goya took Moratín's advice and returned to Bordeaux by September. Later that month Leocadia arrived with her two youngest children, thirteen-year old Guillermo and ten-year-old Rosario, who would thrill Goya with her budding gifts as an artist. In a letter to Melón, Moratín described their apartment as "good furnished quarters in a good location. I believe they will pass the winter very comfortably in it." Then again, their contentment might have been undermined by a bit of domestic tension. As Moratín reported in another letter to Melón, "Goya is here with his doña Leocadia; I do not perceive the greatest harmony between them." One more reason to suppose they were a couple.

Within a year, Moratín could report that Goya had settled comfortably in Bordeaux, though he was still of two minds about expatriate life. He sometimes considered a permanent return to Madrid. This was a plan of action—never realized—that Moratín could not comprehend. After all, he wrote to Melón, "He likes the city, the countryside, the climate, the food, the independence, the tranquility that he enjoys. Since he's here, he's had none of the illnesses that discomfited him there." In a letter Goya had written the previous December to Javier, he even warned his son that his old man might, like Titian, live to be ninety-nine. As we now know, Titian actually only made it to his late eighties, but Goya's point is still clear—in his new circumstances, he was feeling much better.

You can sense the more relaxed Goya in the two drawing albums he produced during the Bordeaux years, the first of them begun very soon after his arrival. It's not that dark imaginings and bitter judgments disappear altogether from the 123 drawings of his last years. Working in crayon, he's still fascinated by madness, and makes a few powerful images inspired by inmates he might have seen in the asylum at Bordeaux. Witches appear in two drawings, executions by guillotine in two others. There's also a weeping man, a procession of flagellants, and a *Bad Husband* with a horsewhip who rides on the shoulders of his bent-over wife. As a climax to Goya's contempt for parasitic clergy first expressed in the *Caprichos*, there's also a gluttonous friar gobbling down his meal and a man murdering a monk with some kind of sharpened tool.

But gone are the tortured victims of the Inquisition and the cannibalistic priests. In these albums, horror isn't the dominant key anymore. Something like bemusement is, the indulgent smile that the younger Goya used to bring to the human comedy. Even when Goya produces a drawing of a winged male demon in flight with his hideous lady, he fends off any genuine dread with a funny title—*They Love Each Other Very Much*.

Working in black crayon this time, instead of the brush and ink washes of his earlier sketchbooks, laying down rapid, thunderbolt lines, Goya casts an amused eye over his new world and its curiosities. (A man on roller skates! A giant snake at the Bordeaux fairground!) His sketches are full of street life observed by an old man chuckling at the unaccustomed sights in his adopted home. Here's a beggar in an early version of a wheelchair. Here's a man toting a woman to the theater in a "shoulder chair," a wooden box strapped to his upper back. The lady gazes out at us from the window of her little compartment. In a drawing like that, or the three others he made of these "new stagecoaches," Goya is operating almost as a cartoonist. Likewise with that man on skates—make that *Crazy Skates*—arms flailing, feet slipping out from under him, about to take an Elmer Fudd pratfall.

And there are tender drawings like *Woman with Two Children* of a smiling young mother cradling one child while the other looks up adoringly from the ground. There's even one, called *Entanglements of Their Lives*, that appears to be a picture—not Goya's first—of lesbian affections. This time he shows us two fully dressed women falling into an embrace while surrounded on all sides by a nest of mysterious faces, some with the features of apes, dogs, and pigs. Symbols of lust? Or creatures of darkness overcome by the forces of love? As so often with Goya, it's impossible to say.

Maybe the drawing that's most telling about Goya's new spirit, at least on the good days, is *Man on a Swing*, in which an old man enters the picture from the left edge of an otherwise blank sheet. He's riding a rope swing, rocketing upward, with his bottom hanging over the rope on the back end and his legs pointing up in the air. On his face there's a manic smile. This picture has been subject to multiple interpretations. A metaphor for sexual intercourse? A reference to the swings of fate? Whatever the intention behind it, this old fellow is clearly enjoying the ride.

Much as he loved to set his new world down on paper—"an old man mad about drawing," he called himself—in Bordeaux Goya had a hand in every kind of picture making. He was often producing oil portraits of his new circle of friends. And remarkably, on the threshold of eighty, he was mastering two new creative practices. In 1825, he dove into lithography, a printmaking process that had been invented in Bavaria around 1796. Unlike etching or engraving, which required a metal tool or acid to incise the lines of a drawing into a copper plate, lithography allowed an artist to draw directly on limestone with a grease crayon.

What would have attracted Goya to lithography was its versatility. Drawing directly in crayon made subtle effects easier to achieve and modify than the laborious process of etching into metal. Working with a skilled lithographer in Bordeaux, Goya was soon exploring this relatively new technique, producing four large prints now called *The Bulls of Bordeaux*. These are visually sumptuous but uncompromising pictures, striking for their blunt imagery of the bullring, where teeming crowds witness chaotic face-offs between man and beast. In some, matadors and picadors are trampled or gored. In others reckless spectators jump into the ring, a practice once permitted in Spain. That graphic violence may help to explain why, like his *Tauromaquia* series of the previous decade, the edition of one hundred failed to sell. Though magnificently produced, they had never been likely to find a market in France. The French cared nothing for bullfighting, and the Spanish exile community there consisted largely of those "enlightened" men and women who looked down on it.

In May 1825, Goya endured another near fatal illness, this one involving a paralysis of the bladder. Yet just one month later, Moratín reported in a letter to Melón that the old man was recovered and back to painting "like nobody's business, without ever wishing to correct anything he paints."

That winter, the seventy-nine-year-old Goya also started down yet another new road in his art. In the previous year he had turned for the first time to making painted miniatures on ivory, working on chips about two inches square or three and three-quarters. Ivory miniatures were a long-established subcategory of picture making, but one he approached in a novel way. The customary technique involved touching the ivory with minute deposits of watercolor, painstakingly applied with the thinnest of brushes. Goya went the other way, using a subtractive method that took advantage of chance and improvisation.

Antonio de Bruguda, a young Spanish painter who became Goya's constant friend and studio mainstay in Bordeaux, described the first steps this way: "He blackened the ivory plaque and let fall on it a drop of water, which removed part of the black ground as it spread out, tracing random light areas." Next Goya would examine these indeterminate blobs of light and dark for their potential to be developed into forms that were decipherable but still evanescent. Only then would he apply his brush, teasing out the details of a face here, a sleeve there, shoring up the emerging image with delicately applied black lines, or producing highlights by scraping away the black ground with a pointed tool to expose the pale ivory underneath. The image that resulted was a dynamic construction of shadow and light, usually in a monochrome of black, white, and grays, with strategic touches of color.

That would describe his masterful little *Reclining Nude*, in which he allowed exposed zones of ivory to represent flesh and added a thin wash of green to define fabric.

What is Goya doing in these ivories if not building art out of random elements, capitalizing on the kind of chance effects that would fascinate the Surrealists a century later? It's possible he had heard of the ink-on-paper "blot paintings" of the British landscape painter Alexander Cozens, who had published a book that included them. But until Goya no one had made miniatures on ivory in quite this way. Explosive forms confined to a small stage, Goya's luscious miniatures are like tiny peals of thunder, and he was quite proud of them. In a letter to Joaquin Maria de Ferrer, a Spanish banker living in Paris, he boasted, with some justification, that he had produced "original miniatures which I have never seen the like of before."

Even in the very last years of his life, Goya was ready for the next thing. In the same letter to Ferrer in which he described his ivory miniatures, he also turned down a suggestion that he produce a new edition of the *Caprichos*. The Spanish banker apparently believed they would find a ready market in Paris, where they were already known by some. (These were the works that Delacroix admired.) But Goya said no. He told Ferrer he had given the plates years earlier to the king, in exchange for an annuity for his son. And besides, he had no interest in repeating himself.

There's an affecting glimpse into Goya's spirit in his last years in one of the most charming drawings he ever made. It shows an old man with long white hair and a flowing beard, similar to the figure he painted beside the door at the quinta. Dressed in a long robe, the man leans on crutches, but he looks out at us with an unwavering eye. Along the bottom Goya, the man who had recently reinvented miniature painting and advanced the new art of lithography, wrote out a caption that was like a declaration of continuing independence. *Aun aprendo*, it says. "I am still learning."

But inevitably, also declining. His hand was getting unsteady. His eyes were weakening. As he closed out that letter to Ferrer he declared glumly, though it wasn't quite true, "All I've got left is will." Having already been granted two extensions to his leave of absence from Ferdinand's court, in May 1826 he made the difficult journey back to Madrid. He went there to retire altogether from his duties as court painter and to visit with his son, daughter-in-law, and grandson. During this stay, in addition to having his

33

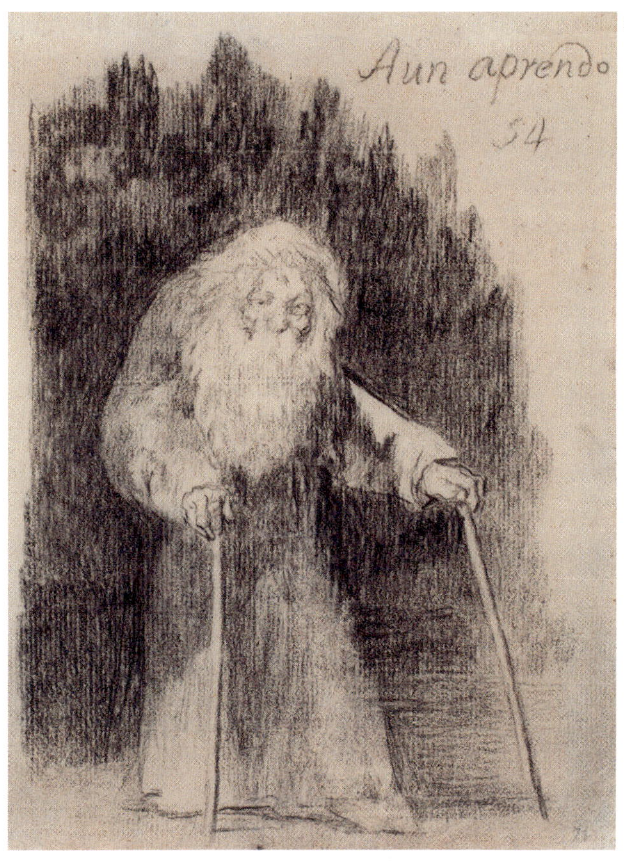

Aun Aprendo (I'm Still Learning), ca. 1826, black chalk and lithographic crayon on grey laid paper, 19.2 × 14.5 cm, Museo Nacional del Prado, Madrid

portrait painted—ironically by the same Vicente Lopez whose work Ferdinand preferred to his—Goya requested a pension from the king. It was granted in June with a blunt observation by one of the king's ministers: "His advanced age promises that, for natural reasons, the period in which he may enjoy these privileges will be short."

Blunt but true. Goya had less than two years to live. In that time, he made one more brief visit to Spain and—perhaps—one last radiant canvas. *The Milkmaid of Bordeaux* is a portrait of a young woman silhouetted against a blue sky. Some scholars think it's by Leocadia's daughter Rosario—the child who may have been Goya's as well. Or was the picture a joint product of Rosario and Goya, who was teaching the girl to paint? If it is indeed entirely or partly his, it's a last burst of sunlight from a dwindling old man, a picture that departs vividly from the restricted palette of most of Goya's late portraits, the range of blacks, browns, and grays that were a Spanish tradition dating back at least to Velázquez.

Goya also endured one last trip to Madrid, which must have been an ordeal—by that time he had developed a sizable tumor on one leg. While there he replied to a letter from Leocadia: "I have just read your most beautiful letter right through and it has made me so happy that even if I tell you it has made me completely better I am not exaggerating at all." He signs off. "A thousand kisses and a thousand things from your most affectionate Goya." These are not words from an employer to his housekeeper.

Somehow Javier never managed to visit his father in Bordeaux, though in March 1828, two days before Goya's eighty-second birthday and a few weeks before his death, Javier's wife arrived with Goya's grandson Mariano. No doubt Javier, who still had no real occupation, had sent them to make sure Goya didn't change his will—which left everything to him and Mariano—so as to make some provision for Leocadia and her children. Goya's daughter-in-law and grandson were there on April 2 when he suffered a stroke. He would linger in bed for two weeks in a state of confusion. The end came on April 16 with Leocadia at his bedside along with his painter friend Brugada.

The estate was sizable. During his five years in Bordeaux, Goya had lived on just a fraction of his salary, consigning the greater share to be invested by his French banker, Jacques Galos. Javier would also inherit Goya's printing plates, as well as many of his paintings and drawings, which he would spend the rest of his aimless life selling off. At his own death what was left went to Mariano, who would go on marketing his grandfather's work while squandering the remaining family money in bad business deals.

As it turned out, there had indeed been an addition to Goya's will providing something for Leocadia. We don't know how much, because in a fit of pique she destroyed the addendum. Was she insulted by how little she got? Javier, who thoroughly disliked her, allowed her the furniture from the Bordeaux apartment and 1,000 francs if she wanted to return to Spain, but he gave her until just the end of the month to vacate. She also got *The Milkmaid of Bordeaux*. In the following year, already nearly destitute, she sold it.

But Goya's real legacy wasn't cash and real estate or pots and pans. It was the profound vision of his art, especially the art of his final decades. We still struggle to understand some of it, as we struggle to understand the demons within ourselves he warns us about and that threaten to reemerge every time history turns another dark corner.

As with Goya, so with ourselves—we're still learning.

34

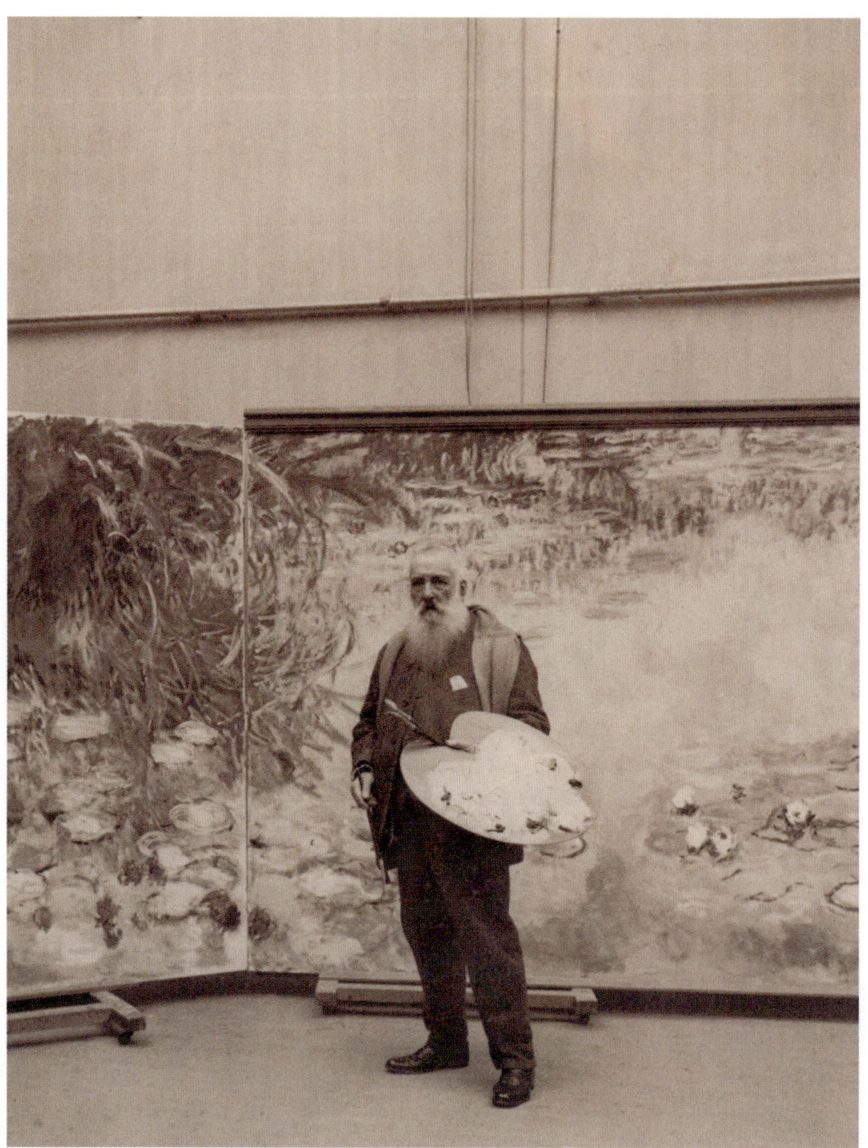

Monet in 1920 in his studio in Giverny, with two adjoining canvases of his *Grandes Décorations*

3

MONET

The Water Cure

The novelist William Burroughs had an apt term for the human body. "The soft machine," he called it. Though just what that meant for him is typically arcane, his phrase has applications that anyone can appreciate. The body really is an apparatus, superb in its complex operations when it's running well, rackety and sluggish when it's not. As Claude Monet entered his seventies, his body was certainly like that, a once peerless mechanism that was winding down. As a younger man he had been inexhaustible. He once said he wanted to paint the way a bird sings, and for most of his life he did. He would set up his easel as soon as the sun rose, pictures flowing from his brush one after another—more than two thousand in his lifetime. In his twenties he wrote to his fellow artist Frédéric Bazille, "I've got such a desire to do everything, my head explodes."

As one of the consummate plein air painters of his time, he had also been a very hardy specimen, working outdoors in every kind of weather. One freezing winter, two journalists came across him laboring at his easel in three overcoats. Over the years his search for new motifs had taken him to London and Venice, the Netherlands and Norway, and to sites all around the coast of Normandy and along the Mediterranean, tying down his easels to work in high winds, clambering around cliffsides to find the right view. Absorbed one day in painting the seaside stone arches at Étretat, he didn't notice the tides rushing in until a heavy swell tossed him hard against the rock and pulled him under. Afterward he wrote to his wife, Alice, "My immediate thought was, I'm a goner, the water was dragging me along." He managed to struggle to safety—in a rage, not because he had nearly drowned but because a day's work had been swept away.

But by the time he turned seventy, in November 1910, month after month would go by in which he never picked up a brush. There had been idle stretches before—one in his early fifties had lasted six months—but nothing like this. The previous December he had complained in a letter to his friend and future biographer, Gustave Geffroy, that he had done nothing for a year. Wet summer weather was part of the reason. As much as any farmer, Monet needed sunlight for his work. Though he had painted winter mists, cloudbursts, and London fogs, sunlight was the real default zone of his art, the mystery he returned to constantly to probe with his brush. But now there was also his faltering health. In his midsixties he had begun to complain about dizziness and blurred vision. More recently there had been recurrent and inexplicable headaches. "Not to mention all the little miseries and problems that accumulate with age," he wrote. "It's hopeless from every point of view."

By February 1910, a few months after he sent that letter, there was another, much more painful development, one that left Monet feeling almost paralyzed. His second wife, Alice, his companion, adviser, and helpmate of more than three decades, was diagnosed with myeloid leukemia. Radiation treatment helped to bring about a few months of remission in the spring and summer, but the hope for any real recovery was slim. Actually there was none. On May 18 of the following year, Monet wrote to his principal dealer, Paul Durand-Ruel, "I have some very sad news for you. My beloved wife is dying. It's only a matter of hours now. I can't tell you what I've been going through, particularly this last fortnight. My strength and courage are giving out." Alice died the next morning. What Monet called "her final agony" lasted until four a.m.

The loss of his wife left Monet crippled with grief. Depressed and withdrawn, he would wander their house at Giverny, miserably rereading her old letters before burning them. Always burdened by self-doubt, now he seemed crushed by it. In the wake of Alice's death, he felt himself unable to put the finishing touches on the paintings that resulted from ten blissful weeks they spent together in Venice in 1908, three dozen or so pictures that his Paris dealers were hoping to exhibit soon. After some half-hearted attempts to complete them, he wrote to Durand-Ruel that he was "completely fed up" with painting. He added the words his friends least wanted to hear. "I am going to pack up my brushes and colors for good."

All his life Monet had been given to melodramatic outbursts about the difficulties he had to struggle with for his art and his frustration over his "failures." Even as a young man he could draw on a bottomless reservoir of self-pity. He was not quite twenty-eight when he complained to Bazille, "Painting is not going well, and I decidedly no longer count on glory." Year after year, in his many letters to friends, family, and dealers, he would sound variations on that theme. ("Ah, how I suffer, how painting makes me suffer!") Always vulnerable to depression, even before Alice's death there were whole days when he didn't get out of bed.

But in the past he had usually bounced back from these episodes after a day or two and returned to his easel. Many years before Samuel Beckett, Monet had arrived on his own at Beckett's bleak motto: "I can't go on. I'll go on." Now those who knew him best worried that this time his black mood was different, that he really seemed like a man ready to bring down the curtain. In September, a succession of old friends traveled to Giverny to plead with him to come back to life. His writer friend Geffroy came. So did Octave Mirbeau, a leading figure of French letters, author of the wonderfully salacious *Diary of a Chambermaid*, and a critic who had championed the impressionists back when few others would. And so did Pierre-Auguste Renoir, Monet's comrade since the earliest days of the impressionist assault on the barricades of the French Academy.

Above all there was Georges Clemenceau, the mighty Jupiter of French politics, former (and future) prime minister of France. One of Monet's most valued intimates, he was a regular visitor to Giverny, especially after he bought a country home nearby. He had already written that summer to rally Monet's spirits by urging him to "remember the old Rembrandt in the Louvre"—meaning Rembrandt as he appeared in a self-portrait from 1660, painted after he had suffered the humiliating collapse of his fortunes. "He clings to his palette," Clemenceau wrote, "determined to battle through to the end despite his terrible ordeal. There is your example."

Monet wasn't ready for Rembrandt's example. As he continued to struggle with the Venice paintings, he went instead through a long sequence of mood swings and self-doubt. In April 1912, roughly a year after Alice's death, he informed Gaston and Joseph Bernheim-Jeune, dealers who had purchased some of the Venice pictures, that he could not supply them with more because the examples still in his studio were "too poor" to exhibit. "I've enough good sense in me to know whether what I'm doing is good or bad, and it's utterly bad." He signed it, "Your very sad and discouraged Claude Monet."

In the following month he wrote to Durand-Ruel, "Now more than ever I realize just how illusory my undeserved success has been . . . I am quite aware that you will think my paintings perfect. I know that the show will be a great success, but all that means nothing to me, for I know myself that they are no good and no one can persuade me otherwise." (Among the several arts Monet mastered in his lifetime, one was plainly humblebragging.) All the same, a few weeks later, with Monet's blessing, the Bernheims mounted an exhibition of twenty-nine of his Venice pictures at their Paris gallery. It was a great success.

In July, just a month after the triumph of that show, Monet's personal misfortunes resumed, when he learned that his elder son, Jean, had suffered a stroke at the age of forty-four. He would die seventeen months later, not long after collapsing in his father's studio. In that same summer an eye doctor for the first time diagnosed cataracts as the cause of Monet's failing sight. To correct them would almost certainly require surgery at some later date, something Monet dreaded because he feared it might distort his all-important color vision. But meanwhile, his doctor assured him, he could slow their growth with eye drops.

That news may have been enough to buoy his spirits, because in August, almost a year after telling Durand-Ruel he was giving up painting, Monet wrote to one of the Bernheims that he was back at work. "I need to paint, and paint unceasingly." He was even working outdoors again, as we know from two views of his house seen from an abundant corner of his garden, as well as an extravagant picture he began the following summer, *Flowering Arches, Giverny,* showing two heavily laden garden trellises and their reflections in his pond. Surely this effusive canvas, a controlled detonation of explosive life, was not the work of a man preparing to pack it all in? But no—by the following January, Monet was back in a funk. Writing to Durand-Ruel that he "no longer felt anything," he promised to complete a few paintings that his dealer admired. "But after that, I really have finished."

He hadn't quite, but in the two years between June 1912 and August 1914 Monet would turn out just five paintings, including three versions of

Flowering Arches. Not until the spring of 1914, after an eternity of suspended animation and mood swings, was he struck by an inspiration powerful enough to renew his spirits. It involved his water garden and an idea he had entertained for some time about how it might be used in pictures unlike any he had ever attempted. What he had in mind was to represent its reflective surface in long panels arrayed all around a curving room, like the cycloramas that were popular Paris attractions, a 360-degree immersion in the infinite that he would soon come to call the *Grandes Décorations*. In a letter to Geffroy five years earlier he had described a first vision of his ambitions. "The illusion of an endless whole, a wave without horizon and without shore; nerves strained by work would relax in its presence, following the reposing example of its stagnant waters."

By 1914, Monet had been painting his lily pond for more than fifteen years, eventually approaching it from a thoroughly radical angle. In a few pictures from as early as 1896, and then in dozens in a series begun ten years later that continued until his death, he started looking down across it in such a way that any view of the surrounding banks was eliminated. All that remained was the water, the lilies that rode on its surface, the reeds and grasses that undulated below, and the reflections of sky and trees. No horizon line, no solid ground, no point at which viewers could situate themselves or find their footing—this was "marine painting" of a very new kind. It was at the same time a profound and haunting culmination of the French landscape tradition, in which the artist advanced into nature to the point of full immersion, and the solid world dematerialized.

What those paintings proved was that, for all his protestations and doubts, in old age Monet still possessed a young man's audacity. But in his last decades it was wedded to an old man's achieved mastery of his art, the fruit of Monet's lifelong "researches" into light, color, and the most potent ways to represent nature. And now, at a low point of life, he was revitalized by the idea that a wraparound installation of water garden panoramas would make them even more dreamlike and compelling. Somewhat like Goya spreading his Black Paintings across every wall of his house, Monet in old age was imagining his art in an immersive environment, his vision projected in all directions.

It was actually an inspiration rediscovered. As early as 1897, Monet had told an interviewer, Maurice Guillemot, of his hope someday to produce a circular installation of water garden paintings. He had even shown Guillemot a few exploratory studies. But for years nothing came of that abortive start. The pictures were stashed away until 1914. As Monet related the story to Geffroy, one day that year he happened upon them while rummaging through his studio and decided . . . they weren't bad. Why not revive this long-neglected project?

That Monet should spend his last years almost literally immersed in a pond was not surprising. It was the final episode in a lifelong fascination with water that may well have begun in the amniotic sac. We think of him mainly as a landscape painter, but most of his landscapes share the canvas with water—the Seine or the Thames, the Atlantic or the Mediterranean, and finally the pond he designed himself on his property at Giverny. He once told Geffroy that when he died he wanted to be buried in a buoy, bobbing all day and night on the swells. In the words of the Normandy boatman who had shuttled him around on one of his painting expeditions, "Only the sea made Monsieur Monet happy. He needed water, great quantities of it."

Water had been Monet's natural element since childhood. Though he was born in Paris in 1840, when he was five his father moved the family to the port city of Le Havre, on the northwestern coast of France. There the elder Monet worked for his brother-in-law as a ships' chandler, supplying merchant vessels with groceries and other provisions. Le Havre sits where the Seine empties into the Atlantic, and Monet grew up on its beaches and estuaries, avoiding school whenever he could. As he recalled in later life, he much preferred spending his days, "when the sun was inviting, the sea beautiful and it felt so good running along the clifftops in the open air, or splashing about in the water."

When Monet was just beginning to form an idea of himself as an artist, his most important influences were two men who would both point him toward the sea. The first was Eugène Boudin, a painter who had also spent most of his boyhood in Le Havre. When they met, Boudin was thirty-two and had made what has turned out to be a lasting name for himself as a painter of the beaches along the Normandy coast and the fashionable people who vacationed there. Monet was around eighteen, already a skilled caricaturist who picked up spending money by selling his witty drawings. He would often credit Boudin as the first to urge him not only to paint but to paint outdoors.

Boudin invited the curious teen to join him on working day trips, which evidently went well. As Monet later recalled of those excursions, "It was as if a veil was suddenly lifted from my eyes and I knew that I could be a painter."

Monet's second mentor would be another marine painter, the Dutch-born artist Johan Barthold Jongkind, whom he would meet in 1862. What especially intrigued him about Jongkind was the free paint handling of his seascapes and harbor scenes, brushwork similar to Boudin's and another precursor to the rapid notation that would become the signature of Monet's art. "My true master," Monet would later call him. "It is to him that I owe the education of my eye."

In the years that followed, Monet was rarely far from a seashore or riverbank. For most of his adult life he lived and worked in towns along the Seine—Argenteuil, Vétheuil, Poissy, and finally Giverny. At thirty-one he also rigged out the first in a succession of boats he would use as floating studios. These allowed him to paint river scenes from a viewpoint directly on the water, most spectacularly in the magnificent 1896–97 sequence known as *Early Mornings on the Seine*. Eighteen violet-toned vistas of delicate mists and dimly apprehended trees, twinned with their mirror-image reflections in the water, they were each produced at different moments around daybreak, fifteen of them from the same vantage point on Monet's anchored boat.

Inevitably he found his way to Venice, on that fondly remembered excursion with his wife Alice, though not until he was nearing seventy. And of course the city on water enchanted him. "What a shame I did not come here when I was a younger man," he wrote to Geffroy. "When I was full of daring!" That's Monet humblebragging again. He was still full of daring—the roughly three dozen canvases that grew out of his stay in Venice were some of the most fearless of his life. Just look at *San Giorgio Maggiore by Twilight*, full of spectacular pink, orange, and yellow harmonies, the work of a man unafraid to hit the afterburners of his palette, but also in full control of them.

Though he didn't realize it at first, those paintings were in a sense his farewell to the wider world. After he and Alice returned to France, late in 1908, the sixty-eight-year old Monet would retreat permanently to his house, his gardens, and his pond. In the eighteen years remaining to him, he would almost never again paint anywhere outside his own gates. He was by no means a hermit. He traveled occasionally to Paris, or to visit friends. He once even ventured on a holiday to Switzerland. But with just a handful of exceptions

35

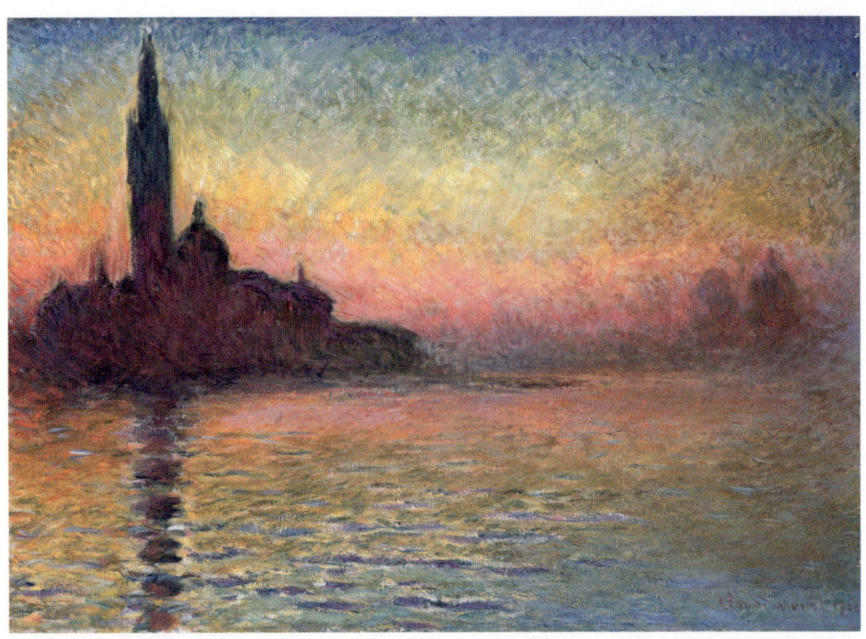

San Giorgio Maggiore by Twilight, oil on canvas, 1908, 65.2 × 92.4 cm, National Museum of Wales, Cardiff

he painted only scenes to be found on his own property. Again, like the aging Goya with the Black Paintings he would set down on the walls of his own house, old man Monet had everything he needed for his final achievement close to hand, above all in the infinite plenitude of his lily pond. "One instant," he would say. "One aspect of nature contains it all."

So in old age Monet's world was closing in, like one of those circular iris fade-outs in the silent films of his last years, a shrinking enclosure of light on a dark screen. But this wasn't happening because his powers were diminishing. It was happening because they were intensifying.

Monet's final withdrawal was not a sudden development. It had been underway in stages for a while. To the extent that impressionism was an art of the present day, of all things new and bustling, the young Monet had been a model impressionist. In 1863, just as he and his friends were first developing their new way of painting, the poet and critic Charles Baudelaire laid out a manifesto for contemporary artists in his essay "The Painter of Modern Life." Nominally about the illustrator Constantin Guys, but actually concerned with the sort of man-about-town Guys epitomized, Baudelaire used his text to call for an art that turned its back on the dead models of antiquity and plunged instead into the delightful maelstrom of the here and now. "The lover of universal life moves into the crowd as though into an enormous reservoir of electricity," the poet enthuses. "And off he goes! And he watches the flow of life move by, majestic and dazzling." That man, Baudelaire tells us, "is looking for that indefinable something we may be allowed to call 'modernity' " And what is that? "The transient, the fleeting, the contingent."

Impressionism was the art that answered that call, and not just because the flickering impressionist brushwork was the sign par excellence for all things fleeting and momentary. From the first, the impressionists sought out as their subjects the life of their times, highbrow and low. Edgar Degas haunted the theaters and racecourses. Renoir set his sights on the cafés and *bal dansants*. Gustave Caillebotte took the measure of the new streets of Paris transformed by Baron Haussmann, Louis-Napoléon's inexhaustible city planner.

In his younger days Monet did the same. In a pair of dazzling oil studies he made in his late twenties, working side by side with Renoir, he immortalized two flickering moments outside La Grenouillère, a fashionable and somewhat racy eatery and boating establishment on the Seine. Like Boudin he also painted vacationers along the Normandy coast. And in Paris he made high-vantage-point views of the new city streets and squares. His *Boulevard des Capucines*, a pale blur teeming with pedestrians and carriages, could almost be his answer to Baudelaire's vision, in his notorious volume of poetry *Les Fleurs du Mal*, of the "ant-swarming city / city full of dreams." That city was Paris, not the primeval warren of Victor Hugo but the emerging metropolis, the one sledgehammered into wide-boulevard modernity by Haussmann just in time for the impressionists to immortalize its new vistas, pleasures, and pastimes.

The Monet of those days was also willing to embrace the multiplying signs of industrialization in the French countryside. When working on scenes like *River Walk at Argenteuil*, he felt no need to edit out the new factory chimneys visible along that stretch of the Seine. For a time in his thirties railway bridges seem to appear in his work almost as often as flowering meadows. In that same decade he even got permission to set up his easel at the Gare Saint-Lazare, one of the busiest train stations in Paris, to paint the heaving steam engines—the last word in full-throttle steel modernity. In the most famous canvas from that series, he shows an arriving train as it barrels down the track directly toward us, plumes of blue vapor belching from its smokestack like the clouds that drift across any of his landscapes.

In any event, his embrace of modernity didn't last. In the late 1870s, as he approached his forties, he began turning away from the contemporary world, at least in his art. It was only landscape that truly interested the middle-aging Monet, and pristine landscape at that, not the modernizing countryside just beyond Paris. Now when he painted along the Seine, he found stretches of the river where no factories intruded—something much easier to do after his move, in 1878, from semi-industrial Argenteuil to rural Vétheuil, about thirty-seven miles northwest of Paris.

In the work of his mid-to-late thirties, you also see a transition in Monet's art that would be crucial to his execution of the *Water Lilies*. He begins to apply his customary mottled brushwork more uniformly across his pictures, with less concern for defining individual things. In that force field of dots and commas and hook-shaped marks, a tree, a house, even a riverbank starts to dissolve into the general commotion, all of them subordinated to the overall weave of color. As the scene begins to dematerialize, the paint itself, meaning the fabric of mingled brushstrokes on the flat surface of the canvas, starts to take precedence over whatever it might be forming a picture of. The colors and surface texture become the things to look at, as much if not more than whatever they're being used to describe.

By the time he started on his "series" paintings in the 1890s—pictures of the same or similar motifs seen at different times of day or in different seasons—Monet had taken the implication of this brushwork to its logical conclusion: that the paint, as much as the thing painted, was the real point of a modern picture. In that case even the plainest scenes could be translated into a canvas packed with complexities. Grain stacks in a farmer's field, a line of poplars at Giverny, the façade of the cathedral of Rouen, morning views along a stretch of the Seine, the Thames riverside in London—in each series the real subject was not just the inherent interest of those scenes but the insights and intensity of his execution. In his forties, Monet had traveled all around France to find new motifs to paint. But by his fifties and early sixties, though he found time for a first trip to Norway and a final trip to London, he was increasingly content to focus repeatedly on the simplest views imaginable, most of them on his own property or nearby.

So nothing could be more prosaic—more dull, really—than the grain stacks that Monet painted over and over again in 1890 and 1891, piles of grain that French farmers fashioned every year at harvest time into circular hut shapes with conical tops. In every one of the dozens of canvases he produced from that motif—which he found in a farmer's field a short walk from his home—Monet shows us just one or two or three stacks in a flat landscape, seen in different seasons and at different times of day. Even the ridge of hills that rise in the background barely undulates, crossing the canvas in something close to a straight line.

Though in nineteenth-century France, grain stacks were often read as symbols of the redoubtable Gallic peasantry and the eternal *France profonde,* Monet does nothing to encourage those associations. Unlike Millet, the great twilight elegist of the French peasantry, he includes no farm laborers in his scenes, no sturdy country folk gathering the grain or building the stacks, no supporting imagery of any kind to play on patriotic sentiment. He simply shows us a few heaps of grain in a bare-bones setting. What makes those pictures compelling is not the unassuming stacks but the gripping way he has painted them, his infinitely nuanced treatment of the light that plays across their bristling surfaces, the mutual infiltration of variously colored brushstrokes to form balanced harmonies. On visits to London, he had found one source for these paintings in the landscapes of J. M. W. Turner, who let fleeting light effects serve as the basis for sizable canvases, paintings in which light itself was the subject. Monet also found another source within himself. Zola had once said that a work of art is "a corner of nature seen through a temperament." Monet was now proving how much the temperament could take precedence over the corner of nature. *L'art, c'est moi.*

By his fifties, even people disappeared from Monet's canvases. In earlier years he had at times literally tried his hand at figure painting. Some of his most ambitious early canvases were of picnickers lounging in the woods or women darting along garden paths, or portraits of his first wife, Camille, posed this way and that. But portraiture never turned out to be a profitable line for him, and scenes of people outdoors were a particular challenge. He struggled to produce "figures out of doors the way I understand them, done like landscapes." He was never satisfied that he had found a way to properly integrate them within the *enveloppe*, the congress of sunlight and atmosphere, and anyway the flowers and greenery were what he really cared about. After making some final attempts at the figure in his late forties, Monet simply stopped trying. In the future, with very few exceptions, he would no longer admit any trace of human presence into his art.

Yet even as Monet barred people from his canvases, he required them in his life. Given his susceptibility to depression, it was probably essential to the great work of his final years that, however much he grieved for his wife, he was not alone at Giverny. Not only were there friends like the ones who came to restore his spirits after Alice passed on, but he also had the company of family. At the time of her death, Monet's younger son, Michel, thirty-three years old but not yet married, lived nearby. Alice had also brought into the homes they shared all six of her children by her first husband, Ernest Hoschedé. Now they were grown and—most of them—enjoying warm relations with their stepfather. So Monet had close at hand his married thirty-four-year-old stepson, Jean-Pierre Hoschedé, as well as his stepdaughter Marthe with her husband, Theodore Earl Butler, an American impressionist painter. In one of the several marital intricacies of the Monet household, Butler had earlier been married to Marthe's younger sister, Suzanne. In 1899, after seven years of marriage, Suzanne fell ill and died, just thirty years old. A year later, content to remain within the agreeable Monet-Hoschedé clan, Butler wed Marthe. Though the couple moved to New York in 1913, eight years later they returned for good to Giverny.

Above all, Monet had the company and assistance of another of his stepdaughters, the devoted and tireless Blanche, herself an impressionist painter who exhibited and sold her work. For the last twelve years of his life she lived at Giverny as his comforter, companion, and studio assistant, carting canvases and easels out to the pond, even helping him to slash the many pictures he found wanting, before they were consigned, like Alice's letters, to the fire. It was because of Blanche above all that Monet was largely spared the loneliness and isolation that many old people suffer when they lose a spouse. And because of her, he never lacked for "assisted living." Clemenceau liked to call her the Blue Angel.

Somewhat remarkably, Blanche was not only Monet's stepdaughter but also his daughter-in-law. (There are times when Monet's family tree makes you think of Woody Allen's.) In 1897, she had married Jean Monet, the painter's elder son by his first wife. Though they were not blood relations, Monet had been uneasy at first when they declared their intention to wed. They were after all stepsiblings, raised under the same roof since their early teens. But he was fond of his stepchildren, Blanche in particular. He eventually relented.

Soon after Jean's untimely death, Blanche, now forty-nine years old, returned to the house at Giverny, which she ran until the end of Monet's life. And afterward too, as it turned out. At his death Monet's properties and other assets all passed to his surviving son, Michel. Having no need to live at Giverny himself, Michel allowed Blanche to stay on. Until 1940, when she moved on to Aix-en-Provence, she would continue to oversee the house and gardens, as well as the many valuable canvases remaining there. Nearly four hundred were Monet's own work, including nineteen wide water lily paintings. Others were by artists he admired, including Manet, Renoir, and Cézanne. For the rest of his life, Michel would support himself largely through selling them off.

Not all of Monet's stepchildren felt so warmly toward him. Alice's elder son, Jacques, had long resented this interloper into his parent's marriage. The loss of his mother did nothing to soften his feelings. The year after Alice's death Jacques sued Monet for the return of property, including several paintings, that he considered part of her estate. In response Monet broke relations. When Jacques organized a sale of the reclaimed items, Monet stepped in and bought most of them himself.

But, if anything, Monet was fortunate to have kept the affection of his other stepchildren, because he had entered their lives by way of a subterfuge, slowly stealing their mother out from under the nose of their father. When Monet first met him, Ernest Hoschedé was a wealthy Paris department store magnate and an art collector drawn to impressionism. In 1876, he commissioned Monet to paint wall decorations at the Château de Rottembourg, the sumptuous country house outside Paris that his then-wife Alice had inherited from her father. That assignment gave Monet the opportunity to linger at the Hoschedé home for months. Alice was always there, but her husband was frequently off in Paris on business. It may be somewhere around this time she and Monet began their affair.

The plot thickened in 1878 after a series of bad decisions led Hoschedé into bankruptcy at a time when Monet and his wife Camille were also struggling with debt. As an economy measure the two families made the unusual decision to move in together. They first put down in a rented house in Vétheuil, a town along the Seine where Monet was already living with Camille, who had been in declining health since the birth, earlier that year, of their second son, Michel.

Because the Hoschedés had six children of their own, Monet would soon find them all a larger place in the same town. But both marriages were entering a new phase. Ernest, who kept an apartment in Paris, was once again away much of the time, attempting to rebuild his fortunes. And in September of 1879, Camille, just thirty-two years old, would suffer a hideous death from what may have been uterine cancer. That same day, as her lifeless body still lay on her deathbed, Monet could not resist the temptation to paint her portrait.

After Camille's death, Monet and Alice were increasingly left to one another, a situation that in time gave rise to gossip. There followed two years of delicate transition. Ernest continued to spend long stretches in Paris. Though Alice wrote him once with a promise to join him there, she never did. Instead, toward the end of 1881, when the lease on the Vétheuil house ran out, she and Monet simply moved on together to the town of Poissy, their eight children in tow. Though they would not marry until 1892, one year after Ernest's death, with their flight to Poissy they acknowledged openly the attachment they had long kept hidden in plain sight. Ernest made no serious effort to end their liaison. By that time most of his children were calling their mother's friend "Papa Monet."

In addition to his immediate family, in old age Monet had another indispensable support in Clemenceau. Monet's contemporary—he was ten months younger—Clemenceau was one of the leading figures of his day. A politician so agile and forceful he was nicknamed "the Tiger," in the years preceding World War I Clemenceau had argued presciently, though without much success, that France must rearm in the face of growing German militarism. A trained physician and a skilled polemicist, often in newspapers he published himself, he was also passionate about art, especially Monet's.

Clemenceau was a key figure in persuading Monet to throw himself into the work that would become the *Grandes Décorations*. The pivotal moment came during a visit to Giverny on April 26, 1914, not long after Monet rediscovered the panels he had put aside seventeen years earlier. Monet took his old friend to see them. Would he agree, Monet asked, that the dream of water lily panoramas in a curving room was one worth pursuing? No doubt knowing what Monet needed most to hear, Clemenceau responded resoundingly. "Stop procrastinating," he told him. "You can still do it, so do it!"

Just four days later, in a letter to Geffroy, Monet sounded like a new man. He described himself as "fired with a desire to paint . . . I am even planning to embark on some big paintings, for which I found some old attempts in a basement. Clemenceau saw them and was amazed." What Monet was planning was not simply a return to work, important as that was, but to produce a fundamentally new kind of work. He would make pictures of great intricacy that were also much larger than anything previously attempted by any impressionist. His panoramas of near abstract "water landscape" would be wider even than the behemoths of French history painting, the wall-size canvases known as *grandes machines*. He was not just resolving to soldier on, he was imagining a final legacy of enormous invention and unheard-of scale. At the age of seventy-three, he too was still a grand machine, and one that was not slowing down after all.

We now realize that Monet's *Water Lilies* were prophetic, their wavering expanses of indistinct form a forecast of the New York School of abstract expressionism that would emerge twenty years after his death. But a paradox of Monet's old age was that he was both a monument of French culture—one of the few living artists to have his work hanging in the Louvre—and at the same time, to the younger avant-garde, more or less irrelevant. As early as the 1880s, just as impressionism was finally beginning to win over some critics and the public, it was losing its position at the forefront of French painting. The new generation of artists whom we now call postimpressionists were already moving on. As that name implies, their work was launched both from and away from the foundations of impressionism. The heightened impressionist palette undoubtedly opened the way for the even more adamant colors of Vincent Van Gogh and Paul Gauguin. And the impressionists' flickering brushwork, as well as their practice of letting pure colors mix in the viewer's eye, rather than blending them first on a palette, were essential precursors to the pointillism of Georges Seurat and Paul Signac.

But for the younger artists, the impressionists' single-minded concern with capturing the appearance of nature was misguided. The postimpressionists didn't want to duplicate the world. They wanted to intensify it. They thought of reality as a bourgeois preoccupation. (Gauguin once sniffed that the impressionists worked "without freedom. Always shackled by the need of probability.") Van Gogh revered Monet but wanted to liberate color and form from the burden of merely accurate description, freeing them to convey personal ecstasies, the way the pulsing blue-white-gold whirlpools do in *Starry Night*. Gauguin also wanted to set color free, but in his case to reach inward to the psyche and outward to the eternal and supernatural. As for the pointillists—or divisionists, as they preferred to be called—they wanted to restore to painting an almost Egyptian weight, stability, and lastingness. To them the impressionists were too focused on setting down the passing moment, their imagery too fugitive and flyaway.

Yet for a time in his fifties Monet would find a way to recover his position in the avant-garde and arrive at something truly new and seminal. That was his age when he produced the "series" pictures of the 1890s, in which he painted the same subject at different times of day or in different seasons. It was an idea he may have gotten from the Japanese printmakers he so much admired, who had sometimes made multiple views of a single motif, like Hokusai's *One Hundred Views of Mount Fuji*. Monet would go them one better by, in most cases, painting each picture from the same spot. Taken together, which is how each series was first exhibited, the individual canvases become episodes in a sequence, each inflecting and amplifying the others. This alone made them prophetic. By the 1960s repetition, sometimes loose, sometimes in the strictly identical forms of "seriality," had become a cornerstone of modern art. The hundreds of iterations of Josef Albers's *Homage to the Square*, Andy Warhol's multiple silkscreens of Jacqueline Kennedy, Sol LeWitt's minimalist grid sculptures of identical cubes—all of them share DNA with Monet's grain stacks, poplars, and views of Rouen Cathedral.

The series pictures also incorporated time within themselves in a way that was new to the art of painting. To produce them Monet kept regular appointments with the sun. On any given day he worked in turn on a number of partly completed pictures—often more than a dozen—revisiting each just as the sun regained the position in the sky it had occupied when he last worked on it. By that method each painting, though he might develop it across a number of days or even weeks, could immortalize a single passing moment, the "instantaneity," as he called it. In this way the series paintings embedded time within themselves and distributed it from one canvas to the next. They didn't show clocks. Taken together, they *were* clocks, each series ticking from one image to the next.

For all that, by the start of World War I, when Monet began his *Grandes Décorations*, impressionism once again no longer seemed like a practice with anything new to offer. By then even postimpressionism was an old story, most of its major figures long dead. The new work that counted most was the cubism of Pablo Picasso and Georges Braque. For them it was no longer color and light but form and space that were the important problems to explore—how to take them apart; how to put them back together, often in a subdued palette of browns, grays, black, and white. In that quest, impressionist light and atmosphere were irrelevant. And in the wake of cubism there would follow a whole storm of new "isms"—vorticism, futurism, Dadaism, surrealism. None of them owed much to impressionism. Most owed nothing. So in the very decades he was producing the *Water Lilies*, Monet was both lionized by some, as the patriarch of French painting, and marginalized, as the leading figure of a onetime avant-garde that was long ago outpaced by more radical practices.

We now realize that view of him badly underestimated his continuing vitality. Monet was no extinct volcano. The *Water Lilies* would be some of the most profound and prophetic art of the twentieth century. What's meant here by that name is not just the long panels of the *Grandes Décorations* that consumed his last twelve years, but also the dozens of canvases in square or horizontal format—and very occasionally circular—in which he painted his pond in the same disorienting way he approached it in the *Décorations*, showing only the lilies, the water, and its reflective surface, with the opposite bank excluded. By 1905 and thereafter, the surface of his lily pond, extending across the entire canvas, became by far his most frequent motif.

Why was this so important? As we've seen, by pointing his gaze down onto the reflective water—what his friend Geffroy called "the luminous abyss of the water lily pond"—and eliminating any reference points on land, Monet was entering—was inventing—an entirely new kind of pictorial space. Seen in that way, the pond is simultaneously a mirror that shows us the sky and the trees above it, a membrane that the water lilies ride upon and a window into the depths below, dimly alive with long filaments of moss and wavering grass. Every brushstroke had to imply one or more of those interlocking dimensions. In a way that seems to predict the shock juxtapositions of twentieth-century collage, it's a world of strange, sometimes almost surreal adjacencies. A reflected glimpse of clouds can appear to be thronged with green lily pads like flying saucers. Trees might enter the picture as topsy-turvy reflections, their branches dangling upward. Even the sky, filled with inverted clouds or cropping up improbably along the bottom of a canvas, can be in some sense upside down.

In this multivalent water world there's no recessional space, no horizon line, no vanishing point. The rules of perspective dissolve, giving way to a kind of optical plasma, fluid, immersive, and ripe with potential to suggest ambiguous psychological and spiritual states. Two decades after Monet's death, a very similar kind of shallow, elastic "all over" space would be explored by many of the postwar abstract expressionists. At various times and along different paths, Jackson Pollock and Lee Krasner, Willem de Kooning and Mark Rothko, Clyfford Still and Philip Guston, all arrived at that space. Monet could have greeted every one of them at the door.

There's an irony to the fact Monet would make his great final contribution to modernism through landscape painting—or water landscapes, *pays d'eau*, as he called the water lily pictures—because landscape was once regarded in France as a minor branch of the arts. When the nineteenth century opened, it had long been consigned to the lower rungs of the French Academy's formal hierarchy of genres, just above still lifes and well below the inspiring and morally instructive pinnacle that was history painting. But over time, even as history painting faded as a credible pursuit, the expressive possibilities of humble nature painting were drawn out by a succession of great French artists, Monet among them.

For that to happen those artists first had to throw off the models of the past. In the view of the Academy the twin peaks of French landscape painting were the seventeenth-century masters Nicolas Poussin and Claude Lorrain. Their achievement had been to perfect the neoclassical vision of nature. Balanced, orderly, and exquisitely contrived, it was anything but natural. It was also not something meant to stand on its own, but rather to serve as a backdrop for human action. And not just any humans. Its sacred groves and sylvan glades were usually peopled by figures from the ancient world or the Bible, moving about among classical architectural settings, which leant to hills and lakes the improving touch of civilization. In all it was a very French version of nature, thoroughly rational and shaped by human hands, like the geometric gardens that André Le Nôtre was designing in that same century for Louis XIV at Versailles.

When the neoclassical landscape was new and being executed by men as supremely capable as Poussin and Claude, it could still be something compelling and original. But by the nineteenth century it was a spent force, all too reliant on exhausted conventions, no matter that the French Academy still endorsed them. Even as a utopian fantasy, the "Arcadian landscape" made no sense in a modernizing France where a headlong era of steam engines and steel trusswork was heaving into view.

For a new generation of French painters, working in the first half of the century, a way out was offered by the powerful new spirit of Romanticism, and the Romantic cult of nature, preferably wild nature as perceived through a passionate individual sensibility. It helped that the spread of railway lines eventually made it easier for artists to get to actual countryside. In particular they flocked to the forty-two thousand acres of the forest of Fontainebleau, a onetime royal hunting preserve about thirty-seven miles southeast of Paris that was first reached by railway in 1849. Even before the railroads arrived, that vast, resonant woodland had been attracting the painters who would become the crucial forerunners of impressionism. Known as the Barbizon school, for the nearby town where many of them lodged, they included Théodore Rousseau, Charles-François Daubigny, Jean-François Millet, and, in his different, more opalescent way, Jean-Baptiste-Camille Corot.

In their early twenties Monet, Renoir, Bazille, and Alfred Sisley all made pilgrimages to Fontainebleau, to paint the same ancient oaks and sun-spattered undergrowth the earlier generation had made famous, and in ways they had pioneered. The Barbizon painters were devoted to working outside, *en plein air*. They weren't the first, but they were different in their determination to preserve as much as possible in their completed studio works the immediacy of their outdoor sketches. Sometimes they even took the unheard-of step of producing finished canvases under the open sky. For the budding impressionists, to work *en plein air* also became an article of faith. So much so that well into later life Monet was happy to encourage the fiction that he never worked in a studio, when in truth by that time nearly all his work was completed indoors.

• • •

For all that Monet was devoted to the close observation of the natural world, his ambition was not simply to record the appearance of a scene but to capture a sort of emanation from it, a fluid congress of light and atmosphere surrounding things that he called the *enveloppe*. What exactly he meant by that word is difficult to say. At times it can remind you of the ether, the long-discredited notion of an invisible medium that light supposedly travels through, or would if it existed anywhere other than in the minds of the nineteenth-century physicists who dreamt it up. And yet Monet's search for the *enveloppe* indisputably led him to produce pictures that our eyes agree to as persuasive—to say nothing of enchanting—representations of the world. He once tried to explain himself this way: "Other painters paint a bridge, a house, a boat . . . I want to paint the air in which the bridge, the house, the boat are to be found—the beauty of the air around them." He also liked to repeat an account of his work provided in 1890 by his friend Geffroy, who wrote that Monet "does not want to represent the reality of things, he wants to record the light which lies between him and the objects."

To do that, Monet relied on practices he had developed in common with the other impressionists, and that he would bring to a last fulfillment in the late *Water Lily* pictures. First there was their distinctive, sensuous paint handling, the many flickering effects they employed to describe an elusive world—a bustle of little semaphore dabs to represent a flowering meadow, or a few brisk strokes in alternating colors to suggest the play of sunlight on rippling water. Then there was the exuberant impressionist palette, made possible by new synthetic paints that were brighter than traditional pigments based on powdered spices or ground minerals. Alizarin crimson, cadmium yellow, chromium oxide green, and the rich Cerulean blue that floods Monet's skies—with that explosive chemical ordnance, the impressionists could convey their sense that light was more than simply illumination. It was a vital, pulsing element.

In their devotion to light, Monet and the other impressionists largely banished black from their canvases altogether, using multiple colors to create shadows. In Monet's famous painting of a locomotive at the Gare Saint-Lazare, the cast-iron framework and cables of the train shed are actually built up from pigments that include emerald, vermilion, and ultramarine. To Monet, the very air had a detectable tint. "I have finally discovered the true color of the atmosphere," he once announced. "It's violet. Fresh air is violet. Twenty years from now everyone will work in violet."

To tastes accustomed to the blended brushwork, nuanced transitions, high finish, and subdued palette of academic painters, the impressionist pyrotechnics simply produced fractured imagery and chromatic overload, like a symphony made of nothing but bugle calls. It was their fondness for strident colors in particular that led one conservative critic to come up with yet another label for the group. *Éclatistes* he called them—"dazzlers." He didn't mean it as a compliment.

In the first decades of what could fairly be called the impressionist revolution, compliments didn't come often. They weren't entirely without their defenders. There were always writers, some of them prominent, who took up their cause, notably Mirbeau, as well as the great and pugnacious Émile Zola. As early as the Salon of 1866 he praised Monet's portrait of his future wife, *Camille, or The Woman in the Green Dress*, as the painting there that had held him longest. "Here is a temperament to reckon with," he announced. "Here is a real man among a crowd of eunuchs." But in its early years impressionism was more commonly treated by critics, and by the public, too, as a joke, a puzzlement, or an outrage. In 1875, when Monet, Renoir, Sisley, and Berthe Morisot auctioned off seventy-three of their paintings at a hotel, the police had to be called in to restrain the jeering audience. One critic said their pictures could have been produced by "a monkey who has got hold of a box of paints." Year after year, impressionist works were also marginalized by the all-important annual Salon of the French Academy, a crucial showcase for any painter hoping to make a name, or for that matter a living. Mostly conservative juries decided which submissions would gain entry, and they greatly preferred artists who upheld the traditions of Academic painting, skilled illusionists like William-Adolphe Bouguereau and Alexandre Cabanel.

No doubt the young Monet followed all this with interest, but in his early twenties, as a new student in the atelier of the Academic painter Charles Gleyre, he was still no more than a would-be member of the Paris art world. It was at Gleyre's that he first met fellow students Renoir, Bazille, and Sisley, who shared his instincts as an artist. After classes the future impressionists ate and drank together, discussed painting, and encouraged one another's initial impulse to embrace unorthodoxy.

Not until 1865 would Monet dare to make his first submissions to the Salon jury. Remarkably, he had two large beachscapes accepted. They even earned him some favorable press. One critic called him "a young Realist who promises much." Another praised his "bold manner of perceiving things" and "the taste displayed by the harmonious colors within the range of similar tones."

Monet would be accepted twice more by Salon juries—in 1866 and 1868—before giving up on the Salons in 1870. In that same decade he and the other impressionists began mounting their own group shows, eight in all between 1874 and 1886. Then in 1880 he abruptly submitted two paintings again to the Salon. One was accepted—the one Monet considered "more bourgeois." A third canvas in a much more freely worked fashion he decided against submitting at all—it would have been pointless. After that, he gave up on trying for Salon recognition. Resigning himself to a career outside the circles of official approval, the ones that laid prizes at the feet of Bouguereau and Cabanel, he would go on painting the only way he could.

That dedication, at least in his first decades as an artist, would cost Monet dearly. Of the core group of impressionists, only Bazille and Morisot, both from prosperous families, avoided hardship in their early days. Renoir, Pissarro, and Sisley all struggled. Sisley struggled to the end. But at the outset Monet was probably the poorest, always in debt, always leaning on friends for handouts, regularly pursued by creditors who sometimes confiscated his work. When he was twenty-seven, along with Camille, and their infant son, Jean, he even suffered the humiliation of being evicted from the village inn where they were lodgers—"naked as a worm," as he memorably described himself in a letter to Bazille, in what we must hope was just a metaphor. The next summer, when the Monets had fetched up near the Seine resort of Bougival, Renoir paid them regular visits, sometimes bringing much-needed gifts of food. After one he reported back grimly to a friend, "Some days they don't get to eat."

That same summer a despairing Monet threw himself into the Seine—or so he claimed in another letter to Bazille. ("Fortunately," he added, a bit mysteriously, "no harm was done.") Over the next decade or so there would be some years less discouraging than others, especially for a time in his early thirties, when Durand-Ruel first began buying impressionist work. But after a financial panic in 1873 even the supportive dealer had to pull back, not resuming purchases until 1880. That left Monet to try as best he could to find buyers on his own. No doubt he sometimes exaggerated the depth of his poverty. For much of his threadbare thirties he and Camille still kept a maid. (They had finally married in 1870, three years after Jean's birth.) All the same, even in the best of those years his income fluctuated in a low range. In his early thirties he was still begging for loans from artist friends and collectors. "It's getting more and more difficult," he lamented to Manet. "Not a penny left since the day before yesterday and no more credit at the butcher's or the baker's."

In his forties, however, things began to change, and not just because Durand-Ruel started buying again. The critical consensus on the impressionists, and Monet in particular, began to shift. Impressionist brushwork that had once seemed slapdash and incomprehensible was now better understood, accepted as a legitimate way of representing the world, in pictures that were vital, pleasurable, and altogether legible. By 1885, even Albert Wolff, the powerful critic of *Le Figaro* and ordinarily a dedicated Monet antagonist, had a change of heart. The same man who six years earlier had sneered that Monet's contribution to an impressionist group show was proof that "he is stuck in this mess and will never get out of it," now decided he had "much talent" and that his color choices, however unconventional, "caught the larger aspects of the landscape with surprising truth."

And in those years Monet was often identified as the key figure of impressionism, "the impressionist par excellence" as the critic Théodore Duret had already called him in his 1878 account of the movement. Not only had Monet been present at the creation, he had never deviated from impressionist practice, even as it evolved under his brush. As Paul Cézanne would say of him, "Monet sticks to a single vision of things; he gets where he's going and stays there." In 1889, on the threshold of fifty, this dogged traveler would be admitted into the pantheon of art history by no less a rising star of French letters than Mirbeau. He had first taken up Monet's cause five years earlier in the pages of the conservative weekly *La France*, where he didn't hesitate to claim that Monet was superior even to the much-loved Corot, that he possessed a "more delicately sensitive and in some sense more impressionable eye." Now Mirbeau, writing in the same *Le Figaro* that once treated Monet with contempt, felt comfortable situating his good friend at the very top of the art historical hierarchy. Monet, he assured his readers, was "equal to the greatest painters of all time."

• • •

And where the critics led, the market followed, slowly at first, and then at a gallop. Over time Monet would become seriously wealthy, an essential precondition for the costly gardens where he would produce his final masterworks. In 1877, a low point of his thirties, the annual income from his pictures was a paltry 4,000 francs. Five years later it had risen to 24,700, and twice in his forties it shot up to around 45,000. By 1890, with the help of a loan from Durand-Ruel, Monet could even afford to buy the home he had been renting for the previous seven years. It would eventually become a very famous one. "Le Pressoir"—the Cider Press—was a long pink house on about two acres in Giverny, a village near the larger town of Vernon. It had plenty of room for the children, ample space for gardening, and an attached barn on its eastern end that Monet would convert into a studio, the first of three he would establish on his property over time. After an eternity of cadging loans, dodging bill collectors, and hiding his paintings from bailiffs, he was becoming at last the man he would be for the rest of his life—a country squire.

And that was only the beginning. The real money started in his fifties, in particular with the series paintings. Whatever the subject, they found buyers quickly, so that throughout the 1890s Monet's annual income regularly reached into six figures. American collectors were a big reason why. Indifferent to the orthodoxies of the faraway French Academy—if they knew about them at all—they responded eagerly to the light and color of impressionism, so eagerly they sometimes bought in quantity. In a single two-year stretch the Chicago collectors Bertha and Potter Palmer purchased thirty-three Monets from Durand-Ruel, including nine of Monet's thirty grain stacks. Eventually they would own ninety of his canvases. James Fountain Sutton in New York owned at least thirty. Pissarro claimed the real number was 120.

Monet once bridled at the idea of his pictures disappearing over to what he dismissively called "the land of the Yankees," but the canny Durand-Ruel knew better. "The American public does not laugh," he liked to say. "It buys!" He had taken the first step to create a transatlantic market in 1886, when he helped to organize and promote the very successful American "debut" of impressionism, a group show in Manhattan of nearly three hundred works, including forty-six Monets. After that he arranged for Monet's work to be exhibited often in Boston, Chicago, and New York, where he soon opened his own gallery on Fifth Avenue.

As the twentieth century got underway, the money only came in faster, with income from investments and bank interest supplementing Monet's very robust sales. Now in his sixties, he had the means to indulge his taste for the latest in fancy playthings—sporty cars. Monet had little use for the telephone and no interest at all in the movies or radio, once those came along, but fast automobiles he adored. He owned several, though he left the driving to his chauffeur, Sylvain. Since he loved to eat but thought vegetable patches were unsightly, he kept a second house just to have a place nearby for a kitchen garden that he wouldn't have to look at. Somewhat to his dismay, he also found himself becoming a cult figure for young artists. They thronged the inns of Giverny, hoping to catch a glimpse of the master and to paint the same countryside he had immortalized, straining to see the *enveloppe* with his eyes.

Settling into his role as one of the prized ornaments of French culture, Monet now welcomed a succession of admiring journalists into his home and gardens. Almost always they would be treated to a sumptuous lunch in the famous yellow dining room with its yellow chairs and its walls covered with the Japanese prints Monet loved for their flatness, their high color, and their novel lines of perspective. Having come of age with the first explosion of mass media and lived into the era of the photo press, Monet became one of the first artists to cultivate his public persona in the way that Picasso and Salvador Dalí, Andy Warhol, and Louise Nevelson would later perfect. He became the Grand Old Man of Giverny. Bearded since his twenties, in his sixties the increasingly bearish Monet sported whiskers so long they cascaded toward his chest. In photographs—there are many—posed amid his abundant vegetation, the combination of his flowing facial hair and his expanding gut makes him look like a cross between Gandalf the wizard and a garden gnome. Somehow both images worked in his favor.

In those photographs Monet routinely appeared in worsted wool jackets and floppy hats, the signifiers of a yeoman artist, "the peasant of Vernon" as Clemenceau called him. But he often paired them with pleated linen shirts and ruffled cuffs, the flourishes of a high-living and very prosperous painter, a man who, when in London, stayed at the Savoy. He drank good wines, ate with relish, assembled a personal cookbook of recipes from his travels, and laid a rich spread for guests. In 1904, a visiting journalist could report that the table was set for lunch by "a butler in full regalia." By that time his wife had a pet name for him. *Le marquis.*

• • •

One other thing Monet could well afford in his sixties was the expansion of his gardens at Giverny, the setting that would be the subject of nearly every one of the great works of his old age. For all the forty-three years he lived there, half his life, Monet's gardens were his other prime passion, his other ongoing work of art. "Apart from painting and gardening, I am good for nothing," he once said. "My greatest masterpiece is my garden."

Even at the homes he had merely rented in his thirties and early forties, at Argenteuil and Vétheuil, Monet had established gardens. But at Giverny, especially once he owned the place, he could realize his most extravagant ambitions. His gardens would become an intricately balanced groundswell of literally living color. His perennials, bulbs, and annuals, grouped among flowering shrubs and trees, were chosen to bloom in sequence in a constantly shifting array. Over time he also amassed a sizable gardening library, including a bound set of *Flore des Serres et des Jardins de l'Europe*, a journal famous for the sumptuous color illustrations published in its pages between 1844 and 1888. For the true devotee it was the last word in horticultural porn. Monet owned all twenty-three volumes.

He started his garden in the property just outside his house, where he ripped out an existing orchard and kitchen plot while keeping a few large trees. In their place would go flowering fruit trees. Nearby he would lay down brilliantly colored planting beds, whole battalions of asters, gladioli, larkspur, and phlox, most surrounded by borders of his much-loved irises, a flower that so intrigued him he created his own hybrids. To form an allée leading to his front door, long beds were dug on either side of a straight pathway, which was flanked by tall yew trees, then vaulted by trellis arches to support climbing roses and wisteria. Later he would add a heated greenhouse for his orchids, dwarf trees, and Korean chrysanthemums.

In a day before he could afford the six or more gardeners who would eventually tend Giverny, it was Monet and his family who first turned the soil. "All of us worked in the garden," he later recalled. "I dug, planted, weeded, and hoed myself. In the evenings the children watered." Before he was done—and he was never really done—Monet had remade his surroundings into a private botanical park and a fantasia on floral themes, his very own Fontainebleau. Like his canvases, his garden was a carefully woven fabric, not of colored brushstrokes but of roses, daffodils and narcissus, tulips and petunias, rhododendrons and sweet peas. In 1891, when his friend Mirbeau produced the first published account of the place, he could not resist a riot of hothouse language. Poppies in spring, he told his readers, "splay on their hairy stalks huge gobletfuls of vermilion blood." In summer "fanfares of blazing copper ring, reds bleed and flare, violets disport themselves." And so on. But if you've seen Monet's gardens in full bloom—and by now they attract some half million visitors a year—you can understand Mirbeau's rhetorical overdrive. Effusion suits the place.

Not until his early fifties did Monet feel prepared to embark on the next major phase of his project—a water feature. Not just a fountain or a reflecting pool, but a good-size body of water in a lush setting, with vistas he plotted out himself, the way nature had fashioned the Seine. What he wanted was a lily pond, the one that would serve as laboratory for the great experiments of his old age, putting nature on canvas in an unheard-of new way.

Not nature as he found it, of course, but nature as he manufactured it. How many people today, losing themselves in the blue depths of Monet's water lily panels at the Orangerie, remember that this *grande décoration* is a grand illusion, pictures of a man-made pond with a sluice gate to control water flow? It's an irony of his late work that in a sense his garden scenes returned French landscape painting to the idealized seventeenth-century views of Poussin and Lorrain. But with an important difference—instead of creating fictional landscapes in the studio, as they did, Monet built a synthetic landscape outdoors, at full scale and in three dimensions, in a carefully perfected "nature" that he created just to paint. Then he stepped inside.

Monet made the first move toward establishing his water garden in February 1893, when he acquired a parcel of meadow on the other side of the railroad track that ran along the southern end of his property. (And carried four trains a day past his house—Giverny was rural but by no means pristine.) To supply the pond he intended to put there, he petitioned his local district commissioner for permission to divert a flow from a narrow arm of the nearby River Epte, a small tributary of the Seine. But there were objections. Municipal engineers wanted to be sure his diversion wouldn't deprive farmers downstream of water for their crops. Some of those farmers also worried that Monet's water lilies—which would be non-native hybrids and therefore suspicious foreigners—could somehow contaminate the river and poison their cattle. All this led to delays that infuriated Monet. At one point he wrote to

Alice from Rouen, where he was working on his cathedral series, telling her to simply toss his new planting stock into the river. "Shit on the Giverny natives," he added, "and the engineers."

He only needed a bit of patience—not always one of Monet's virtues. By July, with the authorities finally satisfied that his plans posed no threat, he set to work. He had countless options for what his water garden might become. Thanks partly to the inroads of French colonialism into Africa and Asia, the nineteenth century had seen an explosion in the number and variety of flowers available in France. Early in 1894 Monet ordered a relatively recent innovation—yellow and pink water lilies from the specialized nursery of Joseph Bory Latour-Marliac. By crossbreeding hardy white European specimens with dazzling wild varieties from around the world, Latour-Marliac had managed to produce blossoms that could survive European winters yet ranged in tropical colors from yellow to deep crimson. In 1889, he had displayed his novel hybrids at the Paris International Exhibition, just across from the new Eiffel Tower. Monet saw them there and took note.

Though he once told the local authorities he would be developing his water garden to provide himself with scenes to paint, it would be some time before Monet felt ready to point a brush at it. Not until 1895 did he make his first sustained attempts, three studies of the pond and the arching wooden "Japanese" bridge he had introduced across it at a narrow point. Four years later he returned to the bridge motif in a more sustained way, so that by 1900 he had completed enough of those to include a dozen in a show of twenty-six recent paintings at Durand-Ruel's gallery. These may be some of Monet's best-known and best-loved works. Amid densely woven vistas of foliage and reflecting water, the elegant parabola of the bridge cuts across the canvas, a near-abstract evidence of human presence, a viewing platform inside a view.

But unlike his later and more radical images of his pond, with their downward-looking perspective, these early bridge pictures don't represent any departure from the stable recessional space common to almost every Western painting since the Renaissance. Looking straight across the water, Monet shows us a foreground of floating lilies before a middle-ground view of the bridge at eye level. Behind it we see greenery that sometimes frames a patch of sky in the final distance. And in most of those scenes, on one or both sides of the canvas, he includes the banks of the pond to provide us coordinates and confirm our bearings.

36

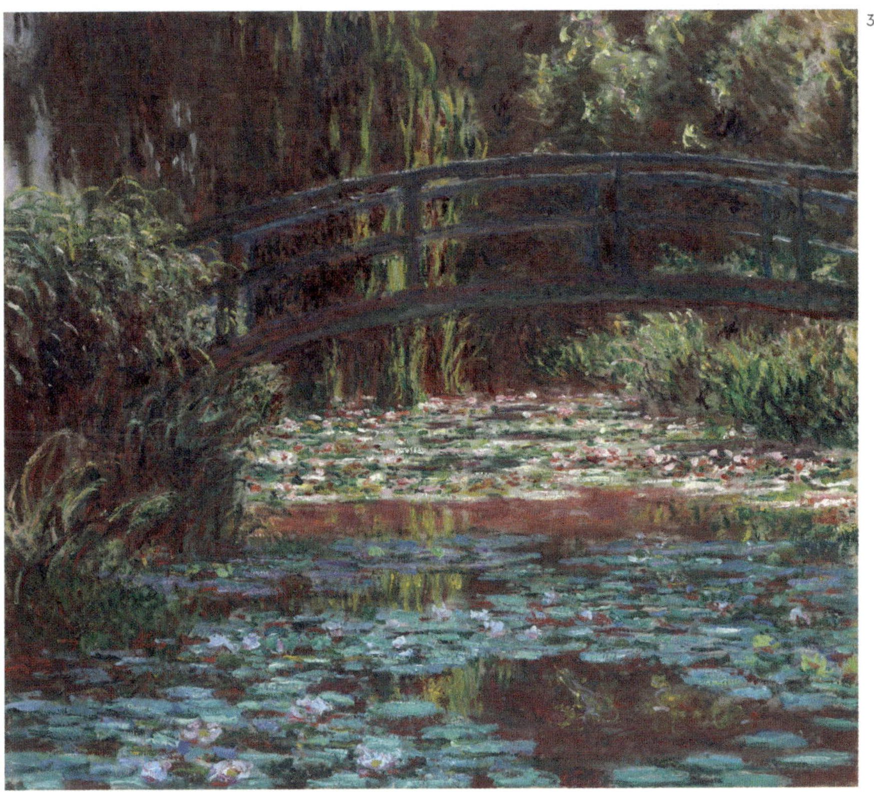

Water Lily Pond, 1900, oil on canvas, 89.8 × 101 cm, Art Institute of Chicago

Interestingly, a few years before making these more conventional views, Monet had produced a handful of pictures looking directly down onto the water, the revolutionary perspective he would later bring to nearly all his water garden paintings. These were probably the canvases he "rediscovered" in 1914. But for whatever reason, he didn't then choose to pursue the new idea they represented—at least not yet.

Monet completed the last of those bridge views in 1900. In the following year he put his pond imagery on hold, after buying additional land adjoining his water garden with the intention of expanding it. That project would take almost two years to complete. When it was done the pond had nearly tripled in size. The bridge sported a new trellis to hold climbing wisteria. And not long after Monet returned to painting his water garden, in 1903, he would be ready to knock down altogether the centuries-old pictorial guardrails, to make the water alone the field he would act across and within.

In the years that followed, and even after embarking on the immense panoramas of the *Grandes Décorations* in 1914, Monet would produce dozens of profoundly inventive and pleasurable views of his pond in smaller but still sizable formats, square, rectangular, or round. In these he almost always eliminated all reference to anything beyond the water's surface and whatever it reflected, as he did in *Water Lilies*, 1906, with its lily pad islands afloat on a field of reflected sky and inverted trees.

Even without conventional solid landscape elements, Monet could arrive at endlessly satisfying compositions, as he did in an elegant series of vertical

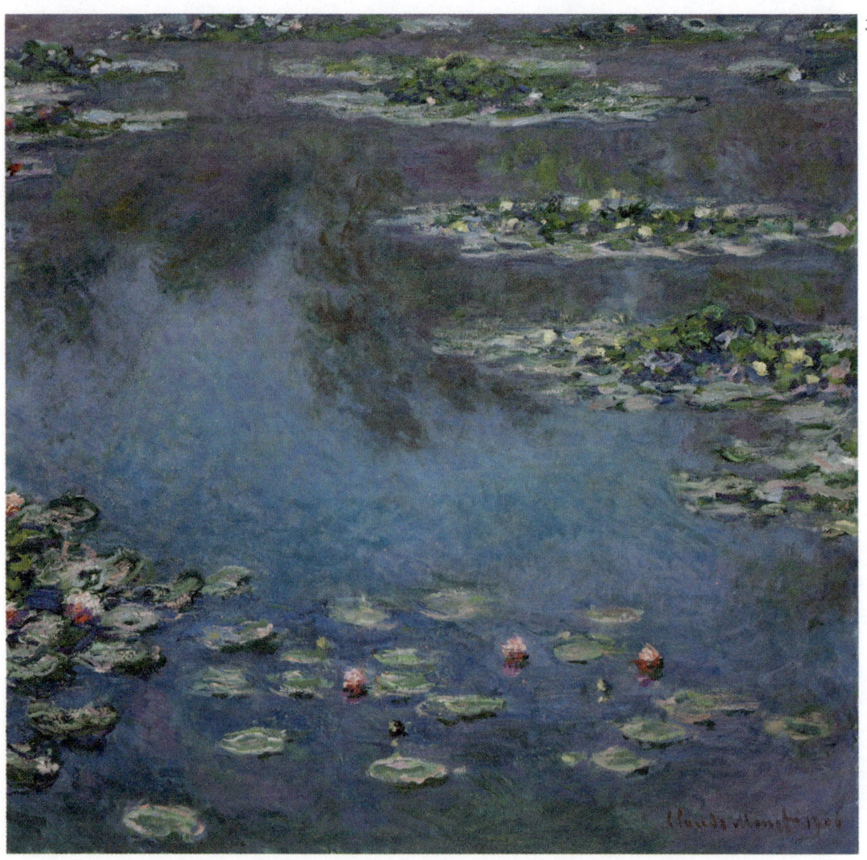 37

Water Lilies, 1906, oil on canvas, 89.9 × 94.1 cm, Art Institute of Chicago

canvases like *Water Lilies*, 1907, in which a white and violet sky cascades down the middle of the image and spreads out in its lower half between deep green reflections of inverted trees.

Monet was fascinated by the challenge these pictures offered. In 1908 he wrote to Geffroy, "These landscapes of water and reflections have become an obsession. They are beyond the strength of an old man, and yet I am determined to set down what I feel. . . . I hope that something will come of so much effort."

38

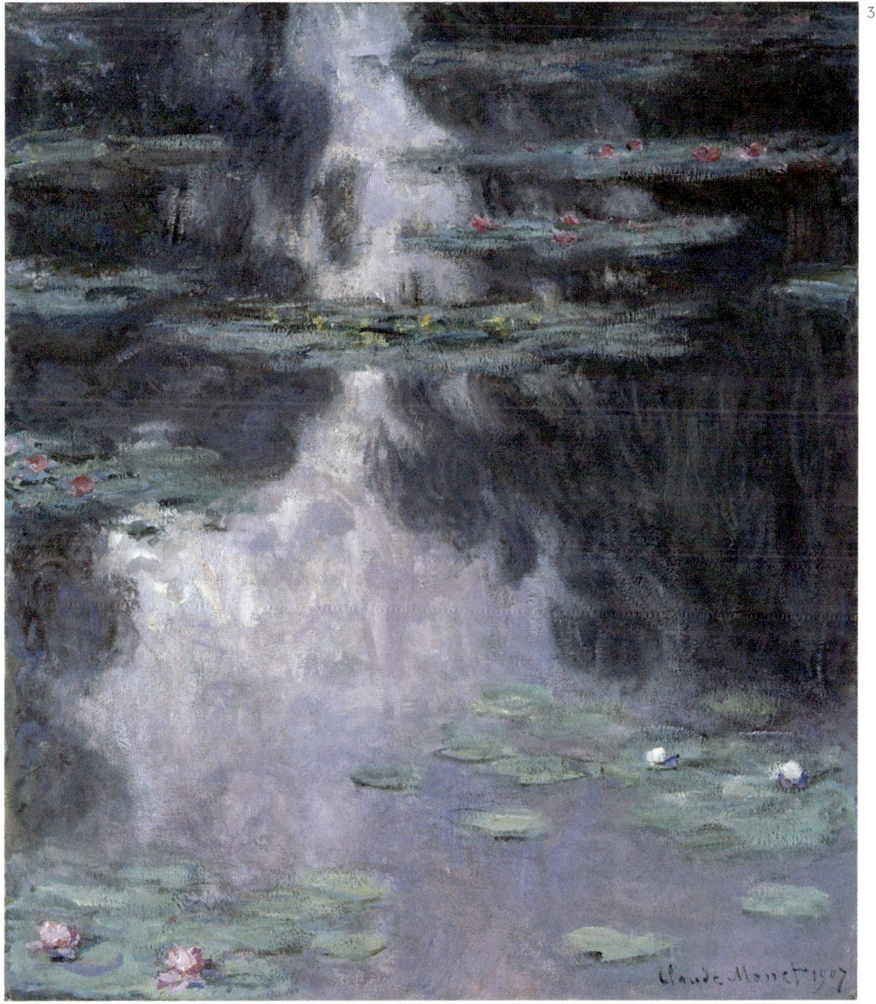

Water Lilies, 1907, oil on canvas, 92.1 × 82.1 cm, Houston Museum of Fine Arts

After many months of the customary hesitations, postponements, and cris de coeur, in May 1909 Monet exhibited forty-eight of his "water landscapes" in an immensely successful show at Durand-Ruel's Paris gallery. By that year his shimmering work and French taste had long since come into perfect accord. The opening was a social event. The reviews were a chorus of hurrahs. By then the idea that Monet ranked among the immortals had become the conventional wisdom. Or as one critic put it: "For as long as mankind has been around, and for as long as artists have painted, no one has ever painted better than this."

The last months of that same year, of course, also marked the beginning of the prolonged stretch of inactivity that Monet drifted through before and after his wife's death. But by the summer of 1914, not long after Clemenceau had encouraged him to attempt what would become the *Grandes Décorations*, Monet was thoroughly reenergized. Once again he was making pictures of his water garden, but on much larger canvases, often six feet by six feet, a preview of the even larger scale of the panoramas he would later produce. "Getting up at 4 in the morning, I slave away all day until by the evening I'm exhausted," he wrote Durand-Ruel. "Thanks to my work everythings going well."

Monet sent that letter in late June of 1914. He had no way of knowing then how badly everything would soon be going again, but not for reasons connected to his work. On June 28, Archduke Franz Ferdinand, heir to the throne of the Austro-Hungarian Empire, was assassinated in Sarajevo. With that began the chain of events that within weeks would pit the armies of Germany, Austria-Hungary, and later the Ottoman Empire against those of England, France, and Russia. The endless calamity of World War I would overturn the old European order and bring the sound of German cannon within earshot of Giverny.

In the first weeks of the fighting the swift German advance led to panic among the people of Monet's little town. In a letter to Geffroy, he complained that many had fled, including most of his family, leaving him alone with Blanche. "As for myself," he wrote, "I'm staying here regardless, and if those savages insist on killing me, they'll have to do it in the middle of my paintings, before my life's work."

Until the war Monet was rarely much absorbed in the events of his day. Though deeply attached to Clemenceau, one of the political giants of his era, he apparently never voted in a French election. We do know that his politics, such as they were, were anti-monarchist, as republican, in the French meaning of the term, as Clemenceau's. He privately deplored the brutal suppression of the Paris Commune after the Franco-Prussian War and publicly supported Alfred Dreyfus in the affair that consumed and divided all of France. For years he even stopped speaking to Degas, an anti-Semite and "anti-Dreyfusard." But Monet was no *engagé*. It's arguable that his deepest involvement with the world beyond his easel had come when he enlisted in the French army at the age of twenty—to avoid the draft—and served an apparently contented year in Algeria. As Delacroix found before him and Matisse would find after, the vivid colors and brilliant sunlight of North Africa were catnip to any painter with a receptive eye. Even then he escaped serving his full tour of duty. While at home the next year on temporary sick leave he convinced a supportive aunt to buy out the remaining five and a half years of his enlistment.

Even when the fighting did not threaten Giverny itself, the new war would cast a constant shadow. Monet's stepson, Jean-Pierre Hoschedé, left almost at once for the front. His son Michel would at first be rejected for service for medical reasons. But by early the following year, when the need to rebuild a French army suffering huge casualties made recruiters less selective, he was allowed to enlist, eventually spending what his father called "three terrible weeks" at the slaughterhouse of Verdun. Though Michel would make it through, for the duration of the war Monet would worry about his son's survival and bemoan the psychic costs of "this terrible, unbearable war."

However much he may have been tormented by concerns about his son and stepson, Monet was not so distressed as to neglect the immense undertaking of his water lily panels. (Immense and difficult, "continual torture," as he—inevitably—described it in a letter to Geffroy.) In early December he would write Geffroy again. "I am back at work; it is still the best way not to think of current woes, even though I would be a bit ashamed to think of little investigations into forms and colors while so many people suffer and die for us."

Did he really think them so little? "Water, water lilies, plants, spread over a huge surface," as he explained his project in a letter to an admirer in January 1915, where, in a notable development, Monet referred to it for the first time as a *Grande Décoration*. To French artists, *décoration* was not a term used dismissively. Some of the great monuments of French painting, like the wall-size rococo confections of Fragonard, were conceived as decorations for

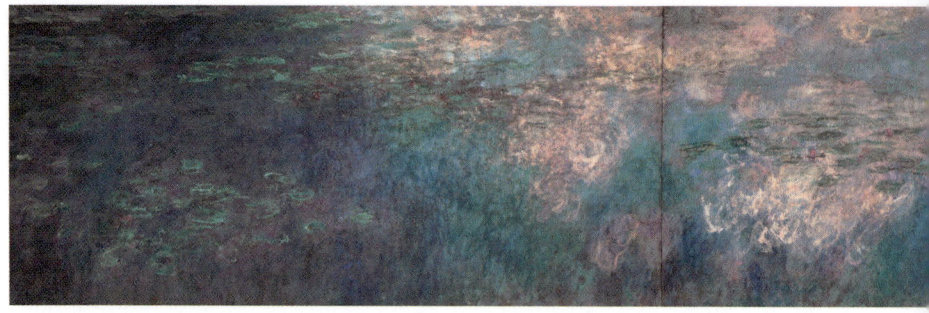

Water Lilies, 1914–26, oil on canvas, 200 × 1276 cm, Museum of Modern Art, New York

aristocratic houses. And the embellishment of public buildings with larger-than-life wall paintings was a highly regarded tradition carried forward by artists as esteemed as Eugene Delacroix and Pierre Puvis de Chavannes.

That decorative art generally tends toward flatness made it especially appealing to impressionists, whose paint application emphasized the surface of the canvas. Yet commissions for large public works had always eluded them, even after their easel paintings came into fashion. Their methods and subjects seemed better suited to an intimate, more domestic scale. Even Monet, who had twice tried and failed to secure a commission to decorate the Hôtel de Ville in Paris, had originally imagined his water lily panels installed in the dining room of a private home. But when he started to call his ambitious work-in-progress the *Grandes Décorations*, he was signaling a bold new possibility, that it might be arrayed across the walls of a great public space—much like the galleries of the Orangerie where it hangs today.

With that name he may also have been sounding a deliberate echo of *les grandes machines*, the term for the behemoths of French history painting, and by that means implying that decorative landscape could rightly claim equivalent wall space. With tongue only slightly in cheek, he even sometimes actually called his water lily panels *machines*. By that Monet would not have meant to imply that he was aiming for the posturing and high rhetoric of history painting. Leave all that to pictures crowded with Roman generals or medieval kings. He too would be working at epic scale—but for the purpose of representing humble flowers on reflecting water, a daring substitution of the lyrical for the declamatory.

This turn toward epic scale was a significant departure for Monet. In the

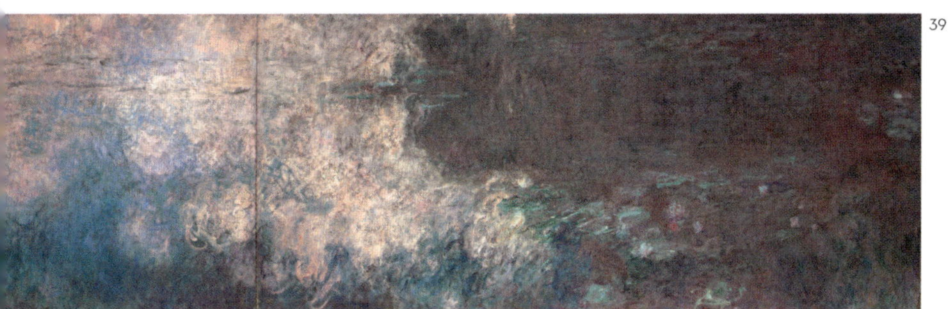

39

mid-1860s he had struggled with two very large outdoor scenes, *Luncheon on the Grass* and *Women in the Garden*. For decades after that he stepped away from working at such dimensions. The nuanced effects of the impressionist style he was just developing in those years seemed better suited to smaller canvases. But in old age, having proved the force of impressionist practices in hundreds of more modest-size canvases, he felt ready to return to the challenge of impressionism at monumental scale.

And the dimensions that Monet's new paintings would eventually reach really are monumental. In pictures constructed from two or three connected panels, each typically about 14 feet wide, he could create panoramas like the one now owned by the Museum of Modern Art in New York. An expanse of water almost 42 feet wide, its surface shimmer is produced by thousands of small incidents of color, shadow, and light.

Monet understood that paintings of the size he was embarked on would require a new studio on his property, his third. It needed to be large, and by the time it was completed, in the fall of 1915, it was—2,925 square feet of floor space; forty-nine feet tall at its highest point, big enough to hold canvases up to fifteen feet wide that could be joined to form panoramas as large as fifty-six feet across. To Monet's dismay, it was also ugly, at least from the outside. His second studio, completed fourteen years earlier, had been designed to look like a house, with a hip roof, bay windows, and a second-story covered porch. This new one was a boxy, bare-bones affair, with stark, windowless walls and a skylit slanted roof. "I am ashamed to have made this myself," he told his stepson. But it got the job done. Inside this vast space, Monet's numerous wide canvases were mounted on casters, allowing him to roll them

40

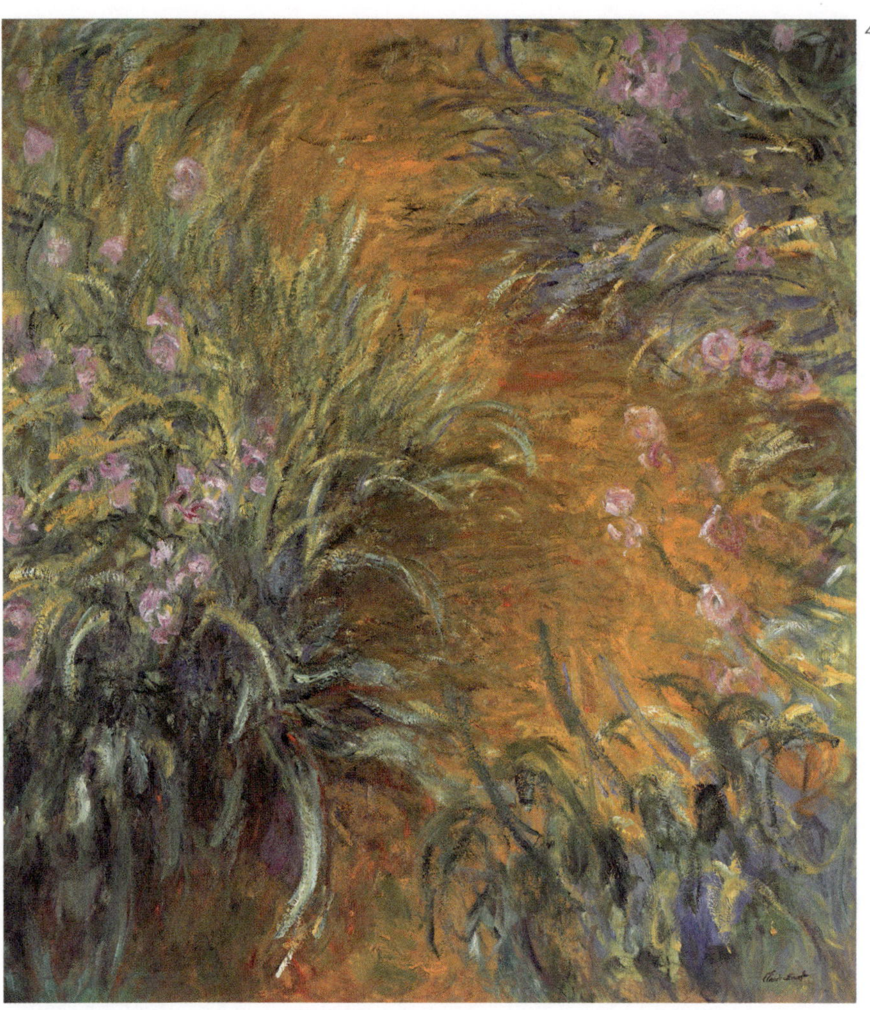

Irises, 1914–17, oil on canvas, 220.3 × 180 cm, The Metropolitan Museum of Art

around or position them side by side to ensure that his imagery was flowing seamlessly from one to the next.

With his studio completed Monet could concentrate on painting, as much as his inevitable mood swings allowed. Work also kept his mind off the horrors of the war. His most frequent subject would be the surface of his lily pond, but he would turn his attention at times to other motifs, like the pictures of irises he produced between 1914 and 1917, again from a downward perspective that eliminates any horizon line.

41

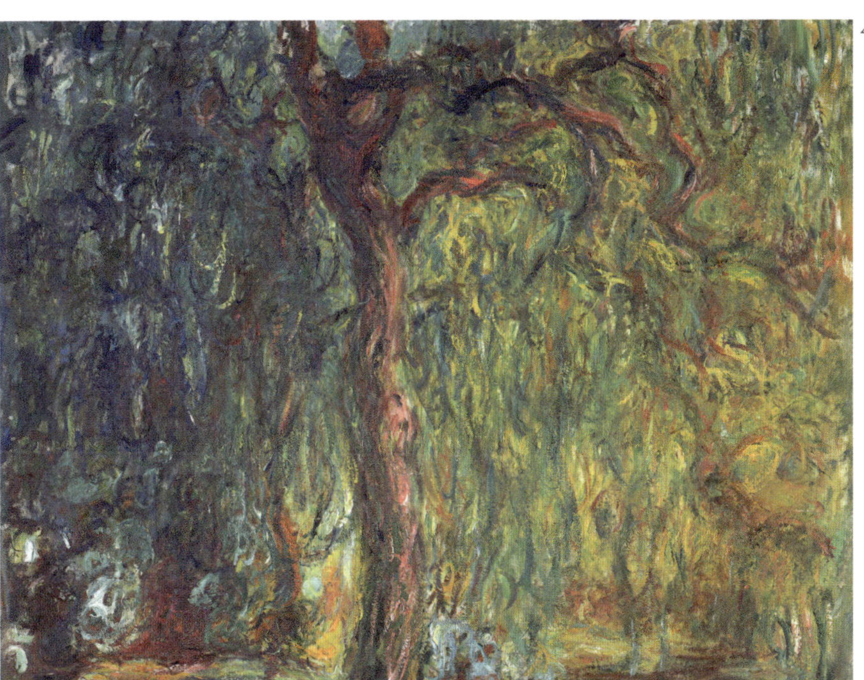

Weeping Willow, 1918–19, oil on canvas, 99.7 × 120 cm, Kimbell Art Museum, Fort Worth, Texas

In the spring or summer of 1918, he also embarked on two strangely uncharacteristic series. The first was a return to his Japanese bridge, but this time rendered in a deeply somber and nearly monochrome palette of dark blues and greens, or in an opposite, eye-searing palette in which reds, yellows and violets predominate. The paint handling was very different too, a loose and wavering brushwork that suggests either the deliberate exploration of a new painterly "signature" or an unintended byproduct of his disintegrating eyesight. Possibly both.

Around the same time, Monet also began what would be a series of ten views of a weeping willow, executed with long, undulant brushstrokes. In many of them a sizable part of the tree is shrouded in shadows built from a somber palette of dark blues, greens, and violets. Those mournful colors may have been intended to express the anguish of both the artist and his countrymen during the exhausting last year of the war, in pictures of a weeping willow, a tree that was already a well-established symbol of grief.

• • •

The end of the war in 1918 provided a major inflection point in the fate of the *Grandes Décorations*. On November 12, one day after Germany signed the armistice that ended the fighting, Monet wrote Clemenceau, by then in his second stint as prime minister, to offer two of his recent paintings as gifts to the French state. He suggested they should be displayed in the Museum of Decorative Arts, where they could serve as both a tribute to France and a memorial to its fallen servicemen. "It's not much," he told him, "but it's the only way I have of taking part in the victory." He invited Clemenceau to choose the pictures himself.

Clemenceau had bigger plans in mind. Six days later he arrived at Giverny with Geffroy. During his year as wartime prime minister—he had returned to the office in November 1917—he had been immensely popular, especially with the troops, whom he visited often on the front lines. With the Allied victory he was lionized. Though on the day of his visit he chose a water lily picture and a weeping willow, he soon felt empowered to present Monet with a much more ambitious proposal: Monet should donate not two pictures to the nation but twelve, and they should all be from among his water lily panels. Years earlier Clemenceau had urged the French government to purchase and keep together Monet's full series of the Rouen Cathedral. That didn't happen. Now, as the man who had led France to victory, he very nearly *was* the French government. This even more sizable project seemed possible.

But not easily. The problem, of course, would be Monet. Within months of agreeing to Clemenceau's plan he was grinding to a halt again, bedeviled by health problems, worsening vision and his own ever recurring insecurities. Before long he was complaining that "I feel that everything is breaking down, my sight and all else, and that I'm no longer capable of doing anything worthwhile." It was the start of the familiar cycle of mood swings that had burdened Monet all his life and that would persistently complicate the remaining eight years of work on the *Grandes Décorations*.

By the summer of 1919 he was on an upward trajectory again, spending most of each day painting outdoors under a parasol, so energetically that Blanche worried he would exhaust himself. Though Monet was no mystic, by his own description the *Grandes Décorations* had taken on something of a metaphysical character. As he put it in a letter that year to Clemenceau, "I am simply expending my efforts upon a maximum of appearances in close correlation with unknown realities." But now he labored under an increasing physical obstacle—his weakening vision, which had not been helped by staring intently for several hours each day at a sun-drenched pond.

Ten years earlier, though he was approaching sixty-nine, Monet had felt able to write confidently to Geffroy that "far from decreasing, my sensitivity has sharpened with age. As long as constant commerce with the outside world can maintain the ardor of my curiosity, and my hand remains the prompt and faithful servant of my perception, I have nothing to fear from old age." But unlike Renoir, whose hands had been bent into claws by arthritis, it would not be Monet's hands that failed him.

After complaining for some time about blurred vision, Monet had finally been diagnosed in 1912 as suffering from cataracts. Just a year after Alice's death, while still coming to terms with that heartbreaking event, he was facing the possibility of another incalculable loss—his eyesight. "The right eye no longer sees anything," he wrote at the time to Geffroy, "the other is also slightly affected." He was relieved when his doctor told him that for the time being his condition could be treated with eye drops. But surgery still loomed as an eventual necessity. Clemenceau, who had medical training, tried to reassure him about its effects. "The cataract on the bad eye will certainly soon ripen, and then one could operate. But that is nothing."

Monet was not so sure. Despite his diagnosis he spent much of the next year conferring with various doctors in the hope that one could offer a permanent solution that did not require surgery. Meanwhile the drops were helpful. As he recalled much later, by the time Monet hit upon the idea for the *Grandes Décorations*, he felt "that my malady was provisionally checked. . . . I was still insensitive to the finer shades and tonalities of colors seen close up, nevertheless my eyes did not betray me when I stepped back and took in the motif in large masses."

That optimism was premature. Throughout the war years Monet's vision continued to deteriorate, though he claimed to one visitor that "my infirmity has sometimes gone into remittance and that on more than one occasion my color vision has come back as it was before." But after the sustained labors of the summer of 1919 the problem was worsening.

Once again Clemenceau was urging Monet to undergo surgery. Seven years had passed since the first diagnosis, and the inevitable could not be postponed forever. Monet was still worried an operation could result in total blindness. "I prefer to make the most of my poor sight," he wrote to Clemenceau, "and even give up painting if necessary, but at least be able to see a little of these things that I love."

But the continuing deterioration of his eyesight could not be ignored. In January 1921, Monet gave an interview—one he soon regretted—in which he admitted, "Alas, I see less and less." After adding that he could no longer paint facing the sun, he vowed to persevere all the same, to "paint almost blind, as Beethoven composed almost deaf."

For more than a year after Clemenceau first proposed the gift idea to Monet, negotiations with the government languished. But in 1920 they picked up speed—unexpectedly, since in January of that year Clemenceau stepped down as prime minister after failing to win election as president, and it was by no means certain that his pet project would be a priority for his successor, Alexandre Millerand. For a while the art critic François Thiébault-Sisson, a close friend of Millerand's, kept the idea alive by acting as the government's unofficial liaison to Monet, until he annoyed the painter by his overly aggressive pursuit of a final deal. At that point the role passed to another writer, Arsène Alexandre, who was working on an authorized biography of Monet.

Thanks to Alexandre's persistence, on September 27, Monet reached an agreement in principle at Giverny with Paul Léon, director general of the government's department of fine arts. When the terms were finalized, it was settled that Monet would donate twelve panels, each of them roughly fourteen feet wide and six and a half feet high, which would be joined together into four panoramas. One of the four would consist of two panels, measuring twenty-eight feet across. Two others would be triptychs forty-two feet wide. The fourth and largest would join four panels and span almost fifty-six feet—a *grande décoration* indeed.

The plan at that stage called for the panels to be housed in an oval gallery in a custom-built pavilion on the grounds of the Hôtel Biron. An eighteenth-century mansion near Les Invalides, it had been converted to a museum dedicated to Rodin not long after the sculptor's death, a purpose it still serves. The architect for the Monet pavilion would be Louis Bonnier, an esteemed practitioner and city planner, chief architect of civil buildings and national palaces and a man chosen by Monet himself—Bonnier had once consulted with Monet on the design of his second studio at Giverny.

As part of the deal, the government also agreed, subject to parliamentary approval, to purchase from Monet a very early work of his for an enormous price: 200,000 francs. But this was no mere juvenilia. It was one of the two very large canvases he had attempted in the 1860s. *Women in the Garden,* a picture from 1866, was more than eight feet tall. In good impressionist fashion he had produced it mostly outdoors, but it was so large that, to bring its upper portions within reach of his brush, he supposedly had to use pulleys that lowered the canvas into a trench. Though completed, it had never been exhibited, much less sold.

That painting was so sizable because Monet had hoped it would be accepted by the jury for the Salon of 1867, and Salon juries were partial to the large canvases favored by French history painters. That ploy didn't work. The subject was too contemporary—four fashionable young women at leisure amid sunstruck greenery. The brushwork was too free and swift. One juror protested that it was necessary to protect young people from just this kind of painting "and save art!" To sell that picture more than half a century later, for a princely sum, and to the French government no less, would be a sweet vindication of Monet's early years. Today it hangs in the Musée d'Orsay.

The agreement had one more important provision. Monet would have to approve the gallery where his paintings were destined to hang. As he later told his friend René Gimpel, "They'll have to build the room as I want it." With that, the stage was set for a yearslong struggle to produce a space the artist would accept and that the French government, still burdened by the costs of postwar reconstruction, could afford. The architect Bonnier held his first meeting with Monet at Giverny in October, measured the immense canvases the planned gallery would have to accommodate, and returned to Paris to draft a memo: "Foresee great expense for the pavilion."

The problem was Monet's insistence on an oval gallery, which would mean walls with complex curvature at a cost of 790,000 francs. Bonnier tried to persuade him to consider a circular gallery, a simpler design that he calculated could be built for 626,000 francs. When Monet would not budge Bonnier rapidly drew up plans for an oval, with an alternative circular option. Monet was able to see them within just days of that first meeting. To see them and reject them, the start of a monthslong tussle with an increasingly irritable painter who thought a round gallery would be "a circus ring."

By March of the following year, after several modifications of Bonnier's original plans, Monet was proposing that an oval gallery might yet be affordable if produced within a smaller building. But that would mean fewer canvases, down from a dozen to as few as eight, an outcome no one wanted. At this point Léon, the increasingly exasperated arts director general, came up with a way out of the impasse. Instead of putting up a new building on the grounds of the Rodin Museum—a plan that was now running into problems with the Public Buildings Council, which had rejected Bonnier's spare design as too modern—why not pursue the less expensive option of adapting an existing building?

The two best candidates were the Jeu de Paume and the Orangerie, paired neoclassical structures in the Tuileries Gardens, just across from the Louvre, that were built during the reign of Louis-Napoléon. The first was an indoor tennis court. The other began life as a place to shelter the park's orange trees in winter, though it was soon turned to other uses—musical events, industry and agricultural shows, and, by 1921, art exhibitions and dog shows. By this time Clemenceau had returned from a six-month trip around Asia and was available once more to cajole and reason with Monet. At the beginning of April, he joined Léon, Bonnier, and Geffroy in an inspection of the two buildings. Clemenceau then wrote Monet that the Jeu de Paume seemed a tad small but the somewhat wider Orangerie would work. "I suggest you call it a deal."

Monet arrived in Paris a week later to get a look at the building himself. To the great relief of all concerned, he gave the site his tentative endorsement. It was not to last. On reflection the space was too narrow and the ceilings too low, which would mean eliminating a decorative frieze of wisteria paintings he had intended to run above the water lily canvases. Worse, the gallery walls were straight, not the elliptical curves he still required. Late in April, he wrote to Léon to say that with regret he was withdrawing his gift. Some months later he changed gears again and told Léon he would go ahead with the gift after all if the display space could be lengthened by ten feet or so. He would even be willing to donate a larger number of panels, as many as eighteen, enough to fill two galleries.

It was not until a year later, in April 1922, that a final authorization of the gift was at last signed by both Léon and Monet. True to his word—at least this time—Monet now agreed to provide nineteen panels to be organized into eight panoramas in two galleries, with the stipulation that they could never be removed or exhibited with other works. By that time the beleaguered Bonnier had been removed from the job of gallery designer. Camille LeFèvre, chief architect of the Louvre, had been chosen by Léon as his replacement on a project expected to cost 600,000 francs.

Should we be surprised Monet fought so hard to defend his vision for those galleries? When he signed that agreement, he was the last surviving member of the original impressionist cohort, a distinction he had unhappily achieved two and a half years earlier with the death of Renoir in December 1919. Bazille, Caillebotte, Morisot, Sisley, and Pissarro had all gone before. His status as the last man standing gave the *Grandes Décorations* a special importance. It conferred upon him the obligation, in his very last years, not just to carry on their legacy but also to confirm that impressionism, a practice that first emerged in the 1860s, remained a vital department of modern art in the twentieth century. To him fell the task of gathering the impressionist discoveries about color, light, and form into a final, irrefutable climax. For a project of such importance, the setting had to be perfect.

In his agreement with Léon, Monet also promised to deliver the paintings within two years, by April 1924. But already there were reasons to wonder if he could meet that deadline. Because now, at the worst possible time, his eyesight was rapidly worsening. Though many of the promised panels were already near completion, Monet was telling friends that he had ruined some by overworking them. The slashed remnants of abortive canvases were piling up at the studio. With constant encouragement from Clemenceau, who was a regular luncheon guest at Giverny, he persevered, but in a state of foreboding. In late June, he could describe himself to Joseph Durand-Ruel, Paul's son, as "hard at work. I want to paint everything before my sight is completely gone."

By September things were bad enough that Monet was resigned at last to visiting a prestigious ophthalmologist in Paris as a prelude to surgery. Dr. Charles Coutela, a friend of Clemenceau's, examined Monet and concluded that in his left eye he had only about 10 percent vision. In his right he was effectively blind, with "perception of light only." To Monet's relief, the doctor provided him with new eye drops that significantly improved the vision in his left eye, leading him to hope he might finish the *Grandes Décorations* before the inevitable operation.

That optimism was misplaced. In January 1923, after more than one postponement by the reluctant patient, Monet underwent two surgeries on his right eye at Coutela's clinic in Neuilly. The postprocedure recoveries were difficult. The first operation left him nauseated and vomiting. The second required a lengthy convalescence in which Monet was expected to remain bandaged and immobilized, a regimen the irritable artist was by no means suited to follow. His repeated attempts to get up and move around, to say nothing of the time he ripped off his bandages, complicated his recovery and required him to endure an additional week in the hospital.

By mid-February he was at last well enough to go home, but 1923 would be a year in which not much painting would get done, though a great deal of anguishing would. While the near vision in his right eye was somewhat improved, his distance vision was feeble. When he stepped back from a canvas to evaluate his work it became a blur. Worse still, just as he had feared, his color vision was distorted. As he put it in a letter to Coutela, "I continue to see green as yellow and all the rest is more or less blue." For a painter, much less one with Monet's exquisite sensitivity to color, this was no small matter.

Coutela, who had already prescribed eyeglasses for Monet, thought a solution could be found through corrective tinted lenses. Tracking down ones that worked became a monthslong project. All the while both Coutela and Clemenceau were pressing Monet to agree to surgery on his other eye, which they both felt was essential if his vision was to improve once and for all. Monet refused to hear of it. By June, six months after the January surgeries, he was sure they had been a mistake. He wrote to Coutela in a fury: "I can see nothing outside or in the distance, either with or without my spectacles." If he hadn't had the operation he could have used those six months to complete his *Décorations*. Instead, he had done nothing. "I think it's criminal to have placed me in such a predicament."

Then the clouds parted again—somewhat. In July, Monet underwent a third surgery on his right eye to correct a new cataract, this operation performed at his home. Within a few weeks he was telling the Bernheim-Jeunes "my condition seems to be improving, the doctors are very satisfied. I'm the only one who's finding it very slow." On a visit to Giverny in late September Coutela brought tinted lenses that appeared to do some good for the color vision problems. Even better were a pair of German eyeglasses that arrived in October. "The results are very good," Monet told Coutela. "I can see green again, red and, at last, an attenuated blue."

In that same month, Monet was visited by two sons of Joseph and

Georges Durand-Ruel, sons of his longtime dealer. Even before their father's death in 1922 they had assumed control of his business. Now they were looking for paintings to buy. But when Monet offered them some recent garden pictures, they were appalled. The new works, they said, were "atrocious and violent." These were very likely to have been produced in the summer of 1922, when his eyesight had begun to fail again. They would include views of his Japanese footbridge and the trellised allee leading up to his house, executed with pulsing colors and rapid, almost reckless, paint handling. Some of these works, based on whatever trickle of light was still making its way into Monet's occluded eyes, are utterly startling, a whiplashing storm of tangled brushstrokes. Expressionist would be one way to describe them. Blurry and borderline illegible might be another.

Even so, in our own time, with eyes long accustomed to expressionist distortion, these same pictures don't seem so much like aesthetic outliers. Thirty years after Monet's death their electric strands of color would find

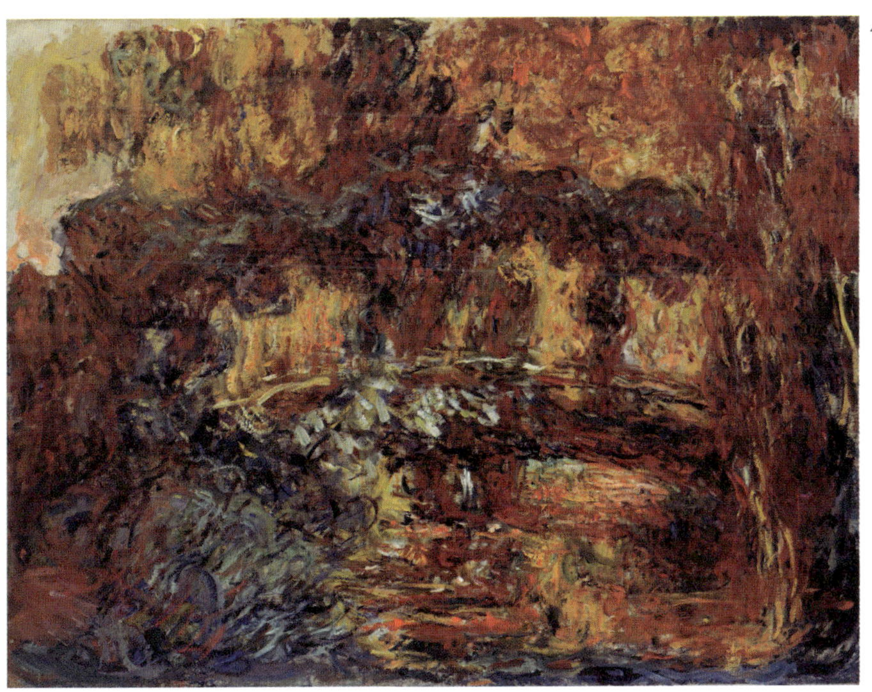
42

The Japanese Footbridge, c. 1920–22, oil on canvas, 89.5 × 116.3 cm, Museum of Modern Art, New York

their way into the work of second generation American abstract painters. Artists like Joan Mitchell, Sam Francis, and Nell Blaine—all of whom came of age in the 1950s, when Monet's last works were resurfacing—were adopting a hectic, scribbled brushwork that bore a plain resemblance to his in these startling late paintings. We can also see how Monet's wild pictures seem to share the impulses of some of the most advanced painting of his own time, the same writhing energies that flow through certain corners of Italian futurism or the portraits of Oskar Kokoschka. But was this a result Monet knew he was arriving at when he painted them? How much of that effect was fully intentional, and how much a byproduct of his disability, the work of an old man squinting at a familiar motif, is impossible to say.

Yet it's also true that Monet, an artist who had no hesitation about destroying paintings that didn't satisfy him, preserved quite a few of these. In 1922, after Dr. Coutela had prescribed the eye drops that temporarily improved the vision in his left eye, Monet wrote the doctor to say he wished he had consulted him sooner. "It would have meant that I could have painted some passable work instead of the daubs I persisted in doing when I could see nothing but a fog." He even admitted to the Durand-Ruel brothers that his problems with color vision may indeed have affected the pictures they found so unacceptable on the day of their visit. But it appears he was unwilling to disown all of them, since many survive.

To further complicate our understanding of Monet's capabilities in late

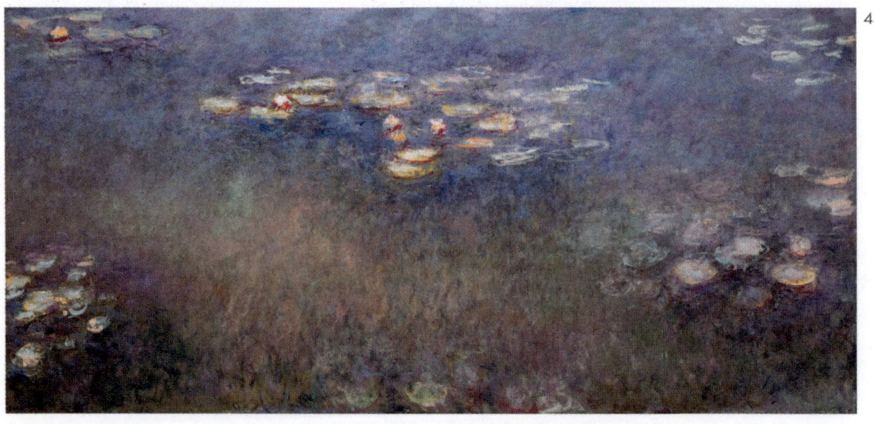 43

Water Lilies, central panel of the now-divided triptych *Agapanthus*, c. 1915–26, oil on canvas, 200 × 426.1 cm, St. Louis Art Museum

life, amid the ups and downs of his vision problems, he continued to fine-tune water lily panels of the utmost delicacy, like the three that make up the triptych once called *Agapanthus*. Conceived for the Orangerie, after Monet's death it was instead divided among three American museums. The central panel, now titled *Water Lilies* and in the collection of the St. Louis Art Museum, is an enchanting stretch of vaporous color. A blooming expanse of rose, ochre, and pale green vibrates within a larger field of blue and violet water, all traversed by white discs of lily pad, here and there flecked with red and orange.

Even so, by April 1924, the very month the *Grandes Décorations* were due to be installed in the Orangerie, Monet was despondent. "For months I've been slaving away and have achieved nothing worthwhile," he wrote Coutela. "Is it my age or my faulty sight? Both no doubt, but my sight most of all. . . . Life is a torture to me." Through the influence of Clemenceau, Monet was granted more time by an increasingly impatient Léon. But the next months would be filled with more ups and downs, as Monet kept reworking canvases that were essentially finished, thinking he could see well enough to add more finishing touches.

In May he learned from Coutela of yet another new German lens, this one from the famed optics company Zeiss, designed specifically for patients who had undergone cataract surgery. Coutela ordered the lenses, but the precision task of measuring Monet's eyes for the new glasses fell not to him but to a Dr. Mawas recommended by Zeiss. While they waited for the arrival of the custom-made lenses, Mawas also arranged for yet another pair of glasses for Monet, these by the Paris optician E. B. Meyerowitz, which in a sense worked all too well. When they arrived in late July, they improved Monet's vision sufficiently to allow him to decide that the "improvements" he had made to his canvases in recent months were a botch. This conclusion sent him into yet another trough of depression and inactivity that lasted through the summer and fall, notwithstanding that numerous visitors to his studio that year were thrilled by the beauty and ambition of his panels.

With this new round of lamentations and paralysis even Clemenceau—who was another among the many who thought Monet's panoramas were "masterpieces"—began to lose patience. In letters that were also full of encouragement and praise he sometimes let his irritation show, telling Monet in one that because he couldn't complain now about his sight he was bellyaching instead about his misbegotten work, "because complaining gives you the greatest joy of your life."

All the same, by November Monet had plunged back into work again—until the next crisis, the worst one yet. Around the New Year of 1925, Monet wrote to Léon to inform him that he was abandoning the attempt altogether and once again withdrew the offer of his gift—this when the French government had already completed the costly Orangerie galleries. He appeared to think he could treat the French nation in the high-handed way he had often treated his dealers when he had told them he could not bring himself to produce paintings he had promised for his next show—though eventually he always did.

When word of this reversal got to Clemenceau he was furious. He wrote Monet in a rage: "However old, however weak he may be, a man, whether he is an artist or not, has no right to go back on his word of honor—above all when it was to France that he gave it." For a time it seemed he was not only through with assisting in this hopeless project, he was through with Monet. He told Blanche by mail that if Monet did not change his mind, "I shall never see him again."

It helps to understand Monet's frame of mind that when he withdrew his gift he was suffering yet another of the endless postoperative setbacks. Every improvement to his sight brought about by new lenses had been short lived, and so had the respite offered by the Meyerowitz glasses that had arrived the previous summer. In February 1925, he was visited by the painter Maurice de Vlaminck, who regarded Monet with awe, as the great precursor of the color-infatuated fauvism Vlaminck had unleashed two decades earlier with Matisse and André Derain. Vlaminck arrived with a friend, the critic Florent Fels, who later described the Monet they met that day as "a proud, small old man, who dodged the obstacles in his path uncertainly. Behind the thick lenses of his spectacles, his eyes appeared enormous, like those of an insect, searching for the last light." Monet told Vlaminck, "I am looking at you, but I cannot see you. . . . With my eyes as they are, it is useless for me to continue painting."

Curiously, around the same time, despite having taken back his gift, Monet was telling others that he was working on his panels all the time and miserable about the fact that he would soon be releasing them to the Orangerie. Perhaps his claim to Léon that he was retracting the donation was a ploy, however ill-conceived, simply to gain time. Inevitably, by March he and

Clemenceau had reconciled and even gotten together at Giverny for one of their customary lunches, though with the understanding that they would not discuss the touchy matter of Monet's gift. Monet even resumed work after a devastating personal loss in May, the death at age sixty-one of another of his stepdaughters, Marthe, the second wife of Theodore Earl Butler, the American painter who had earlier been the husband of Marthe's sister Suzanne.

Monet was still contending with severe vision problems at the time of her death. The Zeiss lenses had finally arrived in the spring but failed to improve the situation. This led Dr. Mawas, who was still involved in Monet's care, to arrive at the idea of completely covering his patient's left eye with an opaque black lens. This had the remarkable effect of significantly improving the vision in his right eye. Monet was elated. He had regained his vision "virtually at a stroke," as he described it in a letter to Dr. Coutela, who was also still on the case. "Am overjoyed to see everything once more."

The lasting return of Monet's sight—at least in one eye—opened the way to a final burst of activity on his canvases. Having told Clemenceau he had decided to go forward after all with his gift to the nation, he worked steadily all through the summer and fall of 1925, with the aim of delivering the paintings the following spring. He had very little time to lose. In April, when his writer friend Geffroy died suddenly of a cerebral aneurysm at age seventy, Clemenceau came to Giverny to give Monet the news. He found his old friend physically unable, at least on that day, to stroll about his gardens. "The human machine is coming apart at the seams," he later wrote. "His panels are finished and will not be touched again. But it is beyond his powers to separate them from himself." Like the elderly Titian, as he drew nearer to his last days, Monet could not bring himself to release his last works. Though the *Grandes Décorations* were effectively complete, he could not admit as much—because if they were finished, so was he. As early as 1917 he had signaled a growing awareness of his own mortality in a letter to his friend Sacha Guitry, the French actor, director, and playwright: "Each day I get nearer the end".

In August 1926, during a summer when Monet was steadily losing weight and in frequent pain, an X-ray showed signs of pulmonary sclerosis—hardened tissue—and a tumor on his left lung. The discovery was remarkable only in that Monet had evaded lung disease for so long. A heavy smoker, he was never at his easel without the bright dot of a cigarette glowing in the middle of his enormous beard. His family decided not to tell him the exact nature of his illness, but he plainly knew his life was drawing to a close. On a visit in November, around the time of Monet's eighty-sixth birthday, Clemenceau spoke with him about the bulbs and seeds he had recently ordered for next year's planting at Giverny. "You will see all that in the spring," the dwindling painter said. "I shall not be here."

Monet died at around noon on December 5, with his son Michel and stepdaughter Blanche at his bedside. Also in attendance was Clemenceau, who had raced up that morning by car from Paris. The previous September, after several months in which he had done no painting, Monet had written hopefully to Clemenceau that he was feeling better, sleeping well, and had been "thinking of preparing my palette and brushes to resume work." He never did paint again, but in a sense he may indeed have worked until the end. By one account of Monet's last moments, his final gesture was to hold up two fingers—to indicate the width he wanted for the frames of the *Grandes Décorations*. With that, the life and the work concluded together.

With the artist departed, his art could finally go as well. It took until the following spring to complete the installation at the Orangerie of Monet's final great achievement. Comprising twenty-two panels, the *Grandes Décorations* are divided into eight separate and separately titled panoramas, four in each of the two galleries, the canvases attached directly to the curving walls with an adhesive. They depict Monet's pond at several times of day, from morning to sunset. Most show just the surface of the water and its complex reflections, but a few, like *The Two Willows, Morning with Willows,* and *Bright Morning with Willows*, foreground the trunks of upright trees and their drooping, feathery branches. Across the entire series the palette varies, from the blooms of white vapor tinged with pale violet in *The Clouds*, to brilliant yellows that flood the lower left of *Sunset,* to the murky blues and purples of the densely painted *Tree Reflections*.

The Monet galleries opened to the public on May 20, 1927. Now visitors could see for themselves the final visions of a man enthralled by the mysteries of vision itself. Yet while some of the first reviews were strong, many critics, especially younger ones, were dismissive. To them Monet's panels were too soft and indistinct, too absorbed in outdated issues of color harmony. The advanced painting of the 1920s was more firmly defined, even when it might be surreal. For others the problem was that Monet's last work was too

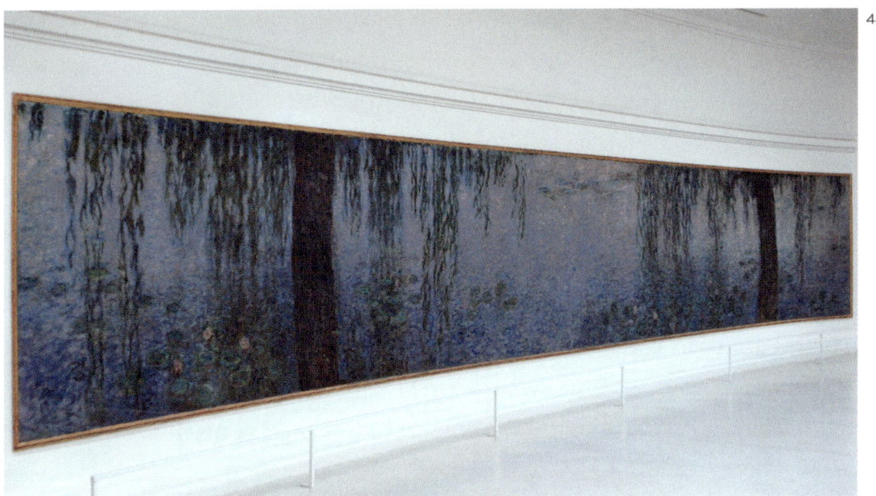

Bright Morning with Willows, a part of the *Grandes Décorations*, 1915–26, oil on canvas, 200 × 425 cm, Musée de l'Orangerie, Paris

avant-garde, "a sort of expedition," as one critic put it, "a raid, on the extreme, outermost reaches of painting." For the next twenty years and more, visitors dwindled and the Monet galleries fell into worsening neglect. A ceiling leak dripped water onto some of the canvases. New galleries added above them blocked whatever sunlight used to reach the windowless rooms from that direction. During the liberation of Paris, Allied artillery shells struck the Orangerie and left one painting speckled with shrapnel.

All of that changed in the 1950s, and not just because of a major renovation, completed in 1952, that led the painter André Masson to pronounce the restored spaces "the Sistine Chapel of impressionism." No less important, beginning in 1949, Monet's son Michel, who had inherited Giverny and the hundreds of late Monets still there, began for the first time to arrange for their exhibition and sale. Some of the largest water lily pictures would be snapped up by American museums. One of those was the Museum of Modern Art in New York, the city that was home to most of the new cohort of abstract expressionists that included Pollock, de Kooning, Rothko, and Barnett Newman. Now the affinities between their art and Monet's were recognized at last.

Because most of those artists knew little about his late works when they were making their initial moves into abstraction, it would not be true to call Monet's last pictures influential, at least not for that first AbEx generation. The pictures were, all the same, prophetic. By 1960, a Monet show at the Modern was mounted partly to make that very point. Years later Andy Warhol remembered it as a watershed rebuke to the presumptions of AbEx painters that their art was without precedent. "It was as if somebody said, 'Why look at Monet, that sweet old man. He was doing all these wild things before you were born.'"

There's a final and unexpected strength of Monet's late *Water Lilies*, one that shows how wrong his critics were who thought them too pretty and ingratiating. Monet arrived at his last decades with an acute awareness of time, the great discovery of old age. We're conscious of it of course even when we're young. Even twentysomethings sense the melancholy gap that separates them from childhood and widens by the hour. But as we grow older we hear more acutely what the poet John Ashbery called "the roar of time plunging unchecked through the sluices."

Even in his fifties, Monet had embedded a profound sense of time's irresistible flow into the very fabric of his series paintings, the grain stacks and poplars, the misty mornings on the Seine and the western façade of Rouen Cathedral. Each series had been like a great sundial, using light to register the ineluctable passage of the hours. Though the water lily canvases, which were not all painted from the same spot, don't constitute a series in that sense, they can still be said to acknowledge time, in their passage from morning to evening. But more than that, to transcend it. Their vaporous, indistinct imagery suggests a state beyond time, one arrived at through the dissolution of the material world into the obscure solvents of eternity. Put plainly, Monet's complex water scenes carry an unmistakable implication of death.

He might have objected to this reading, and not just because, by their liquid complexity and abundance of living forms, his water garden scenes are highly animate, plain emblems of life. Plus he was not generally one to import philosophical statements into his work or to see his images as metaphors. Setting down the intricacies of vision was almost always enough for him. Thus Cézanne's famous remark that Monet was "just an eye—but what an eye!" Yet even Monet understood that his water lily paintings were not merely pictures of a pond, but views into a fundamental condition of all creation. As he once said of them, "They reveal the instability of a universe transforming itself every moment before our eyes."

Look closely into the darker passages of these great pictures—especially in the most dimly shadowed panels like *Tree Reflections*—and it's impossible not to see how often the world Monet shows us there does more than merely transform. It dematerializes, even to the point of extinction. In that way the *Grandes Décorations* are surely the work of an old man, one whose long years had given him at the end a privileged glimpse of a terminal entropy, the complete unraveling of life. Is it too much to suppose that in his last works, Monet embedded this final insight of old age—a frank recognition of death, a serene acknowledgment of the ultimate "unknown reality?"

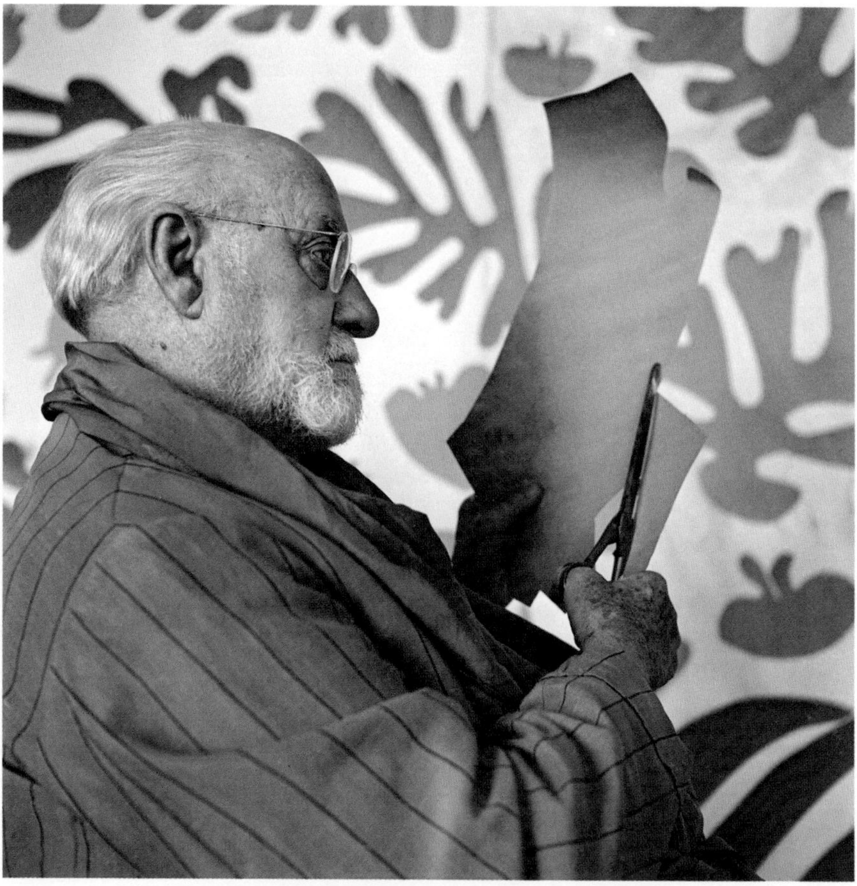

Matisse in 1952 in his Nice apartment and studio, at work on a paper “cut-out.”

4

MATISSE

Henri Scissorhands

46

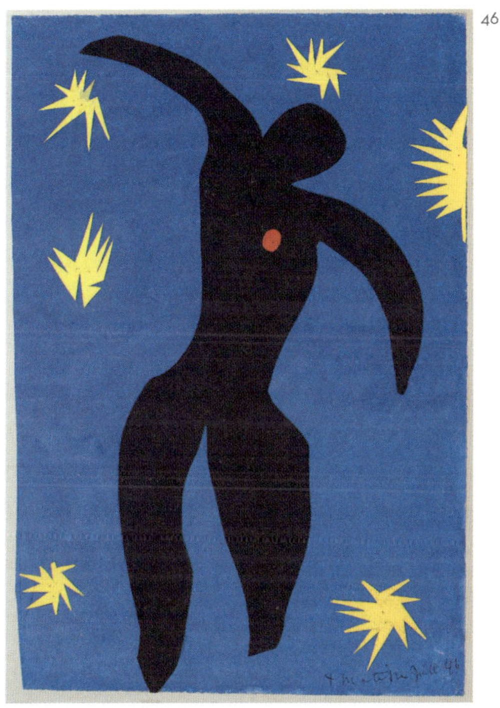

Icarus, maquette for plate 8 from *Jazz*, 1943, gouache on paper, cut and pasted, mounted on canvas, 35 × 27 cm, Centre Georges Pompidou, Paris

During the last years of World War II, Henri Matisse took refuge in Vence, a hillside town above the Mediterranean coast of France. It was there that he produced a now famous image in cut paper called *Icarus*, for the mythical boy who flew too close to the sun. We see that boy plummeting feetfirst back to earth, one arm raised above his head, his tapering silhouette upright against a dark-blue sky. An insistent red dot on his chest represents his fluttering heart. In the sky all around him is a scattering of yellow saw-toothed explosions. Though they seem at first like stars, Matisse told the French poet Louis Aragon they were inspired by the bursts of artillery fire he had seen in the night sky above Nice, the city he had abandoned for Vence when the fighting got too close. So this picture is in part a coded memory of wartime. But might it not also be an implied self-portrait of the elderly Matisse? With his heart on fire, he tumbles through the turmoil of his last years, a man of high ambition, now feeling himself in freefall.

By the time he arrived at the threshold of old age—a New Year's Eve baby, he had turned seventy on the last day of 1939—Matisse was universally regarded as one of the foremost artists of the twentieth century. Like Monet before him, he was a onetime laughingstock who had the last laugh, who now occupied a position atop the art world that Picasso alone shared. He had the museum shows and gallery prices to prove it. He had the rosette of the Légion d'honneur in the buttonhole of his English cloth jackets, a rambling apartment in Nice and another in Paris. He also had the companionship of a lovely young Russian émigré, Lydia Delectorskaya, who was his studio assistant, business manager, and model—as well as perhaps something more.

So Matisse was a man on top of the world. But as the entered his seventies maybe he was also the falling boy, one whose world was coming undone on three fronts. Europe was at war, he was about to endure a life-changing medical crisis, and his wife's suspicions that Lydia was indeed "something more" had recently cost him his marriage.

Their split was the first of his misfortunes to arrive, in 1939. It was a bitter development after more than forty years together, even if by then their stale union was a torment for them both. In their first years of marriage Amélie Matisse had been her husband's indispensable companion, offering tireless encouragement, financial support, and herself as a frequent model. We see her in some of his most fearless early canvases, like the portrait known as *The Green Line*, where the mysterious line runs down her forehead and the bridge of her nose. Or *Woman with a Hat*, an outburst of wayward color so puzzling that even Gertrude Stein and her brother Leo, connoisseurs of the new, hesitated at first to buy it. (They did.) In Matisse's leanest years, when he was too obscure even to rank as infamous, his wife sewed hats to put food on the table. When the critics treated him as a joke, she hid his press clippings so he wouldn't dwell on them. When he couldn't afford a small Cézanne he badly wanted, she found the money by selling her favorite piece of jewelry.

For all that, long before their final separation, their marriage was showing signs of strain. We can see that from *The Conversation*, a portrait of a paralyzed relationship that Matisse began in 1909, eleven years after they wed, but didn't complete until 1912. On the left is the stiffly upright figure of a bearded man who plainly resembles him. On the right he's confronted by a no less rigidly seated woman. Both are in profile against a dark blue background and as immobile as Egyptian statuary, as though their impasse were eternal. Between them is a window looking onto a garden, a zone of contentment beyond the reach of either party to this grim face-off. Despite the title there is plainly no conversation here. You can see very well that their mouths are shut tight.

That picture lets us in on something that Matisse would one day tell his son Pierre. "The great defect of our family is a lack of candor, a fear of what ought to be said." However much we think of him as the painter of pleasure and light, of lounging women, airborne dancers, and windows that open onto bright gardens, the artist could be much darker than his art. "If one was happy," he once shrugged, "one wouldn't paint." All his life he suffered chronic anxiety. Insomnia was a nightly struggle and acute nervous tension was the prelude to his daylight hours at the easel or sculpture table. "In the morning," he once said, "to begin the day well, I have to feel like killing someone." (What exactly he meant by that has never been clear, but it can't have been a happy thought.) Georges Duthuit, an art historian who was the husband and then the estranged husband of Matisse's daughter Marguerite—they separated but never divorced—once lamented his father-in-law's "inability to relax . . . his absolute incapacity, if only for the space of a tear or a smile, to sit down with his neighbor."

Five years after he finished *The Conversation*, the forty-seven-year-old Matisse, who was still living with his wife and children in the Paris suburb of Issy-les-Moulineaux, opened a new chapter in his life. He ran away from home. To be specific, he headed for the irresistible sunlight of the

Mediterranean. He had first encountered it on a honeymoon trip to his wife's family in Corsica in 1898, again in subsequent stays in Saint-Tropez and Collioure, and then during trips to North Africa that also introduced him to the Arab motifs that would ebb and flow through his work ever after. That profound, vivid light, so unlike the gray northern skies he grew up with, left him delighted and infatuated. Determined to let it nourish his art, in 1917 he began to spend a good part of every year in Nice, while returning most summers to Issy. At the outset he lived in a series of hotels, painting his narrow sunlit rooms with their tall French windows looking onto the sea. By 1921, he was ready to rent a two-room apartment on the Place Charles-Félix, later taking more space in the same building, enough for Amélie to relocate to Nice in 1928. With that, the house in Issy would be rented out, while an apartment on the rue du Montparnasse would serve as the family's Paris pied-à-terre.

Without doubt the sunlight was part of his motive for moving south, but was it his only one? Tensions at home were growing, and by the time he first decamped for Nice Matisse was feeling trapped in an unbearable situation. Decades later, after the breakup, he would defend himself in a long letter to his son Pierre, who had moved to New York in 1925 and become a successful art dealer: "I love my family, truly, dearly, and profoundly, but from a distance. . . . A hypersensitive organism like mine can find human contacts unendurable and deeply wounding, even if the heart remains tender."

Even before her move to Nice, Amélie came down in most years to join Matisse for all or part of his stay in the south. But Matisse was often on his own, working with a succession of attractive models, lingering on favorites for years at a time. Yet if his wife had her suspicions, she didn't give them free play or allow them to undermine the sanctum of their family. They had two sons, Jean and Pierre, as well as a daughter, Marguerite, whom Matisse had fathered out of wedlock by an earlier companion and model, Caroline Joblaud. The circumstances of Marguerite's birth mattered not at all to Amélie, who fully embraced the girl as her own, a devotion her stepdaughter very much returned.

But Lydia was the last straw, no matter that it was at Amélie's suggestion that the young woman had entered the Matisse household in the first place. Amélie had gotten to know Lydia after she arrived in 1932 to work as a studio assistant for Matisse. Finding her to be reliable, she decided that Lydia would do as the next in a series of her own live-in helpmates. By that time Madame Matisse had been a semi-invalid for years, requiring constant care, subject to long indispositions and prone to foul moods—maybe for good reason, given her husband's unorthodox ideas about marriage. She was happy at first to be cared for by Lydia, who was then twenty-four. A physician's daughter, she was born in the Siberian city of Tomsk in 1910, orphaned at an early age, taken to China by an aunt and sent to school in Harbin. In the 1920s, she fetched up in Paris, entered and escaped a bad marriage, and made her way to Nice. There she worked variously as a bit-part actress and baby nurse, as well as an artist's model and assistant, eventually for Matisse.

By the time Lydia entered their lives, dealings between Matisse and his wife were grim. Amélie had long since sensed herself being pushed to the margins of her husband's life and begun dwelling on whether his relations with his models were really all that chaste, however much he insisted they were. And the pain in their marriage went both ways. In a 1934 letter to Pierre, Matisse described their life in Nice, where by that year they met only at meals conducted in silence. The previous winter, he wrote, Amélie had experienced "fits of rage that even she herself found frightening." He went on: "To continue with my work I need complete calm. I cannot go on living as I have lived for a long time now—haunted by a mortal disquiet that pursues me day and night."

Was Matisse in fact sleeping with any of his models in Nice, where he sometimes painted the same woman repeatedly before moving on to the next? What exactly were his relations with Antoinette Arnoux, who was nineteen when she began to sit for him, or with Henriette Darricarrère, the movie extra who posed for him for years? And of course people wondered about his dealings with Lydia. Picasso and his postwar companion Françoise Gilot certainly wondered, especially after they surprised an embarrassed Matisse, who was playing hide-and-seek with her in his Paris apartment. Matisse scholars have been divided. In her meticulous two-volume biography, Hilary Spurling, who interviewed Lydia before her death in 1998, is inclined to accept her lifelong insistence that she and Matisse were never lovers. Matisse stuck to the same story. After his surgeries, sex may have been too challenging for Matisse to pursue much, if at all. Meanwhile, Jack Flam, one of the foremost American authorities on Matisse, takes for granted that the pair were intimates during some part of their more than twenty years together. In any case, his relations with Lydia seemed more companionate than professional. More like spousal.

So Lydia is to Matisse what Leocadia Weiss was to Goya, the late-life companion whose exact role is impossible to establish beyond doubt. It was not until about a year after she entered his household that Matisse finally asked her to pose for him. We see her first in *The Blue Eyes*, from 1935, an inward-looking young woman with her head nestled in her folded arms. It's a picture that brings to mind, perhaps deliberately, the infatuated portraits Picasso began making in the early 1930s of his very young new lover Marie-Thérèse Walter. After the war Picasso told Gilot he always suspected that first portrait of Lydia was a clue to the real depth of her intimacy with Matisse. "It had a definite feeling," he told her. "In any case I can't understand how Matisse can manage not to lose his head in front of a model like that."

Soon after *The Blue Eyes* was completed Lydia began posing for Matisse undressed. That's her in his 1935 painting now known as *The Large Pink Nude*. Within a few years of that picture, Amélie's suspicions had turned to Lydia. Whether or not the young woman had become Matisse's bedmate, she had plainly supplanted his increasingly bedridden wife as his indispensable life support. Now it was Lydia who was studio assistant, supply manager, record keeper, and—the most delicate usurpation of all—artist's model, a role Amélie had last served for an abstracted sketch of her head in 1915. "For more than a month we have not known how to go on living," Matisse reported miserably in a letter to Pierre, written just before their final split. "[My doctors] told me that I might have had a stroke. That meant nothing to her. She was like a woman possessed." In October 1938, after months of raging at her husband, Amélie presented him with an ultimatum. "It's me or her," she told him. With the utmost reluctance Matisse sent Lydia away. Amélie left him anyway. Seizing the opportunity, he called Lydia back.

In July 1939, with their divorce being finalized and a division of property underway that included all of his art still held by Matisse, he and Amélie met in Paris, at a café at the Gare Saint-Lazare. The fraught sit-down had been arranged by a mutual friend, the art dealer Paul Rosenberg, who was at their table hoping to act as a go-between. Instead Amélie spoke the whole time only with him, never so much as looking at the mortified Matisse, who said almost nothing. He wrote soon after to a friend, "I remained as if carved out of wood."

There it was again, the family's great defect. "A fear of what ought to be said." It would be more than six years before they saw one another again, and then not until after enduring a war that would engulf them both.

On September 1, 1939, Germany invaded Poland. Two days later Britain and France declared war on Germany. By the following May the Germans had invaded France. Six weeks later Hitler was riding in triumph down the Champs-Élysées.

This would be the second invasion of France in Matisse's adult lifetime. Rejected for service during World War I—he was forty-four when it started—he sat out that war mostly in Paris. That was where he waited anxiously for any news of his younger brother Auguste, who for a time was taken hostage by the Germans. As for his aged mother, she was trapped behind enemy lines in his boyhood town, Bohain, where she was even jailed briefly for resisting a German order to evacuate.

Matisse would see out World War II in the south with Lydia. In its first years, they remained in Cimiez, a hillside neighborhood of Nice. His sizable apartment there was in a six-story building called La Régina, a belle epoque confection that was originally a hotel where Queen Victoria—La Régina—used to stay on Mediterranean holiday. Matisse lived on the third floor, with Lydia, at her own insistence, in a maid's room a few floors above. In June 1943, after Nice became a target of Allied shells and aircraft, they moved on to a rented villa in the nearby hilltop town of Vence. The house was called Le Rêve—The Dream. For years it amounted to just that, a willed fantasy realm, its garden planted with lemon trees, palms, and pomegranates, its rooms crammed with tribal sculpture, Moorish textiles, and Chinese pottery, its walls overflowing with his cut-outs and paintings. A bulwark against the world outside, Le Rêve would be a bubble no artillery could burst.

From the first Matisse had offers of assistance to flee to the United States or elsewhere. In 1940, he even obtained a visa for Brazil but decided he couldn't go. As he wrote to Pierre: "If everyone of any worth leaves the country, what will become of France? I would feel myself a deserter if I left." Besides, away from home he had trouble focusing on his art, and single-minded productivity was how he planned to survive the war. "Each one of us must find his own way to limit the moral shock of this catastrophe," is how he put it in a letter to Marguerite. "I'm trying to distract myself from it as far as possible by clinging to the side of the future work I could do if I don't let myself be destroyed."

And when it came to his art, Matisse could be remarkably cold-blooded. Let Europe implode, his work came first. He wrote Pierre to report that Nice was still full of suitable young women happy to pose for him: "I have arranged with some motion picture agents to send me their prettiest." In the same letter he turned to discuss his latest canvas, *The Dream*. At its center, he wrote, was a young woman, "an angel fast asleep on a violet surface—the most beautiful violet I ever saw. . . . I won't say that this painting made me forget everything else, but at least it brought me some relief."

However many pretty models he could hire during the war, however well his work was going, the worst realities of wartime would eventually penetrate his world. His estranged wife and two of their three adult children would become active in the Resistance, work that put their very lives in jeopardy. His son Jean, who joined a clandestine network in Antibes, would manage to stay one step ahead of the Gestapo, escaping back to Paris just before the Germans rounded up his comrades. But Amélie, whose contribution was to type up reports to be sent on to British intelligence in London, would be arrested in April 1944, then jailed for nearly six months outside Paris.

Marguerite, who dared to carry concealed messages among Paris, Bordeaux, and Rennes, endured much worse. She could. This was a formidable woman. At the age of six she survived the horror of an emergency tracheotomy on a kitchen table, her father pinning her down while a doctor thrust an incision into her throat. For the rest of her life, she wore high-necked blouses or a velvet ribbon to hide the signs of her impromptu surgery. In 1923, she married Georges Duthuit, an art historian, and together they had a son, Claude. But their marriage fell apart in the early 1930s when she learned Georges was having an affair with the wife of the British writer Sacheverell Sitwell, of the stridently visible Sitwell clan. During the war Duthuit decamped to New York, where Marguerite would send Claude to join him. She remained in France, growing ever more determined to somehow fight the Nazi invaders. She wrote to her father: "As for me, I am made of the stuff of warriors, fanatics, and all those consumed by ardor."

She would need it. In April 1944, six weeks before the D-Day landings, the forty-nine-year-old Marguerite was arrested in Rennes. Delivered to the Gestapo, who thought she might know something about the Allied invasion plans, she would be tortured for days. Bound to a table or suspended from a ceiling by her wrists, she was beaten with fists, a leather whip, and a steel truncheon, then submerged till near-drowning in freezing water. In despair she tried to kill herself with a piece of broken glass. In August, with Allied troops poised to enter Rennes, she was herded with other prisoners into cattle cars bound for the German concentration camp at Ravensbrück. Allied air raids forced the train to halt in open country near the German border. In the ensuing chaos she somehow got free and was later harbored by the local Resistance.

For months after Marguerite's arrest her anxious father could learn nothing about her whereabouts. After her escape he finally got word that she had turned up in Paris, but it would not be until January 1945 that they would reunite in Vence. For fifteen days they convened every afternoon at Le Rêve, where Matisse listened in horror as she described the details of her imprisonment and torture. He wrote to Pierre: "I saw in reality, and materially, the atrocious scenes she described and acted out for me." Though an artillery barrage had once forced him and Lydia to retreat into their basement, Le Rêve was supposed to defend him against nightmares like this. For the first time, and appallingly, the war truly came home.

By then, Matisse was well into the third ordeal of his old age. In 1940, he had begun to experience a recurrence of severe gastric pain he had suffered on and off since boyhood. By December he was hospitalized in Nice, where his doctors were unsure what was causing the trouble this time. At Lydia's urging, Marguerite transferred her father to a clinic in Lyon, where doctors suspected a tumor and surgery was recommended. Perhaps to avoid alarming Pierre with the word *cancer*, Matisse wrote him from the hospital to report that his diagnosis was diverticulitis. Ever the artist, he enclosed a bumpy drawing of his diseased digestive track.

In January 1941, surgeons in Lyon would perform two operations on Matisse over four days, the first removing fourteen inches of his intestine. The procedures were successful but at no small cost. They burdened him for life with a colostomy, or as he soon called it, with maybe a dash of sangfroid, "an artificial anus." He confided to Pierre: "I promised myself that I would never tell a soul, but I broke down and told one or two people, and they told their best friends, and so on . . ."

Well into middle age Matisse had been a physically active man. In his late fifties he discovered rowing, joined a boating club in Nice, and was awarded a gold medal as the member who took out his little skiff most often in the previous year—for an hour every morning, weather permitting. Now for the rest of his life he would be a semi-invalid. The surgeries weakened his abdominal muscles, which badly interfered with his ability to paint. Though he still had full dexterity in his hands, he could not stand up for long before an easel or even sit upright in a chair for any length of time. On good days he was able to rise and even walk for a while. On bad days, and there were more of them as he got older, he was confined to his bed or a wheelchair, sometimes for months.

In the weeks following his surgery, Matisse nearly died due to complications from two blood clots in his lungs. His recovery, first in Lyon, then back in Nice, would be long and difficult. It would be months before he felt well enough to so much as drag a pen across paper. But after having ridden out the worst of it, his brush with death revitalized him. The nuns who nursed him in Lyon used to call him Le Ressuscité, the man back from the dead. Matisse felt that way himself. He wrote to friends telling them he had been granted "a second life."

Matisse asked his doctors to give him three years to complete the work he hoped to do. He got almost fourteen and put that time to spectacular use. His old age would not be some pale epilogue to his glory years. They would be his glory years, or rather another string of them in the life of a man who had already had quite a few. Before his death, on November 3, 1954, Matisse would enjoy one of the most powerful final chapters in the life of any artist since the Renaissance.

And this would happen in almost every area of his art. Sculpture was the sole exception. Even before his surgeries Matisse had stopped making bronzes for almost a decade, and in the years afterward he produced just three small figures. But in every other practice he discovered new strengths. In his sweetly seductive late drawings Matisse arrived at a taut, buoyant line that has made them to this day emblems of the very idea of the modern. As for painting, though his infirmities meant that he worked less frequently at his easel, when he did it was often with a spectacular final authority, especially in his studio interiors of the late 1940s, exercises in deeply saturated color that intricately reconciled the flatness that had always fascinated him with the pleasures of deep space. At the end of his life, he also ventured unexpectedly into the creation of an entire sacred space, designing every element of a chapel in Vence. As if all this were not enough, in his last years he dove into the complex and delightful paper cut-outs. An unheard-of pursuit for a "serious" artist, they combined a profound distillation of form and a sophisticated application of color with a childlike sense of delight. Matisse may have been a near-invalid, but in old age he was a man in full. Or as he once put it: "Only the work I did after my illness is truly myself."

"Me," he said. "Free and detached."

Matisse had an early model for this kind of fearless old age. Around 1918, the year after he first arrived in Nice, he began to visit often with Pierre-Auguste Renoir at his villa in the nearby hill town of Cagnes-sur-Mer. Then in his mid-seventies and confined to a wheelchair, his hands bent into claws by arthritis, the implacable old impressionist still painted every day, often another of the sunny nudes that constitute so much of his final output. All the same, on one of his visits even Matisse had to ask the old man, why go on working in such pain? Renoir had his answer ready. "The pain passes, Matisse, but the beauty endures."

Decades later, after his surgeries, the newly disabled Matisse found himself thinking back often on their times together. As he told an interviewer, they had made him realize "that even after a long working life, an artist's curiosity could remain unquenched. The hope of some further progress, something to be added to his oeuvre, was what kept Renoir alive." Of course this spoke to Matisse, who all his life treated his art as his personal land of opportunity, a realm of constant reinvention. If anything, old age only made that prospect more gratifying.

Perseverance was a virtue Matisse had always understood. From his early twenties his life had been dedicated to the day-and-night demands of his art. Everything else—money, health, reputation, even family—came second. However much he had been distracted by the grief and anxiety of World War I, it hadn't prevented him from completing some of his greatest pictures in the same years. *The Piano Lesson* and *The Moroccans*, the intimate quasi-cubist *Goldfish and Palette* and the monumental tour de force *Bathers by a River*—all were done while the Great War ground on, some when German guns sounded over the rooftops of Paris. When the painter Henri Manguin, an old friend, ran into some problems in his art, Matisse had simple advice: "All you have to do is work. If you're in trouble, it's through work that you will get out of it."

Late in 1943, Matisse wrote to Marguerite to defend his determination to go on working. Though she never broke with her father after the divorce, she sided with her stepmother on the issue of Lydia, whose name she refused to speak. Matisse claimed that after the split his daughter occasionally "pin-pricked" him in her letters. So maybe it was another bit of passive-aggression on her part when she wrote that year to remind her father about the pitfalls awaiting artists who persevered into old age, when their gifts can flag and no one around them is qualified to warn against it. (She meant Lydia.) He wouldn't hear of it. "Must I stop work even if the quality deteriorates?" he shot back. "Each age has its own beauty—in any case I still work with interest and pleasure. It's the only thing I have left."

However much Matisse prized his daughter's judgments, we should be glad he didn't take that warning to heart. Divorce, war, and disability—old age had brought him a trifecta of calamities. Who would have blamed him if he had sunk into despair and taken his art with him? But none of them could undermine his faith in the infallible tonic of work. If anything, they made single-minded effort more attractive as a refuge from dark realities. After the health crisis that consumed most of 1941—and his sense, in its aftermath, of a new lease on life, however long it might last—work seemed to him the only way to justify the reprieve he had been granted.

And not just any work. Matisse being Matisse, he would commit himself to efforts that were an unapologetic expression of joy. The man behind the most sensuous department of French modernism was not about to allow despair to gain any lasting foothold in his art. This was not a matter of living in denial. As a reply to the tragedies of his time, it was both an instinctive countermove—Matisse just being Matisse—but also a plausible strategy. His answer to the plain reality of suffering would be to resupply the world's dwindling store of pleasure. It was both the role he was born for and the only one he knew how to fill.

The doctrine of constant work reverberated with a lifelong axiom of Matisse's philosophy, the prospect of endless potential and endless change, that any development in his art could always give rise to a further one. Like Picasso, Matisse had repeatedly reinvented himself. He had begun doing that as a young man simply by deciding to be an artist, not the lawyer he had already trained to become. Like Monet, Matisse was the son of a small businessman.

Émile Matisse and his wife, Anna, ran a successful hardware and seed store in Bohain, a small but fast-growing textile town in the north of France, not far from the border with Belgium. Naturally his ambition for his eldest son was to see him launched into a profession. At his father's insistence Matisse went to Paris to study law at the Sorbonne, then came back to work miserably as a law clerk in the nearby town of Saint-Quentin. While he was at his parent's home recovering from an early episode of his lifelong stomach pain, a neighbor showed him the paint box he used when making copies of Swiss landscapes. Matisse was intrigued. Why not try his hand at painting? As soon as he did, or so he liked to recall it, he found his vocation. "Like an animal that plunges headlong toward what it loves, I dived in—to the understandable despair of my father."

However skeptical his father may have been, he agreed to pay for his son to take art classes in Paris, though only for one year. Once there Matisse would stretch out his allowance for two years by putting himself on half rations. What followed was a long apprenticeship of youthful work, competent but by no means revolutionary, before his next great reinvention, which began in 1905, when he was in his midthirties. Along with André Derain, Maurice de Vlaminck, and a few others, Matisse would become a member of the twentieth-century's first avant-garde. *Les Fauves*—the Wild Beasts—was a name applied to them as a joke by a hostile critic but one that they, like the impressionists before them, proudly adopted. Over the space of a few years, they pushed the dissonant palette of postimpressionism into fever territory. And at their head was Matisse, "King of the Beasts," ramping up the broken brushwork of Cézanne into maelstroms of pyrotechnic color, building pictures from staccato dashes of magenta and ultramarine that melted foreground into background, absorbing people and things into their churning surroundings, turning up all the knobs. "We thought it was necessary to exalt all colors together," he would later say, "sacrificing none of them."

Yet fauvism occupied him only through 1907. When he was through with its hectic charms he abruptly changed gears. To distill and stabilize his art he conjured a stripped-bare world of mythic antiquity, an imaginary place that was one part Arcadia, one part Land that Time Forgot. This was where he set enigmatic pictures like *Bathers with a Turtle*, from 1908, or *Nymph and Satyr*, from the following year, both featuring bluntly rendered, almost cartoonish nudes. In those he put aside altogether the energetic paint handling of fauvism. Partly with an eye to the zones of pure color in the work of Gauguin, he disposed his figures among wide stretches of blue and green, nearly abstract bands of pigment that signified—just barely—land, sea, and air. You find those again in his famous paintings from 1910 and 1911, *The Dance, I* and *II,* with their whirling circles of naked revelers.

Was it with his very bourgeois father in mind that in this same period Matisse made his most notorious and self-sabotaging pronouncement? In his first published essay, "Notes of a Painter," a lengthy mission statement that appeared in 1908 in the arts journal *La Grande Revue*, he announced that it was his dream to produce "an art of balance, of purity and serenity, devoid of troubling or depressing subject matter, an art that could be for every mental worker, for the business man as well as the man of letters, a soothing, calming influence on the mind, something like a good armchair which provides relaxation from physical fatigue."

No matter that in that very year his art was at its most uncompromising, an eyesore to any right-thinking collector, and that he would continue down even more radical paths well into World War I—that "armchair" credo made him sound timid and philistine.

When his father died two years later, his then forty-year-old son had attained a few markers of success. He had recently moved his family out of their cramped Paris apartment to a rented two-story house and garden in the suburb of Issy-les-Moulineaux, a home he would later buy. He had one very wealthy patron, the Russian textile magnate Sergei Shchukin, who filled his Moscow mansion with Matisse's wildest pictures while Russian society snickered. He also had a contract with the prestigious Bernheim-Jeune Gallery that ensured him a predictable income. But he had nothing like the money and acclaim that would come his way over the next decades. In old age he was still haunted by the sense he had failed to make his father proud, and worse, had caused him "great suffering."

And then in the next decade he was off in other directions, especially as he tried to reckon with cubism. With their large, highly simplified forms, semi-abstract paintings like his *View of Notre Dame* or *Bathers by a River* put him at yet another remove from conventional representation. "Details lessen the purity of the lines and harm the emotional intensity," he said. "We reject them." In the previous century Van Gogh and Gauguin had dismissed realistic color, but even in their work free expression had been held in check by the discipline of the visible world, by the conviction that a picture should still resemble the scene it depicted. Matisse felt less obligated. He liked to repeat Delacroix's maxim: "Exactitude is not truth."

This was an important part of what made him modern—his insistence that reality was a necessary starting point but only a starting point for work that in the end would bear the stamp of his own sensibility. Yet at the same time he always insisted that what he did on canvas or in bronze was no thoughtless explosion of reality but a controlled demolition. Its purpose was to arrive at a new kind of likeness, in an equilibrium produced by passing what he saw through what he felt and submitting both to the internal demands of the composition. No doubt the results were strange, at least to many of his contemporaries, but they were also powerful, fascinating, and, in their own way, plausible. By casting aside exact representation, he broke through to a new kind of beauty.

By his own account, his search for the new even played a role in his midlife decision to step back toward the old. As he approached his fifties, Matisse retreated from near abstraction to the more realistic odalisques of the 1920s, sensuous women in vaguely Moorish dress. Posed among cushions, patterned carpets, and floral wallpaper, these were full-bodied figures with recognizably human faces, a convention he had sometimes put aside in his earlier, more radical work. As he insisted later to an interviewer, "If I had continued down the other road, which I knew so well, I would have ended up a mannerist. One must always keep one's eye, one's feeling, fresh."

It was in these years, when he truly let slip for a time his claim to any place in the avant-garde, that his "comfortable armchair" remarks would come back to haunt him again and again. In the decades after World War I, the new art meant Delaunay, Braque, Kandinsky, and Klee. It meant Dada, surrealism, futurism, and expressionism, plus the droll anti-art of Marcel Duchamp and whatever Picasso was doing on any given day. At that very moment Matisse was content to become the former provocateur who now painted half-naked women in harem pants that rich collectors wholeheartedly approved of. Eventually no less a rich collector than David Rockefeller would own one of the best, *Reclining Odalisque with Magnolias*, from 1923. After Rockefeller's death, his son recalled how his father had made sure to hang the picture in a special place—where he could see it from his favorite armchair.

The odalisques have enjoyed a reassessment in recent decades. They're admired now for their synthesis of modernist distortion with the traditions of representation. All the same, it's a fairly housebroken modernism you find in them, one in which walls meet at the corner and the women are as fully modeled and tangible as apples. After the work of his earlier years, this was undeniably a step back. For most of the first two decades of the century, Matisse's every new canvas had been like a bulletin from the front. But his sultry odalisques, and there were dozens of them, were more like postcards from the beach. *Greetings from Nice. Don't you wish you could be here?*

In any event, as evidence of a well-charged libido, that long line of odalisques certified Matisse's reputation as a connoisseur of female flesh. Was it as an antidote to that image that he cultivated the detached air of his adult life? Matisse the great voluptuary took pains to present himself to the world as the ultimate buttoned-up bourgeois. However radical his art may sometimes have been, however offensive to conventional taste, there was nothing bohemian about the man. With his neatly trimmed reddish beard, his wire-rimmed spectacles, his vested tweed suits, he was always groomed, at least for the camera, like the lawyer he once trained to be. No matter that, even in the years before he was confined to his bed, he actually spent many working days in pajamas, a Hugh Hefner avant la lettre. To the outside world he would always present himself as the man his friends liked to call "the Professor."

The most telling picture we have of Matisse at work in old age—a stark illustration of the "male gaze," decades before the term was coined—is a famous photo from 1939 by the renowned photographer Brassaï. In the center stands a very naked woman. We know her name. She's Wilma Javor, a Hungarian model Matisse worked with often. Perhaps on that day she even chatted for a while in her native tongue with Brassaï, who was also Hungarian. But in the photo she's an anonymous specimen being scrutinized by a famous man, torqued in our direction in a three-quarter pose, legs crossed at the ankles. With both arms raised to rest her hands on the top of her head, her face is pointed demurely toward the floor.

Directly across from her, no more than three feet away, sits a severely appraising Matisse. Dressed in cuffed trousers, a necktie, and vest beneath a long white studio coat, he looks like a cross between a banker and a laboratory scientist, with maybe a sideline as a poultry inspector. His gaze is directed plainly at her vaginal area, which is partly turned toward us as well.

A large sketch pad in his left hand blocks our view of his right, his drawing hand, which dips down behind the pad, into the area of his groin. Is this meant to hint at the source of his vigor as an artist? In an earlier self-portrait Matisse had already linked his art to his genitals by having an obviously phallic thumb poke through the thumbhole of his palette. As an image of male cluelessness, on the part of both Matisse and Brassaï, the photo is absurdly comical. As a raw diagram of the power dynamic between artists and their models, a hieroglyph of male privilege and froideur, it's not so funny.

So Matisse was a divided soul. The good family man contained the struggling sensualist. The tweed-suited professor was the mask of the simmering id. As we've already guessed, his libidinous side may have played some role in his midlife decision to spend so much of every year in Nice, sometimes with his wife, sometimes without. However much his motive was to avail himself of the southern light and atmosphere he loved, his regular back-and-forth also looks like the stratagem of a man intent on escaping family life while hoping to hold on to it. There was something about domesticity that he could not bear but could not do without. He once pleaded with an interviewer to make sure to convey to her readers "that I am a normal man; that I am a devoted husband and father, that I have three fine children, that I go to the theater, ride horseback, that I have a comfortable home, a fine garden that I love." It sounds as though he was trying to convince himself.

For all their relative conservatism, the odalisques stand as more evidence of Matisse's constant willingness to change, to move into new territory. That belief in endless renewal was still very much with him in old age. It was behind his hope that his "second life," after his surgeries, would carry his art into new realms. When it did, and quickly, it was first through drawing. In the years just after his surgeries, when painting was too difficult but pens and charcoal were lightweight tools he could manage in bed, he drew. And drew. With mortality now a near-term prospect, he no doubt remembered something he used to tell his students at the Académie Matisse in Paris, a one-man school he established and ran for a few years in his late thirties. "Drawing," he advised them, "is like making an expressive gesture with the advantage of permanence." Years later, with one wary eye on the grave, it was no small matter for him that any line he set down on paper could commemorate the living hand that once made it, that every drawing was done in indelible ink.

In April 1942, Matisse wrote to his son Pierre to exult about the work he would publish a year later as *Drawings: Themes and Variations*. "For the past year I have been working with great effort at drawing. I say effort but it is not correct, what happened was a flowering after fifty years of effort." He wrote in the same vein to Marguerite. "I have made a very important exertion, one of the most important of my life. I have perfected my drawing, making surprising progress in ease, expressing emotion freely with a large variety of feeling and a minimum of means." To make sure she got the point, he added, "This is one of the things for which I wished to continue to live."

As with most artists before the late-twentieth century, when all the rulebooks were tossed aside, drawing had been fundamental to Matisse's work from the beginning, all the more so in the years before and during World War I, as his paintings became more abstract and distilled and each line counted for more. There were times throughout his career, however, when drawing was secondary for Matisse, when he was more absorbed by

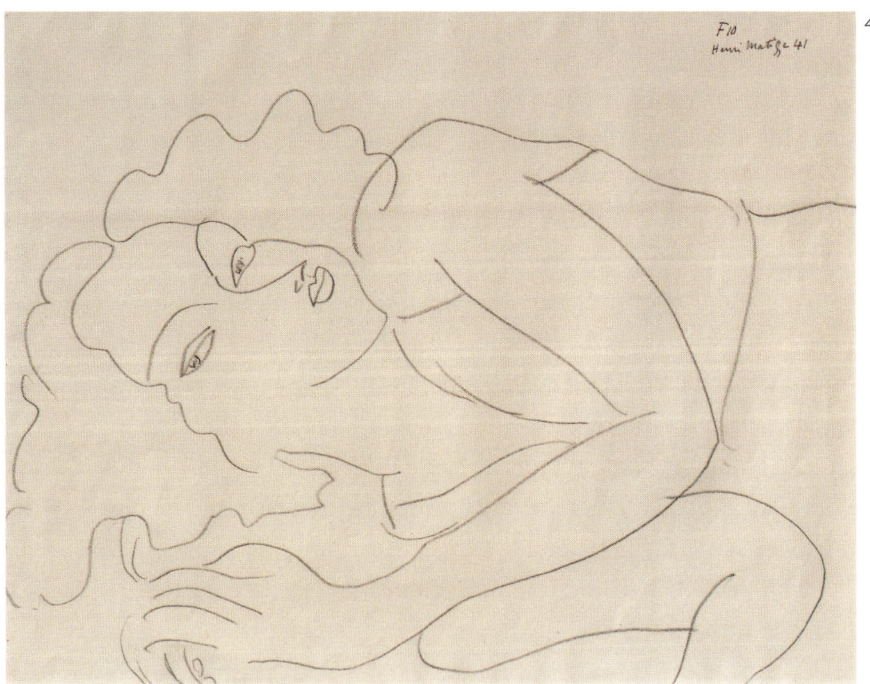

47

F-10. From *Themes and Variations*, 1941, crayon on paper, 40 × 52 cm, Musée de Grenoble

the interplay of colors as his means to construct, bring to life, and stabilize a picture. But in his sixties, even before his surgeries, he returned to his drawing pad with a new vigor, embarking on an elegant pen-and-ink-series on the eternal subject—his eternal subject—of artist and model. By then his fluid lines, with their immense brio and sense of unbroken motion, were like jet stream trails. In his seventies, despite his new physical limitations, that same fluency was still his to call upon, and it delighted him as never before.

Themes and Variations, the collection he boasted about to Pierre and Marguerite, is a volume of 158 drawings produced in seventeen sequences, each beginning with a theme image followed by anywhere from six to nineteen variations. The first drawing, always done in charcoal, is sometimes a still life but much more often a portrait of a languid young woman. Matisse developed each of these patiently over several sessions, often with the charcoal worked and rubbed into clouds of gray tonal passages, shadows, and atmospheres. By contrast the variations that follow are crisp black on white, as clean as a signature. Rapidly executed in thin lines of ink or pencil, the variations flowed from his hand so freely that Matisse said he had made them "like a medium in a trance."

The Swiss artist Paul Klee, whom Matisse admired, once said that a drawing was "a line going for a walk." In his new drawings, Matisse took his line for something more like a stroll, down the curving paths that he particularly loved. Matisse loved coiling lines—arabesques. He had long relied on them to invest his compositions with both buoyancy and tensile strength, the qualities needed to produce "the coordination of controlled rhythms" that was fundamental to his definition of a picture. In *Themes and Variations*, his rolling arabesques express a full-bodied sensuality, not only of the women but even, in the still lifes, of cut flowers and fruit, as though "ripeness" might be a liquid condition coursing through everything, one that Matisse has found just the springing line to convey.

In his later years, Matisse also fulfilled numerous commissions to illustrate works by French poets, including Charles Baudelaire, Pierre de Ronsard, Charles d'Orléans, and Pierre Reverdy. Perhaps the most exquisite of these volumes was *Pasiphaé*, a play by Henry de Montherlant based on the Greek myth of the queen who coupled with a bull and gave birth to the Minotaur. For that book he worked in linocuts, engravings on linoleum. That process produced delicate white lines against a black background, the fine threads slicing the page like fireworks in a nighttime sky.

It wasn't just the external world his drawings were meant to approximate. It was his inner life as well, or rather some conflation of the two. As he said as far back as 1912, "I do not paint a table, but the emotion it produces upon me." He would tell the students at his short-lived academy to inspect closely the model posed before them, but then to "close your eyes and hold the vision, and then do the work with your own sensibility." And in this effort, the swiftness and immediacy of drawing, that quick exchange among eyes, brain, and hand, made it an ideal medium. By the time he reached his seventies, he had settled on drawing as "the purest and most direct translation of my emotion." Or as he would put it, just so, in one of the texts he provided for *Jazz*, "my drawing hand paraphrases my feelings."

One other thing about Matisse's late drawings—they're the last word in pillow talk. As we know, sensuality had always been key to his art. Old age made no difference to that. His presentation of sex as a younger man could be blunt and abrasive, as with his *Blue Nude* from 1906, with her twisted anatomy, or the ropy, distorted women of his bronze sculpture. But his later women, whether painted or drawn, were different. With their pliant poses and sleepy-eyed concupiscence, they were, at least for his heterosexual male audience, a kind of anatomical pastoral, a languid natural paradise. Given the physical disabilities of his last years, it's unlikely that Matisse could indulge much in actual sex, which made his quasi-erotic drawings all the more important as a sublimation of sexual desire. But it wasn't merely Matisse's subject matter that could have a sexual charge. His draftsmanship in old age was sensual in and of itself. In the fluid swells of his late drawings, he perfected an instantly persuasive sign for the erotic. Quite apart from whatever it depicted—a woman, a pomegranate, or a palm leaf—his liquid line was suggestive of arousal and flow.

If at age seventy, war, illness, and the end of his marriage divided his life into a before and after, that may have made it easier in his last years for Matisse to arrive at a new kind of art, the paper cut-outs. Cut paper creations had been produced in China and Egypt for nearly fifteen hundred years, and in Europe for at least three centuries, sometimes in works of phenomenal intricacy. But for Matisse it was new, an art form unlike any he had worked in before. At the same time, the cut-outs weren't entirely a departure from his past. For most of his life Matisse had been intrigued by decorative art of the kind they epitomized. In Bohain, the textile town where he grew up, cut and pinned cloth was everywhere, and the patterned fabric and wallpaper all around him in those days would have provided his first glimpse of the flat imagery basic to the cut-outs. He carried a taste for such things into adulthood when he collected fabrics to use as backdrops in his paintings. Then in his early forties he discovered the two-dimensional intricacies of Islamic tile work, which led him to search out the Moorish monuments of southern Spain, Algeria, and Morocco.

When Matisse first turned to cut paper around age fifty, it was not as an independent art form but as a working tool, a way to plot out projects that he would execute later in some other medium. As early as 1919, working with a dollhouse-style "theater" in a wooden crate, he made paper miniatures as a way to develop sets and costumes for Igor Stravinsky's *The Song of the Nightingale*, a dance choreographed by Léonide Massine for Serge Diaghelev's Ballets Russes.

Eleven years after that he used paper again to arrive at his final composition for *The Dance*, a mural at the private museum in Merion, Pennsylvania, that the brusque and idiosyncratic Dr. Albert Barnes had just built for his immense art collection. That pivotal commission called for Matisse to fill three irregular bays in the ceiling of the museum's long entrance gallery. Dome-shaped lunettes that were linked to one another along the bottom, each was positioned so as to crown a floor-to-ceiling window that rose from the room below. *The Dance* would be by far the largest painting Matisse had attempted to that time, thirty-four feet wide and almost seventeen high at its uppermost curves. So big he had to rent a garage in Nice as a temporary studio, it required endless revisions, on an image so tall he needed a ladder to reach the highest parts. In a photograph from 1930, we see Matisse resorting to a sort of fly-casting draftsmanship. Standing on a low bench, he's tracing a line across the wall-mounted canvas with a charcoal at the end of a bamboo stick longer than a fishing pole. Or a "magician's wand," as his friend the artist André Masson called it.

After a trip to Italy the next year to contemplate Giotto's large frescos in Padua, Matisse returned to Nice with a new idea for how to proceed with this challenging canvas. Why not plot out the image at full scale with pieces of colored paper, much as he had done with his far smaller designs for the ballet?

His assistants could pin those to the canvas at his direction. As his thinking evolved, he could add to, trim, or rearrange his cut paper until he arrived at a composition he was ready to translate into paint. That system allowed Matisse to endlessly experiment. It led him to realize that the very fact that the lunettes confined his figures so tightly could be put to advantage. They could be compression chambers for the bouncing energies of his dancers.

In his final tableau, an airborne ensemble of nearly flat, gray figures leaped and tumbled against a backdrop of wide panels in pink, blue, and black. Every one of them overflowed the bubbles built to contain them. But in February 1932, just as he was preparing to let go of the finished painting, Matisse learned that the lunette measurements he had been working with for nearly two years were off by several inches. Matisse being Matisse, it would not do simply to adjust the first design by a bit here and there. He spent a year producing a substantially new composition, sized to the true dimensions, but with the same explosive vitality.

By the time the final version was ready to ship, cut and pinned paper had become a permanent part of Matisse's working kit. He used it next to plot the changing iterations of *The Pink Nude,* the 1935 painting that Lydia had posed for. Three years later he went back to it again for *Red and Black*, another design collaboration with Massine and the Ballets Russes, then took it up once more to produce magazine covers for *Cahiers d'Art* and *Verve*. But it wasn't until his seventies that he realized at last that cut paper could be more than a device for developing projects in some other medium. He could use it to create works of art in their own right, the kind you sign and frame.

That recognition began in the early 1940s when the Greek-born publisher of *Verve,* an art world impresario who went by the single name Tériade, persuaded Matisse to produce a whole album of cut paper art. Distracted as he was by the war, his lingering family turmoil, and the upward climb that was any given day for a man in his condition, it would take until 1943 before he dug up two old cut-outs he had used years earlier in his curtain design for *Red and Black*. These would become the basis for the first and last plates of *Jazz,* the debut volume of cut-paper pictures he would produce for Tériade.

The first plate for that book would be called *The Clown*. He's a faceless white figure gesturing like a dancer against a black background, with stylized limbs ending in tapering points. All around the edges of his costume, red patches of flame point inward, as though embracing him from behind. Or is it his back he's showing us, turning away in a gesture of farewell, an old man taking his leave from the stage? The flames appear on Matisse's original curtain design, but, interestingly, they also match the inward, licking tongues of fire in the famous woodcarvings of salamanders at Fontainebleau, the royal château near Paris that we know Matisse once visited. Because salamanders were long ago believed to be impervious to fire, they were hallmarks for the sixteenth-century king François I, one of Fontainebleau's succession of builders. He made them emblems of his personal fortitude. Four centuries later, did the durable Matisse quote them as a symbol of his own survival?

The last image of *Jazz* is the one we now know as *The Toboggan*. This

48

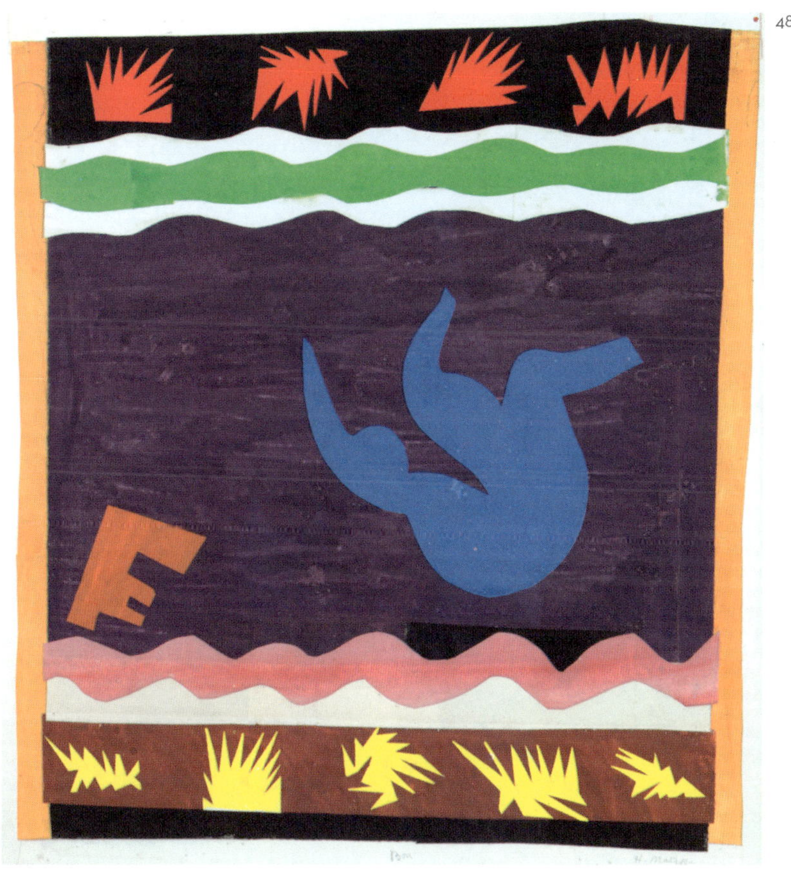

The Toboggan, maquette for plate 20 from *Jazz*, 1943, gouache on paper, cut and pasted, mounted on canvas, 63.2 × 53.3 cm, Musée National d'Art Moderne, Centre Georges Pompidou, Paris

time the featureless silhouette is a plump blue woman tumbling backward in a way that recalls the somersaulting figures in the Barnes *Dance*. Unlike them, she's lost control. A curious *F*-shape in the lower left is her overturned toboggan in the distance. And the flames are back, this time as a frieze along the top and bottom of the image.

What these pictures tell us is that *Jazz* is a book that operates on two emotional wavelengths. One is joyous and buoyant. The palette is gleeful. The mood is fizzy. The acrobats, trapeze artists, and tightrope walkers defy gravity. This is the spirit of a wonderfully intricate image called *The Codomas,* named for a famous family of trapeze artists. Their trapezes, one blue, one white, swing into the picture from the upper corners, while the Codoma brothers themselves appear as wormy yellow quiggles heading toward one another in midair. The net far below them appears as ranks of black boxes sprinkled across a yellow field and spilling into the adjacent zones of green, white, and orange. Vegetal tendrils in violet and blue float all around the edges of the picture, not representations of anything more specific than the spirit of the circus that animates so much of this book.

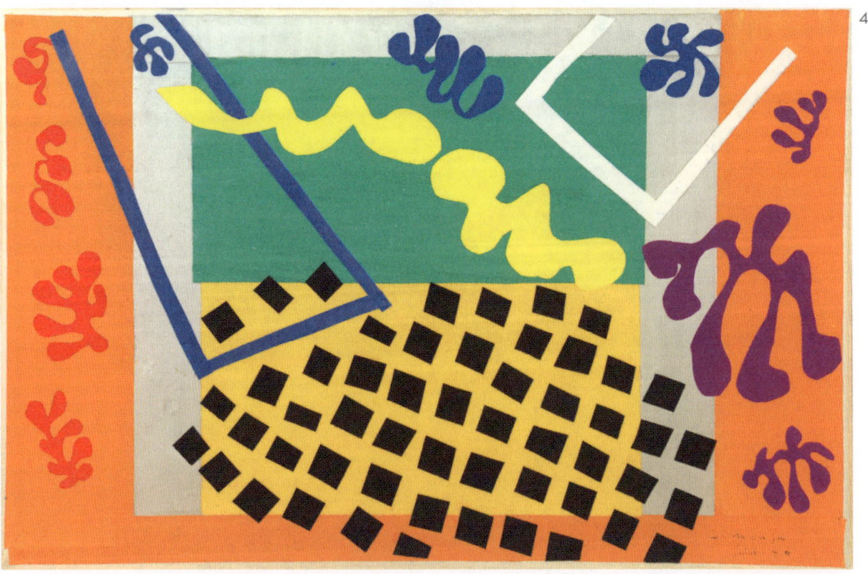
49

The Codomas, maquette for plate 11 from *Jazz*, 1943, gouache on paper, cut and pasted, mounted on canvas, 43.5 × 67.1 cm, Musée National d'Art Moderne, Centre Georges Pompidou, Paris

But among—even within—some of these images of pleasure and playtime, of the circus and the music hall, you find a touch of doubt and even dread. That's when you realize that Matisse has smuggled an anxious counternarrative into this otherwise merry volume—so much so that parts of *Jazz* feel like he's working variations on Death's tart reminder to humanity—*et in Arcadio ego*. "Even in Paradise, there am I."

Surely that's because the book was produced during World War II and just after. Matisse was no Goya, not a man to call up the debris field of wartime. All the same, the anxieties of that moment appear to have infiltrated his pleasure dome. How else should we decode the picture called *Pierrot's Funeral*? If his first *Clown* was a stand-in for himself, the death of this clown might represent the fate Matisse had recently sidestepped, and the comical pageantry of this cortege would be a way for him to make light of his own mortality. Then there's *Destiny*, in which a boxed-in couple cowers before an immense head based on an African carving. And there's the tour de force called *The Knife Thrower*. The title figure is a rippling purple dynamo, a cyclone barely human but somehow still recognizably so. He aims his deadly point at the simplified silhouette of a woman. Is this a metaphor for the artist's fraught former marriage? Possibly. To complicate the matter, an unlikely motif of acanthus leaves, a lighthearted favorite of Matisse, is scattered like parsley across the entire page. If it's there to counteract the tension, there's only so much it can do.

Interspersed among the twenty color plates in *Jazz* are whole pages of text handwritten by Matisse using an oversize coiling script. In a wind-borne penmanship with the bouncing spirit of his drawings—a literal signature style—his words circulate all around the unlined pages. Indifferent to the conventions of linear text, he riffs freely on whatever interests him. In musings that are entirely upbeat, he rhapsodizes about air travel. He explains that he trusts his drawing hand because "when I was training it to serve me I resolved never to let it overshadow my feelings." He states the lifelong principle that will continue to guide his final years: an artist must never be a "prisoner of himself, prisoner of a style, prisoner of a reputation, prisoner of success."

In July 1945, after the final surrender of Germany, Matisse and Lydia returned to Paris for a Matisse family gathering, their first trip back since 1940.

They stayed at his apartment on the rue du Montparnasse, with the others all gathered nearby. His elder son, Jean, and his family were at the old house in Issy. Amélie was living with Marguerite elsewhere in Paris. Pierre flew in from New York.

Of course it was an uncomfortable stay. No one among Matisse's family or friends knew just how to treat Lydia, whose place in the old man's life remained, in the Matisse family way, unspoken. Though Matisse had hoped for a short visit, he was obliged to deal with an unforeseen development. Before fleeing Paris at the start of the war, he had stored a sizable cache of his artworks in a room-size vault at the Bank of France, entrusting Picasso with the key. But over time a leak had developed, resulting in serious water damage to many of the paintings and etchings. The rescue and repair efforts, for the pictures that could be saved at all, would keep him in Paris until November.

Once back in Vence, even before the publication of *Jazz*, Matisse made the first cut-outs he thought of as works in their own right, unlike the images for *Jazz*, which were made to be reproduced on the printed page. Lydia tells us his first was a blot he called *The Lyre*, with slender stripes in its middle that qualified it as a stringed instrument. Then came playful shapes drawn from some wriggly but not always identifiable realm of the plant or animal world. These owe something to Matisse's memories of a 1930 trip to Tahiti, where he had been thrilled by the exotic plant life, the palms and banana trees, the poinsettias and hibiscus. It's the South Pacific he was remembering when he made cut-paper "palmettes"—young palm leaves—and bulbous algae, or long fingers of acanthus leaf or swelling vertebrae based on who knows what exactly. Other forms have the lengthy appendages and inlets of the philodendron plants that filled his apartments. Some he framed as freestanding images, aubergine tendrils of algae against a green backdrop, or a violet palmette against orange. Without being sure of what to do with them, other than enjoy their idiosyncratic charm, he took to attaching them all around the emerging jungle walls of his hillside villa Le Rêve.

As he made more and more of his intriguing new cut-outs, it became plain that they were a way for Matisse to transfer his remaining vitality directly into color, the element that had obsessed him since his twenties. Like Titian with pigment, rubbing paint into the canvas with his fingers, the elderly Matisse could now dig directly into the primal stuff of his dreams. And like the aged Monet seated before an easel at his lily pond, engrossed in his final encounters with light and water, Matisse could now immerse himself in the substance he had spent a lifetime trying to comprehend and unite with.

The cut-outs may also have been therapeutic for Matisse in other ways. No matter that he had experimented with cut paper for years: after his surgeries the act of cutting would have resonated differently for him. Having endured so much at the hands of his surgeons, was he drawn unconsciously to scissors as a way to sublimate the ordeal of their scalpels, to gain control over the very idea of cutting? Now he was the one wielding the sharp edges, using them to produce vitality instead of surrendering it, turning instruments of pain into instruments of pleasure.

What could be more like Matisse than that?

In the spring of 1946, still in Vence, Matisse suffered a long bout of painful intestinal spasms. These may have encouraged the nightmares he began to complain about around that time. His lifelong sleeplessness was already a given. His biographer Hilary Spurling tells us that in these restless hours, attended by night nurses who massaged him and read to him in his semiwakeful, "twilight" state, he began to imagine a new kind of space for his art, one transcending the boundaries of the canvas. Like Monet in the same decade of his life, contemplating the boundless infinitude of his lily pond, Matisse would envision a space, as he put it, "beyond any subject or motif . . . a cosmic space in which I was no more aware of walls than a fish in the sea." This was not unlike the space he first produced in the near abstractions of 1912–1916 like *The Red Studio*, and adapted for the overflowing lunettes of the Barnes *Dance*. Now, in his exhausted late-night reveries, he was drifting back into it once more.

Matisse and Lydia returned to Paris in June of that year, staying this time until the following April. Once again unable to sleep, he went on making cut-outs. First came a long-winged swallow. Deciding it was too interesting to discard, he had his night nurse pin it to a wall to hide a stain. More followed, spilling on to the next wall and over a doorway, with sea creatures joining the birds, flowing like brightly colored kudzu all around his apartment until each wall became a vast canvas.

Or maybe a "cosmic space?" Certainly it was a personal phantasmagoria. Like Goya with his Black Paintings and Monet surrounded by his water lily panels, in old age Matisse encircled himself with projections of his interior life. All across the walls of his homes in Paris, Vence, or Nice, he launched his latest imaginings—"installation art" before the term was coined. The growing assemblage of cut-outs was also a simulacrum of the natural world outdoors, the place he could only now and then visit in his semi-invalid condition. As he would explain, when he could no longer walk in his garden, he made a garden on his own walls.

Something of the same purpose was served by the hundreds of birds that the elderly Matisse kept at home in a room-size aviary and even sometimes traveled with. At their peak population there were roughly three hundred, many of them rare white Milanese pigeons. Matisse had once loved to travel by air. In *Jazz* he described how it offered "a vision of the world that our imagination could not have revealed otherwise." Now that flight was no longer possible for him, his birds were beloved surrogates. The more earthbound he was, the more he needed their wings. This was why he often let them out of their cages. In old age, when he could barely get out of bed, much less board a plane, he could fly vicariously through them. Not just pets, they were avatars.

If the individual cut-outs were still modest in size, Matisse was ready to combine them into something larger, nearer the dimensions of epic canvases like *Dance* or *The Red Studio*. The opportunity to do that came in the summer of 1946. Not long after he and Lydia had returned once more to Paris, he was approached by Zika Ascher, a Czech-born, London-based textile designer who sought out collaborations with major artists and hoped Matisse would agree to be one. After he saw the playful cut-outs all around the rue du Montparnasse apartment he and Matisse arrived at a plan. Why not produce a whole array of them that could be translated into large fabric wall hangings?

Matisse rose to the idea. He even had a notion already of what his theme might be. At seventy-six, with the floodgates of his memory opening, he often found himself dwelling on the past. Lately he was thinking back a great deal on his extended visit to Tahiti in 1930, when he was sixty and at an impasse in his art. The long series of odalisques had largely run its course, but the way forward wasn't clear, so much so that he had effectively stopped painting. In the previous year he had written to Marguerite: "In front of the canvas I have no ideas whatever." He hoped the light of the South Seas would set off something within him, the way the brilliant sun of North Africa and the South of France had excited him as a younger man.

On that score French Polynesia at first disappointed. He was there for nearly three months, after first making stops in New York, Chicago, Los Angeles, and San Francisco. And though he found the light fascinating—a "deep, golden goblet"—the light of Manhattan had enthralled him just as much, "so dry, so crystalline, like no other." And though he loved the beauty and stylishness of the Maori people, he found the French colonials petty, boorish, and tiresome. He made many drawings of the exotic plant life that so intrigued him, but he found himself unable to paint more than a single oil sketch. He later said the beauty of French Polynesia was such it sapped his will to work, but that sounds like an excuse.

What truly excited him were the days he spent diving among the fish and coral reefs in a lagoon off the little atoll of Fakarava. He loved to float in this three-dimensional water world shot through with fiery color, "in an undersea light," as he put it, "which is like a second sky." Years later he recalled how "I would plunge my head into the water, transparent above the absinthe bottom of the lagoon, my eyes wide open." On another day he studied the waters through a glass-bottom boat. In effect it was a "picture plane," like the surface of a canvas, opening onto a view of an endless depth. Again like Monet, he was discovering through water a limitless, all-encompassing space, one that felt free of conventional spatial coordinates.

His encounter with French Polynesia did nothing to bring Matisse back to painting. Except for a few pictures completed in 1934, it would be another five years before he returned in earnest to his easel to produce *The Pink Nude*. But the experience lingered in some liquid compartment of memory. In his midseventies it resurfaced in his imagination, dredged out of oblivion and embellished by time, returning him to the waters of Fakarava and the greenery of Tahiti. Just as the nineteenth-century French painter Corot produced his limpid scenes of Lake Maggiore a full two decades after his final trip to Italy, Matisse would make new works from the residue of old recollections, setting them within the indistinct space he had begun to intuit during those restless nights at Le Rêve.

As a first example, he had already included among the final plates of the still-to-be-published *Jazz* three semi-abstract cut-outs he called "Lagoons." Now, in his collaboration with Ascher, he would return once more to Tahiti. His wall hangings would be two rectangles of beige linen, each more than twelve feet wide. Both would be silk-screened with dozens of white silhouettes of birds, plants, and sea life, all afloat within undulating white borders.

He would call one *Oceania, the Sky* and the other *Oceania, the Sea.* Perhaps to signify the mingling of sky and sea he had experienced in Tahiti, a few birds appear unexpectedly in the *Sea* tapestry. Some fish also frolic in the *Sky.* The world was coming undone again, but this time in a good way.

The Ascher textiles, which came to market in 1948 in a signed and numbered edition of thirty, would help Matisse to see that any single cut-out could be an element within a much larger array, and that the dancing interplay of those forms could spread out into a whole field of fluttering activity, much as they did across the walls of his homes. These all-over compositions could have no end of visual incidents but at the same time no central image—a bit like wallpaper, no doubt, but much more interesting. Soon he designed a pair of thin woven tapestries for the state-owned Gobelin textile works. Called *Polynesia, the Sky* and *Polynesia, the Sea,* they were on a checkerboard ground of dark and light blue squares. By then he had also been making smaller compositions, mostly of vegetal forms on backgrounds of eye-popping color, plasmic curves wiggling on panels of crimson, pink, green, and violet.

Some months before the wall hangings appeared, in September 1947, *Jazz* was published at last, both as an album of twenty color plates, issued in an edition of one hundred, and as 250 copies of a book that included Matisse's texts. However modest its first print run—there would be many more—it was a considerable succès d'estime. Over time it would be recognized as one of the greatest, most radical, and delightful artist's books of the twentieth century. It was also a first announcement that in old age Matisse had embarked on a thoroughly new line of pursuit.

But *Jazz* was also crucial to the evolution of the cut-outs because Matisse wasn't happy with it. He even called it, unfairly, "a complete flop," despite the fact that it had been meticulously produced. Using the expensive and time-consuming process known as pochoir, craftsmen had hand-cut stencils to match each form of the cut-paper originals—the maquettes—then applied the printer's inks with brushes, not the customary rollers or spray guns. And to ensure that the colors on the page matched the originals as closely as possible, the maquettes had been coated in Matisse's studio with opaque watercolor paints, called gouache, that were produced by the same company whose inks would be used by the printers.

Even so, and with reason, Matisse felt the maquettes had a vitality, a physical presence, that was lost in reproduction. To get a second opinion he enlisted an old friend, André Rouveyre. In his youth, he had studied beside Matisse in the atelier of the symbolist painter Gustave Moreau. Knowing that Rouveyre had seen the paper originals, Matisse asked him to look into a Paris exhibition of the stencil-printed plates. After his visit Rouveyre agreed. The force of the maquettes had somehow trickled away in the prints. That was enough for Matisse. He wrote back, "I know these things must stay as they are, originals."

By that time he was producing new "originals" at a constant pace, using the working method he had developed for the Barnes *Dance*. Studio assistants brushed sheets of white paper with gouache in colors of his choosing, let them dry, then brought them to his bed or wheelchair to cut. Though he sometimes made preliminary sketches of whatever forms he had in mind, he never drew on the coated paper itself. He wanted his cutting to be spontaneous and instinctive. He called his book *Jazz* to draw attention to his improvisational style of cutting. It was important to him to feel himself carving directly into pure color, as though it were a substance that could be taken in hand the way Michelangelo had hammered stone. Smaller cut-outs Matisse arranged by hand and pinned lightly to a lapboard, where he could enjoy their fluttering movements. His assistants would attach larger works piece by piece to a wall. To keep things moving they wore pincushions on their wrists.

You can get a sense of Matisse's great dexterity in some color film footage he sat for in the 1950s that's available on YouTube. There we see him suavely snipping away at one of his paper forms, a veritable Henri Scissorhands. And though we know that his infirmities made his work difficult, the irony of that film is that he makes it all look easy.

Over the years Matisse had often worried that what he did in his art, summarizing the world with a few brushstrokes or broad areas of color, might seem to the public too easy. To prove that every picture was a struggle, he hit upon the idea of photographing the evolving stages of his *Large Pink Nude*. This served his purpose so well he did the same with several subsequent paintings. For his first gallery show after the war every canvas was surrounded by a suite of framed black-and-white photos charting its progress over time.

All the same, with the cut-outs he worked with what really did look like an effortless virtuosity, what he called "the purity of my scissor stroke." By his own description, in the preliminary drawings he made for his Barnes murals in the early 1930s, Matisse had learned not simply to sketch a dancer's movements but to internalize them, so that his pen imitated some leaping impulse within himself. Two decades later, though age had made his legs unsteady, that internal guidance system was still available to his hands. On YouTube you see him slicing smoothly through the paper, rotating the scrap with his free hand until some pulsing form emerges in a frictionless glide, through a gesture he once described as "one movement linking line with color, contour with surface." Though we know years of practice lay behind that miracle of prestidigitation, in its combination of firm guidance and spontaneity it seems magical all the same. Awed by Matisse's command of his tools, one afternoon Picasso and his companion Françoise Gilot brought a tribute to his bedside—an actual magician. Two masters of the sleight of hand; it seemed only right they should meet.

It was after the war that Matisse renewed his wary attachment to Picasso, a complex friendship that had weathered four decades of parry and thrust, borrowings and critiques, sometimes affectionate, sometimes not. After they reconnected, Picasso became an important friend in Matisse's last years. Having spent the war in Paris, by 1946 Picasso was living in a rented house in Golfe-Juan, a harbor town not far from Cannes and within driving distance of Matisse's villa in Vence. With him was Gilot, a twenty-four-year-old artist he had met three years earlier.

By that time Picasso was very ready to reach out again to Matisse, his sometime mentor, sometime follower—both roles unacknowledged by both men—and his only real equal. In her 1990 memoir *Matisse and Picasso: A Friendship in Art*, Gilot recalls that on the morning of their first visit to Matisse, when her cohabitation with Picasso was still in its first tricky days, she became a pawn in their envious dealings. Picasso advised her to wear a blouse of mauve silk with almond green slacks. "He will like such colors together," he told her. Apparently he did, because not long after they arrived at Le Rêve, Matisse told Gilot he might like her to pose for a portrait. Then he turned to Picasso and asked, "You could bring her back for some sittings, couldn't you?" A bemused Gilot tells us Picasso squirmed. The old friends were still old rivals, just as they had been forty years earlier in Paris, vying for the approval and patronage of Gertrude Stein and her brother Leo.

In 1946, the first year that Picasso and Gilot were living nearby, their visits to Le Rêve were limited by Matisse's frequent spells of weakness and ill health, when everyone but Lydia and his nurses were kept away. The next year was different. In May 1947 they returned to Golfe-Juan, where they remained into the winter while Picasso pursued his new interest in ceramics at the nearby Madoura pottery works. Gilot found Matisse delightful, funny, and mischievous. He had an ever-ready supply of the painkillers he called "happiness pills." To keep his pencils and drawing pads in easy reach he stationed a small rotating bookshelf next to his bed. It would soon hold a photo of Picasso, a gesture that greatly moved the aging Spaniard.

In the first aftermath of his 1940 surgeries, Matisse was usually too weak to support himself in front of an easel. A few years later, having completed just a few canvases, he told Marguerite he was through with painting altogether. From now on he would devote himself to decorative arts. That was a premature judgment. There would be times during his seventies when he was strong enough to resume painting and he did, to spectacular effect, especially in his last great series of canvases, the "Vence interiors."

Begun in 1946, these pictures are chamber operas, enclosed, intimate, and forceful. Vivid reimaginings of his workrooms at Le Rêve, they reopen the majestic spillways of color from the great canvases of his forties, like *The Red Studio*, *View of Notre Dame*, and *The Blue Window*. In new pictures like *The Black Fern* and *The Pineapple*, wide swathes of pulsing color flatten and obliterate conventional space. Whole rooms are absorbed into the colors that blanket them.

Interior with Egyptian Curtain is one of those, built along the lines of his early cut-outs of vegetal shapes on adjoining panels of solid color, a boxy "zone construction" that points up that the picture is a fiction, a design, however much it may be based on a real scene. This picture has three zones. Down the right side there's a length of black curtain, boldly patterned in red, green, white, and yellow. To its left is a large window filled by the bristling fronds of a palm tree, a starburst of vegetation in stripes of green, black, and yellow. In the rectangle below is an almost conventional still life, a white bowl of pomegranates on a pink-and-ocher tray. Is that more realistic bowl of fruit meant to be a reminder of the palpable world in this deeply imagined setting, one in which the real tree outside the window is barely distinguishable from the patterns on the curtain you see next to it? To double down on the ambiguities, the black of that curtain, as potent as any in Velázquez, has invaded the walls and window frame, where it's bordered by a ghostly filament of white. As the painting's dominant color, black insists that the scene is unreal, then makes every other color come to terms with the unreality it lays down.

In these Vence interiors Matisse often uses black to blur the border between the "real" world, already distilled by him to a decorative fiction, and its representations, mostly prints and paintings we see on the walls of the

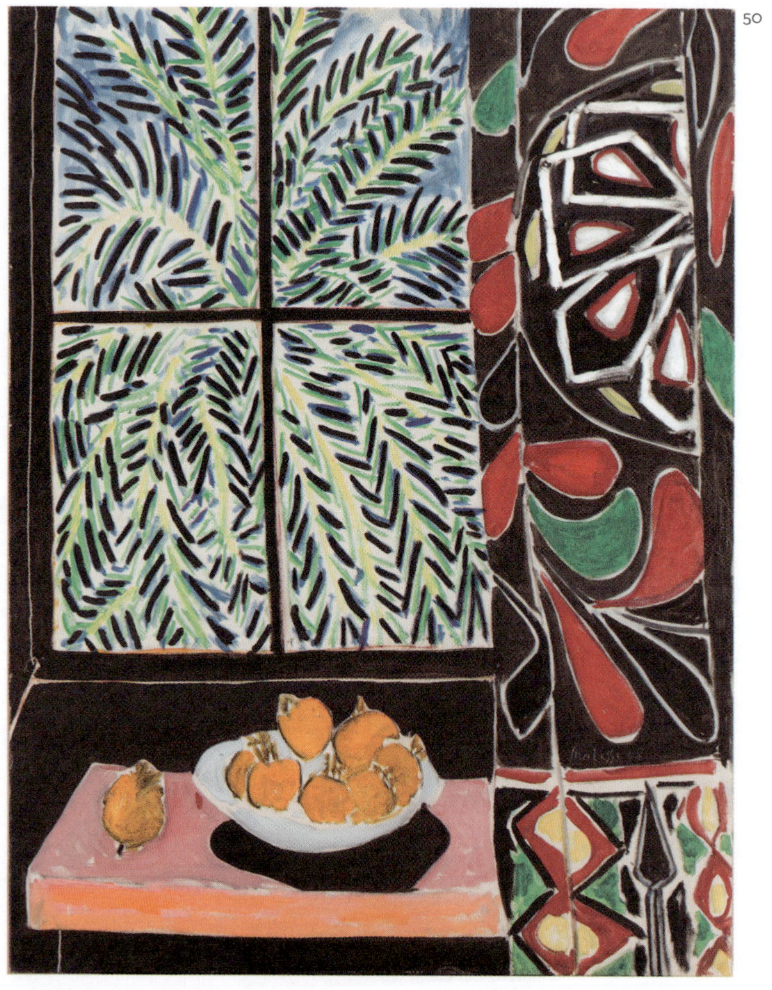
50

Interior with Egyptian Curtain, 1948, oil on canvas, 116.2 × 89.2 cm, The Phillips Collection, Washington, D.C.

studio he is showing us, pictures within a picture that are fictions from the get-go. Is that a window in the corner of *Interior in Yellow and Blue*, giving onto a view of black vegetation? Or is it one of the large ink drawings Matisse made in the same years? Tables and chairs, meanwhile, are just open drawings, transparent black outlines that colored backgrounds show through, as they had in *The Red Studio* forty-five years earlier. Faces are blank ovals, filled in by the color of the room they inhabit.

And as so often with the elderly Matisse, memory is its own fluctuating

51

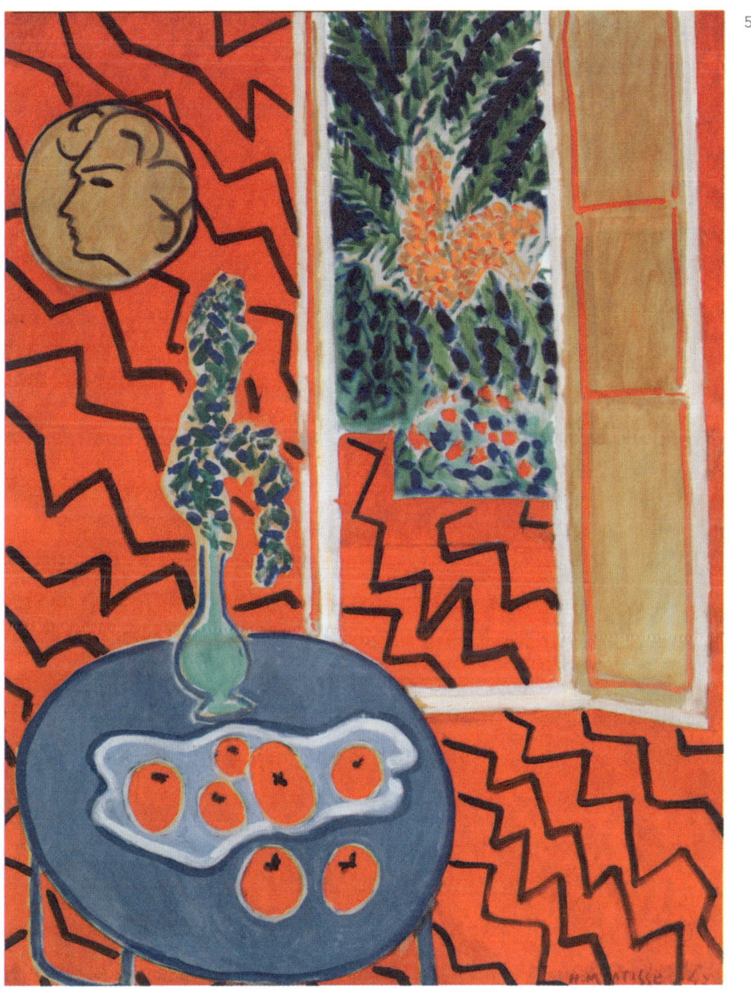

Red Interior: Still Life on a Blue Table, 1947, oil on canvas, 116 × 89 cm, Kunstsammlung Nordrhein-Westfalen, Dusseldorf

medium, a flexible transit zone between reality and fantasy. This is why, in several of these canvases, we see the same token of the past. It's an image of Matisse's first sculpture, a circular clay medallion of Camille Joblaud, his long-ago companion who gave birth to Marguerite. A simple profile head, it had been kept for decades by one of his oldest friends and first collectors, Dr. Léon Vassaux. When Vassaux brought it with him on a visit to Le Rêve, Matisse hung it on a wall, which is where it appears in some of the Vence interiors.

In the most electrifying of these pictures, *Red Interior: Still Life on a Blue Table*, Joblaud's head presides like a beacon from her little circle, a household deity in a room of a uniformly brilliant red. (You think of Matisse, commanding his domestic universe from his bed.) This crimson sea is swept by a surf of jagged lines that furrow it like black lightning. Forces no mere household could confine, both the red pigment and the wild wires that traverse it spill out an open doorway and into the garden beyond. Is this a signal from the ever-agitated artist that he's still running away from home?

Matisse knew that these pictures, done after he thought easel painting was over for him, were one more proof the old man was still alive. When they were exhibited for the first time, at Pierre's Manhattan gallery, no less a critic than Clement Greenberg, then the most influential voice in the American discourse around modern art, decided they were evidence that Matisse was painting "as well as he ever has painted before, and, in some respects perhaps, even better." It was an understatement.

In the summer of 1947, just before the publication of *Jazz*, Matisse took what turned out to be the first step in the project he would one day call "his masterpiece." Certainly it would be his *Gesamtkunstwerk*, his total work of art. The Chapel of the Rosary in Vence would be both a quintessence of his lifelong obsession with color, line, and light, and at the same time unlike anything he had ever done. It would be an entire building, and more than that a sacred space, one that this never very religious artist would design from the ground up. The white marble floor and the stained glass windows, the immense wall drawings, the blunt stone altar, the candlesticks, holy water fonts, and priestly vestments, plus the patterned tile roof and the rooftop cross—every element would be his creation.

The germ of the idea was brought to him that summer by a Dominican nun, Sister Jacques-Marie. Matisse had first met her in Nice five years earlier, when she was Monique Bourgeois, a twenty-one-year-old woman still in secular life. She had arrived at his door in reply to an ad he had posted at a nearby agency for "a young and pretty night nurse." Though she liked to draw and paint, at the time she had never heard of Matisse, and when she saw his work on the walls of his rambling apartment she freely admitted that she found the colors lovely but the forms "horrible." He professed to be delighted by her honesty. He was plainly pleased with her appearance, because he soon persuaded her to pose for him in a low-cut gown with her arms bared, though otherwise fully dressed.

To his great regret, Mlle Bourgeois would not remain for long as his model. Within two years she had entered a Dominican convent in southwestern France. In September 1946, having taken her vows, she returned to Vence as a nursing sister at the Foyer Lacordaire, a Dominican convalescent home where she had been a patient herself the year before, recovering from tuberculosis. The Foyer happened to be just across the road from Le Rêve, the house where Matisse and Lydia had sought refuge from wartime Nice. Though there could be no question of the new sister posing again for the old man, they renewed their affectionate acquaintance. In a letter to his friend Rouveyre, the never-say-never Matisse said he had almost called their "friendly teasing" a *fleur-tation*, "because what happens between us is as if we are throwing flowers—rose petals at each other."

At that time, the twenty Dominican sisters of Vence were holding services in an old garage with a leaking roof, catching the overflow in slop buckets, all the while longing for a real chapel. Sister Jacques knew this on the August night in 1947 when she was keeping vigil at the deathbed of an elderly nun, one who had promised to assist the chapel project from heaven. As she prayed for the nun's soul, Sister Jacques made a watercolor sketch of a stained glass window depicting the Assumption of the Virgin. When she showed it later to Matisse, something she often did with her drawings, he said he could help her translate it into a real window for an eventual chapel. In no time he hit upon the perfect person to design this place—Henri Matisse.

For a while the idea languished. It was a month before Sister Jacques brought his offer to the Mother General and the Prioress General, the superiors of her order. Neither had heard of Matisse or took any interest in his services. There things stood until the arrival of Brother Louis-Bertrand Rayssiguier, a twenty-seven-year-old Dominican friar based in Paris. A bout of pleurisy had landed him in a nearby Dominican convalescent home, from where he paid a visit to the Foyer Lacordaire. Raysigguier had a philosophy degree from the Sorbonne, an interest in contemporary art, and some small experience in architecture. He knew very well who Matisse was and wanted to meet him. Too bad Matisse hated uninvited arrivals. But the Mother Superior, who still scoffed at the idea of a new chapel, was willing to suggest how the novice friar might get a foot in the door: send the artist a note introducing himself as architect of this proposed project and say he wanted to discuss the stained glass.

That ploy worked even better than expected. During their first conversation, on December 4, the pair leaped in no time from discussion of a single window to visions of an entire chapel that could be built on a site the nuns already owned next to the Foyer. As for the window, at the Brother's urging—it didn't take much—it would be designed by Matisse, not Sister Jacques, who in any case wanted no part of the difficulties of translating her drawing into glass. Things moved quickly. At their next meeting, just five days later, Rayssiguier arrived with a preliminary layout of the chapel. Matisse asked him to proceed at once to a three-dimensional model, which Sister Jacques could produce. And the money for this ambitious project? Matisse assured everyone they would find it somehow.

Though any chapel would still require the permission of church authorities, Matisse soon had an important ally in Father Marie-Alain Couturier, editor of the journal *L'Art Sacré*. An urbane, Paris-based Dominican friar, he was a leading figure in the campaign to bring to sacred spaces the work of modern artists, not just Catholic artists but also Jews, Communists, and nonbelievers of every stripe. He had already enlisted Pierre Bonnard, Fernand Léger, and Marc Chagall, later to be joined by Matisse, to decorate a remarkable new church in the French Alpine town of Plateau d'Assy, one that would become a flash point in an ongoing culture war between liberals and conservatives in both the French church and the Vatican. Before his death in 1954 he would also pave the way for Le Corbusier to produce his chapel at Ronchamps, one of the great buildings of the twentieth century. The prospect of an entire chapel by Matisse delighted him. Knowing well how to navigate every byway in the church hierarchy, he quickly secured the necessary approvals, including the grudging assent of the Dominican nuns.

It wasn't long before news of what Matisse was up to reached the mostly left-wing Paris art world, which was both scandalized and amused. (*He's doing a chapel!*) As for Catholic traditionalists, they were merely scandalized. (*He paints nudes!*) Picasso, himself about to become a prize ornament of the French Communist Party, asked Matisse why he didn't design a produce market instead. Matisse sniffed that his greens were already greener than any pears and his oranges were more orange than any pumpkin and went on with his work.

For the next four years Matisse was consumed by his church in progress. Early in 1949, he even gave up Le Rêve and moved back to La Régina, the hotel where his spacious, high-ceilinged studios approximated the planned dimensions of the chapel. Soon the walls were covered with full-scale maquettes of the stained glass windows. To make sure he kept tight control over the project Matisse refused a suggestion to bring on Le Corbusier as collaborating architect. Why cede an ounce of authority to the lordly Corbu? Instead he turned to a distinguished but much less imposing friend, Auguste Perret, who would merely sign the blueprints, with a second architect brought on to supervise the construction phase. Matisse had no interest in making an architectural statement. As he put it, his goal was simply "to insert space and light into an edifice which itself is of no particular interest."

The chapel served Matisse as much as he served it. In early 1948, when he began work in earnest, *Jazz* was behind him and his series of Vence interiors was drawing to a close. This was the perfect moment to take on a new challenge, both to reignite his creative powers and to prove that he could. Just as the Barnes commission had revitalized him when the odalisques had reached a dead end, the chapel recharged him. And especially after his move back to La Régina, the project amped up the life-sustaining energies all around him, a ceaseless bustle of assistants producing a constant flow of cutouts. Long before Andy Warhol came along, Matisse took to calling the apartment his "factory," with its three busy studios that he would move among in a "taxi bed" on wheels.

Before that year was out, his plans for the chapel were largely in place. His layout called for an interior shaped something like a truncated *L*, about fifty feet long but just twenty wide. The shorter expanse would contain an alcove of wooden pews reserved for the Dominican sisters. The longer would accommodate the lay congregation in removable wooden chairs. After much experimentation, Matisse also arrived at a final scheme for the stained glass.

He would combine just three colors—blue, yellow, and emerald green—in three sets of lancet windows. Two sets would share the same design, a suite of slender arched windows separated by thin panels of white masonry that would function visually as "stalks," appearing to sprout colored leaves in the glass on either side. One array of windows would appear behind the pews. The second would line a wall on the longer stretch of the *L*, shedding colored light across the space of the lay congregation.

The third window, actually a single pair of arched windows, Matisse would call *The Tree of Life*. It would be placed in the west wall behind a simple but very powerful marble altar, a rectangular tabletop on a silo pedestal, all resting on a shallow stairstep platform of two semicircular tiers. In a marked departure from tradition, the altar would be placed diagonally, at the bend of the *L*, to face both the nuns and the lay worshippers. In contrast to the orderly regiment of the other windows, *The Tree of Life* would have a much freer pattern of yellow blossoms and blue succulents modeled after local prickly pear figs. These would be scattered across green glass shaped to resemble a long curtain hanging before a yellow background.

The windowless north and east walls would hold the chapel's other major

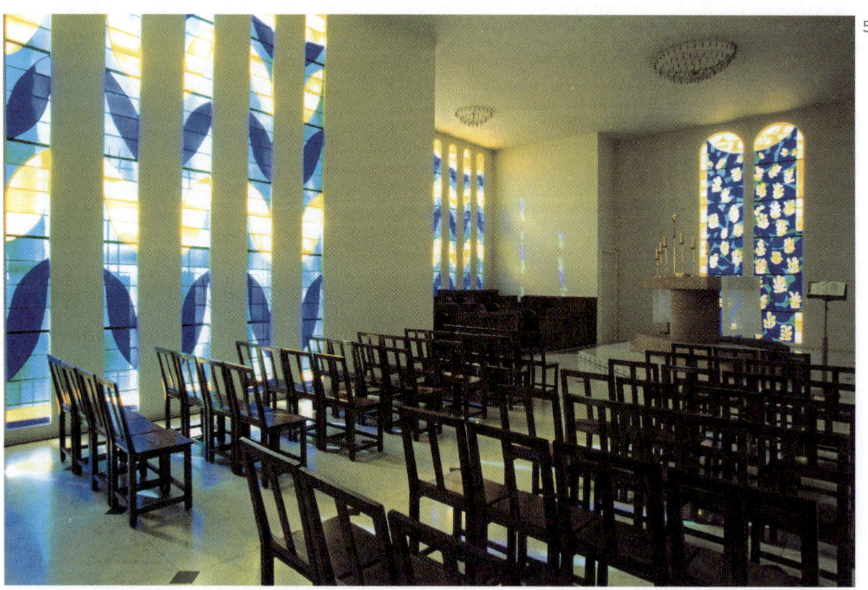
52

Chapel of the Rosary dedicated in 1951, with *The Tree of Life* at right, Vence, France

decorative elements, three large drawings in black ink on white ceramic tile. Closest to the altar would be an immense standing figure of Saint Dominic, fifteen and a half feet tall when completed. A deliberately oversize hand emerges from his robe, with long flowing fingers that cradle a copy of the Gospels.

For the wide expanse of wall to Dominic's right, Matisse planned a full-length figure of the Virgin with a Christ child old enough to stand on her lap. In the completed drawing there are puffy forms all around them that suggest clouds but are stylized flowers. In the upper left corner, in slender uppercase letters, is the word *ave*, meaning "hail." The first word the Angel of the Annunciation spoke to Mary, it's also an acronym for the three tenets of Dominican preaching—*Amor, Verbum, Eternitas*—Love, the Word, Eternity.

The third and much more abrasive drawing takes up most of the east wall behind the congregation, where a turbulent sequence of figures drawn in featureless outline depict the Stations of the Cross in fourteen numbered scenes. While Saint Dominic and the Virgin are beautifully simplified, and all the more powerful for that, the Stations are a hectic scrawl, a bent pipe-cleaner pantomime in which Matisse so abbreviates the episodes of Christ's Passion that some of them are barely legible.

Though it's possible to see in those drawings an echo of the graffiti-style art being made after the war by Jean Dubuffet—and even a forecast of Cy Twombly and Jean-Michel Basquiat—the Stations still represent a failure on the part of Matisse, the lifelong artist of the pleasure principle, to develop a sufficient language for suffering. Whatever anxieties were embedded throughout *Jazz*, most of them were disguised within deceptively lighthearted images. No such subterfuge would work to represent the tragic drama of Christ's Passion, but it appears Matisse never arrived at any clear idea of what would.

He had always been an unlikely church designer. Catholic by upbringing, for most of his adult life he was so dismissive of religion that his daughter, Marguerite, was apparently baptized without his knowledge. Perhaps both his sons as well. And at no point in middle age did he sound like a man much concerned about the eventual whereabouts of his immortal soul. But in old age his sentiments seem to have shifted a bit, even before taking on the chapel. In one of the written texts of *Jazz* he offered a brief account of the ambivalent faith of his later life. "Do I believe in God?" he asked. "Yes, when I am working. When I am submissive and modest, I feel myself to be greatly helped by someone who causes me to do things that exceed my capabilities." Even then he added an escape clause. "However, I cannot acknowledge *him* because it is as if I were to find myself before a conjuror whose sleight of hand eludes me."

This was not exactly the testament of a pious Catholic. More like the opening gambit of an agnostic's entente cordiale with some numinous Creator. When Sister Jacques reminded him in a letter that there is no salvation outside the church and its sacraments, Matisse shot back: "I haven't needed the sacraments to glorify the name of God throughout my life. I went as far as Tahiti to admire the beauty of the light He created so I could share it with others through my work."

Yet in his last years, as he threw himself into completing the chapel, he spoke often about a God who somehow supervised his art. "Basically I do nothing myself," he explained, "as it is God who guides my hand." Matisse also developed an uncharacteristic concern for visual orthodoxy. Because he wanted to be sure that the imagery of his chapel should not depart too far from Church tradition, however much it would offend conservative taste, he looked often to Father Couturier for advice on Catholic iconography. For his Stations of the Cross, he wanted to know what was acceptable in representing the Veil of Veronica, the handkerchief that bore a miraculous image of Christ after he used it to wipe his face on the route to Golgotha. Could he show Christ's impression on that cloth with his eyes closed? This was a delicate matter, because it would be the only detailed face in any of the chapel drawings. On every other figure the head was a featureless outline. Then there was his image of the Virgin and Child. Could he represent Christ not as an infant but as a boy of around three or four, standing upright on his mother's lap, old enough to comprehend the sacrifice he was called upon to make? Could the child's arms spread out from his sides to suggest both his embrace of the world and the cross he would hang upon?

The answers from Couturier were always yes, as you might expect from a man who believed the best art was "the fruit of uncontrollable spontaneities." As for Brother Rayssiguier, if anything he pushed for even more departures from convention. Why not show the Virgin in modern dress? Matisse wouldn't hear of it. He didn't want "a fashion print." Well, why not at least represent her without a halo, perhaps even without the Christ child? Matisse scoffed. "You'd need an explanatory note," he said, to tell visitors who this woman was. "We mustn't completely disconcert the faithful."

Given his regular exchanges with men of the cloth, maybe it comes as no surprise that one day Matisse thought nothing of writing his daughter a letter that included the phrase "if such is the will of God." Her father's tilt into piety left Marguerite amused and puzzled. "When one remembers what you used to think about religion," she needled him, "one has trouble seeing you surrounded by white robes now." Lydia joked to Rayssiguier, "Matisse is starting to convert."

Not quite. To the end he refused the sacraments. The man who would design a lovely Moroccan-style wooden door for the confessional in his chapel refused to enter that little room himself, at least not for the purpose it was designed for. No doubt after a complicated life there were things he didn't want to talk about, but without confession and absolution, the cleansing of the soul, there was no question of his taking communion. In any event, he showed no interest in kneeling to accept the Host, not even at an altar of his own design.

Theological fine points weren't the only problems that kept the "Great Insomniac" awake at night. Financing to keep the project moving forward was a constant struggle. A proposed deluxe picture book went nowhere, but funds came in from ticket sales for a Matisse retrospective in Japan, from occasional donors, and from Matisse himself, money he raised by selling off his own work, despite the fact he took no design fee for the chapel.

He also had literally material concerns. He agonized over the ceramic tiles, searching for someone who could make the large tiles he insisted upon, to minimize the inevitable gridwork pattern beneath his drawings. Picasso recommended his trusted ceramicists, Suzanne and Georges Ramié in Vallauris, the small coastal town where he had recently moved to stay close to their workshop. Matisse gave them the job, but their first attempt at firing the tiles, in June 1949, was a failure. Their second, in August, was a disaster. Three-quarters of the two hundred tiles cracked in the kiln. Matisse accepted it with surprising equanimity. "Life is short," he once said. "Without problems it would go by too quickly." It took a third try, in November, for the Ramiés to produce enough usable tiles for Matisse to at last set them on the floor of his studio and start laying down his drawings. Having modified each drawing dozens of times, refining and simplifying them until he could, literally, sketch them with his eyes closed, he applied the images quickly with another of his "magic wands," a long pole with a loaded brush attached to its end.

With the windows, the main problem was the yellow glass he wanted. It had to be just right, a lemon yellow, not too bright, and frosted to the perfect degree of translucence. Finally, a window maker in Paris was settled upon, which required Matisse to relocate there for four months in 1950 to personally oversee production. He wrote to Couturier: "You know I have given everything to this chapel, and it will all have been useless if it isn't *perfect*."

As he wrapped up his work on the chapel, the priestly vestments, called chasubles, were the last piece of the puzzle—moving pieces, because Matisse expected that as the priest celebrated Mass, his multicolored robes would animate the pristine white chapel just as much as the colored sunlight pooling on the walls and floor. In late 1950 and early '51, he produced six sets, in red, green, violet, rose, black, and white, each matched to a different season of the liturgical calendar. They were hand stitched just in time for the formal dedication of the chapel on June 25, 1951, in a ceremony led by the archbishop of Nice. The event drew hundreds of people—nuns and clerics, locals, tourists, reporters, and newsreel photographers, but the man they most hoped to see sent his regrets. Citing poor health, Matisse dispatched his son Pierre to represent him and issued a formal statement that included his final judgment on his foray into sacred space. "Despite all its imperfections, I consider it my masterpiece."

Matisse had no end of reasons to be pleased with what he had accomplished. Whatever one might think of the Stations, the Vence chapel is in every other respect a unique point on the map of modernism, joining a monastic asceticism to a subtle acknowledgment of earthly pleasures. While the stained glass admits the gifts of Creation—light, color, and the forms of nature—the austere murals bring forward the realm of intangible faith, allowing visitors to contemplate these joint but differing affirmations of God. And even taken simply as a secular visual pleasure, an installation artwork of shifting light and color, this spare white space speckled with dancing reflections can delight believers and nonbelievers alike.

Just not, as expected, the Catholic conservatives of his day, who launched the predictable charges of sacrilege at the by-now very famous new chapel. The Jesuit priest who used a radio address to claim modern art had brought "monsters back into the Church" was typical. For different reasons Picasso is supposed to have said, though not to his old friend's face, that the mostly white interior reminded him of a bathroom. Matisse would not have cared.

He knew the chapel was a sweet valedictory on the terms that mattered to him most. Just as his cut-outs had made it possible for him to grab hold of color, this place had allowed him, at the end of his life, to at last to take possession of light itself. And if light should be a salient attribute of God? So much the better.

Though construction on the chapel lingered into 1951, Matisse's contributions were mostly done the year before. In June 1950, he wrote to Father Couturier, "The Chapel is finished as far as my work is concerned: in other words, I can die." Another premature conclusion, and not just because Matisse would go on for months refining the chasubles. He still had more than four years to live. In that time, he would share first prize at the Venice Biennale and be coronated in New York with a crowded retrospective at the Museum of Modern Art. He would also produce some of the most powerful art of his career.

Stung by French critics who dismissed his cut-outs as a retreat into child's play, Matisse began the new decade intent on proving that cut paper could be a medium as complex as any painting. For the first time he began using it for large figurative works, the centuries-old tradition that had consumed him for most of his life. The first was *Zulma*, a full-length view of a statuesque woman. Her body is mostly flat, like the green and yellow background that frames her, but she's placed in a shallow recessional space, perched between two tables, a hand resting on each—a daring combination of flatness with pockets of linear perspective of the kind he had begun to experiment with as far back as *The Painter's Family*, an ensemble portrait of 1911.

Like an odalisque, *Zulma* wears a blue dressing gown that's fallen open from top to bottom to reveal her naked body, which is represented by a length of orange paper on which her legs, vagina, and breasts are lightly outlined in charcoal. That orange column terminates in the featureless trapezoid that represents her face, surrounded by a round helmet of black hair. Nearly seven feet, eight inches tall, this is a picture that could be placed against any of Matisse's most ambitious portraits on canvas. That said, by sketching in her genitals but not her face, does Matisse not deprive this stately woman of any identity other than her sex? At the age of eighty-one, he's still the white-coated professor of desire we see in that telling photo by Brassaï, eyes riveted on the erogenous zone.

Next came *Creole Dancer*, a mad detonation of form and color that owed something to his memories of Katherine Dunham, the great Black American dancer and choreographer who brought Caribbean rhythms to a receptive Paris after the war. As much a firecracker as a woman, the green body is set along a precarious diagonal and across a background of rectangles in orange, red, yellow, black, and pinkish-purple. Her spindly white skirt and headdress are so explosively designed that at first glance you could easily mistake her for an actual fireworks display. Then you notice, in the upper right-hand corner, the hurtling green pellet of her head, untethered to the rest of her, making her something like a circus clown shot from her own cannon.

Creole Dancer is a banner of life, all flags flying. Elsewhere, Matisse admits

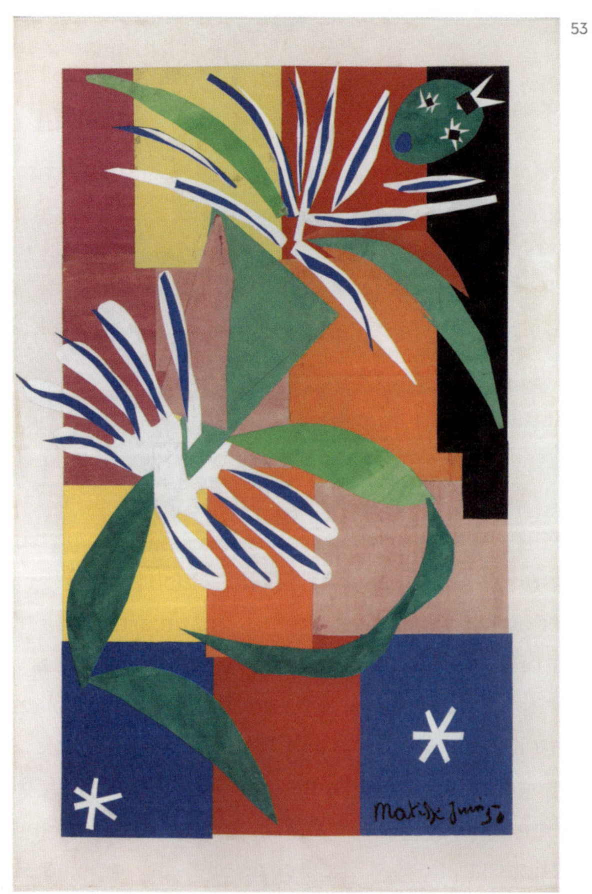

53

Creole Dancer, 1950, gouache on paper, cut and pasted, mounted on canvas, 205 × 120 cm, Musée Matisse, Nice, France

to a looming awareness of death. *The Thousand and One Nights*, again from 1950, grows out of the tale of Scheherazade, who endlessly postponed her execution at the hands of an indifferent king by tempting him each night with a story she promised to finish the next. Matisse doesn't retell her story. He simply evokes it in a series of colored panels overlain with images of lamps, leaves, starbursts, and abstract forms, bordered along the top and bottom by double rows of hearts. But surely in his madly productive final years, the elderly insomniac saw himself in this woman who spent sleepless nights inventing new works to fend off the grave.

In 1952, two years before his death, Matisse would produce his last and most bittersweet reckoning with mortality. His elegiac magnum opus, *Sorrow of the King*, is mounted on a canvas twelve feet, eight inches wide and nine feet, seven inches high. It offers three faceless figures against a background of colored rectangles. At left is a seated green man cradling an orange circle that appears to be a drum. In the center stands a guitarist in a black robe

54

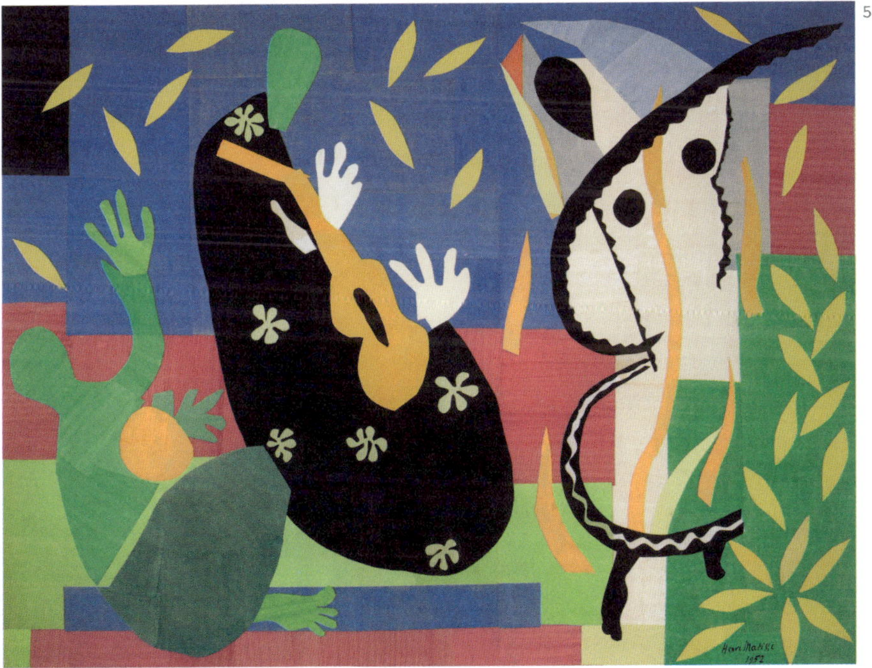

Sorrow of the King, 1952, gouache on paper, cut and pasted, mounted on canvas, 292 x 386 cm., Musée National d'Art Moderne, Centre Georges Pompidou, Paris

spangled with pale green flowers. To the right of him is a black-and-white dancing girl loosely derived from a figure in Delacroix's *Women of Algiers*. All around them is a blizzard of yellow leaves. Matisse called them "a shower of flying saucers" released by the guitar, like musical notes, fluttering in the air but also drifting to the ground. The music of life has been lovely but it's coming to a close. You know as much from the ominous black rectangle in the upper left corner, standing sentry over this colorful scene. *Et in Arcadia ego*.

It was around this time that Janet Flanner, the *New Yorker* writer who dispatched the magazine's splendid "Letter from Paris" from 1925 until 1975, paid a visit to Matisse. She found him "a massive, well-preserved ruin, like an important structure that had been undermined mostly by the weight of time, but the upper and lower stories—his heavy torso, his dwindling limbs—maintained a precarious, majestic balance, with some inner girders of will power holding the whole together."

Yet for all his worsening infirmities, that year, 1952, is always and rightly understood as the pinnacle of Matisse's old age, a last blaze of glory in which his cut-outs took on a complexity, size, and ambition no one could mistake for "child's play." And very often these were cut-outs that only made sense as dreams. You only have to look at *The Parakeet and the Mermaid*, another image that had drifted up from his recollections of the South Seas. Against a massive white background, twenty-five feet wide and eleven high, a wild congregation of palmettes, pomegranates, and algae wiggle in shades of red, orange, fuchsia, blue, and green. Inserted among them, one on each side of the picture, are two incongruous blue forms, the bird and mermaid of the title. By their joint presence they make it impossible to say whether this is an image of the jungle or the sea. This of course is the point. It's neither. Art is a fiction that only art can create, and while so doing it can make its own rules.

In April came *The Negress*. An Amazon in an orange grass skirt, close to fifteen feet tall, she was inspired by memories of the American nightclub sensation Josephine Baker, a Black woman who had electrified Paris before and after the war and had been awarded the Croix de Guerre for her clandestine work with the French Resistance. Baker not only gripped Matisse's imagination, she overflowed it. As her form took shape on one wall of his villa, *The Negress* grew so tall that her lower legs and feet spilled onto the floor, as though she were pooling across some larger space in his mind.

Again in that same year, Matisse made his famous series *Blue Nudes*, four cut-outs, each a single woman assembled from bits of blue paper and set against a white background. All of them are in complex bent poses, seated with one arm raised and hooked over their heads, a favorite Matisse device. To energize what would otherwise be unbroken masses of blue, Matisse allowed slender glimpses of the white background to flow among the dense blue elements that compose their limbs and breasts, channels of light that once again made these otherwise solid women as flickering as dreams.

A few months after completing *The Negress*, Matisse began *The Swimming Pool*, his most ambitious use of cut-outs to create both a reimagined mobility, the movements he could no longer make, and an immersive environment, the reality he could no longer inhabit. The idea for this complex panorama had come to him on a summer day when he and Lydia went to Cannes expecting to see divers at a hotel swimming pool, only to find no one there. Matisse told Lydia he didn't care. "I will make myself my own pool." Back at La Régina, he asked her to unfurl a roll of white paper at about the height of his head all around the four walls of the dining room, which were already covered in a tan canvas. This vast ribbon, nearly fifty-four feet long, would become a landing strip for the next flight of his imagination.

The Swimming Pool is literally that, a pool of images that swim and swirl in all directions. They don't just course along the white paper but fly up or spill over onto the canvas above and below it. In most places the bathers are blue figures cutting through white water, but here's a white swimmer silhouetted by choppy strips of blue water, and then a blue head and arm attached to a white body. Sometimes you see them from the side. Elsewhere you're somehow looking down from above. You're everywhere in this watery flux and nowhere precisely. And many of the cut forms don't resemble people at all. They're semi-abstract "signs," abbreviations for flesh, movement, water, and sheer abandon. In this shape-shifting panopticon, where all things solid might yet be soluble, the indistinct depths of Monet's water lily panels inevitably come to mind once again. In the work of his old age the nineteenth-century British painter J. M. W. Turner took a similar turn, into bright torrents of misty light in which solid things were no more than dimly visible. So here perhaps is another characteristic of the "late style," at least for some artists—a spatial euphoria, a deep dive into a zero-gravity environment of their own making.

One of the last of the great works begun in 1952, though not finished till the following year, was *Memory of Oceania*, a wall-size cut-out that harks back yet again to his 1930 trip. And though it's based on a photograph of a docked boat that Matisse took in Tahiti, it's nearly abstract. The boat is suggested, just barely, by a diagonal green panel supporting an upright fuchsia bar that may be a mast. A black swirl hanging from its lower end like a kite's tail might be a rope. What the other cut paper shapes and charcoal lines in this picture represent is almost impossible to say. But by its very slip-sliding ambiguities it superbly represents what it says it is—a memory, with its indistinct elements floating freely in the mind's eye.

55

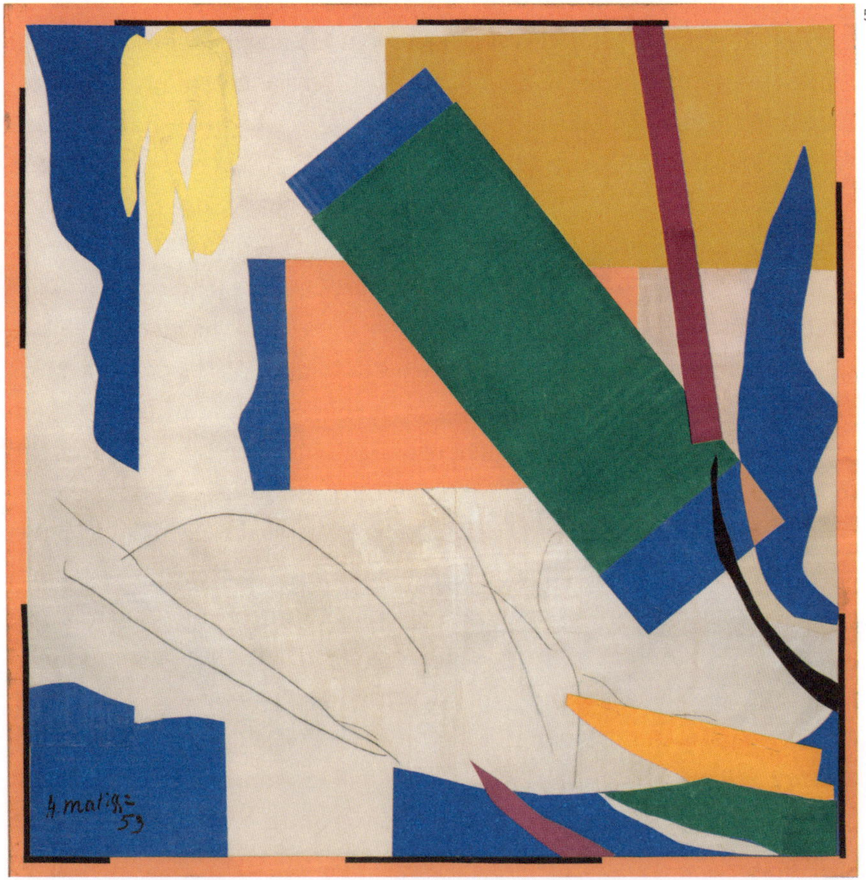

Memory of Oceania, 1952–53, gouache on paper, cut and pasted, and charcoal on paper, mounted on canvas, 284.4 × 286.4 cm, The Museum of Modern Art, New York

Among the last of Matisse's major cut-outs is a delightful visual balancing act from 1953 called *The Snail*. It's a victory of mind over matter, a picture wherein you make out a snail only because the title tells you it must be there. Without that title the image would strike most people as a straightforward abstraction, because the snail's shell is suggested by squares, rectangles, and more irregular shapes in a tumbling array so fragile it seems to fly apart before your eyes.

By the time he completed that picture, Matisse was slowing down and scaling back. He had made his final painting in 1951, the year construction of the chapel was completed. He had cleared out most of the forest of indoor plants in his apartment. He sold or gave away nearly all his birds. That was okay—his walls were still covered with cut-outs of birds and plants and women; an empire of signs had replaced the living things they signified.

But he wasn't through yet. He was still seeking commissions, like the one offered by Sidney Brody, then chairman of the Los Angeles County Museum of Art, and his wife, Frances. They asked Matisse to design a large wall piece for their new home, to be realized in white plaster embedded with colored ceramic tile. But by that time Matisse had moved into an even more radical phase of decorative art, in works that resembled the geometric patterning of Moroccan tile. The Brodys turned down his first proposal for them, *Large Decoration with Masks,* two symmetrical grids of quatrefoil rosettes—like four-leaf clovers seen from above—each grid having an enigmatic oval face looking out from near its center. Matisse was bitterly disappointed. He was extravagantly proud of this work, describing it to Pierre as "a complete success." Even Picasso had loved it, exclaiming when he saw it that "only Matisse can make a thing like that." The Brodys were also not excited about his next proposal, *Decoration, Fruits*, which kept the quatrefoils but replaced the faces with little oranges. And when they visited his studios in Nice in May 1953, they were conspicuously quiet when they saw his third attempt, *Apollo*, a free-floating face drawn in black ink, crowned by a blue-and-orange fan and surrounded by a multicolored blizzard of tumbling tendril forms.

Eventually Matisse salvaged the job by coming up with *La Gerbe—The Sheaf*—a leaping spray of multicolor leaf forms, with nothing symmetrical about it. The Brodys were happy to mount it in their open-air patio above a modern white sofa. But months of work devoted to a project for the widow of a businessman in Rhode Island did not turn out as well. She wanted Matisse to design a stained glass window and bronze door for her husband's mausoleum but rejected the final design she saw only in a color photograph—a waste of precious time for a man with very little left to waste.

That much was evident to Sister Jacques when she paid a visit in the summer of 1954. She was astonished to find Matisse "a poor old man, hunched and huddled. . . . What had happened to my invalid, who had been so lively even in his eighties? Gone was the mischief in his eyes." Yet he had time enough that year for one last undertaking. Alfred Barr, the longtime director of the Museum of Modern Art in New York, relayed a request from Nelson Rockefeller for a stained glass window in memory of his late mother, Abby Aldrich Rockefeller, a founder of the museum. On November 1, Matisse sent off a letter to Barr reporting that the design for the circular window was complete, a central rosette ringed by pomegranates. Within hours he suffered a small stroke.

Matisse died two days later, attended by both Lydia and Marguerite. He once said, "The artist is an actor, the fellow who won't rest until he's told you his life story." He had told his in thousands of paintings, sculptures, drawings, and cut-outs. "Together they constitute Henri Matisse," he said. Naturally the very last of those works were pictures of a woman—four pen-and-ink sketches of Lydia. When she came to his bedside with wet hair bound up in a towel, the dying man reached for a ballpoint pen.

No sooner was he gone than Lydia departed La Régina. Marguerite meanwhile attempted three times to call Picasso with the news about her father, but the famously superstitious old Spaniard refused to come to the phone. He didn't want to hear what he knew she was calling to tell him. A few weeks later he would begin to pay respects his own way, by starting a series of variations on Delacroix's *Women of Algiers*, a scene of harem life that Matisse had drawn on for his odalisques. "When Matisse died," Picasso explained, "he left his odalisques to me, as a legacy."

As for Amélie, she spent the last years of her life on a surprising project, working with Marguerite to track down and preserve any surviving records from the early decades of Matisse's career. Whatever other purposes this reclamation project may have served for her, it was a way to relive the years when they were together, even if not always happily. On November 12, 1958, she would die in Paris at the age of eighty-six. Though she and Matisse had very little contact after their split, in death they were reunited, buried together in Cimiez, not far from La Régina. In the silence of the grave, they no longer needed to worry about the family's great defect. The fear of what ought to be said loses force when there's nothing left to say.

56

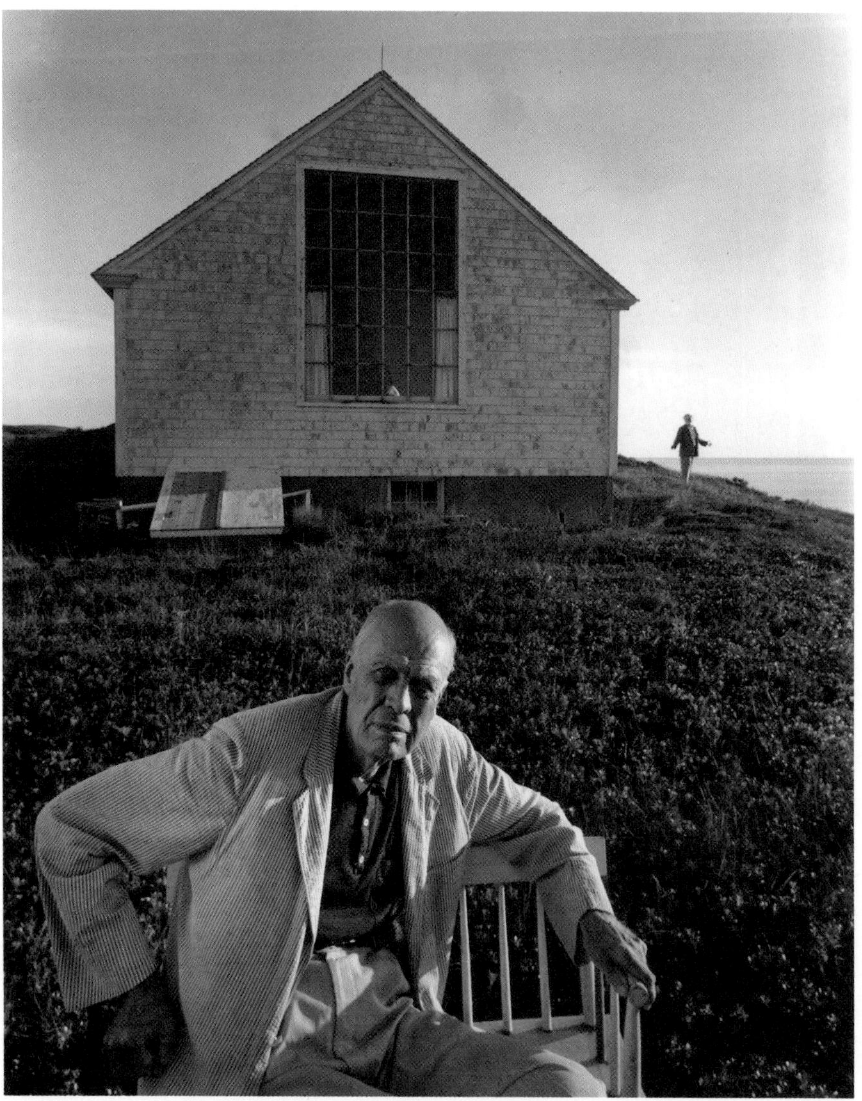

Hopper and his wife, Josephine, outside their house on Cape Cod in 1960

5

EDWARD HOPPER

Into the Light

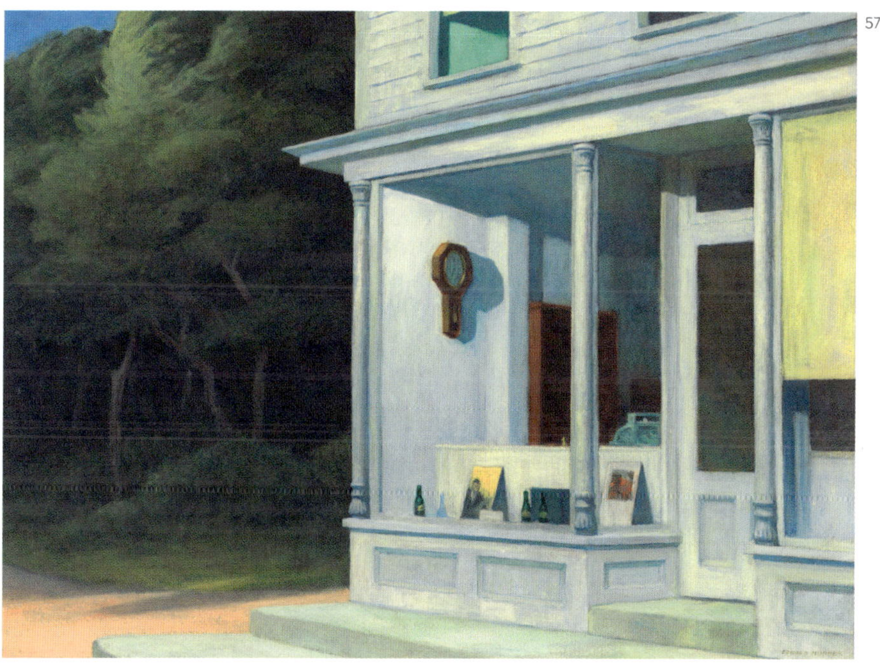 57

Seven A.M., 1948, oil on canvas, 76.7 × 101.9 cm, Whitney Museum of American Art, New York

In September 1948, Edward Hopper put the final touches on the painting he would call *Seven A.M.* As with most of his great pictures—and this is one of them—its quiet power is both plain and a bit mysterious. It shows us a very ordinary scene, a portion of a white storefront, with a partial view of its interior through its wide plate glass windows. It's not clear what kind of business this is. A pharmacy? A barbershop? Even Hopper wasn't sure. But whatever it is, he makes it appear a semi-rural place, set along a dirt road and beside a patch of woods with shadowed undergrowth. Morning sunlight brushes against the upper foliage and spreads across the wooden storefront, where it picks out three slender classical columns that frame the plate glass, a trace memory of the ancient world passed down to a small-town façade. Through the window the same light bends along one white interior wall, showing us a stand of empty shelves and the top filigree of an ornate steel cash register.

What is this painting about? Sunlight and silence, of course. Those are two of Hopper's constants. But a further answer is just to the right of the picture's dead center, where a brown wall clock appears almost to float against the stark white wall where it hangs. Its presence is magnified by the long shadow it casts under the raking morning light. Hopper did nothing by accident, and this clock is nearly central for a reason. It's the keynote of the picture, which, among the other things it's about, is about nothing less than the power of time. Hopper had turned sixty-six in July and had been feeling his age for years. Because time was no longer on his side, it was that much more on his mind.

And as it turns out, this picture is not just a meditation on time but a bit of time recaptured, a painted memory, because the storefront it shows us is based on an actual shop Hopper had first seen in his youth. It was, and still is, just up the road from his childhood home in Nyack, New York, a Hudson River town of about four thousand in the years he grew up there. We know from the journals of his wife, Josephine, that his last addition to this canvas was to delicately brush in the clock's slim hands. He set them to the hour that gives the painting its name, a hushed moment before the shop will open for business. Did Hopper produce this image of an eternal morning as a kind of wish fulfillment, a way to return to the seven A.M. of his own life, to a world at first light, and with it the new beginning promised by each new day? Very possibly, because a new beginning was something the aging Hopper might well have wished for.

Make no mistake, Hopper's last years were gratifying in almost every way an artist could ask for. They were two decades of gold medals, blue ribbons, and academy memberships. The virtuoso of American solitude would represent the United States at the Venice Biennale, appear on the cover of *Time*, and feature in over two hundred gallery and museum shows, including two full retrospectives. And though he stood before his easel less frequently, he would see quick sales of whatever new paintings he could bring himself to produce. More than that, in his old age Hopper would make some of the most profound and moving art of his career, pictures like *Seven A.M.*

More often than in his work as a younger man, a number of these pictures were in some way autobiographical, though almost never directly. Just like Matisse, Hopper often said that the artist always put himself into his own canvases, that his paintings, no matter what they were pictures of—a lighthouse, an empty road, a woman alone over a cup of coffee—were always a projection of his own interior state. But in some of his late work he seems to make coded references to himself that are more specific than a glimpse into some amorphous mood. On a visit to Hopper's studio in 1963, Brian O'Doherty, an arts journalist who was also a friend, had a chance to examine *Sun in an Empty Room*, a then-unfinished painting that would be one of the artist's last. Looking over that scene of two fleeting sunbeams climbing a blank wall—vertical paths of light that surely represent the aging artist and his wife, even as they bring to mind headstones—O'Doherty asked the old man what he was after in that picture. Hopper shot back. "I'm after *ME*!"

That idea of implied self-portrait might even help to explain the woman we see looking out a bay window in *Cape Cod Morning*. It's a painting he made in the autumn of 1950, a few months after turning sixty-eight. We find this searching woman inside one of Hopper's typical houses, both sunlit and isolated, gazing across a sea of tall grasses and a wall of trees that recede into darkness. Though the white exterior clapboard of her house is scoured by a brilliant Cape light, the woman inside is set in a darker compartment, her bay window engulfed in purple shadow and flanked by tall black shutters. Yet while she's as confined as one of the screaming popes that Francis Bacon would start painting a few years later, she's much less anguished and overwhelmed—more questing. Some years before the first astronauts, she's piloting her little capsule like a space explorer.

So is she a stand-in for Hopper, who was a notably shuttered soul, a man who looked out on the world from the chamber of his own solitude? Interviewed with her husband for *Time* magazine, Jo suggested that "it's a woman

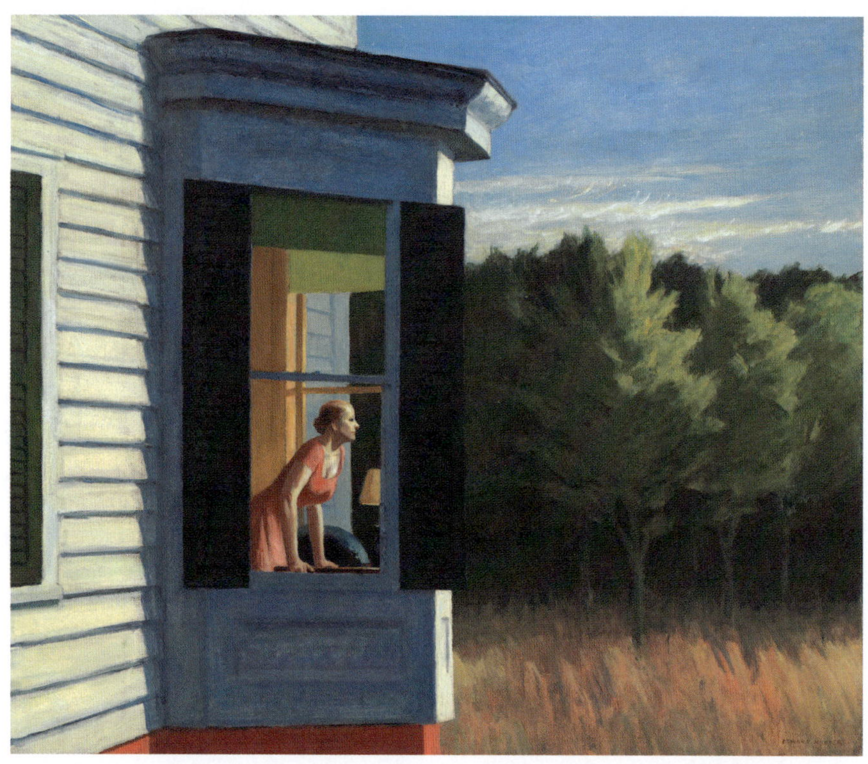

58

Cape Cod Morning, 1950, oil on canvas, 86.7 × 102.3 cm, Smithsonian American Art Museum, Washington, D.C.

looking out to see if the weather's good enough to hang out her wash." Her husband practically winced. "You're making it Norman Rockwell. From my point of view she's just looking out the window, just looking out the window." More than that the laconic Hopper would never tell—he always refused to offer much explanation for his paintings. But on another occasion, he did allow a wonderfully Hopper-esque take on this one, a few parsimonious words that hint she might indeed be a surrogate. *Cape Cod Morning*, he said, "comes nearer to what I feel than some of my other paintings." Because he was Hopper, he still hedged. "I don't believe it's important to know exactly what that is."

In a few of his late canvases Hopper tips his hand even more, with images that hint at particular dilemmas in his life. In this way *Seven A.M.* is plainly the work of a man who hears that insistent wall clock ticking inside his own head. And the twinned bars of light in *Sun in an Empty Room* acknowledge the inevitable slow fade of himself and his wife, Jo. As for the costumed couple in his last painting, *Two Comedians*, holding hands as they take a bow before heading offstage, it's plain they are the Hoppers bidding farewell to the world. By the time he made that picture seventeen years had passed since he completed *Seven A.M.*, and the hands on that clock had come back around to evening.

Yet even as Hopper was continuing to produce some acute and deeply felt paintings, he was making fewer of them. It was the same problem of deceleration the aging Monet once faced. As early as his fifties, when he first started suffering from the chronic fatigue that was misdiagnosed for years as "low thyroid," Hopper's output had begun to sputter. By his sixties it had slowed to a crawl. Where once he might complete four or five oils in a single year, *Seven A.M.* was the only canvas he finished in 1948. In the year that followed there would be four again, but in the 1950s and '60s his output in most years dropped to two, or one, and in some years none.

Some of this was due to what can only be called painter's block, the mysterious condition composed of equal parts exhaustion, ennui, and indecision. Even in his forties Hopper was prone to grumble about how hard it was to find scenes that struck him as worth setting down, but by his mid-sixties inaction had become a chronic condition, if not a kind of philosophical position—a resistance to the idea that life had anything new to offer. Amid the endless variety of Manhattan, where he had lived and prowled since 1908, he found less and less that moved him. As for Cape Cod, where he and Jo had spent every summer since 1930, it was still a source of pleasure but not much inspiration. Months would go by there without a single watercolor to show for it, much less an oil.

This kind of inactivity was sometimes a byproduct of depression, sometimes a cause of it. The long listless stretches made Hopper miserable, then the misery made him even more unproductive. The American realist painter Charles Burchfield, an old friend, once described Hopper as a man who "suffers agony during his dormant periods, so important in him is his need to paint." But as he inched toward seventy, those dormant periods were becoming longer and more frequent.

Hopper's health was also beginning to falter. His periodic inertia was complicated by the persistent fatigue he had suffered for years. Back in 1938 it had led one of his doctors, who rejected the low thyroid diagnosis, to prescribe what was then the new wonder drug Benzedrine—later known to hipsters as "bennies." It's odd to think of Hopper, the laconic Republican in a tweed suit, as an early adopter of the speedball elixir of Beat poets and jazz musicians, but he found it helpful and continued using it into his sixties.

One month after he completed *Seven A.M.*, while still on the Cape, Hopper also suffered a bout of cardiac pain that landed him in the hospital. A few months later, back in New York, he underwent prostate surgery for the second time. Ten months after that, in February 1950, he was hospitalized again. This time the problem was diverticulitis, serious enough to keep him from the opening of his new retrospective at the Whitney, his first since a survey at the Museum of Modern Art in 1933 that had confirmed his rise into the front rank of American artists. Even before that year, the prospect of mortality started to make its way into Hopper's work. Though Hopper would never put it this way, it's easy to think of *Seven A.M.*, a picture of time asserting its power in a wooded setting, as his version of *Et in Arcadia ego*, Poussin's grim masterpiece from around 1638. In Poussin's canvas three idealized shepherds and a very classical maiden are gathered in an open landscape before a tomb carved with death's lethal boast—"Even in Paradise, there am I." Just as that picture also seems to prefigure Matisse's late cut-out *Sorrow of the King*, Poussin's dry-eyed acknowledgement of death's universal dominion feels like a spiritual ancestor of Hopper's imperturbable little clock.

Even more to the point was a small painting that Hopper worked on the next year. The picture we now call *Stairway* was very uncharacteristic for him, and not just because it was on wood panel instead of canvas. It gives us the view from midway down a staircase in a narrow front hallway. At the bottom is a doorway that opens onto a shadowy landscape ending in dark hills silhouetted against a blue sky. Hopper made this painting during a difficult time of depression, illness, and surgeries. Once again it's a memory picture—the staircase and doorway are the ones still to be found at his boyhood home in Nyack. It's also sets down an imagined moment of supernatural power, because Hopper told Jo it was inspired by "a repeated dream of levitation, sailing downstairs & out thru door." Yet, however it is that dreams and memory have blended here, it was to arrive at what may be a bleak premonition, a downward passage into twilight.

As he moved into his late sixties, not all of Hopper's problems involved flagging inspiration or fading health. The most confounding could be called existential. In the years after the war, with the rise of abstract expressionism, American art was changing in ways he scoffed at but that left him in the strangely contradictory position that the aged Monet had also found himself in. He was widely considered one of the greatest living American painters. He was also in danger of becoming yesterday's man, out of step with the new art that was mobilizing critics, curators, and younger artists, plus the collectors who chased after all of them. The rapid emergence of abstract expressionism became one of the great dilemmas of Hopper's old age.

AbEx, to use the shorthand term, was a development Hopper had no use for. Never mind that he was a man many abstractionists admired and even thought of as a kind of fellow traveler, a representational painter whose powerfully constructed pictures, with their complex geometries and force distribution, were abstractions hiding in plain sight. Hopper didn't return the compliment. Sophisticated composition was one thing, but he had no interest in pure abstraction, what he called that "very incomplete means of conveying great emotions."

Hopper also had no sympathy for modern art's fetishization of the new, the idea that, as Marcel Duchamp put it, "A painting that doesn't shock isn't worth painting." Modernism's endless shock corridor, where year after year new "isms" overtook one another, was no place for a man like Hopper. What he wanted was for his work to validate the past, to carry forward the achievements of Winslow Homer and Thomas Eakins, not through imitation but in such a way that their legacy was both preserved and modified under the imprint of his own sensibility. As he saw it, without the ballast of reality and tradition, art would come untethered. This is what he meant when he said he could enjoy certain pictures by Picasso but on the whole found him "capricious." A personal interpretation of the world that still bore the DNA of the past was his very definition of art.

All the same, everywhere he turned in the late 1940s, Hopper was hearing that abstract expressionism was the inevitable next step in the hurtling dialectic of modernism. The painters of the New York School—Jackson Pollock and Willem de Kooning, Robert Motherwell and Mark Rothko, with many more to come—were being credited with at last putting Americans in the vanguard of art history, the cockpit position that for over a century had been occupied by Paris. There was a new thunder in what they were doing on their big canvases, making statements about fate, transcendence, euphoria, and despair. The critic Harold Rosenberg was calling it "action painting" and the canvas "an arena," as though each new picture were the outcome of a titanic throwdown between the artist and the cosmos. By 1949, even middlebrow *Life* magazine, eagerly sniffing the zeitgeist, would headline its famous feature spread on Pollock with the question, "Is he the greatest living painter in the United States?" The magazine didn't actually answer that question. It was enough to have asked it.

The emergence of AbEx did more than merely threaten the status of realism of the kind Hopper practiced. It raised the issue of whether reality itself, at least as a subject for art, was obsolete. What if abstraction wasn't just the next big thing but the final destination, the terminus toward which all art history had been heading and where it would henceforth settle in for good? Critics like Clement Greenberg, a standard bearer for the new art, would soon be suggesting something like that, arguing that the illusion of deep space that had governed Western painting since the Renaissance was being permanently overtaken by the shallow, all-over compositions of artists like Pollock. Henceforth no painting of consequence would pretend to be a window. It would be a surface, and no real artist would violate what Greenberg would call "the integrity of the picture plane."

Even in a climate of opinion so receptive to abstraction, Hopper was too prominent to be entirely marginalized. But the seismic shift in cultural attention was alarming both to him and to his beleaguered fellow realists. It told them everything that in 1945 the Whitney Annual, a yearly survey that was always a bellwether of emerging taste, devoted its entire first floor to abstraction. Representational painters, Hopper included, were kicked upstairs. No matter that the second floor was part of the official show, it must have felt to them like a salon des refusés. Now when an echt-modernist critic like Greenberg bothered to talk about Hopper at all, it was in patronizing tones like these:

> A special category of art should be devised for the kind of thing Hopper does. He is not a painter in the full sense. His means are second-hand, shabby and impersonal. But his rudimentary sense of composition is sufficient for a message that conveys an insight into the present nature of American life. . . . Hopper simply happens to be a bad painter. But if he were a better painter, he would, most likely, not be so superior an artist.

There's a compliment in there somewhere.

By 1952, the same year Hopper would be chosen as one of four artists to represent the United States at the Venice Biennale, status anxiety among American realists was coming to a head. In that year a large group of them banded together in New York to defend their kind of art and to pressure MoMA, which they felt had gone mad for AbEx, to place more focus on them. As part of that pushback, the new group decided to launch a publication, *Reality: A Journal of Artists' Opinions,* with Hopper as co-editor—an unusual case of his taking a public stand on any controversy of his day.

When the first issue appeared, it included a short statement by him that took aim at abstraction. It included this line: "The inner life of a human being is a vast and varied realm and does not concern itself alone with stimulating arrangements of color, form, and design." But the Reality group would manage just two more issues of their journal, with the last appearing in late in 1955. With attendance at their meetings falling into the single digits, by December of that year they had disbanded.

In any event, Hopper didn't need to move into the latest artistic practices. He had his own means of finding his way into new territory. He and his wife, Jo, traveled frequently in search of new light and new scenes along the road. In the spring of 1946, as AbEx was just emerging as a force, they loaded up their old Buick and set off for Mexico. It would be their fourth trip west since they married, their third in just five years, and their second to Mexico, with stops this time in Virginia, Tennessee, Louisiana, Texas, and Wyoming. No matter where it took him, Hopper loved the road for its own sake. A decade later he would tell an interviewer from *Time* that "to me, the important thing is going on. You know how beautiful things are when you are traveling." Jack Kerouac couldn't have said it better.

Whatever the satisfactions of perpetual motion, as a spur to new work these expeditions didn't always turn out as Hopper hoped, and the 1946 trip was one of those. It led to some watercolors, but no oils. Much of the reason had to do with Hopper's very dry sensibilities. In New Orleans Jo found herself charmed by the French Quarter and urged him to find inspiration there. After twenty-two years of marriage, it's surprising she didn't understand he would wince at the suggestion. Hopper hated charm. He hated sentiment. He wouldn't even send Christmas cards. On their first trip to Mexico, he had run into an acquaintance and asked her to recommend someplace they could visit that had nothing "quaint or picturesque." These were qualities he worked hard to avoid in his art, diversions from whatever it was he was looking for in the homely, the commonplace, or even sometimes the repellent. One of his early watercolors was of a small cluster of outhouses. So there should be no mistaking what they were, he called the picture *Outhouses*.

To fully understand the complicated idea of beauty that nourished his work to the end, it helps to go back to 1928, when the forty-six-year-old Hopper published an essay on his painter friend Charles Burchfield. That text is also a kind of self-portrait. He describes Burchfield's aesthetic the way he no doubt hopes his own might be seen: "From what is to the mediocre artist and unseeing layman the boredom of everyday existence in a provincial community, he has extracted a quality that we may call poetic, romantic, lyric, or what you will. By sympathy with the particular he has made it epic and universal."

In that same essay Hopper rose to a bleak peroration, an inventory of Burchfield's favorite motifs that's plainly also an accounting of his own. Reading it you suddenly realize that Hopper, of all people, really was a spiritual precursor of Kerouac. In a passage like this you get a preview of Kerouac's forlorn epiphanies:

> No mood has been so mean as to seem unworthy of interpretation; the look of an asphalt road as it lies in the blazing sun at noon, cars and locomotives lying in God-forsaken railway yards, the steaming summer rain that can fill us with such hopeless boredom, the blank concrete walls and steel constructions of modern industry, midsummer streets with the acid green of close-cut lawns, the dusty Fords and gilded movies—all the sweltering, tawdry life of the American small town, and behind all, the sad desolation of our suburban landscape.

Hopper's approving feel for banality also brought his art into line with the counter-aesthetic of American vernacular photography that began to take hold during his lifetime, first in the baldly and profoundly unbeautiful photos of Walker Evans, and later in the work of Robert Frank, Lee Friedlander, Garry Winogrand, and many others. As he entered old age, their High Prosaic remained the hallmark of his art, too.

This continued to perplex Jo. She was baffled, for instance, as to what drew him to the Cape Cod village of Eastham, "the least attractive township on the Cape," as she called it, when he had "all these marvelous Truro Hills stretched out all around us." In 1950, when he finally settled on a street scene worth immortalizing, it was an unassuming stretch of Orleans, at the time another drive-by Cape hamlet of no great appeal. For the picture he called *Portrait of Orleans* he places the viewer well back in a nearly deserted roadway intersection. That allowed him a sweeping car-windshield view of a few houses and shops, the kind of small-town vista Hopper would have seen many times as he motored around the Cape looking for something to paint. (When he bought his next car, an old Buick, he would have its tinted windows replaced with clear glass. He didn't want a softened view.) In this painting the buildings mostly appear in the middle distance, along with a barely visible woman walking past one of the storefronts. The foreground he reserved for a yellow traffic light on a tall yellow post and a charmless Esso gas station sign hung from a pole. At its base is a jumble of black rubber tires.

Hopper was no doubt satisfied. He had pulled off another exercise in the terse lyricism of the nondescript. And as it happened, for one wealthy collector that Esso sign was not so charmless after all. *Portrait of Orleans* would be bought by Nelson Rockefeller, whose grandfather John D. had founded Esso's corporate ancestor, Standard Oil.

It's been said of Hopper that once he arrived at his characteristic style and concerns as an artist, a journey more or less complete by the mid-1920s, he worked that way for the rest of his life. And certainly there are no quantum leaps in his art, nothing like the constant shape-shifting of Picasso and Matisse, or even Frank Stella's gradual transition from the doctrinaire flatness of his pinstripe paintings to his churning wall reliefs. And it's no less true that once Hopper stopped trying to sell his French landscapes and Paris vignettes, he took a deep breath and allied himself with the painters of his generation who insisted on an American art freed from European models. By 1933 he could write: "The domination of France in the plastic arts has been almost complete for the last thirty years or more in this country [America]. If an apprenticeship to a master has been necessary, I think we have served it."

Plainly this was Hopper talking to himself. He was one of the artists who had served that apprenticeship, then went their own way. Though he hated any attempt to link him to American Scene painters like Thomas Hart Benton and Grant Wood, artists whose notions of the national life looked to him force-fed with period clichés, by the 1930s Hopper had turned his back on whatever was the latest word from Paris. He had pledged himself for good to the kind of nuanced realism, based on the visible world but adjustable to his personal vision, that he considered the great tradition of American painting. And for the rest of his life, he largely remained on that road.

All the same, there's a shift in the art of Hopper's last decades, from his middle sixties until his death at the age of eighty-four. It arrives not by way of a departure from his longtime preoccupations but through an intensification of them. Just as Titian was drawn ever deeper into the very substance of oil paint, the viscous goo he had first discovered as a young man, and Matisse ended his life immersed in the pleasures of pure color, an obsession since the fauvism of his thirties, in his last years Hopper doubled down on his lifelong devotion to light. His biographer Gail Levin has put it this way: "From this time on [1952], sunlight, in its imaginative association with life, became more and more his real subject."

And it's true. Many of his last canvases might as well be called solar panels, so much are they devices to gather light energy and transmit it to the viewer. The older Hopper also chose to introduce light into his canvases in a more aggressive way. Instead of spreading an even illumination across a wall or floor, sunlight arrives in strongly defined beams that contrast sharply with the surfaces they fall on. Sometimes it's a diagonal shaft like the divine light that hits the Virgin in Renaissance annunciations. Sometimes it appears as a glowing square or rectangle. More often it's as the wide trapezoids with angled tops that became a signature of his late work. They appear in at least a third of the twenty-nine oils Hopper completed between *Seven A.M.* and his death seventeen years later. A powerful presence in any of his paintings, in the last of them light is a dazzling intruder, cutting a buzz saw diagonal down any room it enters.

What would be a more natural element for the aging Hopper to be drawn to than light? As the prospect of death became harder to put out of mind, light would have seemed like an antidote, however temporary. Even the names he assigned to the paintings of his old age tell us how his thoughts were turning. In the space of just eleven years, beginning with *Morning Sun* in 1952, he would complete eight canvases that included the words *sun* or *sunlight* in the title. *Sunlight on Brownstones, Sunlight in a Cafeteria, Second Story Sunlight*—none of these are portraits, but taken together their names start to sound like portrait titles, as though sunlight were some fascinating personality Hopper had persuaded to sit for him in one place after another.

And those titles tell us just what these pictures are really about—not people or houses or hills, though any of those might be in the frame, but the infinity of effects produced when light pours across them. The men and women in most of these pictures are also treating this light the way Hopper wants *us* to treat it, as the proper focus of attention. They don't look at us—though people in Hopper's paintings almost never do—or even at one another. Most of them we see in profile, gazing directly into the light. In a kind of human heliotropism, some even bend toward it like sunflowers.

In 1952 alone, the year he turned seventy, Hopper painted two pictures of this kind, rapt exchanges between people and sunlight. In *Morning Sun* we see a woman in profile wearing a pink negligee. Sitting upright in the center of a sunlit bed, she faces an open window that looks onto the distant upper

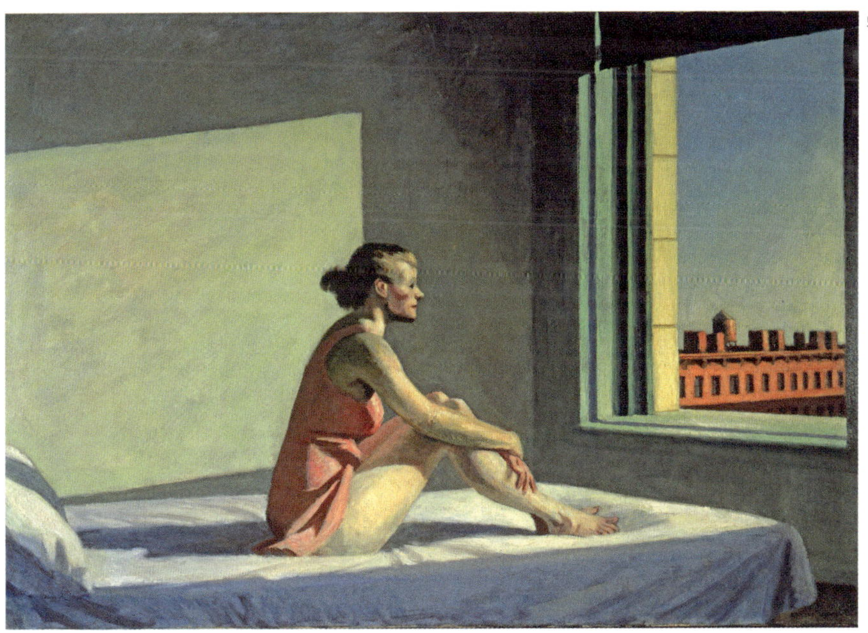
59

Morning Sun, 1952, oil on canvas, 71.4 × 101.9 cm, Columbus Museum of Art, Columbus, Ohio

stories of a long brick building. Her knees are pulled up before her and her arms rest on her lower legs.

Or rather one arm does, her right, the one facing us. Though we can see her left hand on her lower right leg, the arm it would be attached to is nowhere visible, though at this angle it should be, and the disembodied hand appears well below the point it could reach on her leg were it connected to an actual arm. Truth be told, Hopper was only sometimes a skilled figure painter. As early as 1933, the critic Lewis Mumford was complaining that "Hopper has lost his hold on the human figure . . . [his people] are not as real as the furniture." This woman is an especially awkward swipe at the human form, and her face is not much better. It's an impassive mask, with her one visible eye a black dot. But Hopper isn't concerned so much here with giving us a portrait of a woman. It's the sunbeam she's sitting in he cares most about, the one that also spreads itself across a broad patch of the green wall we see behind her. She's here largely to catch the light, and to personify the idea of being drawn to it. It's hard not to think of her as Hopper's Danaë, his

60

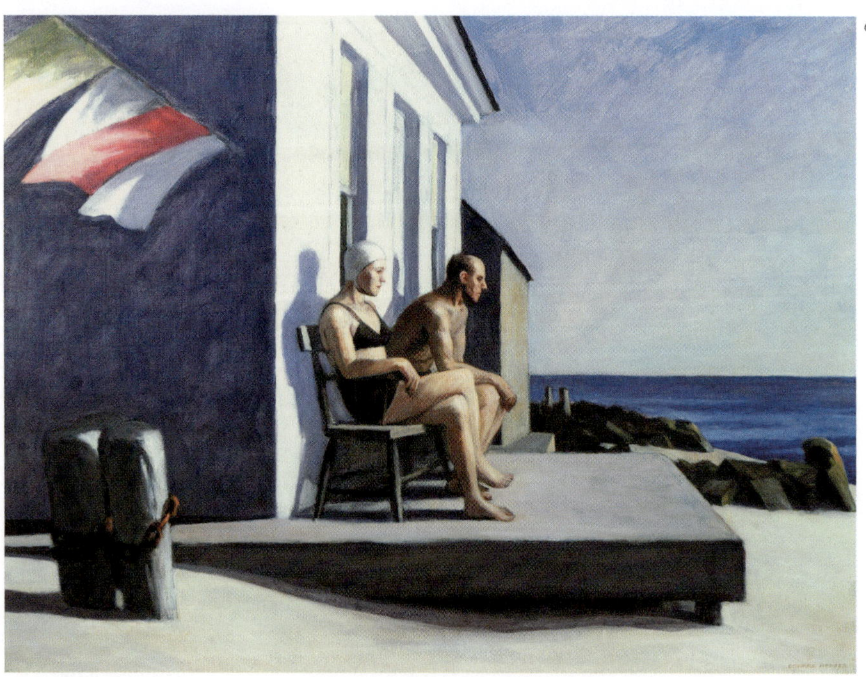

Sea Watchers, 1952, oil on canvas, 76.2 × 101.6 cm, private collection

secular update on Titian's woman in her bed receiving a shower of gold, but with none of the mythical backstory.

In that same year Hopper produced *Sea Watchers*. Now the scene has shifted outdoors. There's a couple seated in profile on the deck of a small white beach cabin, quietly staring out toward the sunlit shore. Both are in swimsuits, so they may have just come from the water, or are ready to go in. But for now they're just sitting, as Hopper people do, silent and impassive, mesmerized by a sun we don't see. Are they married? Maybe they are, because they're not paying the least attention to one another. Whatever is true of them, the pleasures and predicaments of marriage—certainly of the marriage of Edward and Jo Hopper—may well be implied by two thick wooden posts we see in the lower left foreground, sticking up out of the sand. They're chained together.

Along with his work, the consuming fact of Hopper's late life was his enduring but ever combustible marriage. From the start he and Jo were an odd couple, and not just because he was over six-foot-four and she was a birdlike five-foot-one. Though they both loved art, theater, movies, and French literature, she was outgoing, sociable, and talkative. He was inward, solitary, and terse, possessed of what a friend called "a semi-funereal solemnity." Over time these differences would become more pronounced. Interviewers would be surprised and annoyed to find themselves directing questions to Hopper, only to have Jo step in with an answer. It may have been just as well for them. As she knew, if they had him to themselves they would be lucky if he gave them a syllable.

By their last decades together the Hoppers' marriage had long since become a minefield, and this largely because Jo's ambitions as an artist hadn't taken her very far. When they married, in 1924, things were different. She very much thought of herself as a painter, and with good reason. Like Hopper she didn't sell many pictures, but also like him she managed to exhibit enough to sustain her hope that at the age of forty-one she was still on a trajectory toward some kind of recognition. Instead, through whatever combination of the pervasive sexism of the twentieth-century American art world and the limits of her own gifts, Jo's career never took off. Meanwhile Edward became one of the best-known American artists of his generation. This was a state of affairs she would never resign herself to.

• • •

Unlike her husband, who spent his boyhood in small-town Nyack, Josephine Nivison was born and raised in Manhattan, where in 1904 she earned a degree from a New York City teacher's college. By that time, she had already discovered the love of drawing that would decide her next move, to the New York School of Art and Design, a forward-looking alternative to the conservative National Academy of Design.

As it turned out, Hopper was also a student there, though by the time Nivison enrolled he was in his final year and they don't appear to have gotten to know one another well. But her teachers would include one of his favorites, the swashbuckling Robert Henri, a leader among the American painters later known as the Ashcan school. Their frank pictures of city life, its rough edges included, would leave a mark on Hopper's lifelong commitment to the here and now in his own work. Jo would value Henri's guidance enough that in the summer of 1907 she traveled to the Netherlands to take a painting class he was teaching there, making side trips to France and Italy. In the final year of World War I, ever the intrepid young adventurer, she returned to France for a few months as part of an occupational therapy program for American servicemen. At home, she combined stints as a public schoolteacher with occasional work as an illustrator. By 1915 she had also dipped into acting with the Washington Square Players in Greenwich Village. All the while it remained her ambition to make her way as a painter.

Over the years, Hopper and Nivison crossed paths a few times at the New England artist colonies they were both drawn to most summers. They once even stayed at the same guesthouse in Maine. Back home in New York these brief encounters were never something they followed up on. It took until 1923 before they finally locked eyes. This time the setting was Gloucester, Massachusetts. Hopper was turning forty-one and coming off some sort of romance with an older woman we don't know much about except that she was French, he was smitten, and nothing came of it. Nivison was ten months younger and unattached.

At the time, both were still in a state of suspended animation as painters, exhibiting whenever they could but selling very little. After years of commuting between Nyack and New York, Hopper had moved permanently to Manhattan in 1908, in the middle of a period when he was also trying to find himself as an artist through a series of long visits to France. Between 1906 and 1910 he made three trips, each time basing himself in Paris. Though he took excursions to London and around the Continent, it was Paris that kept calling him back. He loved the museums, where he got acquainted firsthand with the work of Manet and Degas. He loved the brilliant cafés, though back home his instinctive melancholy would point him toward lonely diners and automats. And he loved painting outdoors along the Seine, where for a while he took up the bright color and free brushwork of impressionism. It would never be a natural fit for him. Impressionism captured the fleeting moment. In his mature work, Hopper would have the opposite effect, taking momentary scenes and making them feel eternal. But his time in France sharpened his eye and educated his taste, endowing them both with a lifelong sophistication. Much later he would tell an interviewer, "It seemed awfully crude and raw here when I got back. It took me ten years to get over Europe."

It took him even longer to get on his feet as an artist. For years after his return, Hopper would try to sell views of Paris that found no buyers. When he finally made his first sale, in 1913, it was of an all-American boating scene. Remarkably it had been included in that year's infamous New York Armory Show, the traveling exhibition that introduced Americans—many of them puzzled, amused, or horrified—to cubism, futurism, and whatever else the European avant-garde was up to. But the Armory Show still made room for entries like Hopper's *Sailing*, an oil on canvas with some free brushwork but no other summons to the barricades. It was agreeable enough to the common man that after the show a New York textile manufacturer bought it for $50 below the $300 asking price. Hopper was smart to take the discount, because it would be almost ten years before he sold another painting.

In the meantime, having trained as an illustrator, he got by on freelance assignments for books, magazines, and advertising, work he hated but needed. There was also the occasional sale of etchings, a medium he took up in 1915, and powerfully enough that his prints brought him some money and recognition when his paintings brought neither. It was in these that Hopper first developed the scenes and moods of his later work—city views, rooftops, isolated houses, and solitary figures, some sitting at windows, some glimpsed through them, all set within the complex interplay of shadow and light that would one day make him an inspiration to Hollywood cinematographers. Determined all the while to succeed as an artist, he did illustrations just a few days a week. His serious time he gave to etchings and oils.

During their get-acquainted summer in Gloucester, Hopper and Nivison took to going out together on painting excursions. In what turned out to be a crucial bit of advice, she pushed him to give more thought to watercolor, a practice he had mostly used just for his commercial illustrations and may have dismissed for that very reason. In the space of their few months there he completed more than seventeen watercolors of an extraordinary force and fluency. For the next four decades watercolor would be Hopper's other great medium, a discovery he owed in good part to Nivison. This time, when they returned to the city, they were ready to move the dial from friendship to courtship.

Very soon Nivison would be the key to an event on which Hopper's whole future would turn. That fall the Brooklyn Museum invited her to contribute six watercolors to a group show of recent work by European and American artists. She urged the organizers to take a look at some pictures by her new friend Hopper. They did and chose six of his Gloucester scenes. When the reviews of the Brooklyn show came in, it was the "exhilarating" Hopper critics singled out as a discovery. Nivison got an approving mention from the *New York Times* but was otherwise mostly ignored. When the exhibition closed, the museum bought one of Hopper's contributions, *The Mansard Roof,* a watercolor in which he somehow invested a rambling house with both the heft of a mountain range and the majestic lightness of a rolling cloudbank. This was the painting that was his first to find a buyer since *Sailing,* almost a decade earlier. After years of struggle, he was launched.

Within a few months Hopper was invited to join the Manhattan gallery of Frank K. M. Rehn. The prestige venue for American realist painters, it included on its roster of major names George Bellows and Rockwell Kent. They had both gone to the New York School of Art and Design with Hopper and afterward found quick success, the kind that had eluded him. In the autumn of 1924, Rehn gave Hopper a one-artist show of his watercolors, his first in a commercial gallery. Critics loved them. Buyers followed. Not only did all eleven pictures sell, so did five more from the back room. One went to Bellows himself, a sweet vindication. All this was enough to convince Hopper it was time to quit illustration. The next year he delivered his last commercial drawings to *Scribner's Magazine* and never looked back.

By that time his life had changed in another, no less profound way. On July 9, 1924, Hopper and Nivison married. He was two weeks shy of forty-two.

She was forty-one, though on her marriage license she would claim to be thirty-seven. After the wedding, the new couple moved in together to Hopper's place in Greenwich Village, a fourth-floor walk-up in a brick row house on Washington Square Park. Though Hopper had lived there since 1913, it was barely an apartment, with a shared bathroom down the hall and a kitchenette crammed into a corner of the main room, which was a skylit space that doubled as his studio. A coal-burning iron stove did what it could to warm the place in winter. The white walls were kept bare and always would be, the way he liked them.

It seems incredible now, when we expect famous artists to live large, or at least larger than this, but the Hoppers would always remain at that address, even as he became one of the best-known artists of his generation. In the 1950s, he had to decline a visit from the actor and collector Edward G. Robinson, an admirer who already owned one Hopper. The old man didn't want Robinson to see how run-down his apartment was. Though in 1932 he and Jo would relocate to a somewhat larger space on the same floor, one that allowed them a small bedroom, and later expand into an adjacent studio for Jo, not until 1941 would they have the luxury of a private bathroom. And they would climb the seventy-four steps to those spartan arrangements, ever more slowly, for the rest of their lives.

However modestly they lived, by the time they married Hopper was fully embarked on the extraordinary turn in his fortunes as a painter. In 1925, the year that followed his debut at Rehn, the Metropolitan Museum of Art bought fifteen of his etchings and his work was included in nineteen exhibitions. For a long time he had taken part in group shows, but now it was as a name that stood out from the crowd. Now it was not just his watercolors but his oil paintings that began to attract the attention of museums and collectors. *Vanity Fair* came calling to give him some fashionable press. By 1930, a Hopper would become the first painting to enter the permanent collection of the Museum of Modern Art. It was *House by the Railroad*, a gloomy white manse made gloomier by the dated regalia of its Gilded Age windows and roofline, set in isolation against the sky and hemmed in by the crossbar of an empty railway track. Almost thirty years later it would be the picture that Alfred Hitchcock, who knew a haunted house when he saw one, chose as the model for the Norman Bates lair in *Psycho*. Hopper loved that.

To cap off this decade-long ascent, in 1933 MoMA would mount Hopper's first retrospective. By that time his fame had unsettled Jo. *Her* career was going nowhere. There had been some promising years in the early 1920s, when she appeared in many group shows and had been taken on by the short-lived New Gallery. Even then, just like her husband, she sold little, but after the high point of the Brooklyn Museum show that launched him she also exhibited less often. With Edward she was a charter member of the Whitney Studio Club, forerunner of the Whitney Museum of American Art, and she placed paintings in the Whitney Studio Annuals of 1927 and 1928, but no one was taking much notice. In 1931 alone, despite the onset of the Great Depression, Hopper sold thirty works. Jo sold nothing.

Before long, she was asking herself what had gone wrong. Was it that the household chores that came with marriage kept her from her work? Though the Hoppers would never have children, there was still too much to do at home. She wrote to a friend, Bee Blanchard: "For the female of the species, it's a fatal thing for the artist to marry, her consciousness is too much disturbed." God knows she hated to cook. "The ever-recurring treadmill of meals" she called it, that "everlasting eat, eat, eat." In 1934, she wrote Blanchard again. "Time was I would consider myself an artist and would accept no other destiny. Now I know myself as a kitchen slave." In her contribution to a collection of artist's favorite recipes, she admitted that "we like to have cans of the friendly bean on the shelf." With Jo's idea of cookware being a can opener, Hopper ended up doing much of the cooking anyway. When she did venture to the stove, she got varying results. One time she even gamely baked him a birthday cake. He took a bite and told her there was a "faint flavor of haddock."

Even more than their domestic routine, what tormented Jo was what she saw as Hopper's indifference to her stalled ambitions, his unwillingness to help her get attention, or even to sympathize with her frustration when year after year she was largely ignored. Wasn't she the one who got him his first big break? Sensitive to any appearance of a conflict of interest, Hopper resisted leveraging his fame to get curators and dealers to pay attention to his wife. He was so fastidious about professional ethics that he once refused to second the nomination of a friend for membership in the prestigious American Academy of Arts and Letters because the same friend had proposed Hopper for the Academy's gold medal for painting. Hopper didn't want to appear to be trading favors.

All the same, her husband's reticence enraged Jo. Worse still, he didn't hesitate to tell her, repeatedly, that if her pictures had no takers, maybe the problem was with the pictures. Mostly unimpressed by what she did—he once dismissively grouped her as one of those "Lady Flower Painters"—he often found her need for recognition a burden and an embarrassment. She once asked him, "Isn't it nice to have a wife who paints?" He shot back, "It stinks." On another occasion he told her that if she were the famous artist and he were the one who wasn't getting anywhere, after a while he would simply stop trying. She didn't take the hint.

There was also an issue in the bedroom. A virgin when they married, Jo was unacquainted with anal sex and was startled to find it was something her new husband liked. What she called his "attacks from the rear" gave her no pleasure, one more evidence of Hopper's selfishness and indifference to her own needs. To make matters worse he ordered her not to discuss the issue with her women friends. Hopper's unexpected sexual tastes are one more reminder that his psyche was more complicated than his stalwart Yankee image would suggest. It's surely true that his combination of Puritan rectitude and twentieth-century urban weirdness is part of what makes him feel modern. Capable of producing both square-shouldered New England farmhouses and voyeuristic views through city windows, he's part Robert Frost, part Peeping Tom.

As the Hoppers moved through the years together, as he gathered prizes and collectors, sat on exhibition juries, gave tight-lipped interviews, and had one show after another, Jo's unhappiness became a perennial note in her life and theirs. We have a close picture of this because in the summer of 1933, as preparations were underway for Hopper's coronation by MoMA at his first retrospective, she started a diary. It began as an innocuous account of their daily lives—what painting her husband was working on, who came to visit, the movies, plays, and exhibits they saw. But over time a much darker kind of entry joined the mix. Again and again, Jo confided to her book her bitterness about the collapse of her hopes and her husband's inattention. "If E. would only *care*!"

Jo was never shy about airing her grievances directly to her husband. In her seventies she could say, "I am not a silent sufferer. I loathe silent sufferers." But the journal gave her a place to lick her wounds in private. It was in those pages where she asked, "What has become of my world—it's evaporated—I just trudge around in Eddie's." It was there where she set down her "rage" over his "determined opposition to every breath I draw," where she called him "kind of monstrous" and "a sadist" and "a killer," and where she glumly concluded, "He has never wanted me to get anything, to get anywhere." By the early 1950s, when their marriage was entering its fourth strenuous decade, she could look back on their time together with despair. "One had such bright expectations—but with the coming of E. everything went dead."

Hopper's typical response to Jo's episodic anger was to retreat into silence, which in any case was his behavioral default setting. It was also the condition most of his pictures aspired to. Few other artists—Chardin and Morandi in their still lifes, Donald Judd in his hermetic steel boxes—have embedded silence so deeply into their art, have understood so well the paradox that quiet could be a force multiplier, amplifying the power of their work to reach into wordless areas of the viewer's psyche. Hopper may have been a realist but he was not a literary painter, the type whose pictures suggest a clear story. In most of them, narrative, if there is any, is very hard to decipher. Like him.

All the same, what worked for his art merely complicated his life. His very inwardness ill-suited him to answer distress calls from people around him, even when they came from the other side of his own fraught dinner table. To Jo his mute presence was one more provocation. Her journals describe her exasperation with a husband who preferred the quiet company of books to his talkative wife. "E. H. lives to keep his nose in printed matter," she writes. "Any talk with me sends his eye to the clock. It's like taking the attention of an expensive specialist."

It seems pretty clear that Hopper was poking fun at this dynamic in their marriage in *Four Lane Road*, a 1956 painting in which for once there is more than the hint of a story you can guess at. Outside a gas station along a country road, a man sits quietly outdoors in a folding chair facing the sun. Just behind him a woman leans out a first-floor window. She looks to be shouting down to him. He ignores her, staring silently into the distance.

The picture is not Hopper at his best. It's too much the work of Hopper the sometime cartoonist; the satire is too blunt, the faces coarsely fashioned, the "four lane road" so skinny it would barely fit two. But by his midseventies this may have been a statement he needed to get off his chest. Certainly Jo saw it as a portrait of them. She complained to her diary, not without reason, that Hopper had given the hectoring woman "the most evil face . . . a regular shrike, expressive of what he's feeling about me." By that year she had long since formed her own ideas about *his* disposition. Soon she would have her nose in a book, too, the much-talked-about new advice manual by the psychotherapist Albert Ellis, *How to Live with a Neurotic*.

Amid the long silences, Jo's journals also record countless spats and quarrels. Sometimes these came to actual blows, when her much larger husband would hit her or pin her down with one knee, while she bit and clawed. However nonchalantly Jo records some of these battles—and her tone in describing them can range from matter-of-fact to defiant to frightened—these are the hardest parts of her journal to read. The worst of them are nothing short of brutal. In 1942, she describes a fight that resulted in "a good slap in the face and having my head banged up against a shelf in the kitchenette." She adds, "Afraid he'll kill me." Another time she reports, "I get a sound cuff on the side of my face & he got his face scratched in 2 places." She claims she once bit his finger "down to the bone."

Their car, a rolling metaphor for their marriage, was a constant theater of war. Jo wanted to drive. Hopper rarely let her. He thought she was too prone to mishaps on the road, or even the driveway, like the time she accidentally set fire to their secondhand Buick. She had been practicing how to back out of their garage in Truro when motor oil leaked onto the hot blacktop and ignited. Before that there was the time she had swerved to avoid an oncoming car, which resulted in a fender bender on the side of the road. Hopper was so angry he got out of the car and tried to drag her from the driver's seat by her ankles while she held on tightly to the steering wheel. This might all seem like a scene in a screwball comedy if you didn't know it was part of a larger pattern that was not funny.

The Hoppers' eternal deadlock was the governing condition of their old age, peaceful stretches interrupted by outbursts, with Jo's despair always simmering. The painter Raphael Soyer, a family friend, once recalled driving up to Truro in 1954 with his wife, Rebecca, and finding Hopper seated outside at one end of their house, gazing out over the hills. Jo was stationed on the opposite end, looking across the water. She explained this arrangement to Soyer as though it were a diagram of their marriage. "That's what we do all the time. He sits in his spot and looks at the hills all day and I look at the sea. And when we meet there is controversy, controversy, controversy."

As she approached her seventies, Jo found some encouragement again as an artist. In 1952, she had a watercolor portrait accepted for a group show at the Met. Did it help that her husband was on the selection jury? We don't know, but for once he may have nudged his fellow jurors.

Hopper made a few other efforts to promote Jo's work, though typically under duress. In 1946, when his despairing wife went on a two-day hunger strike, he agreed to bring some of her watercolors to his dealer, hoping Rehn would know a gallery that might take an interest. Though he had nothing to suggest, he did promise to show some of her work himself. Six years later, after her failure to be invited to join the realist painters' group led to yet another hunger strike, Hopper brought some of her pictures to another Manhattan dealer, again without results. And soon after the Greenwich Gallery closed, Hopper sent the Whitney's Goodrich a letter with an article about Jo. It reproduced a painting of hers that he called "the best cat and woman picture I have ever seen." Remembering Goodrich's earlier openness to Jo's work, Hopper no doubt hoped to prompt his old friend to give some thought to her again, but nothing came of it.

By the same token, for all her chronic anguish and intermittent rage, there are many entries in Jo's diaries in which she speaks of Hopper with tenderness, admiration, and even raw need. In 1954 she may be able to write, "I yearn to smash his glasses." One year later she's arrived at a complicated recognition: "I can scarcely stand E. H., but how possibly live without him." And the next year she can plead with heaven: "O God, God, so that he stays with me always—always—even if we do fight so much of the time." If there's a signal moment in her journals of their endless predicament, it's the one in which she describes how, in bed after long hours of squabbling, he reached for her across the covers. "We hadn't been in bed long before I felt his arm stretched over mine. 2 hrs. before there had seemed no possible way to go on together."

Reading a passage like that, you find yourself thinking of George and Martha going off to bed at the end of *Who's Afraid of Virginia Woolf?*—exhausted and battle-scarred, but still somehow a couple. The art historian Barbara Novak, a friend of the Hoppers in their later years, once described their marriage as a folie à deux, a joint enterprise of mutual exasperation and reciprocal need. Certainly it was what we might now call a toxic codependency. Given how unlike one another they were, their marriage may have been a mistake from the start. It was also, in some way, and for both of them, indispensable. It was their complicated fate that it would last them a difficult lifetime.

Meanwhile Hopper's other complicated fate was to be an artist. Even in old age, painting remained a kind of mystery to him, a thing that was not entirely in his hands. For this reason he considered *Seven A.M.*, though not a failure, at least a compromised version of his original intention. He felt that way about many of his paintings, even the ones, like *Seven A.M.*, that we now count among his most affecting. He told Jo he had wanted the trees to the left of the stark white shop to be "sturdy oaks." Somehow he ended up painting in locusts instead, with thin, gently curving trunks and tufted foliage. He explained to her that something had steered him in that direction, as though painting were an occult practice over which he exercised only partial control.

Or to put it another way, an unconscious practice. Hopper read Freud with interest, and though he would never invite Freudian interpretations of his work, much less submit to an analyst's couch, he was sufficiently intrigued by the Freudian model of the mind to say this to the artist-photographer Charles H. Sawyer: "So much of every art is an expression of the subconscious that it seems to me that most of the important qualities are put there subconsciously, and little of importance by the conscious intellect." At that point he may have worried he was sounding too high flown, so he added, "But these are things for the psychologist to untangle."

He often spoke of painting that way, as a medium in which each new brushstroke obscured his first intentions, until the picture overtook the man painting it. As early as 1933, he had written that "I find, in working, always the disturbing intrusion of elements not a part of my most interested vision, and the inevitable obliteration and replacement of this vision by the work itself as it proceeds." He later expressed the same idea to his friend Lloyd Goodrich of the Whitney, who observed, "This seems to bother him a great deal."

Hopper would never describe himself as a "metaphysical" painter. Yet however much he addressed himself only to the visible world, he was always in search of some first predicate behind it, some ultimate reality that the things we can see and touch merely hint at. The closest he came to admitting this on canvas was in his awkward 1959 painting *Excursion into Philosophy*. It's the rare Hopper that has an enigmatic title. Ordinarily he went in for the most straightforward naming. *Hotel Lobby, Summer Evening, Four Lane Road*—just-the-facts language, bald indicators of time or place. But this title is more provocative, leaving you to ask, which philosophy? And where is this excursion taking the somber man we see at the center of this canvas?

He sits on a bed—a very odd one, covered almost to the floor by a dark blue bedspread with such crisp edges and sharp corners that it looks like a tightly wrapped package. Behind him is a woman lying on her side, her face to the wall. Is she sleeping, or simply turning away from the man? Though she's wearing shoes and some kind of very short, rose-pink dress, her legs and bare buttocks are fully exposed—a rare example of Hopper representing on canvas his favorite part, if such it was, of a woman's body. But if there had been sex between these two, it must have been a while ago, because now the man is fully dressed, right down to his creased slacks and nearly pointed shoes.

From a window on the right side of the canvas one of Hopper's cascades of light flows into the room and leaves a glowing rectangle on the wall behind them. Another spreads across the floor at the man's feet. He gazes down into it, lost in thought. On the bed beside him is an open book, no doubt a volume of the philosophy the title promised. We can't see whose work it is, but the seventy-seven-year-old Hopper reportedly explained the picture to his dealer by saying the man had been "reading Plato rather late in life."

Did Hopper have in mind the ideal of platonic love that transcends physical desire? In that case this man may be longing to move beyond the pull of flesh, as represented by the half-naked woman whom he has literally put behind him. But it's just as possible that Hopper was thinking of the *Republic,* where Plato lays out his broader theory of an invisible realm of ideals, of absolute truth, that lies behind the visible world. If so, what we may be seeing here is a man—another Hopper surrogate?—torn between the counterfeit reality of the material world, represented again by the woman but also the all-too-solid bed, and whatever transcendent ideal is to be discovered in that captivating pool of light. That the fiction of the visible world was the very illusion Hopper devoted himself to in every painting only makes the man's dilemma more painful.

"Realism" is always a misleading word, at least as it applies to art. No picture, however much it may try, ever simply duplicates what the eye sees. If anything, the closer it gets to that goal, the more dreamlike it becomes. Look at any of the works of optical high-definition produced by photorealist painters, like Richard Estes and Robert Bechtle, who first gained notice in the 1970s. The nearer they got to "picture perfect," the more their images fluctuated in the mind's eye until they tipped into the unreal. To borrow a once fashionable academic term, the paradox of representational art is how easily it can "defamiliarize the familiar."

Hopper of course never attempted the high definition of a cameras lens, or even the ruler-edged look of precisionist painters of the 1920s and 1930s like Charles Sheeler, Charles Demuth, and (sometimes) Georgia O'Keeffe, artists whose taut lines seemed like guy wires holding in place the explosive energies of modernity. Hopper's weighty pictures seem more like emblems of eternity. Yet much of his art surely does defamiliarize the familiar. He bears down on prosaic realities until they release a whiff of the uncanny, suggesting not so much the world we live in but one proximate to it, a place always at a slight remove, always recognizable but somehow otherworldly.

He does this by various kinds of painterly legerdemain. Sometimes he rakes floors down, so that they tilt slightly toward us in a way they shouldn't. Or he toys with perspective in other ways, so that we see things, very subtly, from more than one vantage point. At times his sunlight comes from multiple directions. And sometimes he makes it fall into whatever shape he requires for the effect he's after, no matter how impossible it might be. The point for Hopper was never mere depiction. It was more like transfiguration, to take the raw material of the world and make it somehow mysterious and radiant.

In some of the work of his old age, Hopper, the great realist, actually tiptoes up to the edge of surrealism. As far back as 1942, there had been a hint of Giorgio de Chirico's ominous plazas in the empty train platform of Hopper's *Dawn in Pennsylvania*. But it was only after the war that the most prominent realist painter of his time produced a few pictures that he could not possibly have meant for us to entirely believe. The most teasing example is that 1951 painting called *Rooms by the Sea*, a haunting picture of a nearly empty interior. On the right is an open doorway that gives onto a seemingly

61

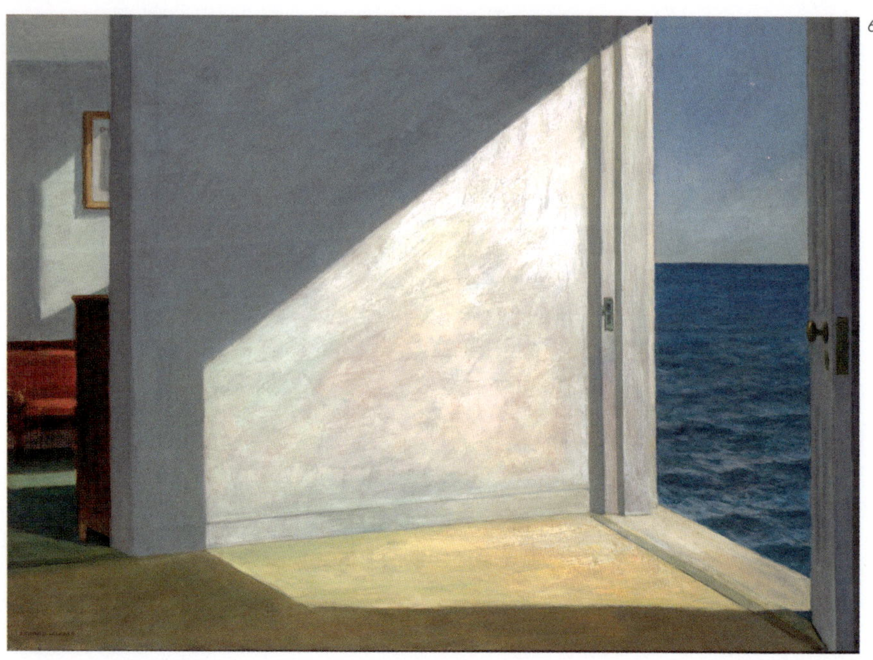

Rooms by the Sea, 1951, oil on canvas, 73.7 × 101.9 cm, Yale University Art Gallery, New Haven, Connecticut

impossible view. It's of a choppy blue sea, looming directly outside the threshold, with no sign of an intervening shore. What we see instead is a wall of water mounted halfway up the doorway, as though we were looking through the glass wall of an aquarium tank. Though the water is somehow held back, sunlight pours through that improbable opening. It deposits a wide trapezoid of light on a bare wall of the front room and spills across the wooden floor beneath it. At left there's a glimpse of the next room, where we see some furniture and a smaller patch of the same angular sunbeam high on the far wall.

In his notebooks, Hopper originally called this work *The Jumping Off Place*, another odd title for him. Certainly it feels as though you could plunge forward through that doorway directly into the sea. But with those enigmatic words Hopper might also have been saying that sunlight—here spread across a bare wall that's like a giant blank canvas—was always the jumping-off place for his imagination. This is after all a picture of what Hopper famously said was the only thing he ever really wanted to paint—"sunlight on the side of a house." This "side of a house" happens to be indoors, but it serves his purpose.

And in another of those autobiographical touches you find in his late work, the house we see here is his. *Rooms by the Sea* is based on an interior view of the Hoppers' summer place in the Cape Cod shore town of Truro. Even more than their apartment in Greenwich Village, the all-white, wood-shingled Truro house was a foursquare extension of both Hoppers. They had designed it together in the early 1930s, even building a three-dimensional model to help them arrange their living spaces and their all-important studios at either end. On its northern side they introduced a single immense window, seventeen feet tall, an outsize declaration that this place was a machine built to capture sunlight. Though they would not have electricity until 1954, meaning two decades without light bulbs, refrigeration, or a telephone, they both loved the final result. When Jo asked her husband if he didn't think their house was as good as Paradise, he had the perfect Hopper comeback: "Better, no people, no harps."

However much he approved it, Hopper never included the house in any of his pictures until *Rooms by the Sea*. It was rare for him even to allow photographers to come by. One famous exception was Arnold Newman, whom Hopper knew and trusted from a portrait Newman had made of him in 1941, in which he is seated pensively before a blank canvas in his Washington Square studio. Nineteen years later Newman hauled his big view camera up to Truro to photograph Hopper for *Horizon* magazine. Quickly becoming aware that Jo wanted to be in the picture, Newman made a now-classic portrait of an implacable-looking Hopper seated in the foreground on a white bench outside the house, its peaked roof forming an arrowhead pointed skyward, the big window looming behind him. In the distance, arms slightly bent at her sides like a dancer, is the much smaller figure of Jo, still broadcasting the energy that insists you look her way too.

Even when Hopper decided to allow his own house into *Rooms by the Sea*, he shows it to us with a few of his customary adjustments. In his painting, the doorway is hinged on the right. The actual door is hinged on the left. And we know from photographs of that space, taken from a perspective similar to the one in the painting, that the ocean, though it would be visible in the middle distance through the open door, would by no means appear pressed right up against it. But there's more. Computer simulations show that only a bizarre five-sided doorway could admit a sunbeam in exactly the trapezoidal shape we see in the foreground. As for the smaller square of light high on the wall of the next room, it could only be formed by a no less misshapen window that bordered the ceiling. If these were the shapes Hopper needed for his purposes then mere reality was a disposable constraint.

So this bizarre image is as brazenly unlikely as that famous Magritte locomotive barreling out of a fireplace. Hopper knew that. He told his dealer the picture was probably too strange to sell. Given his fame, it sold anyway, and quickly, to no less a notable than Stephen Carlton Clark. A founding trustee of the Museum of Modern Art—it was Clark who gave MoMA Hopper's *House by the Railroad*—he was a very ambitious collector, in constant competition with his estranged brother Sterling, who was founder of the Clark Art Institute in Williamstown, Massachusetts. Stephen was always more sympathetic to modernism than his brother, whose taste ran to old masters and impressionism. A Hopper that veered toward the surreal would have suited him fine.

Why the departures of this kind in Hopper's late work? By the 1950s, surrealism was largely a closed chapter in art history. Invoking it would hardly be a way for Hopper to connect with a fashionable department of modernism, which in any case he had no reason to do. A better explanation might be that as he grew older Hopper found that reality didn't always suit his feeling toward life, that there were mysteries the visual world hinted at but never quite divulged. Wasn't this the implied dilemma in *Excursion into Philosophy*? And Hopper could drift outside the boundaries of strict realism more easily than you might suppose, because even his most scrupulous oil paintings weren't executed on the scene but pieced together later in the studio. Hopper was in his early forties when he stopped doing easel paintings directly from nature. Though he would continue to make watercolors that way, all his subsequent oils were studio constructions, assembled from studies, memories, and bits of entirely manufactured detail.

So if some of Hopper's late pictures carry a whiff of the surreal, that was an effect he could accomplish just by moving up the dial a bit on those studio rearrangements. In a memory picture like *South Carolina Morning*, from 1955, the entire scene is a much-after-the-fact re-creation, based on his recollection of a woman he saw briefly some twenty-five years earlier, when he

62

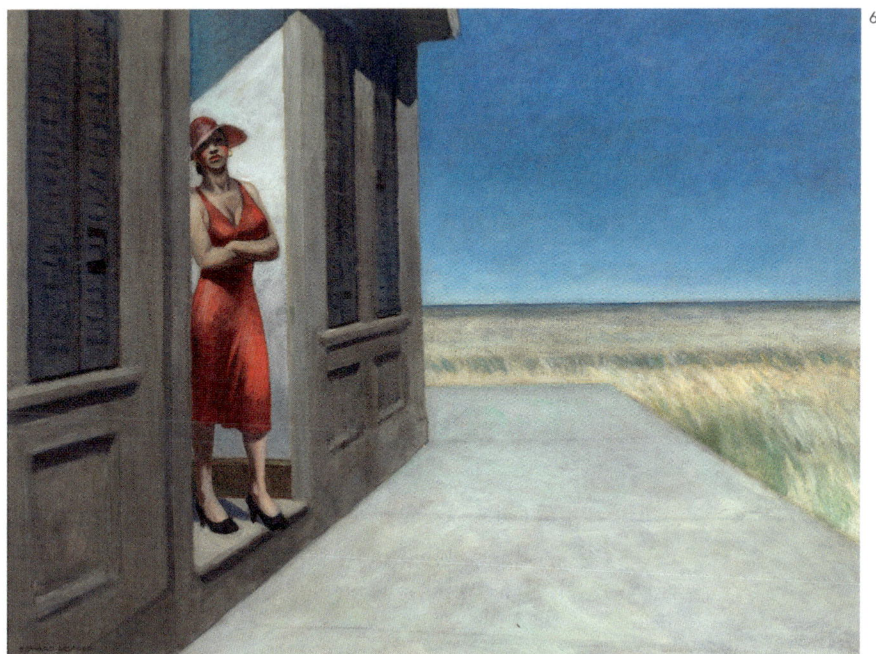

South Carolina Morning, 1955, oil on canvas, 77.2 × 102.2 cm, Whitney Museum of American Art, New York

and Jo were traveling through South Carolina. In the painting, a sumptuous Black woman in a blazing red dress and black high heels stands in the open doorway of a building with a wooden façade. At her feet a very improbable length of pavement sweeps past like a wide runway, then turns left at the corner to disappear behind the isolated building. Unconnected to any road that we can see, the building that frames her is surrounded by fields of yellow and green seagrass. They stretch from the horizon right up to the sidewalk's ruler-straight edges, so that the woman seems to be planted in an impossible place, a concrete island surrounded by a sea of vegetation.

The woman defies you to notice any of this. Lounging with her arms folded beneath her breasts, she has a lordly presence quite beyond the effect produced by her full figure. Her eyes, which may be closed, are just dimly visible in the shade of her wide-brimmed hat. In something like a classic contrapposto pose, weight shifted to her rear leg, her other knee slightly bent, she's absorbed in a drowsy sensuality that literally nods to the dreamlike atmosphere of the entire image.

In the following year, Hopper painted *Sunlight on Brownstones*, a more straightforward scene until you notice how much of it isn't. Now we're in a city, almost certainly New York, where a man and woman once again gaze silently into the light. Both appear on the left side of the canvas, where he stands in the doorway of a low-rise brownstone and she sits on the handrail of the building's stone staircase. On the right we can see across a narrow street into a park. Beneath a patch of blue sky there are some feathery trees, plus a glimpse of lawn behind a rocky ridge. The rocks have a silhouette that's like toppling dominoes, a formation as startling and incongruous as the mountains behind the *Mona Lisa*.

Hopper made his preliminary sketches for this picture on Manhattan's Upper West Side, just across from Central Park, which might present these very elements to someone seeing it from across the street—just not in this way. The avenue that runs between the brownstones and the park is too slender. Meanwhile that rocky ridge is pressed too close to the low wall, and the wall is *too* low, out of scale with the rocks and trees looming behind it. Not so much a park view as an expressionist stage set, this is a scene that even Hopper described as "vague not accurate."

That improbable avenue and that ill-proportioned wall are signs of how far the aging Hopper was willing to go to violate the rules of a convincing illusionism he had long ago mastered. In this he's like the elderly Titian, the man who largely abandoned the smooth finish and firm modeling that made him famous for the broken brushwork of his late style. For both, it can seem that the skills they acquired over a lifetime were insufficient to what they needed to say, and in their last years they were finally willing to throw off any hesitations about putting them aside.

There's one more of Hopper's forays into the semi-surreal worth examining. In his curious 1960 painting *People in the Sun*, three men and two women are seated in wooden folding chairs on a sunstruck pavement. Four of them are ranged side by side, facing sharply right toward another of Hopper's unlikely landscapes. This one starts just across from them, on the other side of yet another disproportionately narrow road. It's a wide field of ocher grassland that ends in the distance along a range of dark foothills. Even by Hopper's relaxed standards, this quartet of fully dressed sunbathers are stiffs, as inanimate as the marionettes that pass for people in a Balthus. They look like attentive playgoers, with the erect posture and fixed expressions of an

63

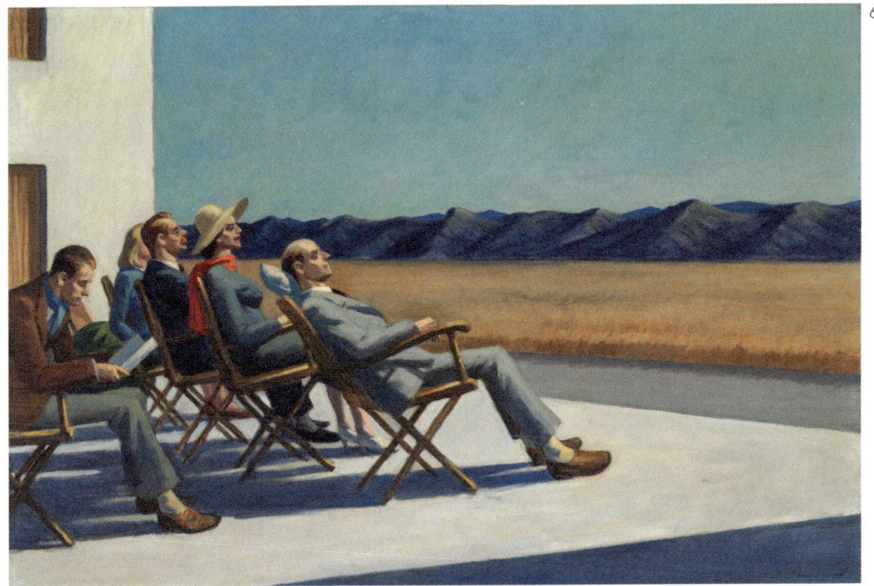

People in the Sun, 1960, oil on canvas, 102. 6 × 153.5 cm, Smithsonian American Art Museum, Washington, D.C.

audience. Even the landscape before them looks more like a painted backdrop than a real view.

Sitting just behind them is the fifth figure in this picture, a young man ignoring the scene that has so captured them. Instead, he's bent over a book. Is he another surrogate for Hopper, the compulsive reader, the man for whom the silent discourse of the printed page was the only kind of discourse he liked? In that case this painting might be Hopper's last word on the grand western vistas that left most tourists transfixed but left him indifferent. He told Jo he found them "too impersonal."

But it's also notable that Hopper has cast this scene as a comedy, a rare thing for him. We know he admired Honoré Daumier, a cartoonist who was also a great painter. At home Hopper liked to make satirical sketches, mostly good-humored commentaries on his fractious marriage, like the sketch of himself and Jo that he captioned "Non-Anger man, Pro-Anger woman." No doubt with an evil grin, he would leave these around the house for Jo to find. Think of *People in the Sun* as another of Hopper's cartoons, dressed up as an oil painting, and it starts to make sense. Maybe it's not just a comment on his failure to appreciate the great western sublime, but also a satire of modern tourism and its compulsory "sight-seeing," in which few sights are ever really seen. Maybe it's Hopper satirizing himself, the self-described "hermit" out of step with the taste of his time. Whatever his intention, there's a whiff of *Mad* magazine in there somewhere.

In the same year he made that picture, 1960, Hopper produced another that was, in classic Hopper fashion, entirely straightforward and utterly enigmatic. No doubt it's for both reasons that *Second Story Sunlight,* completed when he was seventy-eight, has become one of his best-known paintings. It shows us another of his four-square white houses. This time Hopper limits our view to the upper floors, which rise in the form of twin towers—two high gables under sharply pitched roofs that are like matching white spearheads. Each holds a single window within its narrow tip, with two tall windows on the second floor below. On that floor the tower to our left is also fronted by

64

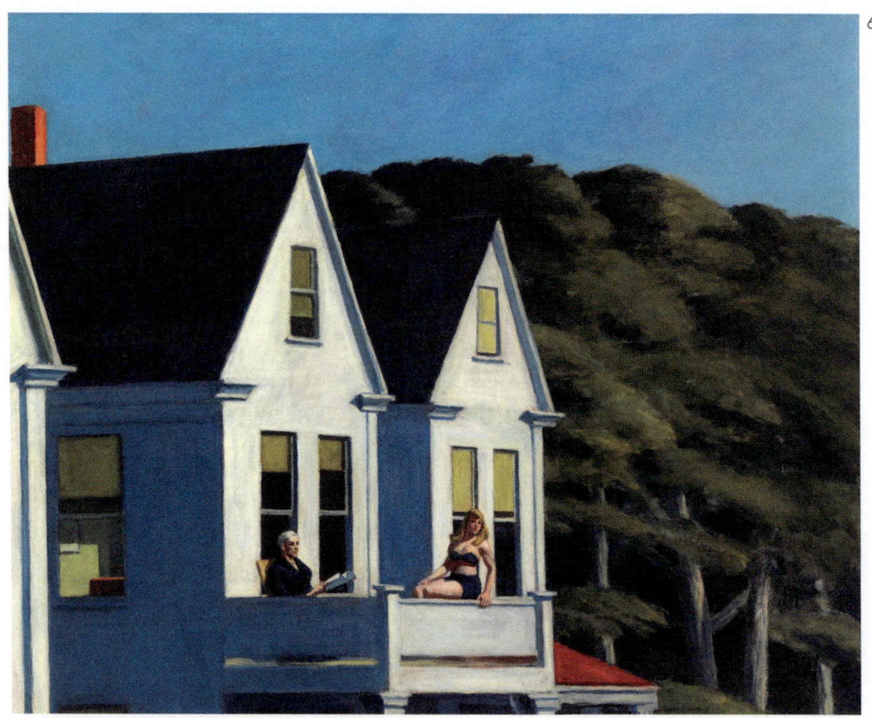

Second Story Sunlight, 1960, oil on canvas, 102.1 × 127.3 cm, Whitney Museum of American Art, New York

a broad balcony with waist-high wooden barriers around three sides. Two silent women are taking in the sun there. One is young, a long-haired blonde wearing dark-blue shorts and a blue halter top that bares her waist. She's perched almost in profile on the upper edge of the porch railing, so that her pink thighs and upper body catch the sun as she gazes out toward whatever there is to see. Farther back is a gray-haired woman in a blue dress, with just a modest slice of neckline bared, sitting in a chair and holding an open magazine.

That sunstruck house is decidedly solid and hard-edged. The flesh-and-blood women seem more related to the shadowy grove of trees that spreads out behind the house. Their branches dense with soft clouds of green leaf, they form another of Hopper's dark, feathery woodlands. Indistinct forests of that kind, playing visual and psychological counterpoint to hard surfaces in the same picture, are one source of the uncanny power of so many of Hopper's paintings. They somehow suggest a realm of the unconscious that surrounds waking experience, like the woods that are "lovely, dark and deep" in Robert Frost's poem. Whether running behind the red fuel pumps at the isolated filling station in *Gas*, alongside the shop window in *Seven A.M.*, behind the searching woman in *Cape Cod Morning*, or outside the somewhat ominous open door in *Stairway*, that silent, beckoning greenery is one reason Hopper's plain reality is never all that plain.

As always with Hopper there's no clear narrative in this painting, just the emotional and psychological vibrations set off by the contrast between the two women, one old and subdued looking, the other much younger and apparently more vital, balanced along her railing as if ready to fly off into life. And as always, Hopper wouldn't say what they might represent, offering only that his picture was "an attempt to paint sunlight as white with almost no yellow pigment."

In the fall of 1956, the Hoppers set off on what would be their final trip west. It was to a different kind of destination this time, not Mexico or the southern states, and not by way of the motels and tourist camps where they usually stopped. They were headed straight to California and the unaccustomed comforts being offered them by the Huntington Hartford foundation in Pacific Palisades. The Foundation had been established eight years earlier by the heir to the once enormous A&P supermarket fortune. A tireless playboy, erratic businessman, and would-be thinker, Hartford detested most modern art and literature. On a 150-acre site in Rustic Canyon, he built a retreat where artists, musicians, and writers who didn't take their lead from Faulkner, de Kooning, or Picasso could produce more-traditional work. Earlier that year, Hopper had been awarded the foundation's annual art prize, which included a six-month residency at the Pacific Palisades campus. For the Hoppers it would mean having a Frank Lloyd Wright–designed house and two studios, one for each of them. At breakfast and dinner there would be a communal dining room where the distinguished guests could trade views over meals prepared by the staff. Jo loved everything about the place, luxuriating in the private studio, the nonstop talk, and the relief of being in a setting where nobody expected her to cook. Hopper appreciated it, too, but kept his customary distance. At meals he stayed to one end of the long dining table, ruminating in silence.

During his time in Pacific Palisades, which lasted from December 1956 through the following June, Hopper did produce one oil painting. Ironically, in this redoubt of traditionalism and his deepening old age, it was one of his most modern in its streamlined feel. In *Western Motel* we find a

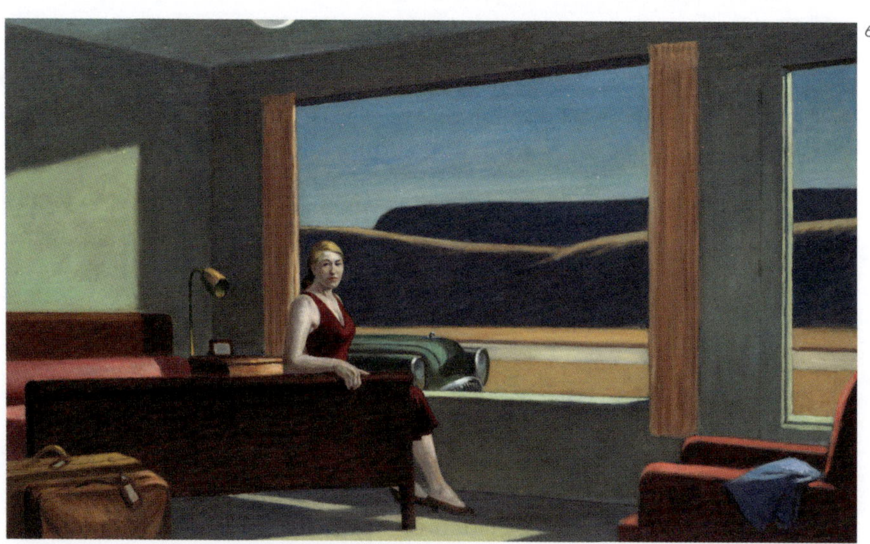
65

Western Motel, 1957, oil on canvas, 77.8 × 128.3 cm, Yale University Art Gallery, New Haven, Connecticut

self-possessed blond woman in a spare, sunny room. Seated at the foot of a large bed, she's wearing a low-cut purple dress, though most of her lower body is blocked from our view by the dark wood footboard where she rests her right arm. That gives her the appearance of one of those half-length Renaissance portraits of a figure leaning on a parapet, a reference Hopper may even have meant us to register, though not to dwell on.

Behind her is a picture window so wide it feels like a CinemaScope movie screen. It looks onto another of Hopper's perfunctory hillside views, the western landscape that left him so unimpressed, reduced here to a few featureless rises, the nearest ones looking like deflated loaves of bread. We also get a glimpse of one more of his impossibly slender roadways and, just outside the window, the hood, grille, and headlights of a green car, one based on the Hoppers' own Buick.

At the foot of the bed are two unopened suitcases. Is this woman arriving or departing? We don't know, but she has paused long enough to do an utterly unexpected thing. She's looking straight at us, one of the very few people to do that in any painting by Hopper. Ordinarily his pictures are full of men and women looking anywhere else, enclosed in their own solitudes and unaware that we're watching them. This woman is watching us. Interestingly, among the very few earlier examples of a direct gaze in Hopper's work, three are self-portraits, including two from his student days and a famous one from his forties. So Hopper reserved eye-to-eye contact almost exclusively for images of himself and for the privileged exchange between artist and viewer. Three decades after last deploying it in a self-portrait, he brings it back for this painting of a woman on the road, one of his favorite places to be. But who is she?

One possibility—she's Hopper. To be clear, this is not a picture of Hopper in drag, and not just because Jo was the model, as she was for all the women in his work after their marriage. But as we know from *Cape Cod Morning*—that image of a woman in a bay window enclosure, a solitary searcher not unlike himself—Hopper was willing sometimes to let a woman serve as a surrogate for himself, a spiritual and psychological stand-in. Ten years before his death, the woman in *Western Motel* is also someone like him, or us, someone passing through life. At the same time, her steady regard is a reminder of the power of the artist's vision—Hopper's vision—to fix in place the passage of time. She may be in transit, but her riveting gaze brings everything around her to a halt.

There's one other hallmark of Hopper's later work that *Western Motel* epitomizes. It's a kind of aesthetic streamlining. To clear the stage for the light shows of his last years, he radically unpacks many of his pictures, sweeping away extraneous detail. That makes his late work feel more of its moment, bringing it into line with the clean-line modern design and architecture that was gaining ground in postwar America. Even as a younger man he was not one to produce cluttered compositions, but in old age he empties out his scenes with a vengeance. Rooms are sparingly furnished, if at all, the better to expose the bare walls that are the landing pads for his broad inroads of sunlight. People disappear. By comparing Hopper's preparatory drawings with the finished canvases, we know that a woman was erased from *Sunlight on Brownstones* and a man from his 1955 lobby scene, *Hotel Window*, leaving an isolated woman to gaze by herself out into the darkness. Another man has exited the orchestra section in *Intermission*, so that once again it's a solitary woman who now passes the time, sitting suspended in the featureless moment. And in *Sun in an Empty Room* it's a woman who's been subtracted from the scene, so the walls can sun themselves with no humans to steal the show.

Landscapes are pared down too. *Road and Trees* is one of just two paintings Hopper completed in 1962, the year he turned eighty. Now it's the outdoors he's stripping down to basics. A straight expanse of pale gray pavement traverses the canvas, forming a slender horizontal band beneath yet another of his walls of dark foliage and an incongruously bright blue sky. Something we don't see are cars. None were needed. As he well understood, this bandsaw of a highway has its own implied momentum. And anyway, the American road is lonely, and what's lonelier than an empty one?

It cannot escape notice how much this picture verges toward abstraction, with broad zones of color and a firm, simplified construction. Even the more detailed trees bring to mind the blast marks of pigment in an Adolph Gottlieb. Though Hopper may have dismissed the work of abstract painters, he always knew what they were up to. Certainly this picture has affinities with Mark Rothko's foggy zones of color. Even more so it rhymes with Barnett Newman's "zip" paintings, tall or wide canvases in a single color with a thin strip of contrasting color cutting down them. Newman usually placed his zips vertically. Hopper lays his down from side to side but still seems to nod toward Newman's stripes slicing along a backdrop of solid color—and with something like the same bracing effect, as if to show that you don't have to resort to abstraction to go down the same road.

In the postwar years of AbEx supremacy, Hopper always maintained that most people still wanted recognizable imagery, that taste would swing back, that abstraction was "a temporary phase in art." At a Manhattan penthouse party in the 1950s, he intervened in an argument between Jackson Pollock and the quasi-abstractionist Stuart Davis by pointing them to a sunset outside the window and telling them, "People are starved for content today." He didn't have to add that painters like them were the ones he held responsible.

As it turned out, Hopper was partly right. Though abstraction would live on as an option for any artist to take up, art would soon make a decided turn back toward the visible world. But when it did, first in the work of Jasper Johns and Robert Rauschenberg, then in the early '60s explosion of pop art, it wasn't in any way Hopper would have predicted. The "realism" of Andy Warhol, Roy Lichtenstein, Claes Oldenburg, and James Rosenquist was heavy with irony, their version of reality the one manufactured by media, advertising, and consumer culture. Missing from any of this was the intrinsic density of Hopper's world, all those weighty rooms and tangible people, though you could find them in the work of artists like David Hockney, Alice Neel, and Lucian Freud. In particular, the impassive people in Hockney's double portraits have a family resemblance to Hopper's.

All the same pop was a watershed moment. It let the world back in, so that in the next decades "realisms" of every kind would proliferate. Photorealism, neo-expressionism, plus work by artists with no "ism" attaching to them and sculpture with the human form once again as its starting point—representational imagery would be the working kit of so many artists that abstraction would again be a minority position. Meanwhile Clement Greenberg's "grand narrative," the one leading to the final triumph of abstraction, dissolved under the pressure of an emerging postmodernism that declared there was no royal road of art history, just a network of infinite byways.

In this transition back to figuration, there were few moments to compare with the grand apostasy of the painter Philip Guston. After three years of quiet experimentation in the seclusion of a new studio in Woodstock, New York, in 1970 Guston stunned the artworld with a Manhattan gallery show of wall-size canvases that weren't the lush abstractions that had made him famous but a return to the cartoonish realism he had abandoned two decades before. He would go on working that way for the rest of his life. What a shame Hopper didn't live to hear Guston's explanation for this about-face: "I got sick and tired of all that Purity! I wanted to tell stories."

By the mid-1960s, Hopper's health was plainly failing. He was repeatedly in and out of hospitals. He even turned down an invitation to Lyndon Johnson's 1965 inaugural. He didn't feel up to it and anyway he was a Republican to the end. Meanwhile he had his final work to attend to. His last painting, produced that year, was *Two Comedians*, that picture in which he and Jo, dressed as commedia dell'arte clowns, take a final bow at the edge of a stage. It's a poignant image, but as a farewell to the world maybe a little too pat. Though not for Frank Sinatra, who would eventually buy it.

More subtle, and for that reason more affecting, is *Sun in an Empty Room*, made two years earlier, in which Hopper returned to one of the nondescript rooms he had painted so many times. Only now he dared at last to arrange it just as he wanted it—emptied out entirely so as to hold nothing but light, rendered with the hard-edged starkness of a minimalist abstraction. It's a

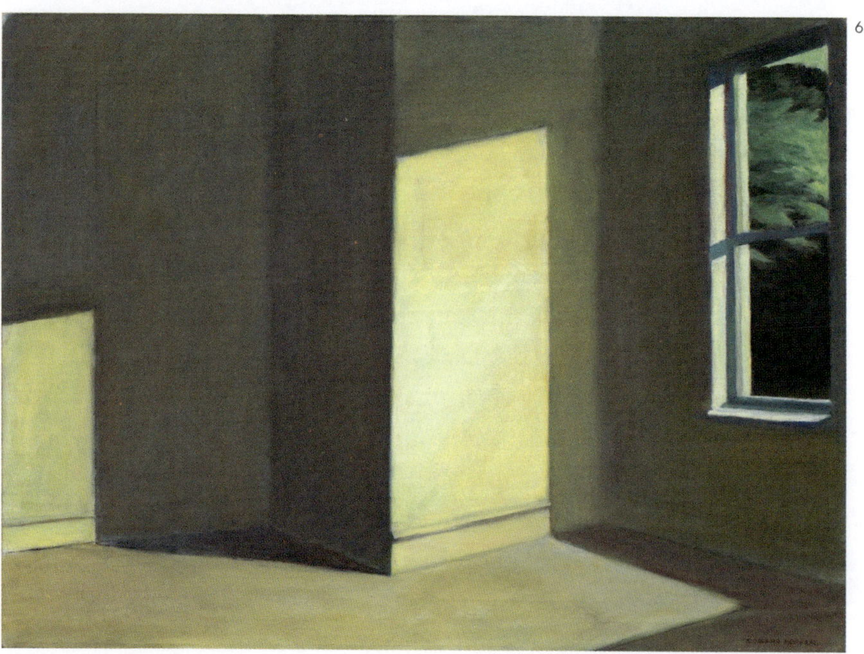
66

Sun in an Empty Room, 1963, oil on canvas, 73 × 100.5 cm, private collection room as bare as his studio in Greenwich Village, the one where no pictures, not even his own, were allowed to spoil the beauty of the empty white walls.

But plainly we're meant to see that this room is not empty after all. It's inhabited by the departing spirits of the artist and his wife, expressed as the two vertical bars of sunlight that climb the walls. Like Hopper and Jo, one is much taller than the other. The husband and wife who used to sun themselves on opposite ends of the house have been brought together one last time, as shimmering cenotaphs. Both these lingering presences are certain soon to fade away, their lives and their disputes dissolving into the last of Hopper's resounding silences. Sunlight and silence, as ever Hopper's constants, the prime elements of *Seven A.M.*, this time brought into service for a memorial to himself and his wife, who would both be gone within a few years.

Hopper would die in his studio on May 15, 1967, at the age of eighty-four. Jo would follow on March 6 of the next year, just short of eighty-five. They would leave behind their art and their complex account of themselves in words and pictures. You might say they also left behind a challenge to us to somehow make our peace with their contradictions. After all, they did.

October 4, 1944

From Jo's diary:

It's been such a happy week, gorgeous weather and we both painting.

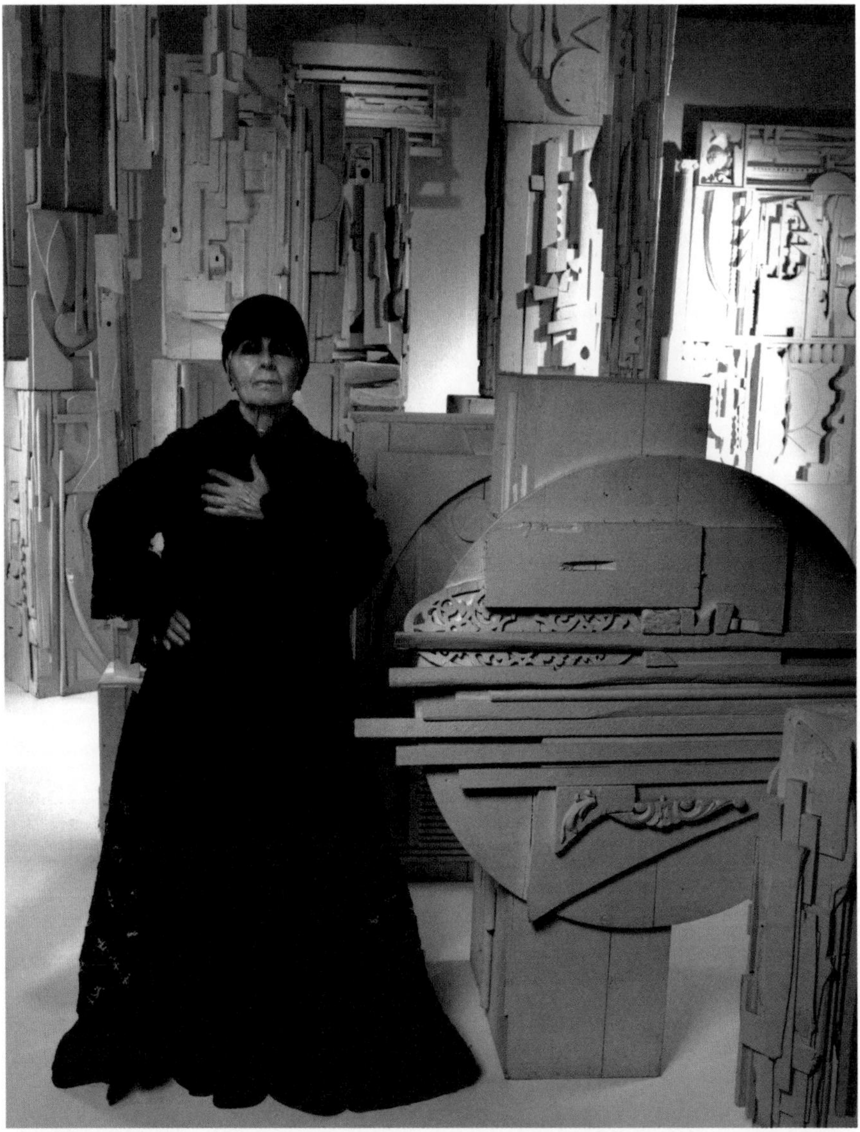

Nevelson in 1972, surrounded by her white wood assemblage sculptures

6

LOUISE NEVELSON

My Whole Life's Been Late

Cézanne and Van Gogh notwithstanding, not many of the artists we remember today had to wait forever to be recognized, much less until after they were dead. Long before the cool kids of the 1980s and '90s, the era of Jean-Michel Basquiat, Keith Haring, and the first stirrings of Damien Hirst, there were any number who found success early. Velázquez was just twenty-four when he was named a court painter for Philip IV of Spain and by one account the king's exclusive portraitist. Jacob Lawrence was the same age the year he finished *The Migration Series,* his chronicle of the twentieth-century Black exodus to northern cities that brought him his first fame. Marcel Duchamp was all of twenty-five when *Nude Descending a Staircase* made him not just famous but notorious at the New York Armory Show.

Then there was Louise Nevelson, the patron saint of late bloomers. It's not merely that, when she finally arrived, she was no longer young. It's that even middle age was behind her. The turning point event of her long climb into the light was "Sixteen Americans," the fifth in a series of group shows mounted every few years by the Museum of Modern Art to single out emerging artists. All of them were organized by Dorothy C. Miller, a MoMA curator supremely attuned to her time and to whoever was doing its most forward-looking work, even if that might be someone well on in years. That would describe Nevelson. When the show opened, on December 16, 1959, she was sixty.

The road to that moment had been full of hard bargains, made at great cost, and not just to herself. Decades earlier she had walked out of a stifling marriage with a husband who had money, at least at first, and even some interest in the arts, just not enough to want an artist as his wife. In an act that never stopped haunting her, she had abandoned her son, Mike, at first when he was nine so that she could study painting in Germany, later to pursue her new life as an artist in Manhattan. This left him for years to shuttle between her immigrant parents in Maine and his downwardly mobile father, with occasional detours back to her in whatever tight circumstance she found herself. She had weathered depression, serious money problems, periods of heavy drinking, and decades of neglect by an art world in which even the most gifted women were marginalized. All the while she held to the idea that she mattered and in due time the world would come around. And she was right. It's just that due time took longer than she expected.

Of the artists chosen for "Sixteen Americans," Nevelson was by far the oldest. Ellsworth Kelly was next, at thirty-six. All the rest were in their twenties and thirties, including Robert Rauschenberg at thirty-four; Jasper Johns, twenty-nine; and Frank Stella, just twenty-three. Typical of the era, there was only one other woman, the San Francisco-based painter Jay DeFeo, who was thirty. Though not nearly so famous as she was about to become, Nevelson was also probably the best known of what was at that time a largely obscure cohort. She had been "emerging" for over a decade, and there were critics who had promoted her work for even longer. Since the mid-1950s in particular, a series of brilliantly inventive gallery shows had brought her what might be called art world fame, meaning enthusiastic reviews in the *New York Times* and in magazines like *Arts*.

But by definition, art world fame has a narrow range of broadcast. MoMA was an altogether larger platform. It was the chief custodian of modern art history, and in those days the arbiter of who mattered in contemporary art. However many smaller venues Nevelson had appeared in, however many critics had paved her way, "Sixteen Americans" would be a debut, a first step onto a world stage and a vindication of her ragged faith that she was an artist to be taken seriously. Hemingway famously said that people went bankrupt "gradually, and then suddenly." Nevelson achieved recognition that way. And though it delighted her to be discovered, even so late in the day, it by no means intimidated her. She was road tested, resilient, and full of ideas and energy. If ever there was an artist who was ready for her close-up, it was Nevelson. She had been ready for it all her life.

. . .

It was only the year before that Nevelson had mounted the breakthrough gallery exhibition that made Dorothy Miller, who had long been following her work, decide it was time to invite her across the threshold of MoMA. "Moon Garden + One," which had opened in January 1958, was a pioneering example of installation art, a creative practice that Nevelson pioneered. In a darkened space barely illuminated under dim blue light, she had combined a massive black wooden wall assemblage with an array of smaller wood constructions in a room-filling interplay. Lining the gallery's perimeter or perched on tabletop platforms, every sculpture in that space was in some enigmatic concert with all the others, one meant to engulf the viewer—the "One" of Nevelson's title—in a unified field of sensory overload. Not just the labor of months, that show was the work of a lifetime. When she was done installing its many parts, Nevelson, who had studied expressive movement for years, broke into an ecstatic dance with her studio assistant Teddy Haseltine.

Apart from the powerful way the show was conceived and mounted, Nevelson's great innovation for "Moon Garden" was its centerpiece, a monumental wooden wall called *Sky Cathedral*. Walls of that kind, intricately assembled jumbotrons of black wood, were an invention she would return to for the rest of her life. Each was a towering message board of crates, sometimes dozens of them, all holding abstract tableaux made from wooden castoffs she found on the curbs and in the trash cans of Manhattan. Combing the predawn streets behind an old wheelbarrow, Nevelson might come upon discarded chairs, broken picture frames and lengths of scallop-cut molding, along with bedposts, balusters, newels, spindles, and piano legs, plus ragged offcuts of all shapes and sizes. She either took them as she found them, cracked, scuffed, and timeworn, or she cut and smoothed them back at home, where she also painted everything a uniform black. She would insert these whatnots inside the crates, composing them according to an arcane syntax all her own, but with a peerless sense of syncopated visual rhythm. Then she would stack the boxes face forward to produce an intricate call-and-response among her multitude of shallow compartments. Seen today, a Nevelson wall can bring to mind a semi-abstract Zoom screen where some tantalizing group chat is underway, one you fully intend to join, as soon as you figure out the multiple passwords.

More than eleven feet high and ten feet long, *Sky Cathedral* was a work so

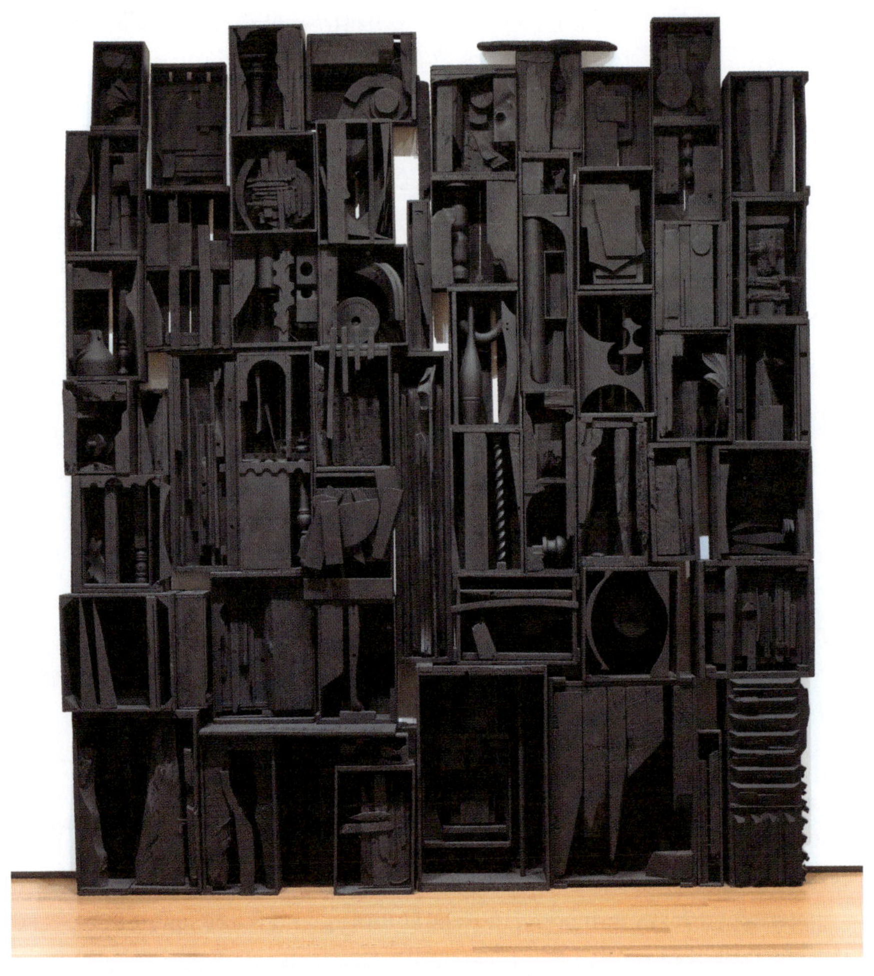

Sky Cathedral, 1958, painted wood, 343.9 x 305.4 × 45.7 cm, The Museum of Modern Art, New York

forceful and original that even before "Sixteen Americans" opened, MoMA acquired a version for its permanent collection. (Nevelson would make at least eight variants.) A young Hilton Kramer, the future *Times* critic and a rising voice in cultural journalism, summed them up well in *Arts* when he said that the various *Sky Cathedral* works were "appalling and marvelous, utterly shocking in the way they violate our received ideas on the limits of sculpture and on the confusion of genres, yet profoundly exhilarating in the way they open an entire realm of possibility."

As Kramer understood, Nevelson's walls drew brilliantly from multiple streams of twentieth-century art, including cubism and cubist collage, with nods to early Soviet-era constructivism and the surrealism that Nevelson had first explored in the 1940s. (The box was a favorite surrealist device, one used most effectively by Joseph Cornell.) Certainly they seemed to have affinities with the street-flotsam collages that the German Dadaist Kurt Schwitters made in the 1920s, and especially his *Merzbau*s, whole rooms with eccentric outcroppings like jagged ice floes. But Nevelson claimed to have been unaware of Schwitters until he was brought to her attention by the Swiss artist Jean Arp, who was so thrilled by his first sight of her work in New York that he published a poem about it in a French art magazine. In any case Nevelson's walls had layers of mythic and psychological resonance that were not part of Schwitters's aim. In her seventies she would say of herself, "I was always a soloist," and certainly her mature work was entirely her own.

Even so, an artist whose influence she was happy to acknowledge was Picasso. She once described cubism—in a typically eccentric locution—as "one of the greatest awarenesses the human mind has ever come to." In her walls she took the fractured, shallow space of cubist paintings and translated it into a no less shallow three dimensions. Because the wooden elements in any box were most often fastened into place near the viewer, some even attached to the outer edges of their box, they lent her walls the surface appearance of a rippling, low-relief carving. By the 1950s, sculpture, like painting, had been tending toward actual flatness for years. Picasso's wood plank assemblies, David Smith's welded steel constructions, and the dangling wafers of sheet metal in Alexander Calder's mobiles were all rejections of the solidity that sculpture had aspired to for centuries. In her own work, Nevelson discovered an ambiguous zone between flatness and depth that she played with in both directions to great effect.

At the same time, however shallow they may have been, her walls were monumental. They rivaled in size the abstract expressionist canvases that dominated postwar American art, the swaggering dimensions of a Jackson Pollock or Mark Rothko. This was after all a woman who would one day come back from a trip to Egypt and say that she found the pyramids "too small." The magnitude of her new work seemed to Nevelson the natural expression of the mad vitality she had called upon to produce it. "I attribute the walls to this," she would say. "I had loads of energy."

Scale wasn't the only characteristic of postwar American abstraction that Nevelson's walls shared. They had the "allover" composition of most abstract expressionist paintings, the centerless space predicted in Monet's late water lily panels. Through their multitude of curved and broken shapes, plus the trickles of light peeking out from between them, they also brought into sculpture a touch of expressionist painterly form. And the way they built something modern out of vintage parts made them steampunk before there was such a thing. Nevelson's wooden walls were devices with endless possibilities, and over the next three decades she would make scores of them, even while also finding her way into other materials and approaches to sculpture.

But Nevelson's ambitions for her art were never merely a matter of space and form, any more than Pollock's or Rothko's were. Though her mysterious walls resisted any final decoding, they invited all kinds of free association. They could bring to mind altarpieces full of sacred niches, grottoes with dark cavities, lines of mysterious hieroglyphs, coffins, tabernacles, circuit boards, and exposed innards of every sort. As complex and contradictory as the human psyche, the walls were places where a regiment of upright shafts in one box might suggest an internal clarity that a jumble of wooden fragments in the next box denied, while in a third box a curving chair leg hinted at some flexible state between order and chaos.

As dark chambers, the boxes were also metaphors for secret places within the self, some of them no doubt her own. Looked at that way, their teasing internal configurations become the insignia of unconscious drives. This suggestion of something concealed was especially true of the boxes that contained drawers with keyholes or had hinged doors left slightly ajar. Others were almost entirely enclosed, like confessionals, obscured by planks or caged behind a peekaboo line of slender pickets. Though none of her boxes would ever contain anything like human forms or features, to look deeply into them can feel as voyeuristic as peering through one of Edward Hopper's city windows to spy on the people inside.

The sheer intricacy of her walls was one reason Nevelson painted them all black. It was a way to unify and subdue them visually. "Black creates harmony" is how she thought of it. It also conferred the mystique of darkness, night, and the unconscious. And it helped to solve a problem created by her use of vintage junk. She knew that might tip her work into the realm of nostalgia, especially in a place like postwar Manhattan, where a new world of glass and steel was overtaking the ornate and fragile past her castoffs called to mind. They were, as she once nicely put it, "the skin that New York has shed." But nostalgia was something she wanted no part of, so she hoped the uniform black would thwart any urge on the part of the viewer to sentimentalize these odds and ends or to dwell on whatever purposes they once served. "That lonely, lowly object is not used anymore for what it was," she would explain. "It becomes a work of art."

As she would certainly have known, this placed her work in a line of descent from Marcel Duchamp and his readymades, found objects like the urinal purchased from a plumbing store that he signed "R. Mutt" and sent off to be exhibited as a work of art. Nevelson's new take on the readymade was to collage her found objects by the dozens in a single work and give free play to their interactions. Yet having reclaimed these things from the scrap heap, even she wasn't always sure at first what new uses they might be good for. Some she squirreled away for years, until she found herself at work on just the wall where they belonged. For this reason, the massive inventory of discards that Nevelson kept stashed at home was always neatly stored and well organized. Her art was only possible because she combined a scavenger's instincts with a librarian's skill set.

"Moon Garden" made enough of a splash that it was covered in both *Time* and *Life*, giving Nevelson a first taste of attention from mass-circulation magazines. And the show's blue twilight vibe was strange enough that *Life* headlined its three page spread "Weird Woodwork of Lunar World." It also led with a photo of Nevelson in what looked like a witch's hat. ("Without resorting to eyes of newts or toes of frogs she has conjured up a spectral sculptured landscape . . .") The spook-show atmospherics of that picture badly misrepresented Nevelson's intentions. Beyond her aesthetic and psychological aims, what she tried to evoke in her environments was not the folktale supernatural but the genuinely spiritual, in the particular way she understood the term. She was not religious in any conventional sense, but she was much drawn to the otherworldly.

It was thanks to that side of herself that she became deeply interested in the teachings of the Indian writer and lecturer Krishnamurti, whom she first heard speak in 1928 and whose emphasis on self-realization resonated in a woman fleeing marriage and motherhood. When explaining her art in interviews Nevelson also pointed frequently, if none too clearly, to the idea of a "fourth dimension." It was not a notion unique to her. Some variety of it had intrigued a number of artists in the twentieth century, whether as a spatial concept, as the cubists understood it, or as some mystical domain. Like so many ideas of that kind, it didn't lend itself to clear description—certainly Nevelson never managed one—but it was plainly an immaterial realm of real importance to her, a world beyond the merely physical that she wanted her art not only to express but to summon.

Nevelson saw her deliberate use of shadow as one means to tune her work to those cosmic frequencies, to scatter phantom traces of the ineffable all around her solid walls. Could she capture in wood the same yearning for transcendence you find in the pulsing vapors of the abstractions of her friend Mark Rothko? She would try. Quite apart from their spiritual potential, Nevelson thought of shadows as artist materials in other ways, both as compositional devices and as signifiers of deep but intangible feeling. She was especially proud of having brought this weightless medium into the working kit of sculpture. As she would put it, and rightly, "I used shadow as if it were made out of stone."

Even before the reviews came in, the year of "Moon Garden" was a personal watershed for Nevelson, one that began with a great purge. For years she had been miserably awaiting eviction from the faded four-story brownstone on East Thirtieth Street that her family had helped her buy in 1945 to put a roof over her head. But by the mid-1950s her old neighborhood was being demolished piecemeal, largely to make way for modernist-grid apartment towers designed by the rising architect I. M. Pei. These were the same years that she made her first walls, and it's hard not to see them in part as an attempt to preserve fragments of her disappearing corner of Manhattan.

Moving would be no simple matter. Her house was stuffed to overflowing with salvaged street finds and hundreds of artworks, both her own and things she collected, like African tribal sculpture and Southwest Indian pottery. When Hilton Kramer paid a visit in the 1950s, he found himself in a dim warren of art and art materials, a "very mysterious world" where even the bathtubs were filled with her works in progress. Much later he remembered that when he stepped back outside he felt much as he had as a child emerging from a Saturday-afternoon movie. There was the same feeling "of shock and surprise upon discovering that the daylight world was still there, going about its business in the usual way." What he learned from that visit was that Nevelson's walls were an outgrowth of the environment she had created at home, a fine-art translation of "its pell-mell profusion of forms, its architectural divisions of space, and its twilight atmosphere."

Nevelson would postpone the inevitable move as long as she could, not only because she hated to leave the old place but because relocating would mean a nightmare packing job. To preempt that fate, in January 1958, the same month "Moon Garden" opened, she decluttered with a vengeance, discarding or donating nearly all her furniture. When it was over, she had allowed herself to keep a dinner table and chairs, a refrigerator, and a bed. She also held on to much of the art, as well as the junk, which to her was just more art waiting to happen.

More than a housecleaning, Nevelson's radical cleanse was a purification ritual, an act of samurai discipline by an artist who knew she had made a breakthrough in her work and was entering a new phase of peak creativity, one that required her to clear away however much of the past she could do without. For a woman of her abrupt disposition, this may not have been as difficult as it seems. Disburdening was something of a motif in Nevelson's life. She had already said goodbye to Russia and Maine, a husband and a child. How hard could it be to toss out a sofa?

Though Nevelson was gaining recognition as an artist, she was still selling very little. Even "Moon Garden + One," a triumph with critics, had disappointing sales. Seven individual boxes went for ninety-five dollars each. But that show led all the same to a turning point in her finances. Since 1955, she had been exhibiting with Grand Central Moderns, a nonprofit gallery on East Fifty-Sixth Street run by Colette Roberts, a critic and art educator who became a close friend and well-connected cheerleader. It was in her annual one-woman shows at Grand Central that Nevelson evolved into the artist the world would soon know, the virtuoso of black wooden sculpture in themed environments.

The success of "Moon Garden," the fourth of those shows, convinced one ambitious New York dealer it was time to get in touch. Martha Jackson had a prestigious gallery on East Sixty-Ninth Street, where she had already exhibited Willem de Kooning and Jim Dine. Through family inheritance and her own success in the art market, she was wealthy enough to offer Nevelson something no previous gallerist had the means to propose, an annual stipend of $20,000 against sales. With Roberts's blessing, Nevelson and Jackson entered talks. By March 1959, they had a contract. By October, two months before her MoMA debut, Nevelson had her first exhibition at Jackson's venue.

Called "Sky Columns Presence," it was another of her all-black installations. Even the gallery was painted black, while across one wall stretched an immense black-box assemblage. Elsewhere were intricately pieced-together columns, four-sided works of a type she had first produced for "Moon Garden." This time some of them even hung from the ceiling like basalt stalactites. Nevelson had long been intrigued by the immense stone steles of the Mayans, tall rectangular shafts carved with images of their kings and deities. In the early 1950s, she had traveled to Mexico and Guatemala to commune with them on-site. Though her own mature sculpture would never admit faces, after returning from those trips she began making abstract sentinels that plainly drew on her encounters with the Mayan carvings. They introduced into her art scaly, freestanding shafts, upright silhouettes that were vaguely human but still otherworldly. Situated within the complex field of a Nevelson environment, they could suggest stately presences taking part in obscure ceremonies. For "Sky Columns Presence" she also debuted two low-relief discs titled *Sun* and *Moon*, emblems of the "sky presences" that were central figures of Mayan religion. She placed them prominently in the gallery, as if to make the whole show seem tuned to their wavelength.

The money from Jackson came just in time. Early in 1958, not much ahead of the bulldozers that had already demolished whole stretches of her neighborhood, Nevelson learned about a five-story redbrick building for sale at 29 Spring Street in Little Italy, just above Chinatown. Reputedly once a private asylum for the mentally ill—or had it been an illegal abortion clinic?—it was old and in need of work. But even with a florist, a barbershop, and a candy store occupying the first floor, it was spacious enough for an artist of her pack rat inclinations. Using loans from her brother, Nate, and her brother-in-law, Ben Mildwoff, the husband of her sister Lillian, she bought it that September. Three years later, using money of her own as well as her sister's, she would add a neighboring building, 31 Spring Street, connecting to it by way of step-up and step-down hallways because the floors of the two places didn't align. Later still she expanded into a third adjacent building, a garage that she converted into an immense studio. Over time her linked houses became another brimming labyrinth of artworks and dumpster finds. She would preside there for the rest of her life.

By the next year, with a new home, a new gallery, her MoMA debut on the horizon, and the first payments from Jackson coming in, Nevelson found herself at last in the life she had always been struggling toward. Though Colette Roberts, who remained a close friend, had placed her work with several private collections and more than a dozen museums, Jackson would launch her into even higher orbits, getting her work shown by galleries and museums around the United States and introducing her to collectors as important as the Rockefellers, who would become lifelong patrons. In 1960, Nevelson turned another corner when Jackson arranged for her to be represented in Europe by Daniel Cordier, a French dealer who was soon getting her into group shows in Germany and giving her a solo exhibition at his Paris gallery. Though she would only remain with him for a few years, it was through Cordier's efforts that Nevelson first became a transatlantic phenomenon. And an increasingly prosperous one. Just like Jackson, he paid her a $20,000 annual stipend.

With that there was even enough money for some deferred maintenance on her relations with the son she had so haphazardly parented. "I never thought I was much of a mother," she admitted to one interviewer. "I dragged him up. But what can you do?" She allowed herself this much. "I did, I must say, give him a great deal of freedom." Yet for all the rough and tumble of their relationship, mother and son never stopped signaling to each other. Sometimes by mail, sometimes during periods when Mike lived with her in Manhattan, they managed to keep up a wary bond. It says something that during World War II, when Mike was serving in the merchant marine, he had sent a much-needed check to his mother every month. With her new prosperity she could now send money to him. By that time, he was back in Maine with a wife and two daughters, trying, with mixed results, to make it as a sculptor himself. To be in a position at last to help him out was one more sign to Nevelson that she had finally arrived, however long the trip had taken. Anyway, as she once said, with a shrug, "My whole life's been late."

Edward Hopper, who waited a long time for critics and the public to find him, took a skeptical view of fame when it came to him. "Recognition doesn't mean so much," he said. "You never get it when you need it." Nevelson, who waited even longer, had more mixed feelings. It pained her that she didn't break through until her sixties. One of her biographers, Laurie Lisle, describes her after she had found success, at the opening of one of her own gallery shows, sitting at the bar and weeping, "It's too late, it's much too late." She was nonetheless thrilled to have emerged at all, and ready, in whatever time remained, to seize the opportunities fame brought with it. The keynote of Nevelson's old age would be a perennial triumphalism. As she made her veni, vidi, vici progress across the cultural landscape of her time, the city of New York, and the wider world, she didn't hesitate to remind anyone who would listen of her own importance as an artist. "Sometimes you have to turn around the things you are taught," she once explained. "For instance: 'You have to be humble and you'll inherit the earth.' I don't believe that." And it worked. She may have spent most of her life in obscurity, but in her last decades she would routinely be described as the foremost living American sculptor. Twelve years after her death, the US Postal Service would even issue five Nevelson stamps.

The "foremost American sculptor" actually began life in Ukraine. Nevelson was born Leah Berliawsky, later Americanized to Louise, in Pereyaslav, a centuries-old city not far from Kyiv with a large Jewish population. At her birth—probably in September 1899; the exact date is uncertain—her family already included an older brother, Nathan. Two sisters, Anita and Lillian, would come along later. Though not wealthy, her parents, Isaac and Minna Berliawsky, had enough money to own land, including woodlands necessary to Isaac's business as a timber merchant. However prosperous they might be, in the fiercely anti-Semitic Russian Empire, of which Ukraine was then still a part, Jews were always in peril and pogroms were a constant danger. Seeing no future for themselves in such a place, by 1902 five of Isaac's siblings had immigrated to the United States. In that year he left as well, taking with him his elderly mother. Until he was ready to send for them, Minna and the children would stay behind, living with her parents in the peasant village of Shusneky. Family lore had it that Louise felt so betrayed by her father's departure that she stopped speaking for six months. If so, it would count as the first of her occasional but lifelong episodes of depression and self-isolation, a condition both parents also suffered from.

In 1905, after a three-month odyssey that took Minna and her children through Hamburg, Liverpool, and Boston, they would at last be reunited with Isaac in the small shipyard town of Rockland, Maine. Its population of eight thousand included just twenty-two other Jewish families. Isaac started out there as a peddler and junk dealer, an occupation many commentators would later seize on as a forecast of his daughter's scavenger art. Nevelson would object that her father's junkyard was so far outside town she rarely went there. In any case, Isaac soon advanced beyond dealing in scraps, by starting his own lumber business. From there he moved into building, buying, and selling houses, which in time allowed the Nevelsons to have one of their own. Even so, Minna never entirely reconciled herself to Rockland. As her daughter later recalled, when she first arrived there she was so devastated to find herself exiled to this *goyishe* backwater that she cried for weeks.

Nevelson would always claim to have known from an early age that she was destined to be an artist. ("Artists are born, you know.") Rockland was not a town where many other kids felt the same, and Waspy, insular Maine was unsuited generally to a headstrong girl with Nevelson's talent and ambition. But with the help of an encouraging art teacher, she made an uneasy peace with the place. Though the family spoke Yiddish at home, she and her siblings mastered English. She would much later tell an interviewer that as a Jew she felt excluded from the social life of the town. Even so, the genteel strain of Yankee anti-Semitism she faced there was nothing compared to the bloodthirsty variety her family had fled. Tall for her age, in ninth grade she was even made captain of the girl's basketball team. But when an opportunity to escape presented itself, she lost no time.

It came in her last year of high school. To satisfy a graduation work requirement, Louise took a six-week job as a stenographer in a local law office. That was where she met Bernard Nevelson, a wealthy New Yorker up on business for the shipping company he owned with his younger brother, Charles. Bernard was very impressed by this striking young woman who had even greeted him in Yiddish. He was also married. Charles was not. Back in New York, Bernard urged his thirty-seven-year-old brother to make his own business trip to Rockland. As soon as he got there he asked Louise out and proposed on the first date. Two years later they married in Boston and honeymooned in New Orleans and Cuba. Charles was plump, bald, and shorter than his new wife. Whether she ever loved him remains a matter of conjecture. What is not in doubt is that, at least at first, she loved where he was taking her, to a big twelfth-floor apartment in Upper Manhattan and a life of theater, opera, and concerts. The marriage also made her an American citizen. However she felt about poky Rockland, she well understood that her adopted nation—and more to the point, the magical city of New York—was where she would find herself.

Within just a couple of years, the perks of her new life began to pale. She wanted a career of some kind in the arts. Her husband wanted a conventional wife, the kind who would be home every night by 7 p.m. She said later she should have recognized early his latent strain of philistinism, however much he enjoyed symphonies and the opera. "I probably gave him more credit than he deserved for really being an intellectual." A crisis came in their first year of marriage, when Louise learned she was pregnant, news that led her to suffer a panic attack in her doctor's office. Her first and only child, Myron, called Mike, was born on February 23, 1922. Because his mother found vaginal birth "revoltingly animalistic" he was delivered by Caesarean. Severe postpartum depression followed.

Was it to convince herself that motherhood didn't mean an end to her ambitions that just a few months after Mike's birth she started singing lessons, her first adult venture into self-expression? For a woman who feared being silenced, it was also a symbolic gesture—she would now be learning to project her voice. Meanwhile, as she was edging into the creative life, the Nevelson brothers' shipping business was heading toward insolvency. By 1924, things were bad enough that Louise and her husband made the first in a series of moves to ever-smaller homes. She particularly hated the one in suburban Mount Vernon, New York, which took her away from Manhattan entirely. No doubt to stay in touch with the city, she enrolled in a drawing class at the Art Students League in Midtown, the well-respected academy that Georgia O'Keeffe had once attended and where the young Jackson Pollock would later study under Thomas Hart Benton.

By 1926, the Nevelsons were back to New York but only its Brooklyn outskirts, where Charles was trying to start over with a metal-stamping business. Though they were never poor, the new venture didn't bring in enough for them to keep live-in servants. To her horror, Louise found herself forced to cook and clean. Determined to sustain her artistic ambitions, even if she wasn't sure yet what they might be, she started acting lessons. Meanwhile, with her in-laws losing patience with her, she retreated to the company of her supportive younger sisters, Anita and Lillian, and to the fascinating new role models she was finding in Manhattan. There were none more fascinating than Princess Norina Matchabelli, an Italian-born actress, "fourth dimension" evangelist, and true exotic. With her husband, a Georgian prince and amateur chemist, she had cofounded the perfume company that for decades would carry the Matchabelli name on its crown-shaped bottles. Through her Nevelson also met the avant-garde Austrian designer and architect Frederick Kiesler, who collaborated with the princess on experimental stage productions. For a while he may also have become Nevelson's lover. However true that may be, his involvement in avant-garde theater design may well have influenced the woman who would one day make sculptural environments that would often be compared to stage sets.

In 1929, she took another important step toward a new life, enrolling full time at the Art Students League. There she would make her fateful discovery of cubism. "When I found cubism," she said later, "it was like when some people find God." In 1931, Nevelson decided she must pursue this new fascination by taking classes in Munich with the famed modernist painter and teacher Hans Hofmann. This was plainly more than a decision to further her art education. Given her feelings about marriage and family life, it was a kind of jailbreak. It was also the thing that led her that September to drop off her son with her parents in Maine. Did she realize at the time that this was a reenactment of her own abandonment by the father who left for America without her? Thereafter she would only sometimes resume the role of on-site parent, during periods when Mike came down to live with her in New York.

Stunned that his wife planned to abandon her family, Charles Nevelson refused to pay for her escape to Germany. Undeterred, she got the money from her mother, who could see how unhappy her daughter had become. But by 1931, the year she arrived in Munich, Hitler was on the rise and Hofmann was absorbed in trying to get back to the safety of the United States, where he had recently been teaching in California. Too absorbed, in Nevelson's view, to pay attention to his students. She stayed on in Europe anyway, continuing to study with him on and off. Meanwhile she picked up work as a café singer in Munich and a film extra in Berlin and Vienna, making enough for excursions around Italy and France. In this transatlantic Wanderjahr she would sail back to New York in June 1932, decide her marriage was still intolerable, and abruptly head off again for Paris six weeks later.

Returning at last to New York in September, Nevelson moved in at times with her husband, but with no intention of resuming married life. Not ever, with anyone, as it would turn out. Years later she would explain her unwillingness to marry again: “I think true love is a dedication . . . and my dedication is art.” She was also dedicated now to whatever came next. After an adventurous new friend, Marjorie Eaton, introduced her to Diego Rivera and Frida Kahlo, she began work as an assistant on the mural Rivera was producing for the New York Workers School. As so many American painters would do, Nevelson may have found in the wall paintings of Rivera and the other Mexican muralists her first glimpse of modern art at a heroic scale, the wide expanse she would later bring to her sculpture. Certainly for a while she fell under the spell of Rivera’s personal charm and outsize personality. She and Eaton saw quite of bit of him and Kahlo, especially after he invited them to move into a vacant studio in a building he was renting in Greenwich Village, one of the many cramped places where Nevelson would live and work over the next dozen or so years.

On her return to New York, Nevelson also took up modern dance with Ellen Kearns, a eurythmics teacher she would continue with for the next twenty years as a student and close friend, but never with any thought of becoming a dancer. She knew now that visual art was her true path, but in that pursuit she saw dance as a way to internalize her understanding of forms in space. The woman who would later gyrate before “Moon Garden” was an artist in every fiber of her being. Plus, the former acting student and silent film bit player loved the sheer drama of expressive gestures. All her life she would talk with her hands.

Meanwhile Nevelson found regular paychecks teaching art, jobs she got through the Works Progress Administration of FDR’s New Deal. She studied sculpture for a while with Chaim Gross, a prominent American artist in those days who admired her works. These were mostly small terra-cotta figures of animals or people in a Jenga-style cubism of jutting, asymmetrical blocks and planes, some of them painted. One subject she returned to often was mothers and children. Given her fraught history with Mike, it may have been her way of probing an old wound.

In 1939, the WPA sharply cut its budget and cut Nevelson, too. That left her more than ever reliant on handouts from her sisters and especially her older brother, Nate, a lively character who had gone from running illegal slot machines to becoming owner of a profitable hotel in Rockland. There was still no question of making her living through art. Though she had started to exhibit in group shows as early as 1934, she could not find a dealer willing to represent her. Feeling desperate, in September 1941, she walked into the prestigious Fifty-Seventh Street gallery of Karl Nierendorf and effectively demanded that he give her a one-woman show. It was an act of pure, eye-batting chutzpah on her part—she later claimed to have sat herself on Nierendorf's desk and demurely crossed her legs—but it succeeded in getting him to come by her apartment to look at her work. On the spot he offered her a show. For what was probably just a short while they also became lovers.

In the same year she met Nierendorf, Nevelson finally divorced the husband she had put aside a decade earlier. Charles had long since left his family's shipping business, tried selling air conditioners in Texas, then moved on to California, where he ran a men's clothing store. Meanwhile, Nevelson had been taking on lovers, as she would continue to do after their formal split. Some were long-term, like the abstract painter Ralph Rosenborg. Though fourteen years younger, he would influence her thinking in two important areas. He got her to consider working with wood, a material most advanced artists considered too traditional, if not folkloric, but which she knew well from her years in Maine. He also nudged her toward abstraction, the working language she would make her own. They were well suited to one another, in ways good and bad, both passionate about art and both heavy drinkers. They lasted six years together, until his drinking got to be too much even for her, and she passed him along to her sister, Anita.

Not all her men were the kind you come home to. Quite a few were the kind you kick out in the morning. However much she dismissed the idea of marriage, Nevelson was an enthusiastic heterosexual, and casual sex represented to her an aspect of her freedom as an artist. This remained true even after the trauma of a near rape in 1937. Her attacker was a new friend, one she thought of as mild mannered until he came by one day for a visit, suddenly threw her on a sofa and tried forcing himself upon her. He failed but she was shaken, though with her characteristic resilience she collected herself enough to go out that evening to see a new play by Sherwood Anderson.

That grim episode aside, she continued to like sex for its own sake. Her niece Corinne told the Nevelson biographer Laurie Lisle that her aunt once took leave of her suddenly on the street to chase after a stevedore she had just spotted. Nevelson herself told how a police officer who caught her scavenging a city-owned trellis said he would need to stop by her house to confirm her claim that she was an artist. She suggested he arrive with a bottle of whiskey. He did. Merriment ensued.

In the years when she was just scraping along, she was also happy to accommodate men, like Nierendorf, who could help her career, or even to be picked up by strangers with an open wallet. Having parted from her husband, she still liked to dress in the style he had accustomed her to. To that end she was not averse to the kindness of strangers, like the gentleman who spotted her admiring an outfit in the window of the luxury retailer Bergdorf Goodman. He whisked her inside to buy it, all as prelude to a weekend together in Atlantic City. At lunch one afternoon in the middle of the Depression, the painter Alice Neel asked Nevelson how she could afford to dress so beautifully. She didn't mince words. "Fucking, dear, fucking."

For six years, until his sudden death from a heart attack in October 1947, Nierendorf would be Nevelson's faithful supporter, career strategist, and bankroll. At his gallery, he gave her five solo exhibitions that rescued her from the relative anonymity of group shows. After his death she drifted into a long period of dissolution, drinking heavily and working sporadically, mostly on small terra-cotta figures she would later cut from her résumé. But toward the end of those low years she would make her electrifying encounter with Mayan stone sculpture. It happened during trips in 1950 and 1951 to Mexico and Guatemala with her sister Anita, who paid their way.

Those immense carvings were for Nevelson catalysts of the kind African tribal sculpture had been decades earlier for Picasso, works that seemed invested with an occult power that Western art, even the most daring productions of twentieth-century modernism, had not shown her. Like Rivera's murals, the Mayan carvings were big, and prompted her to think along the same lines, to wonder how to bring the same force and mystery into her own sculpture. Though she would continue for a few years making small terra cottas, the seeds of much larger and more potent things had been planted.

It took until 1951 before Nevelson fully crawled back into the light, rallying enough to return regularly to group shows. A year later she also took up printmaking at an atelier in Greenwich Village. As a process that's hard to control, one that requires an artist to surrender a bit to chance once the paper meets the etched plate, lithography appealed to her surrealist taste for spontaneity and the sublime accident. Over time she would return periodically to making works on paper, often with quasi-representational images of kings and queens, figures she identified with and would translate more abstractly into sculpture.

The 1950s would be the decade when Nevelson would finally arrive at herself. In 1952, Colette Roberts invited her to take part in a group show at Grand Central Moderns. By 1954, she had the first of the solo exhibitions there that would put her on the path to "Sixteen Americans" and everything that followed.

About a year after she tossed out most of her furniture, Nevelson was ready for a housecleaning of another kind. Having made her name with work all in black, she decided to reach for its opposite color. When she was first asked by Dorothy Miller to take part in "Sixteen Americans," she abruptly declared that for her MoMA debut she wanted to produce her first all-white environment. Surprised but intrigued, Miller went along, even giving her the largest gallery in the show. Nevelson filled it with "Dawn's Wedding Feast," another multipart ensemble meant this time to suggest some mythic nuptial. The largest element in this white-on-white flotilla was *Dawn's Wedding Chapel II*, a sixteen-foot-long assemblage that filled most of the gallery's back wall. Nearby were more of her tall, intricately pieced-together columns. Encrusted, even scaly looking, they were similar to forms she had included in "Moon Garden + One" and "Sky Columns Presence." At MoMA some hung from the ceiling like icicles, or like celestial beings shooting skyward, but most were ranged upright from the floor like members of some very unusual wedding party.

No matter that her MoMA gallery struck a festive note, Nevelson didn't go entirely soft there on the question of marriage, an institution that had certainly not worked for her. "No more marriages for me," she would vow. "Because I recognized the bondage." So this "Wedding Feast" had its mischievous elements, like the three-tiered, stair-step box that was *Dawn's Wedding Pillow*. With layers of jagged offcuts and a painful-looking triangular point at its center, it wasn't meant for sweet dreams. As for *Dawn's Wedding Mirror*, its central element was a toilet seat cover surrounded by an oval frame.

So if not her own, what was the marriage she was celebrating here? As

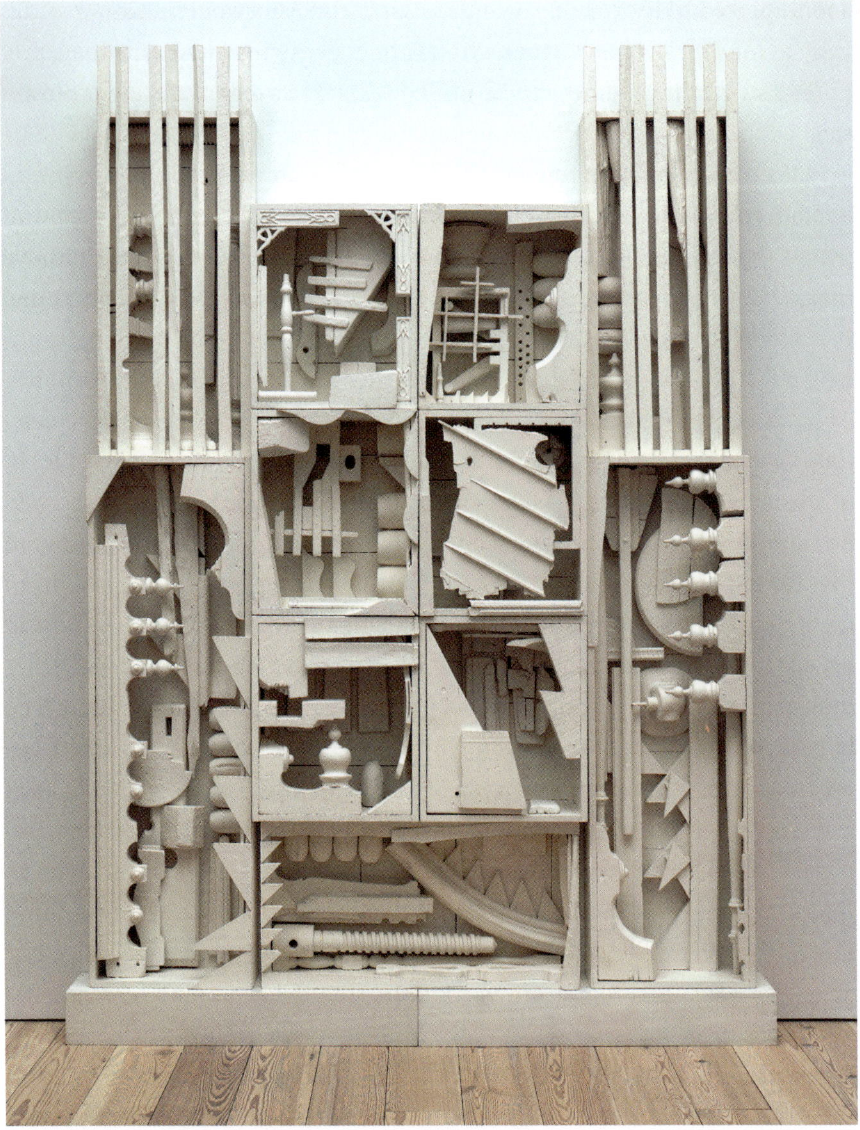

Dawn's Wedding Chapel II, 1959, painted wood, 115.8 × 83.5 x 26.7 cm, The Whitney Museum of American Art, New York

she would explain, in this year when she at last emerged, it *was* her own marriage after all, just not the one she had left behind. Instead it was a symbolic nuptial that she would variously describe as a marriage with her own art, the partnership that gave her the most satisfaction, or better still, "a transition to a marriage with the world." Having escaped a conventional union, Nevelson was only interested now in mystical alliances on a majestic scale.

Her switch from black to white had been a gamble, but it paid off. It proved that with a new color she could operate freely in a new, more jubilant key. She explained the change in typically head-scratching terms: "For me, the black contains the silhouette, the essence of the universe. But the white moves out a little bit into outer space with more freedom." Whatever that might have meant, Nevelson in white was as open and joyous as Nevelson in black had been secretive and brooding. In black her totems had been looming sentinels. In white, they evoked classical columns and even bubbling fountains. Everywhere in her white gallery were hints of rebirth and transfiguration, heavenly ceremonies and cascades of celestial light.

And if white could invest her work with so many new associations, why not reach for gold? With her recent success Nevelson was in an expansive mood, ready to play with signifiers of power and majesty. She had long been fascinated by gold. She claimed that in the 1920s she had fully emerged from her postpartum depression only after seeing a show of gold-threaded Japanese kimonos at the Metropolitan Museum. Having entertained thoughts of suicide, she was brought to tears by their glittering thread. "I said, 'Oh, my God, life is worth living if a civilization can give us this great weave of gold and pattern." So even as she was preparing "Dawn's Wedding Feast," she began experimenting with metallic gold spray paint.

Throughout 1960 she would debut the gold works scattershot in group shows at Jackson's gallery and others, as well as in a solo exhibition at Cordier's Paris gallery that combined work from all three of her color phases. In April 1961, at her second one-woman show for Jackson, she rolled out another selection of works in black, white, and gold. She called that exhibition "The Royal Tides" and saw it as a visual account of her progress from darkness and confusion to white daybreak and then the full flush of golden noonday sun. For her that color also invoked the alchemist's quest to change lead into gold, the way she transformed junk into art. Pride in her power to elevate the mundane may help to explain why toilet seats appear so often in the gold series. Plainly Nevelson enjoyed demonstrating that as an artist she could transform anything, even those. She claimed that once they had been subjected to her golden touch they resembled halos. And why not? Duchamp's title for his famous urinal was *Fountain*.

Nevelson never disowned the gold assemblages, but it appears that after 1962 she stopped making them. There had been favorable reviews, quite a few, and most critics had noted with approval how the works echoed the gilded Spanish baroque. But some, including her great supporter Hilton Kramer, had been cool to the new direction. If they were looking for grandeur, what they kept seeing was glamour. Or worse, glitz. Perhaps the problem was that her gold wasn't golden enough, not the precious metal but a counterfeit—a coat of Spray-O-Namel that could edge the new sculpture to the brink of kitsch. And by the very act of changing her palette so often she risked trivializing her art, making it appear like some adjunct to the world of fashion, where they were always rolling out this year's hot new color.

However mixed the reception of her gold work may have been, the early 1960s were still an extraordinary time for Nevelson, with shows in London and across West Germany and at the Los Angeles County Museum of Art. And one of her gold walls brought her once more into MoMA, where *Royal Tide I* was included in a group survey of assemblage art. Then came an enormous opportunity. Early in 1962, Dorothy Miller asked her to be one of four artists who would represent the United States at the upcoming Venice Biennale. From 1954 to 1964 MoMA owned the American pavilion there and chose the artists who would fill it at each Biennale. However gratifying it had been for Nevelson to be anointed by MoMA for "Sixteen Americans," it was something else again to represent her adopted nation at the world's most famous international art exhibition.

Nevelson would be given three galleries in the pavilion, a one-story Palladian-style building constructed in 1930 in the Giardini, the public park that's one of the two principal venues of the Biennale. Each of those rooms she would devote separately to sculpture in black, white, or gold. Her gold work would hold the central space, the circular entry where visitors would pass first. To dazzle them on arrival she painted the entire space gold and covered its glass ceiling with gold gauze. In the black-and-white galleries to either side she covered the skylights with cloth of the same colors. Because there was no time to produce any new art for Venice, some of the works she brought there were repurposed from "Dawn's Wedding Feast." Others would be diverted from the Nevelson show that was still in the middle of a seven-city German tour arranged by her new French dealer.

For three weeks Nevelson and Miller led a team of Italian workmen to prepare her spaces. As was her practice, she improvised much of the installation on the spot. Even when creating individual assemblages, Nevelson valued spontaneity, adding and subtracting parts as her instincts dictated. Only in later years would she rely sometimes on maquettes or look back to older works as templates for new ones, but in larger or smaller versions. In the American pavilion she went so far as to seize upon a chunk of wood extracted from one gallery's wooden archway, paint it gold and introduce it on the spot into one of her sculptures. She even took apart some of the works requisitioned from Cordier's touring show. To the despair of her dealers at that time, she rarely considered any of her walls truly finished. Not until later did she begin securing her boxes permanently into position. Until then, they were simply stacked and could be endlessly rearranged, something she encouraged her collectors to do. She didn't even hesitate to remake walls that had already been purchased. To submit to the inspiration of the moment was an article of faith for her. Even in Venice, with so much on the line, she saw no reason to change.

Though there was speculation that the first prize for sculpture at that year's Biennale might go to Nevelson, the winner would be Alberto Giacometti. This was not surprising. Giacometti was one of the emblematic artists of the postwar era. His famished bronze figures, both fragile and resolute, had become mascots of the Western intelligentsia, instantly recognizable signposts for human endurance and existential dread. But Nevelson, who bonded with Giacometti over drinks, got from him a personal consolation prize that pleased her no end. Giacometti was fascinated by her walls. He understood them at once as a rich new department of sculptural possibilities. He even said that his Biennale prize should have gone to her.

Nevelson was enormously gratified. She had admired Giacometti's work for decades. You see that in some of her Surrealist-influenced work of the 1940s and 1950s, which bore a debt to his table sculpture of the previous decade. To have his personal endorsement was a powerful gift. In the 1930s, when the embattled New York avant-garde was forming into affinity groups like "The Ten," she was never invited to join. It was a slight that stayed with her. Now one of the world's most respected artists was treating her as an equal.

So midway through her third year in the spotlight, Venice offered yet another vindication of her faith in herself and another grace note in an ever more gratifying chapter of her life. As she returned very late one night from a party, things reached an elegant crescendo. On the vaporetto taking her back to the apartment she was sharing with Dorothy Miller, drifting at first light along the waterways that Titian had spent a lifetime beside and Monet had captured in old age, she had a moment of pure bliss. Decades later she still remembered it with a sigh. "The dawn was just beginning to break, so that those islands with the great cathedrals were darker than the light. It was so perfect, if I can use the word there, as I had ever seen on earth."

Came the dawn. Though she could not have known it at the time, that enchanted moment was the prelude to more than a year of turmoil, most of it stemming from Nevelson's ambition to sign on with one of New York's most prestigious galleries and her failure to read the fine print. A few months before she left for Venice her contracts with both Jackson and Cordier expired. The rising star was a free agent.

By that time two potential successors had appeared. The first would turn out to be a lifelong friend, adviser, and evangel. Arne Glimcher was a young graduate of the Massachusetts College of Art and Design who had recently opened a gallery in Boston called Pace. Over time he would emerge as one of the most important dealers in the world, representing Alexander Calder, David Hockney, Maya Lin, Richard Avedon, and Kiki Smith, among many others. In his spare time he would also produce the film *Gorillas in the Mist* and direct three, including *The Mambo Kings*. But in 1961 he was just twenty-two years old and a nobody.

All the same, a smart and ambitious nobody. That May he asked Jackson if he could bring some of Nevelson's work to his Boston outpost. "The Royal Tides," Nevelson's most recent show at Jackson, had just closed, with only a few things sold. Glimcher borrowed seventeen of the remaining works for an exhibition that opened on Memorial Day. Six or seven sold at once. Nevelson was thrilled. It was the beginning of a beautiful friendship, but not yet an ongoing business relationship—not until she had passed through a long ordeal with the other gallerist who was courting her that year.

Sidney Janis was a wealthy former shirt manufacturer. In the late 1920s, as his shirt company took off, he and his new wife, Harriet, became passionate collectors of European modernists like Picasso, Matisse, de Chirico, and

Mondrian. By 1939, he was chairman of MoMA's art committee. Nine years later he and his wife opened the Sidney Janis Gallery on East Fifty-Seventh Street, which would soon become a launchpad for the emerging cohort of abstract expressionists. Its importance in that connection can hardly be overstated. At various times Janis represented Pollock, de Kooning, Rothko, Guston, Arshile Gorky, Robert Motherwell, and Franz Kline. But like most successful dealers he had an eye for the next thing. By the early 1960s that was pop art. In 1962, he even mounted one of the new movement's first and most explosive group shows, complete with two Warhol soup cans, a development that led some of his AbEx artists to leave his gallery in disgust. Nevelson was never pop, but she was plainly something new, and something big, two qualities Janis understood. She was also very interested in joining up with him. He was open to that.

For her part Nevelson was ready for his attentions. Not only was he in the forefront of New York dealers, but to her great satisfaction she would be the first woman added to his all-male roster. A mutual friend introduced her to Janis's attorney, Sam Kurzman, who promised to connect her to Janis. In return she promised Kurzman one of her walls. Very soon Kurzman was her lawyer as well. Before Nevelson left for Venice, she had a deal with Janis to take her on. In a peculiar side arrangement, she also agreed to buy from Kurzman a small clapboard house in Westport, Connecticut, part of a compound that included his own home. At the time, Nevelson was not aware that the house had a lien on it, meaning she had no clear title. Meanwhile, Kurzman held the mortgage, which she unwisely—she claimed unknowingly—pledged to pay off in full within a year.

Apart from the convoluted issues surrounding the house, it would quickly turn out that Nevelson and Janis were not a good fit. There were disagreements over money. There were disputes over whether sculpture still held by Jackson was now the property of Janis. Worse still, Nevelson's first and only show at the Janis Gallery, which opened on New Year's Eve, 1962, was a bust. Almost nothing sold, leaving Nevelson in debt to Janis for funds he had advanced her.

All this guaranteed that 1963 would be a nightmare year of legal battles with both Janis and Kurtzman about money and contested ownership of her art, especially three unsold walls that Janis was refusing to return. There were also mounting payments on the Westport house, where at Nevelson's invitation her son and his family were living. Inevitably her fight with both men ended up in court. Before the whole costly mess was over, she had to sell her houses on Spring Street, an enormous sacrifice. Though the buyer allowed her to stay on as a tenant, the sudden decline in her fortunes so soon after her sudden rise was devastating. Amid bouts of serious depression, she took refuge again in heavy drinking.

Thanks to Martha Jackson, who remained a friend and could see that Nevelson was floundering, in late April she escaped for three months with her sister Anita to Los Angeles, where a grant from the Ford Foundation would allow her to spend the spring making works on paper at the Tamarind Lithography Workshop. "I wouldn't ordinarily have gone," she said later. "I didn't care so much about the idea of prints at that time. But I desperately needed to get out of town and all of my expenses were paid."

Yet, as always for Nevelson, work was a tonic. Throughout May and June, she produced twenty-six lithograph editions, full of experiments with unorthodox materials like cheesecloth and lace that she layered across the printing plates to produce surprising marks and new tonal effects. You think of the aged Goya in exile in Bordeaux, mastering the process of lithography and delighting in the novel results he could achieve, and then going on to invent a unique way to create ink miniatures on ivory. So old dogs can learn new tricks after all. They just have to dive in.

Her experience at the Tamarind Workshop helped Nevelson to regain her equilibrium and cut down on her drinking, at least during the day. (Nights could be a different story.) Yet even despite that break, there were times in her struggles with Kurzman and Janis when Nevelson was suicidal. In July, back in Manhattan, she missed the deadline to pay off the mortgage on the Westport house, leading to lawsuits between Kurzman and herself. But the whole mess had just a few more months to play out. In November, the New York State Supreme Court handed down a ruling that dismissed Kurzman's claims over the house and ordered Janis to return Nevelson's walls. In a grotesque coincidence her victory came on November 22, 1963, the day of John F. Kennedy's assassination, a moment of shock and grief all over America, and no doubt for her as well. But at last she could move on. After agreeing to pay Janis $18,920 to get out of her contract, she was in a position to join another gallery.

She had already found one. While she was in limbo, her young friend

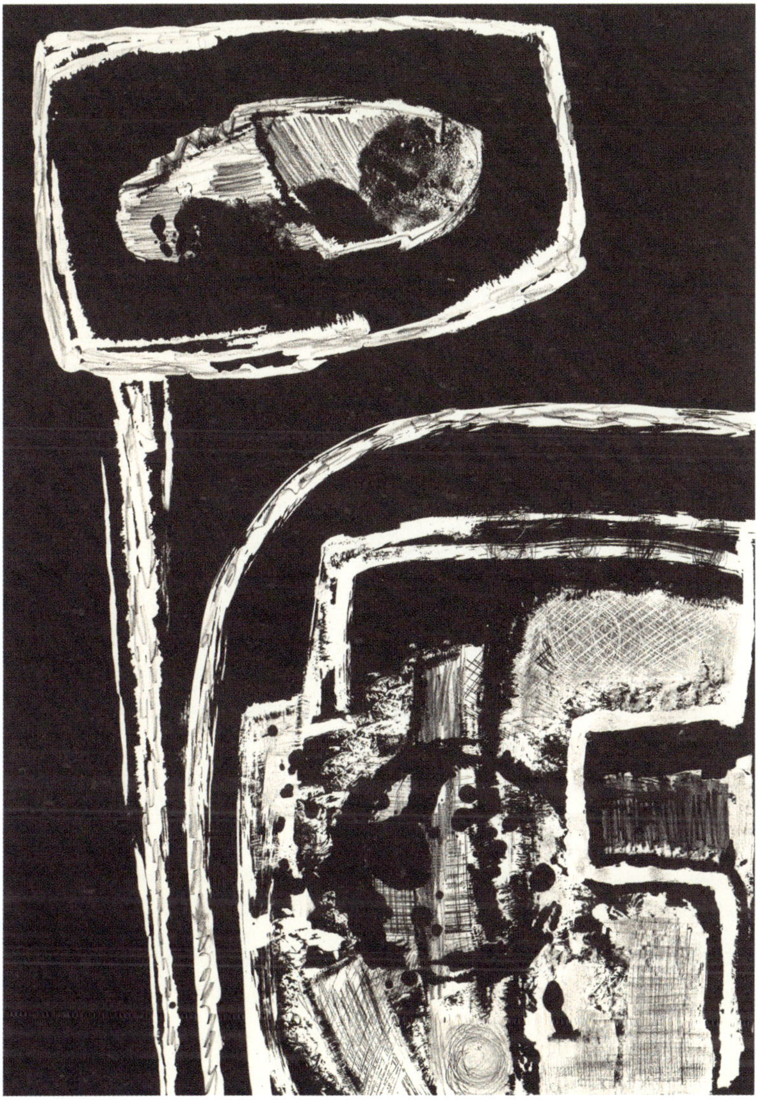

Untitled, 1963, lithograph, 82.6 × 58.4 cm, National Gallery of Art, Washington, D.C.

Glimcher had realized his ambition to set up shop in New York, on the prestigious gallery row along Fifty-Seventh Street. Not caring that he was an unknown, Nevelson quickly signed on to become his first marquee name and a magnet for others. More than a dealer, Glimcher would be a rescuer for Nevelson. He came up with the money to repay Janis and gave her thousands more to help put her back on her feet. For the rest of Nevelson's life,

Glimcher would be her confidant, wise counselor, promoter, and shrewd appraiser. When his mother, Eva, opened a Pace gallery in Columbus, Ohio, it gave Nevelson a regular showplace and salesroom in the Midwest. She would even let Glimcher install her work, a remarkable vote of confidence from an artist who ordinarily relied only on her own instincts.

Best of all, they would very soon start making one another a great deal of money. By the mid-1960s Nevelson was earning hundreds of thousands of dollars a year, a sizable sum in those days, more than enough to allow her to buy back her houses on Spring Street in 1967. The cash flow was important, not only because it meant an end to the financial headaches she had suffered since the 1930s, but because it was yet another thing that certified her importance as an artist. That she was making this kind of money from recycled junk just made her success all the sweeter. "I enjoy the fact that a woman artist in America can collect wooden scraps from the street, put them together, and sell them to the Rockefellers for $100,000."

In that same period there were other big developments in Nevelson's life and art. For years her live-in studio assistant had been Teddy Haseltine, the trained dancer who had joined her in those ritual gyrations after they finished installing "Moon Garden." Haseltine was gay, had a good eye that Nevelson respected, and like her could drink too much. More than an assistant, he was effectively part of the family. In the summer of 1964 he had health problems, possibly drug- and alcohol-related, that were serious enough to require surgery. Back home on Spring Street, he came by her bedroom one day to say good morning and abruptly collapsed and died, probably of a cerebral blood clot. He was thirty-six.

Nevelson responded to that loss in a way typical of her. She refused to speak of it. She would donate some works on paper to the Brooklyn Museum in Haseltine's memory, but she did not attend his funeral. For a long time, to deny death had been her way of dealing with it. She had skipped her mother's funeral in 1943 and did the same when her father died three years later. Like Picasso, who wouldn't come to the phone when Matisse's daughter called with news of her father passing, Nevelson could not face the loss of people she loved. Her own progress into old age would do nothing to make it easier. In 1976, her sister Lillian would die of pancreatic cancer. She passed on that funeral too.

Even before Haseltine's death, Nevelson had begun working with Diana MacKown, a twenty-eight-year-old Yale arts graduate who soon assumed an even larger place in her life than the one Haseltine had occupied. Until Nevelson's death in 1988, MacKown would be her studio assistant, live-in companion, confidante, and gatekeeper. She would also be archivist and amanuensis, recording and transcribing dozens of conversations with Nevelson that became the basis of *Dawns + Dusks*, the artist's 1976 monologue-memoir. Nevelson would never take up with another male partner, but in MacKown she would have a kind of surrogate spouse, an ever-present helpmate and plus-one for her frequent New York socializing. And in later years, a caregiver. So much would they be in one another's company that many people just assumed—or whispered—that they were a lesbian couple. If that were true, in an era when gays were routinely stigmatized and worse, there would have been plenty of reasons to be circumspect about their relationship. But it was something they always denied, and people who knew them best always took them at their word. The playwright Edward Albee, who was gay and one of Nevelson's closest friends, told her biographer Laurie Wilson that "I wouldn't have minded what their relationship was, for God's sake, but I think they were just drinking buddies." Arne Glimcher told Wilson bluntly, "Trust me, Louise was a predatory heterosexual into her eighties."

By the early sixties, Nevelson was pursuing some significant new directions in her art. At some point in 1962, when she was working on the walls that would go into her ill-fated Janis show, she made a change to one of their most important elements. Instead of using salvaged crates of different sizes, she introduced newly made boxes of uniform dimension. American art was in ferment and the first stirrings of minimalism were in the air. The young Donald Judd, the new art's representative practitioner as well as its chief polemicist, would make the box a building block of his work, too, but in ways very different from hers and for different purposes. Above all, a box by Judd was just a box, an obdurate thing that seemed to have come into the world chiefly to display its own implacable thing-ness. As silent and unflinching as a sentry at Buckingham Palace, its salient properties—really, its only properties—were its dimensions, its color, and the materials it was made from, sometimes plywood but more often steel, aluminum, or sheets of colored plexiglass. Curves appeared occasionally in Judd's works, but most were chaste right-angled boxes. And most sat on the floor, daring you like

Melville's Bartleby to draw them out. As a category, Judd called the things he made "specific objects," but any given one he termed "Untitled." More title than that would nudge it into the realm of meanings, something he wanted no part of. As the painter Frank Stella would famously say of his own echt-minimalist white pinstripes on black fields, "What you see is what you see."

For all their high-minded refusals, or rather because of them, Judd's boxes can be strangely potent. But plainly the minimalist ideal of the hermetic object, a sealed-off thing that allowed for no reference to anything outside itself except the space surrounding it, would not be of much interest to Nevelson. To her, the psychological and spiritual implications of her art, its multiple means of outreach to the viewer's imagination, were the very qualities that made it worth making and worth contemplating. She also didn't care much about the "integrity" of her materials, a minimalist fetish. She painted her wood so you could forget it was wood.

71

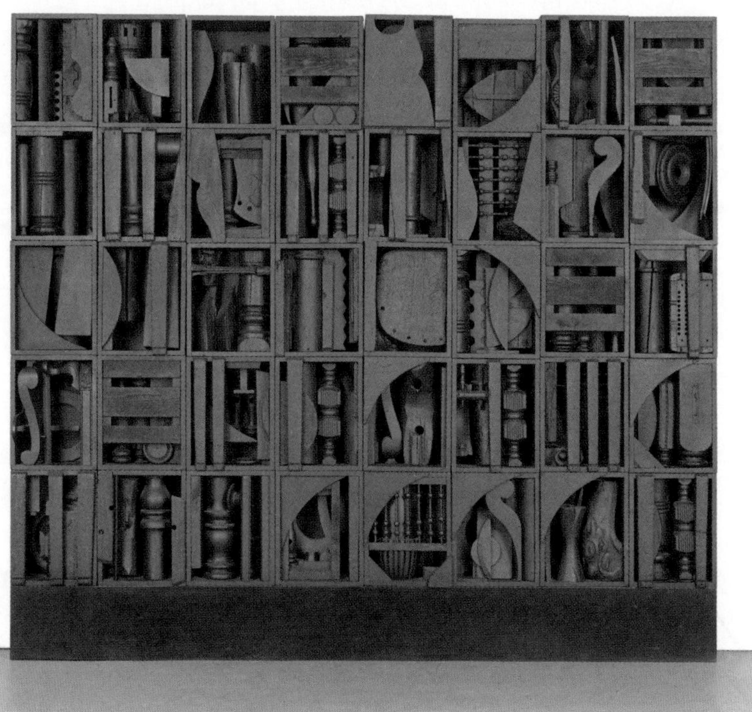

Black Chord, 1964, painted wood, 265.4 × 299.1 x 31.1 cm, The Whitney Museum of American Art, New York

Nevelson would still take what she could use from this new kind of art. Once she started building her walls from matching boxes of equal size, they became more right-angled and straight-edged, so that an entire work might have the silhouette of a single rectangle formed from uniform compartments, like a bookcase. That could open the way to a very productive interplay between the simplified geometry of the framework and the irregular wooden elements that still filled each box, a counterpoint of classical structure and baroque intricacy. This is what you find in *Black Chord*, a wall from 1964, where Nevelson plays with the contrast between her square-shouldered grid of vertical rectangles and the unruly compositions they hold—hold so tightly that the ascending rows of boxes are like cellblock tiers. You half expect the wayward things inside them to rattle the bars.

Nevelson also found uses for the blunt force of minimalist austerity, the way it makes any small variation within a work carry outsize weight. In *Silent Music II*, also from 1964, she built a Cartesian grid of twenty identical rectangles, five high and four across. But on the left and right sides she pushed six of her boxes a bit off to the diagonal. Having them literally step out of line was all it took to provide an escape clause from the work's classical order and maybe from the grip of rationality itself. Nevelson the romantic, the believer in the fourth dimension, would always be open to that. If *Silent Music II* can be read in several ways, and it can, a winking critique of pure reason is one of them.

Nevelson didn't merely borrow from minimalism. She was effectively a codeveloper, however unorthodox, the creator of a hybrid outgrowth that played minimalist rigor, its simplified forms and economy of means, against the internal intricacies that were necessary to art as she understood it. Judd the great purifier saw such things as contaminants. She considered them essential devices. Though Nevelson would circle back often to her earlier practice of using boxes of varying sizes, the minimalist grid of uniform compartments would remain for her an alternative framework, but almost always filled with her mysterious fragments and their elusive hints of meaning.

Adapting aspects of minimalism was also a way for Nevelson to move her art forward without resorting to yet another new color. After the mixed response to her gold walls, she returned to black for the rest of her life, with occasional forays into white. In her sixties, she also produced her first curved walls, semicircular arrays that partly enwrap the viewer, an effect that could be either embracing or faintly ominous. And she started to incorporate mirrored surfaces into her walls, which offered one more way to dematerialize them and hint at the fourth dimension.

With Glimcher's encouragement, in 1967 and 1968 she even made whole works from clear plexiglass. Nevelson was by no means the first artist to dabble in acrylics, which had appeared in the 1930s and were soon being used by the constructivist Naum Gabo for transparent sculpture. But three decades later they still had a futuristic vibe that she could draw upon. Her plexiglass works also let her deploy light as she did shadow, as one more weightless artist's material, letting it flow through and across the clear solids. And of course their very transparency could make them ideal conduits to the fourth dimension, whatever that was. Hilton Kramer, who had been cool to the gold walls, was fascinated by her efforts in plexiglass and "their combination of a

72

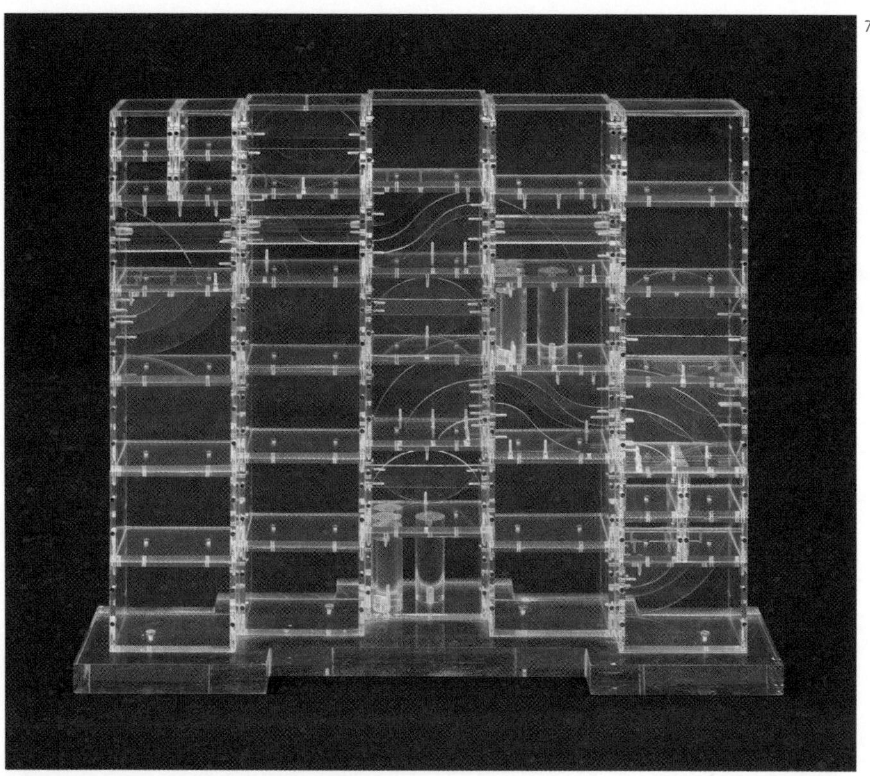

Transparent Sculpture VI, 1967–68, acrylic with metal hardware, 48.3 × 55.9 x 21.9 cm, The Whitney Museum of American Art, New York

strict, unembellished syntax and a cool, detached glamor." He called them a "vivid realization" of the old constructivist ideal "of a transparent structure, in which space, mass, and light, are identical and indistinguishable." True enough, but given that most of them were tabletop objects, with a footprint roughly between one and two feet square, some could also feel a bit like space-age crystal knickknacks, impeccably modern but with a whiff of the Swarovski gift shop.

For whatever reason, Nevelson's detour into acrylics, like her experiment with gold, was short lived. Yet it was one more sign that she meant to move forward. Adopting a transparent material was also a way to show that, though she might be pushing seventy, she was in step with much younger artists. Donald Judd had been using sheets of Lucite since the early 1960s, around the time the Los Angeles minimalist Larry Bell began producing his tinted glass cubes. For four weeks in 1967, the year Nevelson took up plexiglass, the Museum of Modern Art would display *The Star Garden (A Place)* by the thirty-year-old Les Levine. It was made from sheets of Acrylite heated and then air blown into immense clear swells and hemispheres, large enough for visitors to walk between. As part of a Manhattan-wide exhibition of outdoor sculpture, Levine would soon install a similar work, *All Star Cast*, in front of the nearby Time & Life Building. Nevelson would certainly have been aware of it, because she was included in the same show on a site just two blocks north, where a pair of her first works in enameled aluminum, *Offering* and *Exclosure*, sat in front of CBS headquarters.

In later years, Nevelson was sometimes accused of repetition, but what's striking about so much of the art of her sixties and seventies is her refusal to stagnate. Mirrors, acrylics, aluminum—just a few years after having made her name with wood, she had moved on to all of them. Because she had found success so late, did she feel she had to play her cards quickly? No matter that she was in good health in those years, there was still no time to lose.

By 1964, Nevelson had also made her first venture into art that made reference to a historical event, not a mythical kingdom. *Homage to 6,000,000* is a Holocaust memorial. A curving black wall, twenty feet wide, it's built from sixty equal-size vertical boxes in four tiers, which she debuted at her first one-woman show at Pace. (She would also make a second, very different and more irregular version, now in the Israel Museum in Jerusalem.) None of its salvaged wood arrangements allude plainly to the mass murder of European Jewry. She counted largely on the work's name to make people see it as a cenotaph for a calamity. But because of that title, things that are aspects of any of her black walls—the dark recesses, the suggestions of charred rubble and abandoned belongings—suddenly carry a more haunting resonance. And the concave curvature of the entire work is just enough to make it feel engulfing and ominous, a thing closing in.

Nevelson had never been an observant Jew. Neither had her parents. But in a world that had witnessed the Holocaust, a woman who grew up in a Jewish household, even speaking Yiddish at home, could never forget who she was. In her sixties, her thoughts were almost certainly turned in that direction by a 1964 trip with Arne Glimcher to Kassel, Germany, where four of her walls had been included in Documenta III, the international survey of new art. It was her first visit to Germany since 1931, the year she had bolted to Munich, when Hitler's rising Nazi Party was headquartered there. More than three decades later, after a new encounter with Germany's ghosts, and maybe her own, and in the wake of the enormity of the Shoah, how could she fail to revisit her Jewish identity, if only as part of the wider spirituality that was always important to her?

Nevelson would return to the Holocaust as a subject in 1971, this time to create *The White Flame of the Six Million* for Temple Beth-El of Great Neck, in Great Neck, New York. A very wide wall, measuring fifty-five feet, it runs along the back of the synagogue's lengthy bema, the raised platform where the Torah is read during services. Once again Nevelson adopts a minimalist grid, this time consisting of three tiers of narrow vertical boxes. Each holds an arrangement of sinuous white slats, custom-cut to produce a shimmering illusion of waving forms, all of them silhouetted against the shadowy recess behind them.

Nevelson had made use of this kind of rippling repetition in two black walls from 1969. One of them, *Night-Focus-Dawn*, consists of twenty equal-size black boxes. All of them hold similar arrangements in which two or three long spikes, pointing up or down, rest on wooden rectangles. At the front of each box there's also a single concave triangle of flat wood, fitted into the upper left or lower right corner so as to form a long, gentle curve. Multiplied by twenty, those arcs join to produce a cascade effect down the entire wall, a flowing visual field where the interplay of daggers and curves is both

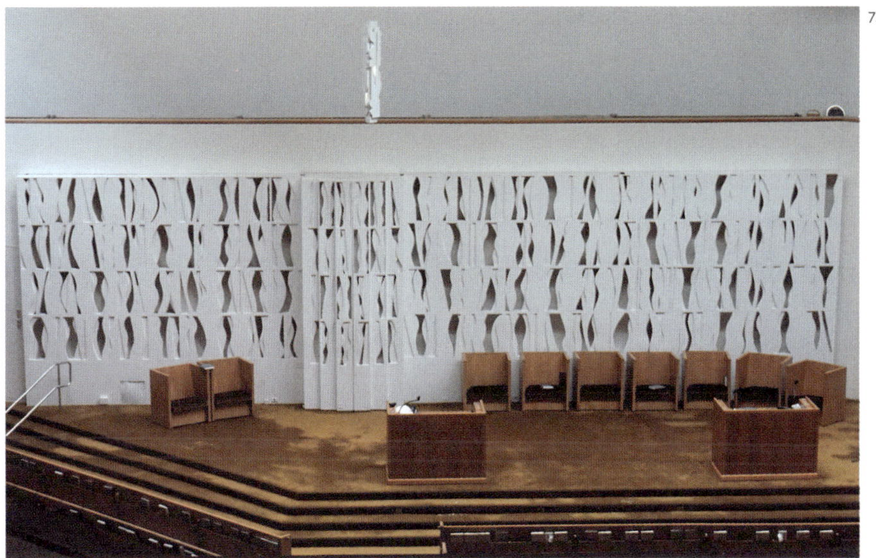

73

The White Flame of the Six Million, 1971, painted wood, 1676.4 cm wide, Temple Beth-El of Great Neck, Great Neck, New York

hypnotic and a touch sinister. In *The White Flame* she returns to that kind of repetition, of undulating solids and shadowy depths, but this time to create a flickering panorama that's literally uplifting, one that suggests both tongues of fire and ascending souls.

White was a daring choice. Nevelson's customary black, the color she had used for *Homage to 6,000,000*, might have seemed more suited to a tragic event. But white offers a better means of transcending the sufferings of the Holocaust and the memories of the crematoria. Not unlike the biblical story of Shadrach, Meshach, and Abednego, the Israelites cast into a furnace who are delivered by an angel of God, *The White Flame* draws out of a grotesque ordeal a testament of endurance. Not salvation—the Jews who died in Hitler's camps were not saved and no work of art could say otherwise. But the affirming fire of Nevelson's white wall grants a symbolic triumph, one amplified by the fact that the wall contains a closet enclosure that serves as the temple's Torah Ark, where the ancient and enduring Hebrew scripture is kept. And hanging above it, in one of Nevelson's white "stalactites," is the temple's eternal flame, the symbol of God's abiding presence.

• • •

In the spring of 1967, the Whitney Museum in New York certified Nevelson as an artist of consequence by mounting her first full-career retrospective. Or rather, she mounted it. As always, she insisted on installing her own work, and she wanted to be sure the Whitney show made clear to younger artists that she was a pioneer of the immersive art installations some of them were also now producing. To that end, how she arranged the work in each gallery was as important as any individual piece. As she made plain in a letter to the show's curator, Jack Gordon, such matters could only be decided by her. So completely was she in charge that when Gordon wanted to include an early plaster figure she no longer cared for, she told Glimcher and a colleague of his to just drop it on the Whitney's stone floor, where it shattered. They all laughed.

The Whitney retrospective was a triumph, another one, in the ever more visible career of an ever more visible woman. In the early 1960s, the *New York Times* critic John Canaday could write that Nevelson's work "seems to be everywhere these days." By the later part of the decade so was Nevelson—attending openings, accepting prizes, appearing on panels, giving lectures and interviews. That was when she started to cultivate her public image as shrewdly as Mae West. Knowing how easily women artists were overlooked, she decided that to make her art more visible she should do the same with herself. Even in earlier years, when she was producing her gold assemblages, she sometimes went about in gold lamé clothing and gold shoes, turning herself into something like a brand extension. Now she would build the brand every time she walked out the door.

In her choice of wardrobe Nevelson might have opted for simple lines in austere black, the color of so much of her art, but Georgia O'Keeffe had already laid claim to that look. And besides, pure sobriety would have been out of character for a woman who had once been dressed by her immigrant mother in Old World plumage that startled the prim Yankees of Rockland, Maine. So while Nevelson would wear plenty of black, she also doubled down on layered abundance and chromatic overload. She mixed the flowing scarf finery later adopted by Stevie Nicks with a Tartar opulence of the kind the Ballets Russes had used to conquer Paris around the First World War. "The Nevelson," as her friend Edward Albee called the face she showed to the world, was a phenomenon built from embroidered jackets, Chinese silks, cowboy boots, and necklaces of boar's teeth, plus the two or three pairs of sable false eyelashes she was never in public without. As she told a reporter for the *Washington Post*, "Look, when I meet someone, I want people to enjoy something, not just an old hag."

Though pop culture was never a point of reference in her wardrobe, the rock star regalia of the 1960s and 1970s—Janis Joplin's boas, Mick Jagger's sequined jumpsuits, almost anything worn by Elton John or David Bowie—offered Nevelson a kind of cultural permission slip. It meant that an artist who liked her gypsy blouses and ankle-length furs wasn't so much of a fashion outlier. And while her wardrobe was plainly calculated for effect, it was still the true expression of who she was and had always been. Even when she was broke she had dressed with do-it-yourself panache, improvising outfits from dyed sheets, ribbons, and tablecloths. And the onetime acting student and movie bit player had no fear of seeming theatrical. As she said: "I think that some of us are made for the grand gesture."

A signal event in the construction of the public Nevelson came when she was preparing for her Whitney retrospective. Knowing it would mean a new flood of media coverage, Glimcher introduced her to the designer Arnold Scaasi, hoping Scaasi might want to dress this very visible art star. He became a good friend. Nevelson became his sometime muse. Once she had made clear to him she wasn't interested in subdued style—"I'm just *not* a Scarsdale matron!"—he would produce clothes for her that were eye-catching without edging into camp. (There was always the cautionary example of Salvador Dalí, who by the late 1960s was more famous for his moustache than for any of his recent work.) For special occasions, Scaasi might costume her in a green silk jumpsuit under a velour lace poncho. To keep her warm in the studio he made a coat from paisley Persian shawls lined with great panels of chinchilla. Not one to farm out entirely the important business of her image, she always customized his outfits, adding her own scarves and boots, plus the chunky, faux-barbaric jewelry she designed herself, jagged pieces made from black wood, stone, hammered metal, and ivory.

The decision to become an eccentric fashion plate worked, and not just because by 1977 it had landed her on the International Best-Dressed List. In old age she was one of the most recognizable figures in American cultural life. Not as famous as Andy Warhol—who was?—but a face familiar to people who wouldn't know Jasper Johns if he was at the next table. Every major portrait photographer wanted her to sit for them. Cecil Beaton, Arnold Newman,

Richard Avedon, and Robert Mapplethorpe were a few she obliged. And it helped to ensure her high visibility that "the Nevelson" was often out and about, to parties and openings, as well as to dinner most nights with Diana MacKown at their favorite spots in Little Italy. The local Mafiosi, who hung out at the same places, all knew her on sight. They called her "La Principessa."

The mid-1960s saw the beginning of an explosion of public sculpture all around the United States. Most of that was due to new city, state, and federal programs designed to fund art for major government construction projects. These set aside a slice of the budget, typically one-half or one percent, to buy or commission works. Matching grants from the newly established National Endowment for the Arts could also enter the equation. Not since the WPA grants of the Depression had there been so much government money available for art. At the same time, the postwar boom in modernist office towers set on broad plazas spiked demand for something eye-catching to fill all those concrete prairies. So while the classic WPA projects were murals, like the one by Diego Rivera that Nevelson had long ago assisted on, the art being sought three decades later was large-scale outdoor sculpture, preferably made from materials that could withstand all kinds of weather. Already famous for her big wooden walls, Nevelson would soon become one of the most sought-after producers of monumental steel, a nationwide brand name along with Alexander Calder, Claes Oldenburg, Ellsworth Kelly, George Sugarman, and others. No corporate headquarters or windswept government plaza would be complete without its bolt-fastened Calder, its big comical Oldenburg, its monochrome Kelly, or a sizable Nevelson, either in grid format or the irregular formations she turned to in the 1970s.

Even after she began making public art, she would never be a political artist in the manner of Rivera. It's not that she kept quiet about her mostly left-liberal views. She supported the civil rights movement and Native American causes, opposed the Vietnam War, and donated art for a George McGovern fundraiser at Pace. One of her wooden walls is titled *Homage to Martin Luther King, Jr.* But she would never attempt anything like *F-111,* James Rosenquist's massive lampoon of American militarism and materialism, much less Leon Golub's raw scenes of napalmed bodies and snarling death squads. Most of her outdoor sculpture ended up in office plazas, parks, or city squares, or beside museums, where it carried uncontroversial titles like *Dawn's Forest* or *Summer Night Tree.*

As those names suggest, in the steel sculpture of her old age Nevelson became at times a kind of landscape artist, albeit one who worked with materials that measured by the ton. It took her a while to warm to metal as a medium. As the daughter of a man who once owned a lumber yard, she had known wood as an organic material since childhood. Metal was something hard and cold she once associated with war, in part because her son spent World War II on cargo ships in the merchant marine. She also considered welding too masculine a practice for a woman. But in 1965, Arne Glimcher, who could see the public art boom that was getting underway, began urging her to reconsider. Wood didn't withstand the elements well. And by that year welded metal had long been the medium of choice for advanced sculptors like Anthony Caro and David Smith. The hard-edge geometric sculptor Tony Smith was even having his immense polyhedrons fabricated by industrial metal shops. To show her what was possible, Glimcher brought Nevelson along on a trip to one such place in St. Louis. Within a year she was showing works in aluminum at Pace.

Metal made Nevelson a different kind of artist. Whether produced from aluminum or steel, which she adopted around 1970, many of her metal walls are spare and linear, almost like diagrams of her much denser constructions in wood. Their minimalist-style boxes, upright rectangles with crisply manufactured corners, contain less complicated innards. Many are backless and see-through, or largely so—ready to frame views of the outdoor settings they were destined for. Some hold a bolted interior crosspiece that splits the empty rectangle into quadrants. They might also have circular discs or quarter-discs attached at front or back, or undulating cuts of the kind that produce the cascade effect of *Night-Focus-Dawn*.

All those ingredients are at work in *Atmosphere and Environment XII*, a sculpture from 1970 that's now on the campus of the University of Pennsylvania. Composed of thirty boxes in six attached columns, it has a stair-step footprint, so that, when seen face on from one side, one column advances toward the viewer while the others recede on either side. Though its interior imagery is much less intricate than what you might find in her wooden walls, the discs, curves, and semicircles that play across the surface of the open boxes are enough to hint at the clouds, water, sun, and moon that the

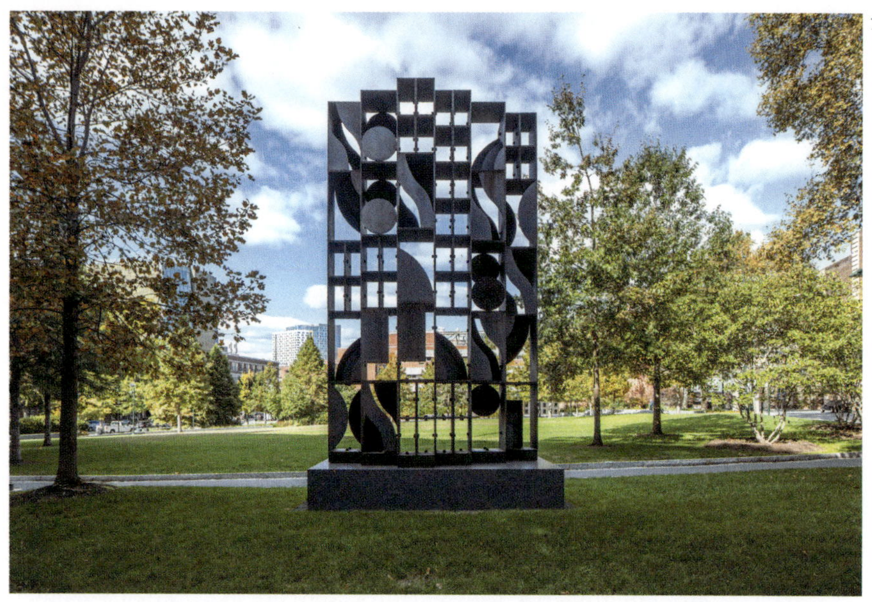

Atmosphere and Environment XII, 1970, Cor-Ten steel on granite base, 538.6 × 304.8 x 152.4 cm, University of Pennsylvania, Philadelphia, Pennsylvania

title suggests. Meanwhile, as a mostly see-through construction, it offers glimpses of the natural and man-made surroundings it was scaled to meet.

However large her wooden walls might be, they remain in effect chamber pieces, things meant to be examined at close range. The metal walls are like artist billboards, with big elements you grasp at once from a distance. By her seventies, going big was second nature to Nevelson. From the time of her "debut" in "Sixteen Americans," the trajectory of her career had taken her to ever larger stages, from galleries to museums, from New York to venues across the United States and in Europe, from occasional reviews to major media coverage and TV appearances. Her move into monumental outdoor sculpture was of a piece with all that, a step out of the gallery into a backdrop of earth and sky. "I had been through the enclosures of wood," is how she explained it. "I had been through the shadows. I had been through the enclosures and come out into the open." And all of this comported of course with her grand sense of self. "A brook is beautiful," she once said. "And a lake you can look at and it's just peaceful and glorious, but I identify with the ocean."

Nevelson's forays into welded metal were made possible by Lippincott,

Inc., a metal fabricator in North Haven, Connecticut, that Glimcher introduced her to in 1969. It had been founded three years earlier by Don Lippincott—whose father helped design the Campbell's soup can—and his business partner Roxanne Everett. Lippincott was a unique operation, the first metal shop devoted entirely to helping artists realize monumental sculpture in steel or aluminum. Most fabricators were geared to turning out industrial products with fixed specifications on predictable schedules. Art doesn't usually get made that way. Especially as carried out by someone as spontaneous as Nevelson, the production process can involve multiple redesigns and on-site adjustments. Lippincott offered a flexible approach, a crew trained to work with artists, and a twenty-two-thousand-square-foot workshop with twenty-five-foot ceilings and overhead cranes. Nevelson was delighted. In this industrial-strength atelier, she said, she found "total harmony and understanding."

Nevelson's imagination was sent down new paths at Lippincott, where she typically came for working visits that lasted several days. Accustomed to making art at home in solitude, or with MacKown as her only helper, at Lippincott she found herself in a place that harked back to the bustling studios of the Renaissance, one where "I can work from six in the morning to as late at night, with as many assistants as I need." The woman who once thought welded sculpture was too masculine for her now roamed the shop floor in a hard hat, making art that had to be engineered, not just assembled. Already trained to spot wooden discards in Manhattan, her eye would settle on scraps of aluminum that had been sheared away to make works by other sculptors. Nevelson started rescuing these for herself. As she did with the scavenged bits of her wooden walls, some she kept as she found them. Others she handed off to the Lippincott crew to be cut and bent at her direction.

Discovering Lippincott encouraged Nevelson literally to think outside the box. Though she would continue to make gridwork steel walls, she turned now as well to much more supple assemblages of flat metal that was curve-cut and joined into irregular silhouettes. One of her early Lippincott projects was a suite of ten tall black assemblages that looked like spectral plant life or trees with ragged foliage. Having recently entered her seventies, she called them *Seventh Decade Garden*. Actually, as they are for anyone, her seventies were her *eighth* decade. But even if her math was off, the *Garden* was one more demonstration that metal was a medium she could literally bend to her own purposes.

Seventh Decade Garden was made from aluminum, a metal relatively light and easy to work with. As Nevelson told MacKown, "I knew if I wanted a half circle [the shop crew] would put it through a machine and in a few seconds, you get it." But at Lippincott she was also introduced to COR-TEN steel, at the time a new alloy designed to express a thin patina of rust as it weathered. By the late 1960s sculpture was moving into its most muscular phase, and steel was its signature material. Early in that decade the English sculptor Anthony Caro was already making very blunt instruments from steel beams. Ten years later a work by Robert Morris might be just a series of COR-TEN trestles. Richard Serra was leaning steel plates against one another, while Mark di Suvero was joining immense I-beams into improbable balancing acts. Nevelson's work would never be as rawboned as theirs, but COR-TEN would soon become the medium for most of her public sculpture. It was heavier than aluminum, but once she took it up she was surprised by how pliant it could be. "It was almost like butter," she said. "Like working with whipped cream on a cake."

Nevelson's adoption of monumental steel was one more reminder, if one more was needed, that there was nothing dainty about her or her art. But she was conflicted about attempts to make her a role model for the more militant women's movement that emerged in the 1970s, when the "second wave feminism" of Betty Friedan, Kate Millett, Germaine Greer, and *Ms.* magazine got underway. As "sexism" and "male chauvinism" became diagnostic terms for toxic male presumption, and Linda Nochlin's quietly devastating essay "Why Have There Been No Great Women Artists?" laid the groundwork for feminist art history, Nevelson was inevitably drawn into the clamor. It was a delicate matter for her. She didn't mind saying that men and women were biologically different and that because of that they should be expected to take different approaches to their art, a view that put her at odds with feminist thinkers looking to minimize those differences. At the same time, she didn't want to be thought of as a "woman artist." She was one of the most important American sculptors of the twentieth century, full stop, and defied anyone to make her part of some women's auxiliary. But as a proud and forceful personality, she also didn't want to claim victim status. Victor status was always more to her taste.

All the same, Nevelson knew that being a woman had made things harder for her. In a now notorious review of her 1941 debut at the Nierendorf Gallery, a show that drew mostly favorable press, the critic for *Cue* felt free to hedge his bets this way: "We learned the artist is a woman, in time to check our enthusiasm. Had it been otherwise, we might have hailed these sculptural expressions as by surely a great figure among moderns."

Even at the tail end of the 1960s, when she was thoroughly famous, she was somehow excluded from two major group shows that she surely belonged in. One was at MoMA, a survey of assemblage art. The other, at the Metropolitan Museum, was a particular sore point. "New York Painting and Sculpture: 1940–1970" was an attempt by the Met, a latecomer to modern art, to get in the game by identifying its own canon of important New York artists from the previous thirty years. A show that would be the talk of the town for months, it was organized by Henry Geldzahler, the museum's pop-infatuated new curator of twentieth-century art and a power broker in New York cultural circles. Bearish, cigar-smoking, openly gay, and by no means press shy, Geldzahler avidly promoted the contemporaries whose work he approved, some of them personal friends like Warhol and David Hockney. When it came to women, he appears to have had a blind spot. There was just one among the forty-three artists in his big Met survey, the color field pioneer Helen Frankenthaler.

After that slight, Nevelson began to view Geldzahler as an obstacle, if not an antagonist, along with the prominent critics he listened to. Though she occasionally hit back at them in interviews, she mostly avoided squabbling in public. By that time, she was too prominent for their views to do her much harm. If anything, many people saw her exclusion from Geldzahler's show as an embarrassment for him, not her.

For years, Nevelson would try both to acknowledge the barriers she had faced as a woman in male-dominated art circles and to shrug them off. She could say, "I'm not a feminist. I'm an artist who happens to be a woman." But she also remembered how it felt to be dismissed. "When I first started, nobody took me seriously. In the galleries—a woman! I'd look in the mirror and see the gestures they made behind my back." She once told Glimcher that even her interest in dressing well was held against her. "It was taken for granted that a woman of that sort couldn't be totally dedicated." Maybe the best summary of her feelings is one she abruptly offered in a 1972 interview she gave to a feminist magazine, *Changes*. When the interviewer mentioned Nevelson's support of women's liberation causes, she shot back, "Of course, because I *am* woman's liberation." Meaning that her life was what liberation looked like, a hard-won fait accompli. To fulfill her ambitions, she had walked away from material comfort, marriage, and conventional family life. "The personal is the political" was a favorite catchphrase of that era. She could have coined it herself, because she knew all about it.

Throughout the 1970s, public art put Nevelson literally on the map all around the United States. And because most of hers was sited outdoors, it was seen by people who might never visit a gallery or museum. Her *Night Presence IV*, which she presented as a gift to the city of New York, was situated in the planted median that divides the uptown and downtown lanes of Park Avenue. Every day, tens of thousands of people passed its oscillating verticals and bisected newel posts. In Scottsdale, Arizona, there was *Windows to the West*, commissioned by the city for its Civic Center Mall. *Dawn's Column* rose up on the Government Plaza in Binghamton, New York. There would be other Nevelsons at Princeton University, the Massachusetts Institute of Technology, and Harvard. A high point came in 1975. Ahead of the two-hundredth anniversary of America's independence, the General Services Administration commissioned Nevelson to make *Bicentennial Dawn*, an indoor suite of white wooden assemblages for the federal courthouse in Philadelphia. When it was unveiled the next year, First Lady Betty Ford attended the ceremony.

In her seventies, Nevelson's energies were unceasing, sufficient to ensure a constant output of wooden walls, monumental steel, wall-mounted assemblages, and lithographs. It was work that sustained her and kept her vital. Early in the decade, she described her creative life to an interviewer in terms that made her sound like an industrious cobbler. "An artist goes to the studio to work. Not when the spirit moves you; you go every day and work—just plain work, physical work—and you keep right on going. The tools are put away at night, and the studio is swept down, and things you want for tomorrow morning are placed out." And when you return the next day, she added, "Everything is clean, is nice. You are very happy. You start working."

Even in this decade of extraordinary productivity, 1977 and 1978 figure as a watershed, years when she completed some of her most ambitious projects.

One was the towering *Sky Tree,* her largest work to that date. A rising sequence of flat and curling elements weighing twenty-nine tons, it climbs fifty-four feet from a sunken plaza at San Francisco's Embarcadero Center, a mixed-use project codeveloped by her longtime patron David Rockefeller. Sited in a reflecting pool, it ascends past several tiers of the underground shopping mall that surrounds it, emerging above street level like the Loch Ness monster.

As *Sky Tree* was getting its festive unveiling in San Francisco in March 1977, with Nevelson on hand, she was at the same time busy preparing for the opening two months later of the first museum show devoted entirely to her work in steel and aluminum. The Neuberger Museum, a Philip Johnson–designed venue on the campus of the State University of New York at Purchase, would host an exhibition of nearly two dozen of Nevelson's recent large-scale sculpture, all of it installed and lighted by Nevelson and Glimcher.

In November of that same year at Pace, she debuted one of the most important works of her career, a magnum opus titled *Mrs. N's Palace,* for the name that neighborhood kids gave to her houses on Spring Street. It carries a date spanning thirteen years, because she first conceived it in 1964, collected its component parts for more than a decade, but didn't complete it until a two-week burst of activity that summer in a rented studio, assisted by Glimcher and two carpenters. Just as with her first walls two decades earlier, Nevelson's *Palace* is indifferent to any rules about what sculpture should be or look like. A massive rectangular box with an open entryway, it's a hybrid of sculpture and architecture, nearly twenty feet long and more than eleven deep. Not quite a palace, except metaphorically, it's more like a flat-roofed house, or perhaps a mausoleum, one stuffed and covered, inside and out, with 130 or so sculptural assemblages.

One source for *Mrs. N's Palace* was Nevelson's yearslong fascination with Edward Albee's 1964 play *Tiny Alice.* A baffling meditation on faith and illusion, much of it takes place in the library of a mansion, a room that contains a detailed model of the same mansion, which in turn holds an even smaller model and so on. With Albee's Chinese box simulacra still in mind, in 1972 and 1973 Nevelson made a series of more than forty black wooden sculptures, each called *Dream House.* Tall, hollow constructions, most between six and eight feet high, some resemble houses stretched to skyscraper heights, with

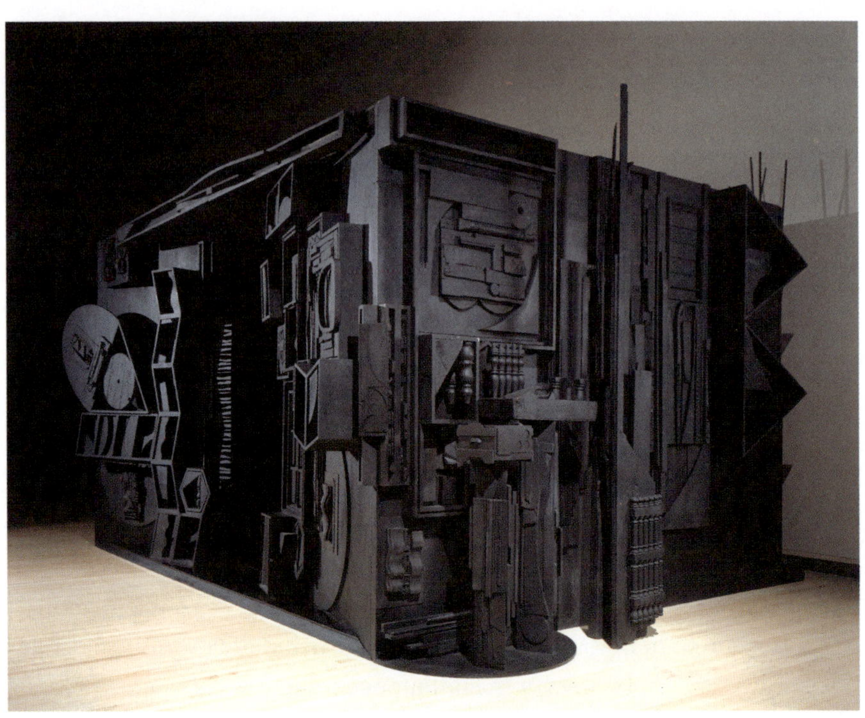

Mrs. N's Palace, 1964–77, painted wood, mirror, 355.6 × 607.1 x 457.2 cm, The Metropolitan Museum of Art, New York

hinged doors, multiple floors, peaked rooflines, and uniform window grids that admit light. Others are more topsy-turvy, like high-rise crates with irregular exterior detailing and patchwork fenestration. All of them carry abstract surface attachments, sometimes hundreds on all four sides. Plain precursors of her *Palace*, they were Nevelson's first attempt to make a dwelling serve as a metaphor for the self and its mingled cargo of memory, fantasy, and desire. Never a devoted homemaker, she still identified strongly with her houses, always adding decorative touches and rearranging what furniture she had. Hilton Kramer was right when he realized that her sculpture was a translation of the spaces she actually occupied.

Though she never described it as such, Nevelson's *Palace* could also be read as her final reply to Judd's austere boxes. Not a minimalist box, but a crazy-quilt box, an eccentric container of hints and near-meanings, with passages that can be menacing, whimsical, lyrical, or all three. Inside her cluttered stronghold, shadows and light seep through slats of horizontal lattice work. Outside, streams of slanting boxes, loaded with cut wood, snake back and forth down the walls. Here and there are round wooden plates the size of chariot wheels. Actually the circular sides of industrial cable spools, they recall the sun and moon discs of her earlier work. And all along the back wall, peering above the roofline, is a sparse palisade made from dozens of long, thin sticks. Are they antennas? Spear shafts? Tall grasses? The answer of course is all of those and none of them. However much *Mrs. N's Palace* looks like a building, it remains a bristling abstraction. It doesn't depict, it suggests, and all its parts are ambiguous.

Like her entire "Moon Garden" show, the *Palace* was conceived as a work of art you can enter and move about in. A tall central threshold opens onto a windowless room thronged with Nevelson sculptures. But in 2019, when the *Palace* was last put on temporary display by its owner, New York's Metropolitan Museum of Art, a rope line blocked entry. From outside you could peer into the darkness to glimpse some of the interior works but you could no longer approach them. Though the barrier was there for the understandable purpose of preventing visitors from damaging the interior or its reflective black glass floor, it had the effect of making the *Palace* a walled-off castle keep, which would not have been Nevelson's intention. It did at least compound the mystery of a work she plainly intended to be mysterious.

In her annus mirabilis of 1977 Nevelson would complete another all-encompassing work. Like Matisse, she would design an entire chapel. Hers would be a room off the main sanctuary of Saint Peter's Church at the corner of Lexington Avenue and Fifty-Fourth Street in New York. An aggressively modern granite building, Saint Peter's rests on the site of a neo-Gothic church from 1903 that was razed to make way for what is now Citigroup Center. As part of the deal that produced the center and its fifty-nine story office tower, the bank agreed to fund construction of a new church. Its pastor, Dr. Ralph Peterson, had a strong interest in the arts. Being aware of the Rothko Chapel in Houston and the chapel created by Matisse in Vence, to say nothing of Michelangelo's Sistine, he wanted the new Saint Peter's to include a contemplative space created by an artist, a quiet refuge in a busy stretch of Midtown Manhattan. Late in 1974, even as construction of the new church was still underway, he chose Nevelson to produce it.

Three years later, Nevelson's Chapel of the Good Shepherd was dedicated, just two weeks after she had unveiled *Mrs. N's Palace*. An irregular, five-sided white room, it measures roughly twenty-eight by twenty-one feet. Though she collaborated with the designers Lella and Massimo Vignelli on the three rows of movable pews and the altar table, every other principal element is hers alone. On the wall behind the altar is her abstract version of a cross, a rectangular field of gold leaf traversed by horizontal gold panels. Running down the center, a cascade of white wood stands in for the figure of Christ. Near the altar, in an echo of the Holy Trinity, three of Nevelson's hanging post assemblages descend from the ceiling. Below them is a boxy, wall-mounted candle holder.

The other walls of the chapel are almost entirely covered with big low-relief wooden friezes that have both the spiky density of a logjam and a baroque sense of flow. The wall-spanning *Sky Vestment—Trinity* even has an airborne feel. Its silhouette—an inverted trapezoid—suggests a wingspread, which in turn brings to mind the white dove of the Holy Spirit. As its title implies, it also suggests an ecclesiastic robe. (Working with Arnold Scaasi, Nevelson, like Matisse, had designed an actual vestment—now lost—to be worn during chapel ceremonies.) Yet for all its very animated surfaces, the chapel's white-on-white palette draws the room back toward the subdued New England churches Nevelson grew up around. Its atmosphere would be well described years later by the actress Mercedes Ruehl, who studied the place in preparation to star as Nevelson in *Edward Albee's Occupant*, his two-person play about Nevelson in which the artist is called back from the dead to sit for an uncomfortable interview. Ruehl said it had "kind of a teeming silence."

Though the chapel is a nondenominational space, Saint Peter's is a Lutheran church, albeit one that dropped the word "Lutheran" from its name. Did it matter that its chapel designer was Jewish? Certainly Pastor Peterson didn't think so. He liked to remind people, "God is not a Lutheran." As for Nevelson, a woman who had looked into any number of belief systems without committing to any of them, her whole effort in the chapel had been to attain the universal, not the sectarian. "Abstraction allows me to transcend Christian imagery to the essential point where all religions meet." And thanks to her gift for forms that are expressive but elusive, she got them to meet snugly at the corner of Lexington Avenue and Fifty-Fourth Street.

In 1977, Nevelson also received a more secular commission, for what amounted to a monument to herself. The City of New York invited her to transform a small triangular park in Lower Manhattan with big new works.

76

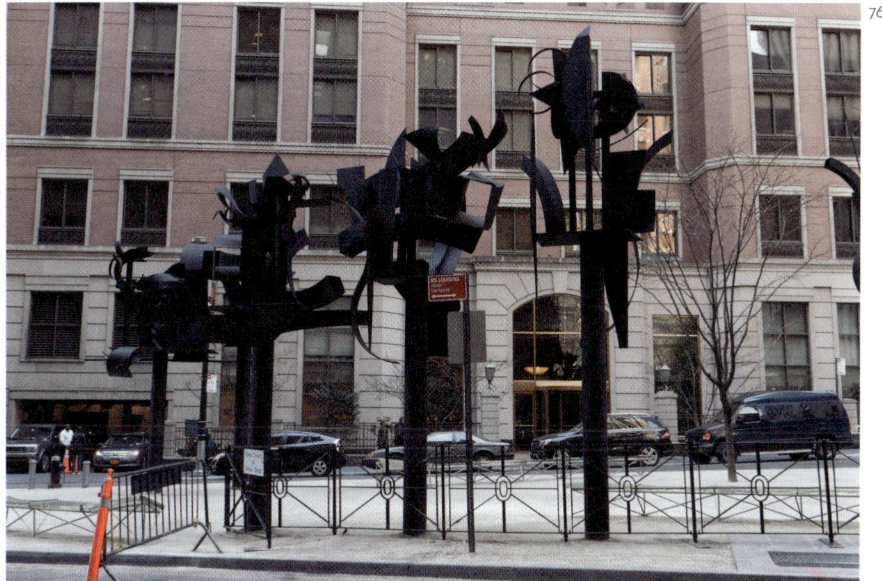

Four sculptures from the series *Shadows and Flags*, painted steel, each approximately 762 cm high, Nevelson Plaza, New York

Better still, the site would be renamed Louise Nevelson Plaza, the first in the city to be named for an artist. Once again, a prime mover of the project was David Rockefeller, whose office on an upper floor of Chase Manhattan headquarters was just a few blocks away. Nevelson adored New York, the city where she had come into herself, a place with the abundance and intricacy that characterized her walls. It seemed only right that a patch of it should bear her name.

Nevelson Plaza, which was dedicated on September 14, 1978, holds seven black steel sculptures collectively titled *Shadows and Flags*. The largest—at seventy feet it's sixteen taller than *Sky Tree*—unfurls majestically against the heavy stone of the Florentine-style Federal Reserve Bank across the street. Arrayed down the two long sides of the plaza are six smaller works. Each around twenty-five feet tall, they recall the ragged silhouettes of Nevelson's *Seventh Decade Garden*. But while those rose directly from the ground, these perch like nesting ospreys on platforms that rest on tall posts. They must be city birds, because one even includes a wide sheet of metal stamped with the diamond plate pattern of sidewalk cellar doors. It's a lowbrow motif so redolent of New York that a year later Talking Heads would make it the cover art for their album *Fear of Music*. With their curving bands of metal spilling over the platform edges, the shorter works also seem vegetal, like hanging ferns. But as her title makes plain, Nevelson thought of them as flags, waving madly in the breeze. Perhaps she even saw them as victory flags, marking her final triumph in the city where she first planted her own flag more than half a century before. *Veni. Vidi. Vici.*

Nevelson still had some unfinished business with the much smaller town she had left behind. Though she had lived in Manhattan for almost sixty years, she had never entirely lost touch with Rockland, Maine. Her brother, Nate, owned a hotel there, where he proudly displayed some of his famous sister's work. Even after leaving for New York in the early 1920s, she went back for occasional visits. But in 1978 she acknowledged to an interviewer that growing up she had felt marginalized there, both as a Jewish girl and a budding artist. "If I never set foot in Rockland again," she said, "it will be fine by me."

As she certainly knew, by the time she gave that interview, a major opportunity for reconciliation was already underway. With her agreement, Rockland's Farnsworth Art Museum was planning a Nevelson retrospective to open in 1979, the first one-artist show the museum had ever mounted. The Farnsworth is a small museum, but its new director, Marius Péladeau, had ambitious plans for his Nevelson show. He also had the cooperation of Pace Gallery and a grant from the National Endowment for the Arts. Those allowed him to assemble a full-career survey that ranged from Nevelson's early terra-cotta figures to her breakthrough wooden assemblages to her later work in plexiglass and metal. When it opened over three days in July, Nevelson herself was in attendance, looking thoroughly pleased to be feted by the town where she had once felt excluded, but where the city council had now declared Louise Nevelson Day. The camera crew that trailed her for a segment on the CBS program *Sunday Morning* caught her beaming as locals flocked to congratulate her. They even paid a literal kind of tribute, presenting her with wood scraps they had gathered for her to use in her work.

It was like that in the last decade of Nevelson's life, when she often had to take time from her art for the agreeable distraction of collecting tributes. All told there would be thirteen honorary degrees from schools that included Brandeis, Harvard, and Columbia. There would be two White House award ceremonies. For the first, in 1979, she joined Alice Neel and Georgia O'Keeffe among five artists chosen by the Women's Caucus for Art to receive their newly established lifetime achievement award and to meet afterward with President Jimmy Carter and First Lady Rosalynn Carter. Nevelson and the Carters were already acquainted. Two years earlier she had been their guest at a White House dinner. In 1985, it would be President Ronald Reagan who presented her with the National Medal of Arts, again as part of the first cohort to be honored, a group that included Ralph Ellison, O'Keeffe again, Martha Graham, and Leontyne Price. Not to be outdone by the Americans, a few months later the French minister of culture would bestow his nation's Order of Arts and Letters.

All the while, with one eye on the clock, she never lost focus on her work. It may no longer have been true, as she once claimed, that she could go for two or three days without sleep. But her waking hours, which began most days before six a.m., were still devoted to planning and making art. "And I wear cotton clothes, so that I can sleep in them or I can work in them—I don't want to waste time." When she wasn't eating out, she kept her meals simple, too. As she told MacKown, she was happy with "a can of sardines and a cup of tea and a piece of stale bread." She was delighted to learn that the writer Isak Dinesen once claimed that in old age she only ate oysters and drank champagne. "I thought what an intelligent solution to ridding oneself of meaningless decision-making."

Nevelson's house in Little Italy reflected the same indifference to bourgeois comforts. When she said, "I don't like a homey home," she meant it. Like her former habitat on East Thirtieth Street, her place on Spring Street overflowed once more with junk and art, but after her household purge of the late 1950s, and another in 1966, there was very little furniture. She slept in an upstairs bedroom in a single twin bed, her clothes neatly stored in industrial metal closets. Though she still collected china, crystal, silver, and pewter, she kept it stashed away. She told a reporter, "Objects have vibrations that intrude." To discourage visitors who might keep her from working, she didn't even like to have comfortable chairs. "I don't want anyone to come and park themselves."

As she entered her eighties, Nevelson had no end of things to keep her busy, including another retrospective at the Whitney. Though it would take its name from her first series of outdoor steel sculptures, "Atmospheres and

Environments" was mostly intended to reproduce earlier work—four of her installation shows of the 1950s and early '60s—plus the more recent *Mrs. N's Palace*. This was no simple matter. By 1980, the only Nevelson environment still fully intact was her Chapel of the Good Shepherd. All the others had long since been broken up and scattered, their walls and other assemblage works sold off piecemeal or returned to her. But the curators managed to retrieve many of the original components, and where they could not they were able to swap in other Nevelsons of a similar kind, enough to remind visitors that Nevelson's great gift was not just the discrete work of art, but the wizardly creation of entire worlds.

At eighty-four Nevelson satisfied a longtime ambition when the Opera Theatre of St. Louis invited her to provide sets and costumes for *Orfeo ed Euridice*, Gluck's stately eighteenth-century retelling of the Orpheus myth. Always fascinated by music and dance, of course she wanted to join the list of artists who had collaborated on stage productions. In 1917, her hero Picasso had provided the extravagantly cubist costumes for Erik Satie's ballet *Parade*. Two years later Matisse designed both costumes and sets for a ballet based on Igor Stravinsky's opera *The Song of the Nightingale*. In 1968, her friend Merce Cunningham had used Andy Warhol's helium-filled Mylar pillows as a floating backdrop for his ballet *RainForest*. And by the 1980s, David Hockney had something like a second career in stage design, having worked on several Stravinsky operas, as well as Mozart's *Magic Flute*.

With her typical take-charge manner, Nevelson did everything but write the music and choreograph the dances for *Orfeo*. She designed the costumes, most of them silk-screened in abstract patterns of black, white, and gray. She produced the jewelry, including necklaces made from flattened beer cans painted black on one side and gilded on the other. She created the cover image for the program, an abstraction in metallic paint and gouache. She even got to approve the stage director. And of course she conceived the set and its centerpiece, a backdrop divided into twelve panels, each containing four rectangular boxes filled with various geometric shapes. In effect, a Nevelson wall, though this one in gold and black, except in Act III, when its central panels turned to present the audience with black forms on a field of gray.

Nevelson's involvement was enough to convince the *New York Times* to send its music critic John Rockwell to check out the St. Louis production. In his review he was respectful toward Nevelson but thought her costumes inhibited the dancers' movements. Knowing how much she admired Martha Graham, he decided her designs owed too much "to the world of modern dance between the world wars" and seemed "to speak of a different era than today"—a gentle way of saying her ideas seemed dated. No matter, Nevelson was thrilled by her experience with the St. Louis company. Her biographer Laurie Wilson describes a high point, a dinner party at which Nevelson was taken by surprise when a newly arrived guest, the celebrated American soprano Eleanor Steber, abruptly serenaded her with the whole of "Vissi d'arte." In that poignant aria from *Tosca*, Puccini's doomed heroine declares that she has lived for art and for love. Nevelson was overcome. Whether she had lived for love was debatable. But that she had lived for art—for her art—was beyond dispute.

Even in her mid-eighties, though she was ever more aware of her advancing age, Nevelson had the energy to complete some major works in both wood and metal. So for the Storm King Art Center, a museum and vast, rolling sculpture park in New Windsor, New York, she made *City on the High*

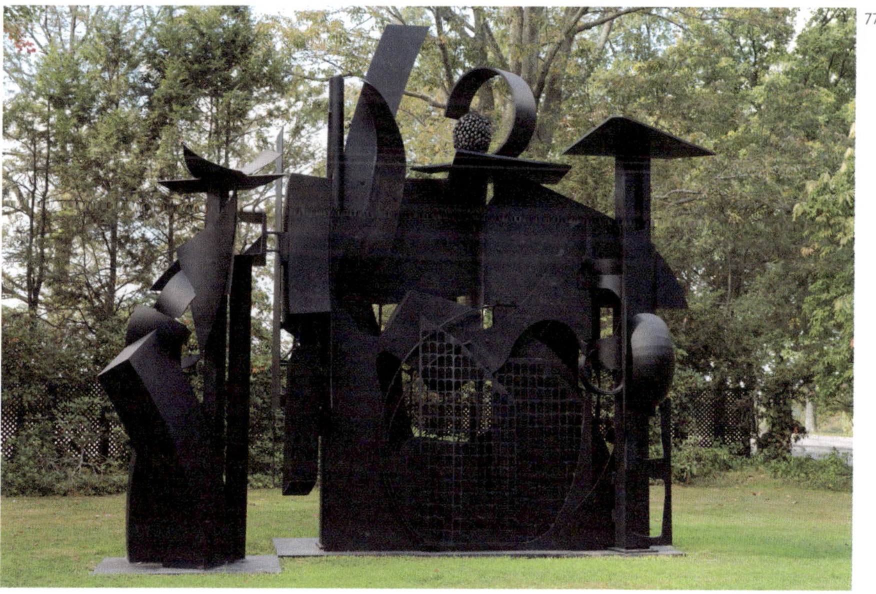 77

City on the High Mountain, 1983, painted steel, 624.8 × 701 x 411.5 cm, Storm King Art Center, New Windsor, New York

Mountain. A two-part exercise in dynamic composition, with elements that rise to a height of nearly twenty-one feet, its principal section is a free-form assembly punctuated near the top by a black ball of railway spikes, like an oversize pincushion, framed within an open curve of black steel. At ground level Nevelson attached two large sheets of scrap metal punctured with arched forms that look like gravestones, though she compared the pattern they made to lace. Set close by is the work's secondary portion, a near-replica, but at reduced scale, of the tallest of her seven sculptures at Nevelson Plaza.

Even if that gravestone motif was unintended, intimations of mortality were creeping into some of Nevelson's other last works. As she was completing *City on the High Mountain,* she was also making a numbered series of more than forty wooden wall reliefs called *Mirror Shadow*. All of them combine familiar Nevelson elements like grids, rings, discs, and table legs. Some are held in her customary boxes, but others are spread out in freely arranged compositions, like the aftermath of some seismic event, with lots of diagonal offshoots across a shallow backdrop of gridwork frames. For all their off-kilter energies, once you know they were produced by an artist in the final stretch of a long life, they have a valedictory feel. You sense that Nevelson was not just revisiting forms she had worked with for decades but combining them in final orchestrations and in the full awareness of that shadow in the mirror. There's nothing especially ominous about the appearance of any of these works. But to call them *Mirror Shadow* hints they were made by an artist who had glimpsed in her reflection the first signs of a gathering darkness.

Gathering fast. In 1986, one year before she wrapped up the *Mirror Shadow* series, Nevelson completed her last monumental steel sculpture, *Sky Horizon,* which would be installed on the grounds of the National Institutes of Health in Bethesda, Maryland. Its tallest element, rising more than thirty feet, is a slender triangle with a narrow tip touching the ground. Looked at one way, from bottom to top, it could easily be read as an exclamation point, but it's doubtful she intended that. Cartoonish imagery was rarely her thing. But from top to bottom it brings to mind a spear tip driving into the ground. That may have been meant deliberately. In its plainspoken way, it points to the grave.

Even before *Sky Horizon* was finished, Nevelson had been putting her affairs in order. With an eye to securing her legacy, she was setting down monumental steel work in prominent locations. For Los Angeles, a city that somehow had never landed a Nevelson, she delivered *Night Sail* to the new Crocker Center (now the Wells Fargo Center). A thirty-foot combination of solid and perforated steel, it has a handle shaped like bull's horns protruding from one expanse of vaguely sail-shaped sheet metal. It makes that element appear to double as a shield, though Nevelson said the work's title was inspired by what was then still the openness of the surrounding neighborhood, which reminded her of the sea. Naturally the city declared Louise Nevelson Day to celebrate. She was also donating works to museums, mostly to first-rank institutions like the Whitney and the Guggenheim, but also to the plucky Farnsworth in Rockland. In 1985 it gave Nevelson her second show in the town where she came of age and where it now pleased her to leave more reminders of herself. That September she even spent her eighty-sixth birthday there.

In her will Nevelson would leave her entire estate to her son, Mike, whom she named as executor. But to her mind, documents she signed in both 1985 and 1986 ensured that a number of her works would go to Diana MacKown, mostly terra-cotta figures from early in her career, as well as the right to make and sell reproductions of those. It's plain she never imagined that very soon after her death her son would try to thwart that bequest. Mike always held MacKown partly responsible for the limited contact he had with his mother in her last years. Within days after her death he would install a metal door in the Spring Street house to lock MacKown out of the third-floor rooms where Nevelson had lived. He would also take from the house twenty-five of the terra-cotta pieces and ten other works that Nevelson had intended MacKown to have.

What would follow would be two years of legal battles before MacKown was finally able to retrieve the terra-cottas, plus two walls. The fight would keep Nevelson's name in the public eye, but not in a good way. Worse still, her son later became embroiled in a yearslong dispute with the IRS over back taxes on Nevelson's work. That protracted struggle, along with his insistence that Pace Gallery return many Nevelsons it had from her on consignment, kept the greater part of her inventory off the market until a 2005 estate sale that resulted in some 1,500 works being divided among three galleries, including Pace. The sale opened the way for Nevelson's work to come back into circulation, but the seventeen-year market hiatus diminished her posthumous name recognition, a stunning setback for a woman who was once so famous. To the extent that Mike's actions played a role in the—temporary—eclipse of his mother's reputation, the neglected son may have gotten his revenge after all.

But in 1987, the last full year of her life, she had no inkling of what lay in the future, a future she would not in any case live to see. With the completion of the *Mirror Shadow* series that year she had wrapped up her last sizable works. Though at the beach house she rented that summer in Westhampton she continued to make small collages from sandpaper, clothespins, and whatever else was at hand, by September, the month in which she turned eighty-eight, she was facing the beginning of the end. Until she quit in her eighties, she had been a smoker for years, both cigarettes and skinny cigarillos. Now tests found evidence of lung cancer. After some hesitation she agreed to surgery that removed half of one lung. Because it appeared the cancer had not spread to other parts of the body, there was some room to hope.

To escape the challenge of another New York winter, MacKown rented a small house for them on St. Martin in the Caribbean. They flew in just after Christmas. A few days later, when they showed up for lunch at the home of Jasper Johns, he was so alarmed by Nevelson's appearance that he called a mutual friend in Manhattan. Johns enlisted him to persuade MacKown that Nevelson must return immediately to New York. On arrival she was taken straight from the airport to the hospital, where she was diagnosed with a brain tumor. Over the next weeks and months, in the hospital and then at home, she gradually descended into a profound silence. She died on April 17, 1988.

Except for her last difficult months, Nevelson was a productive artist for nearly her entire adult life. It was work that sustained her through the many years of obscurity and helped her to keep her bearings during the many years of fame. However much she went out and about, it was her studio she always returned to, where the tools were put away at night, and the place was swept down, and things you'd want for tomorrow morning were laid out. And everything was clean, was nice.

And by means of that devotion, she achieved for herself the full and very gratifying life she had always presumed to be her destiny. In one of the conversations that MacKown recorded for *Dawns + Dusks*, Nevelson confided to her the modest goal she once set for herself.

"I wanted one thing that I thought belonged to me. I wanted the whole show. To me, that is living."

It took single-minded effort, sustained self-confidence—between the bouts of despair—and endless patience, but who can deny that she did it? When she was still vital enough to enjoy every minute of it, Louise Nevelson got the whole show.

SELECT BIBLIOGRAPHY

TITIAN

Books

Ackroyd, Peter. *Venice, Pure City*. New York: Nan A. Talese–Doubleday, 2009.

Clarke, Michael, et al. *Titian and the Golden Age of Venetian Painting*. New Haven and London: Yale University Press, 2010 (exhibition catalogue).

Ferino-Pagden, Sylvia. *Late Titian and the Sensuality of Painting*. Venice: Marsilio Editore, 2008 (exhibition catalogue).

Goffen, Rona. *Renaissance Rivals: Michelangelo, Leonardo, Raphael, Titian*. New Haven and London: Yale University Press, 2002.

Greengrass, Mark. *Christendom Destroyed*. New York: Viking Penguin, 2014.

Hale, Sheila. *Titian: His Life*. New York: Harper Collins, 2012.

Hope, Charles, et al. *Titian*. London: National Gallery, 2003.

Hudson, Mark. *Titian: The Last Days*. New York: Walker & Company, 2009.

Ilchman, Frederick, et al. *Titian, Tintoretto, Veronese: Rivals in Renaissance Venice*. Boston: MFA Publications, 2009 (exhibition catalogue).

McCarthy, Mary. *Venice Observed*. San Diego, New York, and London: Harcourt Books, 1963.

Norwich, John Julius. *Four Princes*. New York: Grove Press, 2017.

———. *A History of Venice*. New York: Knopf, 1982.

Rosand, David. *Painting in Sixteenth Century Venice: Titian, Veronese, Tintoretto*, revised edition. Cambridge: Cambridge University Press, 1997.

———. *Titian*. New York: Harry N. Abrams, 1978.

———. *Titian: His World and His Legacy*. New York: Columbia University Press, 1982.

Sohm, Philip. *The Artist Grows Old: The Aging of Art and Artists in Italy*. New Haven and London: Yale University Press, 2007.

Tietze, Hans. *Titian: The Paintings and Drawings*. London: Phaidon Press, 1950.

Wills, Garry. *Venice, Lion City*. New York: Simon & Schuster, 2001.

Wivel, Matthias, et al. *Titian: Love, Desire, Death*. London: National Gallery Company Ltd., 2020 (exhibition catalogue).

Articles

Berger, John, and Katya Andreadakis. “Titian as Dog.” *The Three Penny Review*, no. 54 (Summer 1993): 6–9.

Carrier, David. “Mrs. Isabella Stewart Gardner’s Titian.” *Source: Notes in the History of Art* 20, no. 2 (Winter 2001): 20–24.

Dunkerton, Jill, Marika Spring, et al. “Titian after 1540: Technique and Style in His Later Works.” *National Gallery Technical Bulletin* 36 (2015), London, National Gallery Company.

Georgievska-Shine, Aneta. “Titian and the Paradoxes of Love and Art in Venus and Adonis.” *Artibus et Historiae* 33, no. 54 (2012): 97–113.

Rosand, David. “Titian in the Frari.” *The Art Bulletin* 53, no. 2 (June 1971): 196–213.

Tanner, Marie. “Chance and Coincidence in Titian’s *Diana and Actaeon*.” *The Art Bulletin* 56, no. 4 (December 1974): 535–50.

Wiseman, Mary. “Words About Women: Interpreting Titian.” *Source: Notes in the History of Art* 17, no. 2 (Winter 1998): 15–25.

GOYA

Books

Bareau, Juliet Wilson, and Manuela B. Mena Marques, et al. *Goya: Truth and Fantasy. The Small Paintings*. London: Royal Academy, 1994 (exhibition catalogue).

Blackburn, Julia. *Old Man Goya*. New York: Vintage Books, 2003.

Brown, Jonathan, with Susan Grace Galassi. *Goya’s Last Works*. New Haven: Yale University Press, 2006 (exhibition catalogue).

Connell, Evan S. *Francisco Goya: A Life*. New York: Counterpoint, 2004.

Esdaile, Charles. *Peninsular Eyewitnesses: The Experience of War in Spain and Portugal*. Barnsley, UK: Pen & Sword Books Ltd., 2008.

———. *The Peninsular War: A New History*. New York: Palgrave Macmillan, 2003.

Goya, Francisco. *The Disasters of War*. Mineola, NY: Dover Publications, 1967.

———. *Los Caprichos*. Mineola, NY: Dover Publications, 1969.

Hughes, Robert. *Goya*. New York: Knopf, 2003.

Ilchman, Frederick, Stephanie Loeb Stepanek, and Janis Tomlinson. *Goya: Order & Disorder*. Boston: MFA Publications, 2014 (exhibition catalogue).

Licht, Fred. *Goya: The Origins of the Modern Temper in Art*. New York: Harper & Row, 1983.

McDonald, Mark. *Goya's Graphic Imagination*. The Metropolitan Museum of Art. New Haven: Yale University Press, 2021 (exhibition catalogue).

Pérez Sánchez, Alfonso E., and Eleanor A. Sayre. *Goya and the Spirit of Enlightenment*. Boston: Little, Brown and Company, 1989 (exhibition catalogue).

Symmons, Sarah. *Goya: A Life in Letters*. London: Pimlico, 2004.

Tomlinson, Janis. *Francisco Goya y Lucientes, 1746–1828*. London: Phaidon, 1994.

———. *From El Greco to Goya, Painting in Spain, 1561–1828*. London: George Weidenfeld and Nicolson Ltd., 1997.

———. *Goya: A Portrait of the Artist*. Princeton and Oxford: Princeton University Press, 2020.

———. *Goya in the Twilight of Enlightenment*. New Haven: Yale University Press, 1992.

Articles

Abrash, Merit. "Use and Misuse of Historical Art." *The History Teacher* 8, No. 4 (August 1975): 557–72.

Baldwin, Robert W. "Healing and Hope in Goya's 'Self-Portrait with Dr. Arrieta.'" *Source: Notes in the History of Art* 4, no. 4 (Summer 1985): 31–36.

Krumrine, Mary Louise. "Goya's 'Maja Desnuda' in Context." *Journal of Aesthetic Education* 28, no. 4 (1994): 36–44.

Levitine, George. "The Elephant of Goya. An Emblematic Basis for a Political Interpretation." *Art Journal* 20, no. 3 (Spring 1961): 145–47.

Licht, Fred. "Goya's Portrait of the Royal Family." *The Art Bulletin* 49, no. 2 (June 1967): 127–28.

Morgan, Jay Scott. "The Mystery of Goya's 'Saturn.'" *New England Review* 22, no. 3 (Summer 2001): 39–43.

Olszewski, Edward J. "Color Coding in Goya's 'Self-Portrait with Dr. Arrieta.'" *Source: Notes in the History of Art* 23, no. 2 (2004): 23–27.

———. "Exorcising Goya's 'The Family of Charles IV.'" *Artibus et Historiae* 20, no. 40 (1999): 169–85.

Salner, David. "Goya, Two Old People, Starving." *The Threepenny Review* 151 (2017): 27–27.

Tal, Guy. "An 'Enlightened' View of Witches: Melancholy and Delusional Experience in Goya's 'Spell.'" *Zeitschrift für Kunstgeschichte* 75, no. 1 (2012): 33–50.

MONET

Books

Assouline, Pierre. *Discovering Impressionism: The Life of Paul Durand-Ruel.* New York: Magowan Publishing and The Vendome Press, 2004.

Ausrig, Helga Kessler, and Tanya Paul. *Monet and the Seine: Impressions of a River*. Houston: The Museum of Fine Arts, 2014 (exhibition catalogue).

Clark, T. J. *The Painting of Modern Life, Paris in the Art of Manet and His Followers*. Princeton: Princeton University Press, 1984.

Dallas, Gregor. *At the Heart of a Tiger: Clemenceau and His World, 1841–1929.* New York: Carroll & Graf, 1993.

House, John. *Monet*. New York: Phaidon, 1977.

———. *Monet: Nature Into Art*. New Haven: Yale University Press, 1986.

Herbert, Robert L. *Impressionism: Art, Leisure, and Parisian Society*. New Haven: Yale University Press, 1988.

Joyes, Claire. *Claude Monet: Life at Giverny.* New York: The Vendome Press, 1985.

Kendall, Richard, ed. *Monet: By Himself.* New York: Knickerbocker Press, 1999.

King, Ross. *Mad Enchantment: Claude Monet and the Painting of the Water Lilies*. London: Bloomsbury, 2016.

Lawrence, Nora, and Ann Temkin. *Claude Monet: Water Lilies*. New York: The Museum of Modern Art, 2009.

Lochnan, Katharine. *Turner, Whistler, Monet: Impressionist Visions*. London: Tate Publishing, 2004 (exhibition catalogue).

Loyrette, Henri, and Gary Tinterow. *Origins of Impressionism*. New York: The Metropolitan Museum of Art, 1994.

Moffett, Charles S., and James N. Wood. *Monet's Years at Giverny: Beyond Impressionism*. New York: The Metropolitan Museum of Art, 1978 (exhibition catalogue).

Orr, Lynn Federle, Elizabeth Murray, and Paul Hayes Tucker. *Monet: Late Paintings of Giverny from the Musée Marmottan*. New Orleans Museum of Art and The Fine Arts Museums of San Francisco, 1994.

Rewald, John, and Frances Weitzenhofer, eds. *Aspects of Monet: A Symposium on the Artist's Life and Times*. New York: Harry N. Abrams, 1984.

Rey, Jean-Dominique, and Denis Rouart. *Monet: Water Lilies, The Complete Series*. Paris: Flammarion, 2008.

Robinson, William H., et al. *Painting the Modern Garden: Monet to Matisse*. London: Royal Academy Publications, 2015 (exhibition catalogue).

Shackelford, George T. M., et al. *Monet: The Early Years*. Kimbell Art Museum. New Haven and London: Yale University Press, 2016 (exhibition catalogue).

———. *Monet: The Late Years*. Kimbell Art Museum. New Haven and London: Yale University Press, 2019 (exhibition catalogue).

Spate, Virginia. *Claude Monet: The Color of Time*. London: Thames & Hudson, 1992.

Stuckey, Charles F. *Monet: 1840 to 1926*. Chicago: The Art Institute of Chicago; New York: Thames and Hudson, 1995 (exhibition catalogue).

Temkin, Ann, and Nora Lawrence. *Claude Monet: Water Lilies*. New York: The Museum of Modern Art, 2009.

Tucker, Paul Hayes. *Claude Monet: Late Work*. New York: Gagosian Gallery, 2010 (exhibition catalogue).

———. *Monet in the 90s, The Series Paintings*. New Haven: Yale University Press, 1989 (exhibition catalogue).

———. *Monet in the 20th Century*. New Haven: Yale University Press, 1998 (exhibition catalogue).

Wildenstein, Daniel. *Monet: The Triumph of Impressionism*. Taschen, 1996.

Articles

Brettell, Richard R. "Monet's Haystacks Reconsidered." *Art Institute of Chicago Museum Studies* 11, no. 1 (Autumn 1984): 4–21.

Cooper, Douglas. "The Monets in the Metropolitan Museum of Art." *Metropolitan Museum Journal* 3 (1970): 281–305.

Levine, Steven Z. "Monet's Series: Repetition, Obsession." *October* 37 (Summer 1986): 65–75.

Lyon, Christopher. "Unveiling Monet." *MOMA*, no. 7 (Spring 1991): 14–23.

Mount, Charles Merrill. November 24, 1873. "The Precise Moment of Impressionism: Claude Monet's 'The Bridge at Argenteuil' at the National Gallery of Art in Washington, D.C." *Records of the Columbia Historical Society of Washington, D.C.* 71/72 (1971/72): 508–47.

Perry, Lilla Cabot. "Reminiscences of Claude Monet from 1889 to 1909." *The American Magazine of Art* 18, no. 3 (March 1927): 119–26.

Roy, Ashok. *Monet's Palette in the Twentieth Century: "Water-Lilies" and "Irises."* National Gallery Technical Bulletin 28 (2007): 58–68.

Schmidt, Anna Seaton. "An Afternoon with Claude Monet." *Modern Art* 5, no. 1 (Winter 1897): 32–35.

Seitz, William. "Monet and Abstract Painting." *College Art Journal* 16, no. 1 (Autumn 1956): 34–46.

Wood, James N. "Monet's Years at Giverny: Beyond Impressionism." *Bulletin (Saint Louis Art Museum)* New Series, vol. 14, no. 3 (July–September 1978): 46–49.

MATISSE

Books

Aagesen, Dorthe, and Rebecca Rabinow, eds. *Matisse: In Search of True Painting*. London: Yale University Press, 2012.

Aragon, Louis. *Henri Matisse.* 2 vols. New York: Harcourt Brace Jovanovich, 1972.

Barr, Alfred. *Matisse: His Art and His Public.* New York: The Museum of Modern Art, 1951.

Blum, Shirley Neilsen. *Henri Matisse: Rooms with a View.* New York: The Monacelli Press, 2010.

Brezzo, Steven, et al. *Henri Matisse: Florilege des Amours de Ronsard*. Laguna Niguel, CA: Contemporary and Modern Print Exhibitions, 1997.

Courthion, Pierre. *Chatting with Henri Matisse, The Lost 1941 Interview*. Los Angeles: the Getty Research Institute, 2013.

Couturier, Marie-Alain, and Louis-Bertrand Rayssiguier. *The Vence Chapel, The Archive of a Creation*. Milan: Skira Editore S.P.A., 1999.

Cowart, Jack, et al. *Henri Matisse: Paper Cut Outs*. The St. Louis Art Museum & The Detroit Institute of Arts, New York: Harry N. Abrams, 1977 (exhibition catalogue).

Elderfield, John. *The Cut Outs of Henri Matisse*. New York: George Braziller, Inc., 1978 (exhibition catalogue).

———. *Henri Matisse: A Retrospective*. New York: The Museum of Modern Art, 1992 (exhibition catalogue).

———. *Henri Matisse, Radical Reinvention 1913–1917*. The Art Institute of Chicago & The Museum of Modern Art, New Haven: Yale University, 2010 (exhibition catalogue).

——— et al. *The Drawings of Henri Matisse*. London: The Arts Council of Great Britain and Thames and Hudson Ltd., 1984 (exhibition catalogue).

——— et al. *Matisse Picasso*. London: Tate Publishing, 2002 (exhibition catalogue).

Flam, Jack. *Matisse: A Retrospective*. New York: Hugh Lauter Levin Associates, Inc., 1988 (exhibition catalogue).

———. *Matisse and Picasso: The Story of Their Rivalry and Friendship*. Cambridge, Mass.: Westview Press, 2003.

———. *Matisse on Art, 1869–1918*. Ithaca and London: Cornell University Press, 1986.

———, ed. *Matisse: The Man and His Art, 1869–1918*, Berkeley and Los Angeles: University of California Press, 1995.

Gilot, Françoise. *Matisse and Picasso, A Friendship in Art*. New York: Doubleday, 1990.

Gowing, Lawrence. *Matisse*. New York: Thames and Hudson, 1979.

Hauptman, Jodi, et al. *Henri Matisse: The Cut Outs*. New York: The Museum of Modern Art, 2014 (exhibition catalogue).

Sister Jacques-Marie. *Henri Matisse: The Vence Chapel*. Paris: Bernard Cheveau/Editeur, 2014.

Matisse, Henri, and Charles Baudelaire. *Les Fleurs de Mal*. Paris: Editions Hazan, 2016.

———. *Drawings: Themes and Variations*. New York: Dover Publications, Inc., 1995.

———. *Jazz*. New York: George Braziller, Inc., 1985.

Pulvenis de Seligny, Marie-Therese. *Matisse: The Chapel at Vence*. London: Royal Academy of Arts, 2013.

Rishel, Joseph. *Gauguin, Cézanne, Matisse: Visions of Arcadia*. Philadelphia: Philadelphia Museum of Art, 2012 (exhibition catalogue).

Russell, John. *Matisse, Father & Son*. New York: Harry N. Abrams, Inc., 1999.

Schneider, Pierre. *Matisse*. New York: Rizzoli International Publications, Inc., 1984.

Sooke, Alastair, *Henri Matisse: A Second Life*. London: Penguin Books Ltd., 2014.

Spurling, Hilary. *Matisse the Master*. New York: Alfred A. Knopf, 2005.

———. *The Unknown Matisse*. New York: Alfred A. Knopf, 1998.

Wheeler, Monroe. *The Last Works of Henri Matisse: Large Cut Gouaches*. Garden City, NY: Doubleday, 1961.

Articles

Greenberg, Clement. "Matisse in 1966." *Boston Museum Bulletin* 64, no. 336 (1966): 66–76.

Tchalenko, John. "Henri Matisse Drawing: An Eye-Hand Interaction Study Based on Archival Film." *Leonardo* 42, no. 5 (2009): 433–38.

Van Adrichem, Jan. "A well-kept secret: Matisse's 'The parakeet and the mermaid' (1952–53) at Amsterdam's Stedelijk Museum." *Simiolus: Netherlands Quarterly for the History of Art* 38, no. 4 (2015–2016): 289–306.

HOPPER

Books

Barr, Alfred H. *Edward Hopper, Retrospective Exhibition*. New York: Museum of Modern Art, Plandome Press, 1933 (exhibition catalogue).

Colleary, Elizabeth Thompson, ed. *Josephine Nivison Hopper: Edward's*

Muse. Nyack, NY: Edward Hopper House & Study Center, 2021 (exhibition catalogue).

———. *My Dear Mr. Hopper*. New York: Whitney Museum of American Art; New Haven and London: Yale University Press, 2013.

Foster, Carter. *Edward Hopper*. New York: Whitney Museum of American Art, 1964 (exhibition catalogue).

———. *Hopper Drawing*. New York: Whitney Museum of American Art; New Haven: Yale University Press, 2013 (exhibition catalogue).

Goodrich, Lloyd. *Edward Hopper, Retrospective Exhibition*. New York: Whitney Museum of American Art, 1950 (exhibition catalogue).

Haskell, Barbara, and Ortrud Westheider. *Modern Life. Edward Hopper and His Time*. Munich: Hirmer Verlag, 2009 (exhibition catalogue).

Levin, Gail. *Edward Hopper: An Intimate Biography* (updated and expanded edition). New York: Rizzoli International Publications, 2007.

———. *Edward Hopper, The Art and the Artist*. New York: W. W. Norton, 1980.

———. *Edward Hopper, The Complete Prints*. New York: Whitney Museum of American Art, W. W. Norton, 1979.

———. *Edward Hopper as Illustrator*. New York: Whitney Museum of American Art, W. W. Norton, 1979.

———. *Hopper's Places*. New York: Alfred A. Knopf, 1989.

Mazow, Leo G., and Sarah G. Powers. *Edward Hopper and the American Hotel*. New Haven: Yale University Press, 2019 (exhibition catalogue).

O'Doherty, Brian. *American Masters*. New York: Universe Books, 1988.

Ottinger, Didier, and Tomás Llorens. *Hopper*. New York: D.A.P./Distributed Art Publishers, 2012 (exhibition catalogue).

Salatino, Kevin. *Edward Hopper's Maine*. New York: Prestel Publishing, 2011 (exhibition catalogue).

Strand, Mark. *Hopper*. New York: Knopf, 2001 (originally published by Ecco Press in 1994).

Troyen, Carol, et al. *Edward Hopper*. Boston: MFA Publications, 2007 (exhibition catalogue).

Articles

Brown, Milton W. "The Early Realism of Hopper and Burchfield." *College Art Journal* 7, no. 1 (Autumn 1947): 3–11.

Doss, Erika. "Hopper's Cool: Modernism and Emotional Restraint." *American Art* 29, no. 3 (2015): 2–27.

Fryd, Vivian Green. "Edward Hopper's 'Girlie Show.'" *American Art* 14, no. 2 (Summer 2000): 52–75.

Geldzahler, Henry. "Edward Hopper." *The Metropolitan Museum of Art Bulletin*, New Series, vol. 21, no. 3 (November 1962): 113–17.

Koob, Pamela M. "States of Being: Edward Hopper and Symbolist Aesthetics." *American Art* 18, no. 3 (Fall 2004): 52–77.

Kramer, Hilton. "The Modern Movement on the Eve of the Second World War." *The American Scholar* 51, no. 2 (Spring 1982): 219–28.

Lacy, Robert. "Office at Night." *The Threepenny Review,* no. 130 (Summer 2012): 18.

Levin, Gail. "Edward Hopper's 'Nighthawks,' Surrealism, and the War." *Art Institute of Chicago Museum Studies* 22, no. 2 (1996): 180–95, 200.

———. "Josephine Versatile Nivison Hopper." *Woman's Art Journal* 1, no. 1 (1980): 28–32.

———, moderator, with William Bailey, Joel Meyerowitz, and George Segal. "Edward Hopper Symposium at the Whitney Museum of American Art." *Art Journal* 41, no. 2 (Summer 1981): 150–54.

Marling, Karal Ann. "Early Sunday Morning." *Smithsonian Studies in American Art* 2, no. 3 (Autumn 1988): 22–53.

Millard, Charles W. "Edward Hopper." *The Hudson Review* 34, no. 3 (Autumn 1981): 390–96.

Mitchell, Dolores. "Edward Hopper's 'Gas': Two Roads Diverge." *RACAR: revue d'art canadienne/Canadian Art Review* 17, no. 1 (1990): 71–76, 107–12.

Nemerov, Alexander. "Ground Swell: Edward Hopper in 1939." *American Art* 22, no. 3 (Fall 2008): 50–71.

Nochlin, Linda. "Edward Hopper and the Imagery of Alienation." *Art Journal* 41, no. 2, Edward Hopper Symposium at the Whitney Museum of American Art (Summer 1981): 136–41.

States, Bert O. "Death as a Fictitious Event." *The Hudson Review* 53, no. 3 (Autumn 2000): 423–32.

Weales, Gerald. "The Year of the Hopper." *The Hudson Review* 25, no. 1 (Spring 1972): 111–18.

NEVELSON

Books

Albee, Edward. *Edward Albee's Occupant*. New York: Samuel French, 2001.

———, and Laurie Wilson. *Louise Nevelson: Atmospheres and Environments*. New York: Clarkson N. Potter, with the Whitney Museum of American Art, 1980 (exhibition catalogue).

Friedman, Martin. *Nevelson Wood Sculptures*. New York: E.P. Dutton, 1973 (exhibition catalogue).

Gilbert, Lynn, and Galen Moore. *Louise Nevelson: Women of Wisdom*, e-book published by Lynn Gilbert, 2012.

Glimcher, Arne. *Louise Nevelson*. New York: E.P. Dutton, 1972.

Gordon, John. *Louise Nevelson*. New York: Whitney Museum of American Art, 1967 (exhibition catalogue).

Lippincott, Jonathan. *Large Scale*. New York: Princeton Architectural Press, 2010.

Lisle, Laurie. *Louise Nevelson: A Passionate Life*. New York: Summit Books, 1990.

MacKown, Diana, with Louise Nevelson. *Dawns + Dusks: Taped Conversations*. New York: Charles Scribner's Sons, 1976.

Miller, Dorothy. *Sixteen Americans*. New York: The Museum of Modern Art/ Doubleday, 1959 (exhibition catalogue).

Munro, Eleanor. *Originals: American Women Artists*. New York: Da Capo Press, 2000.

Rapaport, Brooke Kamin, et al. *The Sculpture of Louise Nevelson: Constructing a Legend*. New York and New Haven: Jewish Museum with Yale University Press, 2007 (exhibition catalogue).

Scaasi, Arnold. *Women I Have Dressed (and Undressed!)*. New York: Scribner, 2004.

Wilson, Laurie. *Louise Nevelson: Art is Life*. New York: Thames & Hudson, 2016.

———. *Louise Nevelson: The Fourth Dimension*. Phoenix: Phoenix Art Museum, 1980.

Articles

Bryan-Wilson, Julia. "Keeping House with Louise Nevelson." *Oxford Art Journal* 40, no. 1 (March 2017): 109–31.

Dupré, Judith. "Renewal of a Manhattan Retreat." *Faith & Form: The Interfaith Journal on Religion, Art, and Architecture* 52, no. 1 (2019).

Henning, Edward B. "Sky Cathedral-Moon Garden Wall by Louise Nevelson." *The Bulletin of the Cleveland Museum of Art* 64, no. 7 (September 1977): 242–51.

Hobbs, Robert C. "Louise Nevelson: A Place That Is an Essence." *Woman's Art Journal* 1, no. 1 (Spring–Summer 1980): 39–43.

Hughes, Robert. "Sculpture's Queen Bee." *Time* 117, no. 2 (January 12, 1981).

Kraus, Rosalind. "Grids." *October* 9 (Summer 1979): 50–64.

Lipman, Jean. "Recalled Encounters: Memorable Meetings with Artists and Collectors." *Archives of American Art Journal* 31, no. 1 (1991): 20–24.

Ott, Cindy. "Visions in Wood: Four Twentieth-Century American Wood Sculptors." *Archives of American Art Journal* 43, no. 3/4 (2003): 18–26.

Siegel, Harmon. "The Black Wallpaper: Louise Nevelson's Gothic Modernism." *The Art Bulletin* 99, no. 4 (December 2017): 168–90.

Speaks, Elyse Deeb. "Experiencing Louise Nevelson's 'Moon Garden.'" *American Art* 21, no. 2 (2007): 96–108.

OLD AGE GENERALLY

Books

Cole, Thomas R., and Mary G. Winkler. *The Oxford Book of Aging*. New York: Oxford University Press, 1994.

de Beauvoir, Simone. *The Coming of Age*. New York: W. W. Norton, 1972.

Dormandy, Thomas. *Old Masters: Great Artists in Old Age*. New York: Hambledon and London, 2000.

Munsterberg, Hugo. *The Crown of Life*. New York: Harcourt Brace Jovanovich, 1983.

Thane, Pat, ed. *A History of Old Age*. London: Thames & Hudson, 2005.

ACKNOWLEDGMENTS

I worked on *Last Light* for more than five years. By the time it was finished I was sixty-nine, old enough to empathize very easily with my six aging artists. But I actually began thinking about the questions this book deals with when I was still fairly young. I was twenty in 1972, when I made my first visit to London. It was there, at the National Gallery, that I discovered Titian's *Death of Actaeon* and was startled by my first encounter with the agitated brushwork of Titian's last years, to say nothing of my first encounter with the very idea of "late style" in the arts.

The event that finally catalyzed this book came more than four decades later. In 2013 I was invited to give one of that year's three Clarice Smith Distinguished Lectures in American Art at the Smithsonian American Art Museum in Washington, DC. Those lectures are an annual series in which an artist, an art historian, and an art critic give talks on separate nights on topics of their own choosing. I knew right away what mine would be. I'm grateful both to the late Clarice Smith and to the staff of the Smithsonian for the opportunity that lecture gave me to start putting in order the ideas developed in this book.

Among people who offered advice and guidance during the research and writing that followed, I owe a special debt to Stephanie Loeb Stepanek, the now retired curator of prints and drawings at the Museum of Fine Arts, Boston. Her comments and suggestions after reading the chapter on Goya were invaluable, and not just for that chapter. It was also largely thanks to her that I was granted access to the Boston museum's rich collection of Goya's works on paper. And it was "Goya: Order and Disorder," the superb 2014 exhibition she co-curated with Frederick Ilchman, the Boston museum's chair for the art of Europe and curator of paintings, that convinced me that Goya had to be one of the artists this book would include.

Last Light required research in museums all around Europe and the United States, and it was also Stephanie who connected me to colleagues in Madrid. One was the estimable Manuela B. Mena Marques, a senior curator and renowned authority on Goya at the Museo Nacional del Prado, now retired. Another was José Manuel Matilla, the museum's senior curator of drawings and prints. With their assistance I was able to spend mornings studying Goya's work in the Prado's great prints collection and afternoons in the galleries devoted to Goya and Titian. I'm grateful as well to Carmen Espinosa Martín, chief curator of Madrid's Museo Lázaro Galdiano, where I was also able to examine Goya's etchings, as well as a number of his late paintings.

Thanks also to Adam Weinberg, director of the Whitney Museum of American Art, and to Farris Wahbeh, the Whitney's director of research resources, who opened the way for me to study materials in the museum's archives relating to Josephine Hopper, the artist-wife of Edward Hopper. During the same yearslong dive into the Hopper story I was also assisted by James Zimmerman, archivist of the Provincetown Art Association and Museum (PAAM), in Provincetown, Massachusetts, and to Seth Abrahamson, the museum's registrar. It was through them that I was able to examine over a dozen paintings at PAAM by Jo Hopper and to read substantial parts of her journals. I was able to see more of her work in an exhibition at Edward Hopper's boyhood home in Nyack, New York, which is now the Edward Hopper House Museum and Study Center. The center's executive director, Kathleen Motes Bennewitz, and its head of visitor services, Eileen White, also alerted me to the places around Nyack that Hopper had used as models for some of his pictures. The noted curator and art historian Barbara Haskell also helped me to identify the owners of a Hopper in a private collection.

At Temple Beth-El of Great Neck, in Great Neck, New York, I owe thanks to Stuart Botwinick, the executive director, and to his executive assistant Joy S. Palevsky, for giving me access to Louise Nevelson's *The White Flame of the Six Million*, a monumental work that serves as both a Holocaust memorial and the synagogue's bema wall, Torah ark, and the case holding its eternal light. When I had difficulty tracking down the dimensions of that enormous work, they even measured it for me.

I'm also greatly obliged to the Archives of American Art for digitizing and making available on line many of Nevelson's letters, business records, and other archival materials, a very useful and convenient resource.

I'm especially grateful to Crary Pullen, a onetime photo editor at *Time* and other publications, and now an independent photo researcher. It was Crary who tracked down the many pictures in this book and secured the reproduction rights, complicated jobs involving dozens of museums, photo agencies, and artist's estates that I could not possibly have done on my own.

This book would probably never have happened if I hadn't been cold-called one day in the late 1990s by Todd Shuster, a New York literary agent. At lunch a few days later he spent part of the afternoon persuading me that I should write a book, and that better still, he should represent me, which very soon he did, and I'm very glad of it. Well, Todd, here it is.

The person most indispensable to this project has been Priscilla Painton, my editor at Simon & Schuster. (No relation to Todd Shuster.) Priscilla was also for some years my editor at *Time*, where I learned to appreciate her gift for not making changes in my copy, except for ones so necessary and to the point that I would happily convince myself they had been my idea all along. This book benefited in countless ways from her close reading and sure sense of how to keep a narrative from wandering off track.

Finally, on every day that I worked on this book, I relied on my very long-time partner, David Anderson, for his care, companionship, and good humor. Not long after I turned in the manuscript we married. So long as we continue down this road together, old age might not be so bad after all.

IMAGE CREDITS

CREDITS

1: H. O. Havemeyer Collection, Bequest of Mrs. H. O. Havemeyer, 1929/ Metropolitan Museum of Art; **12:** Photo © Photo Josse/Bridgeman Images; **23:** Bridgeman Images; **24:** Cameraphoto Arte Venezia/Bridgeman Images; **29:** Wallace Collection, London, UK/Bridgeman Images; **41:** Bridgeman Images; **43:** Luisa Ricciarini/Bridgeman Images; **45:** © Wallace Collection, London, UK/Bridgeman Images; **46:** The National Gallery, London; **47:** National Trust Photographic Library/Bridgeman Images; **49:** National Trust Photographic Library/Bridgeman Images; **50:** Isabella Stewart Gardner Museum/Bridgeman Images; **52:** Bridgeman Images; **53:** Artothek/Bridgeman Images; **58:** Bridgeman Images; **62:** Luisa Ricciarini/Bridgeman Images; **67:** Bridgeman Images; **77:** Purchase, Jacob H. Schiff Bequest, 1922/Metropolitan Museum of Art; **78:** Purchase, Jacob H. Schiff Bequest, 1922/Metropolitan Museum of Art; **79:** Gift of Mrs. Grafton H. Pyne, 1951/Metropolitan Museum of Art; **80:** Purchase, Jacob H. Schiff Bequest, 1922/Metropolitan Museum of Art; **86:** Bridgeman Images; **94;** Photo © Fine Art Images /Bridgeman Images; **101:** © of the image Museo Nacional del Prado/Art Resource, NY; **103:** © of the image Museo Nacional del Prado/Art Resource, NY; **107:** Harris Brisbane Dick Fund, 1924/ Metropolitan Museum of Art; **108:** Katherine E. Bullard Fund in memory of Francis Bullard Museum of Fine Arts Boston; **109:** Minneapolis Institute of Art /The Ethel Morrison Van Derlip Fund/Bridgeman Images; **111:** Bridgeman Images; **113:** Bridgeman Images; **114:** Bridgeman Images; **115:** Bridgeman Images; **123:** © of the image Museo Nacional del Prado/Art Resource, NY; **126:** Henri Manuel/Bridgeman Images; **134:** Bridgeman Images; **155:** Mr. and Mrs. Lewis Larned Coburn Memorial Collection/Art Institute of Chicago; **156:** Mr. and Mrs. Martin A. Ryerson Collection/Art Institute of Chicago; **157:** Museum of Fine Arts, Houston/Gift of Mrs. Harry C. Hanszen/

Bridgeman Images; **160–61:** Digital Image The Museum of Modern Art/Licensed by SCALA/Art Resource, NY; **162:** Bridgeman Images; **163:** © Kimbell Art Museum/Bridgeman Images; **171:** Digital Image © The Museum of Modern Art/Licensed by SCALA/Art Resource, NY; **172:** The Steinberg Charitable Fund 134:1956/Saint Louis Art Museum; **177:** Album/Alamy; **180:** Ralph Gatti/AFP/Getty Images; **181:** © 2022 Succession H. Matisse/Artists Rights Society (ARS), NY/Archives of Henri Matisse, all rights reserved; **198:** © 2022 Succession H. Matisse/Artists Rights Society (ARS), NY/Ville de Grenoble/Musée de Grenoble –J.L. Lacroix; **203:** © 2022 Succession H. Matisse /Artists Rights Society (ARS), NY/Archives of Henri Matisse, all rights reserved; **204:** © 2022 Succession H. Matisse / Artists Rights Society (ARS), NY/Archives of Henri Matisse, all rights reserved; **214:** © 2022 Succession H. Matisse / Artists Rights Society (ARS), NY/© The Phillips Collection, Washington, DC/Bridgeman Images; **215:** © 2022 Succession H. Matisse/Artists Rights Society (ARS), NY/Archives of Henri Matisse, all rights reserved; **220:** © 2022 Succession H. Matisse / Artists Rights Society (ARS), NY/Hemis/Alamy Stock Photo; **226:** © 2022 Succession H. Matisse Artist Rights Society (ARS), NY/Photo © François Fernandez/Gift of Henri Matisse, 1953/Musée Matisse, Nice; **227:** © 2022 Succession H. Matisse/Artists Rights Society (ARS), NY/Photo: Philippe Migeat/RMN-Pompidou/Art Resource, NY; **230:** © 2022 Succession Henri Matisse/Artists Rights Society (ARS), NY/Mrs. Simon Guggenheim Fund/Museum of Modern Art, NY/Art Resource, NY; **234:** Arnold Newman Properties/Getty Images; **235:** © 2022 Heirs of Josephine N. Hopper/Licensed by Artists Rights Society ARS), Digital image © Whitney Museum of American Art/Licensed by Scala/Art Resource, NY; **238:** © 2022 Heirs of Josephine N. Hopper/Licensed by Artists Rights Society (ARS), NY/Smithsonian American Art Museum, Washington, DC/Art Resource, NY; **247:** © 2022 Heirs of Josephine N. Hopper/Licensed by Artists Rights Society (ARS), NY/Artothek/Bridgeman Images; **248:** © 2022 Heirs of Josephine N. Hopper/Licensed by Artists Rights Society (ARS), NY/Lefevre Fine Art Ltd., London/Bridgeman Images; **262:** © 2022 Heirs of Josephine N. Hopper/Licensed by Artists Rights Society (ARS), NY/Yale University Art Gallery/Bequest of Stephen Carlton Clark, B.A. 1903; **265:** © 2022 Heirs of Josephine N. Hopper/Licensed by Artists Rights Society (ARS), NY/Digital image Whitney Museum of American Art/Licensed by Scala/Art Resource, NY; **267:** © 2022 Heirs of Josephine N. Hopper/Licensed by Artists Rights Society (ARS), NY/Smithsonian American Art Museum, Washington,

DC/Art Resource, NY; **268:** © 2022 Heirs of Josephine N. Hopper/Licensed by Artists Rights Society (ARS), NY/Photo Fine Art Images/Bridgeman Images; **270:** © 2022 Heirs of Josephine N. Hopper/Licensed by Artists Rights Society (ARS), NY/Yale University Art Gallery/Bequest of Stephen Carlton Clark, B.A. 1903; **274:** © 2022 Heirs of Josephine N. Hopper/Licensed by Artists Rights Society (ARS), NY/Private Collection; **276:** Arnold Newman Collection/Getty Images; **280:** © 2022 Estate of Louise Nevelson/Artists Rights Society (ARS), NY/Digital Image © The Museum of Modern Art/Licensed by SCALA/Art Resource, NY; **296:** © 2022 Estate of Louise Nevelson/Artists Rights Society (ARS), NY/Digital Image Whitney Museum of American Art/Licensed by SCALA/Art Resource, NY; **303:** © 2022 Estate of Louise Nevelson/Artists Rights Society (ARS), NY/Rosenwald Collection/National 352 Gallery of Art, London; **306:** © 2022 Estate of Louise Nevelson/Artists Rights Society (ARS), NY/Digital image © Whitney Museum of American Art/Licensed by Scala/Art Resource, NY; **308:** © 2022 Estate of Louise Nevelson/Artists Rights Society (ARS), NY/Digital image © Whitney Museum of American Art/Licensed by Scala/Art Resource, NY; **311:** © 2022 Estate of Louise Nevelson/Artists Rights Society (ARS), NY/ Photograph © Samuel Gruber; **316:** © 2022 Estate of Louise Nevelson/Artists Rights Society (ARS), NY/Photograph Gregory Benson © 2019, courtesy Association for Public Art (aPA); **322:** © 2022 Estate of Louise Nevelson/Artists Rights Society (ARS), NY/Image © The Metropolitan Museum of Art. Image source: Art Resource, NY; **325:** © 2022 Estate of Louise Nevelson/Artists Rights Society (ARS), NY/Terese Loeb Kreuzer/Alamy; **329:** © 2022 Estate of Louise Nevelson/Artist Rights Society (ARS), NY/ Photograph by Jerry L. Thompson © Storm King Art Center, Mountainville, New York

ENDPAPER CREDITS

Titian - Archivart /Alamy Stock Photo

Goya - Bequest of Archer M. Huntington, 1956/Courtesy of The Hispanic Society of America, NY

Matisse - © 2022 Succession H. Matisse/Artists Rights Society (ARS), NY/ Photo Jacob Schou-Hansen/Statens Museum for Kunst, National Gallery of Denmark

Nevelson - © 2022 Estate of Louise Nevelson/Artists Rights Society (ARS), NY/ Photograph © Museum of Fine Arts, Boston, Museum purchase with funds donated by Charlotte and Irving Rabb, Thomas H. Lee and Ann Tenenbaum Lee, Robert L. Beal, Enid L. Beal and Bruce A. Beal Acquisition Fund, and the Sophie M. Friedman Fund 1997. 97

BACK COVER IMAGES CREDITS

Titian by Gl Archive/Alamy Stock Photo
Hopper by Oscar White/Corbis/VCG via Getty Images
Matisse by Ralph Gatti/AFP via Getty Images
Nevelson and Monet by Bettmann/Getty Images
Goya by Imagno/Getty Images

INDEX

Page numbers in italics refer to images

ABOUT THE AUTHOR

RICHARD LACAYO was a longtime writer and editor at *Time* and from 2003 the magazine's art and architecture critic. He has also written about arts, media, and cultural affairs for *Life*, *People*, *Foreign Policy*, *Air Mail*, and the *New York Times*. He is the coauthor, with George Russell, of *Eyewitness: 150 Years of Photojournalism*.

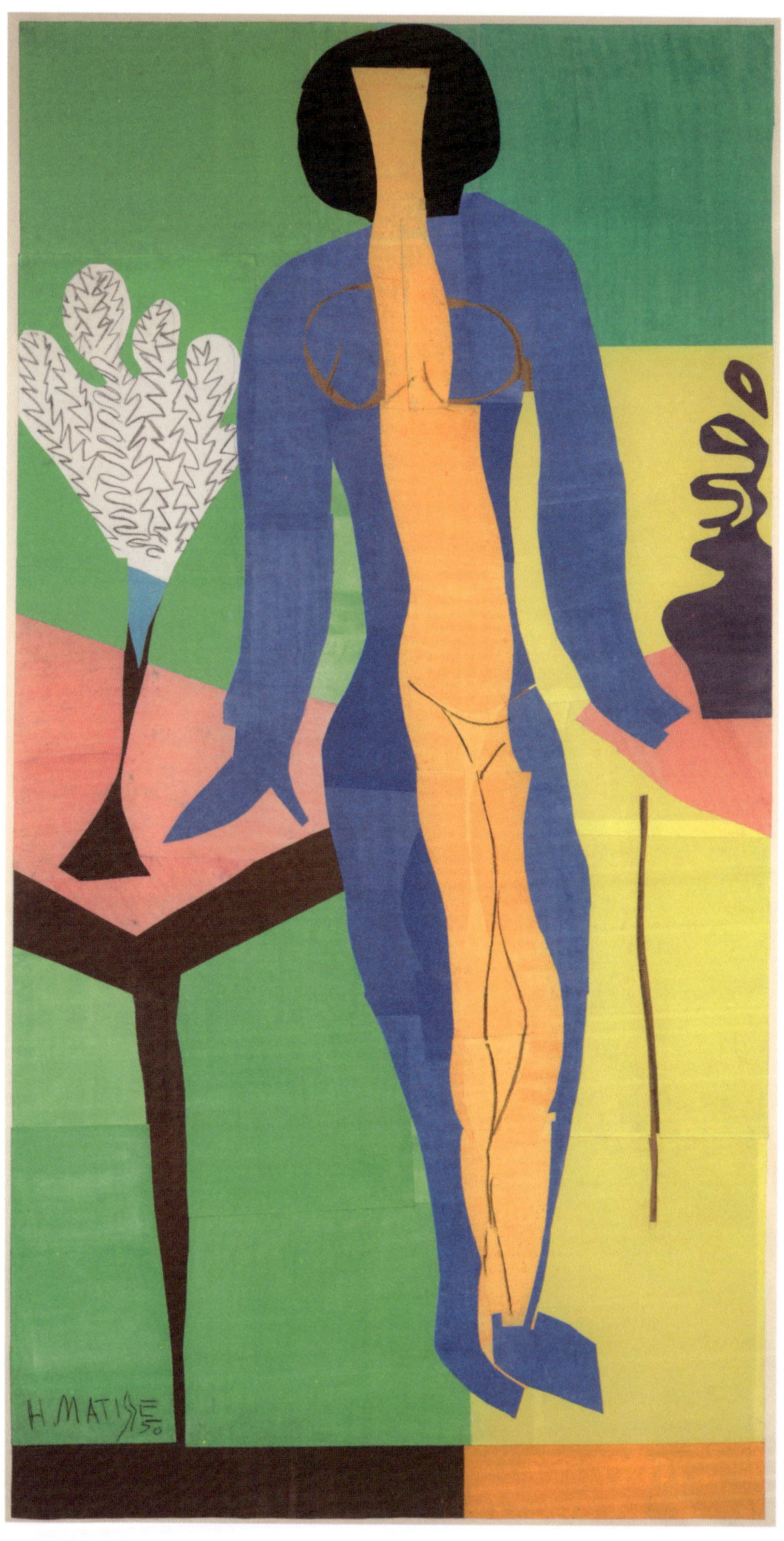

Matisse, *Zulma*, 1950, Statens Museum for Kunst, Copenhagen